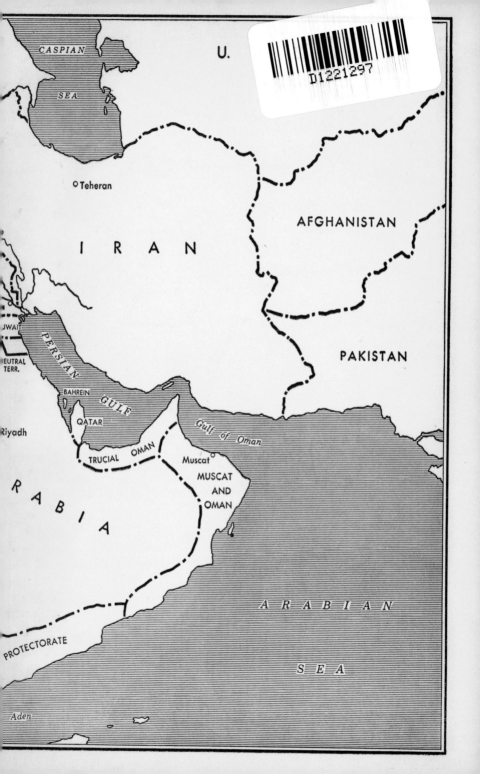

Challenge and Response

in the Middle East

❖

Under the test of a common challenge a certain number of the communities that are exposed to it are apt to succumb, whereas others strike out a successful response through a creative movement of Withdrawal-and-Return, while others, again, neither succeed in responding along original lines nor fail to respond altogether, but manage to survive the crisis by . . . following tamely in the footsteps of the pioneers.

—Arnold J. Toynbee
in *A Study of History*

Challenge and Response in the Middle East

The Quest for Prosperity

1919-1951

❖

By HEDLEY V. COOKE

*Former United States Consul in Palestine
and Turkey; Former Consultant, Middle East Planning
Staff, Economic Cooperation Administration*

Huston - Tillotson Library

Harper & Brothers · Publishers New York

DS57
.C6

CHALLENGE AND RESPONSE IN THE MIDDLE EAST

Copyright, 1952, by Harper & Brothers

Printed in the United States of America

All rights in this book are reserved.
No part of the book may be used or reproduced
in any manner whatsoever without written permission except in the case of brief quotations
embodied in critical articles and reviews. For
information address Harper & Brothers
49 East 33rd Street, New York 16, N. Y.

FIRST EDITION

F-B

Library of Congress catalog card number: 52-8467

F. W. O'Reilly

Gift

2-28-41

To my uncle
Morris Llewellyn Cooke
*in gratitude for his encouragement
of my work*

41323

CONTENTS

LIST OF MAPS

Probably the most significant fact about the story of the Middle East—as it is reflected in our American libraries, current publications, museums, and elsewhere—is the extraordinary lack of balanced perspective in the over-all picture which emerges.

Almost every American with a grade-school education knows at least a few things about ancient Egypt, the ancient and modern lands of Israel, and the Crusades. Also the story of Mohammed's life is a familiar one to many of us. But how many Americans know the more important cultural facts about the golden age of Islam?

The presence of oil deposits and their exploitation by foreign companies are well known. But who knows anything about the political regime in the oil-rich shaikhdom of Qatar? The word *pasha* is reasonably familiar and at least vaguely comprehended by many. But can the same be said of the equally important word *fellah*?

Knowledge of the social and economic aspects of the Middle East is now increasing, though at a painfully slow rate. Since the end of World War I a new institution, namely, the foreign-directed economic survey mission, has played an increasingly prominent role in the affairs of the region. The factual findings of the numerous successive missions have constituted valuable, and often pioneer, contributions to the general fund of regional data. Unfortunately, however, these missions have, with few exceptions, failed to hit upon economic approaches which would be meaningful in their Middle Eastern settings. This shortcoming is apparently attributable to an absence of adequate understanding of the traditions, background, and current thinking of the people in whose interests the surveys were being made.

This book is an attempt, first, to close one or two of the more prominent gaps in our present-day knowledge of the Middle East, and second, to indicate a possible method to be followed in future analyses of regional economic conditions—especially those which are designed to facilitate economic planning.

The material in the first eleven chapters covers events occurring up to January 1, 1951. However, each of those chapters was subsequently reviewed and supplemented by footnotes wherever it was deemed necessary or desirable to include additional relevant data up to December 1, 1951. The discussions in the final chapter take into account all known occurrences in or involving the region up to the second of the two dates mentioned. The conclusions arrived at could, of course, be altered in great measure by such unpredictable events as political assassinations. These have not been at all uncommon in the Middle East in recent years. Another unpredictable factor of importance could be the establishment of effective military dictatorships. As of today, it is still not clear whether the events in Syria since December, 1951, are indicative of a significant development in this sense.

It should also be noted that only the *independent* states of the Middle East have been dealt with in this study. The areas which have not been covered (otherwise than incidentally) are Cyprus, Aden Colony, Aden Protectorate, Muscat and Oman, Trucial Oman, Qatar, Bahrein, and Kuwait. These omissions are probably not of great importance, as far as the total picture is concerned.

Finally, I must take this opportunity of expressing my great gratitude to those who have assisted me in bringing this work to completion, and without whose active help and encouragement there would have been no worth-while accomplishment. In particular, thanks are due to Dr. Bert F. Hoselitz, Chairman of the Committee on International Relations of the University of Chicago, for his guidance and scholarly judgment as to the matters which should be included. Eric H. Biddle, then Director of the Middle East Planning Staff of the Economic Cooperation Administration, was kind enough to devote large amounts of his valuable time to reading over the chapters and making useful suggestions based both on his knowledge and understanding of the Middle East and on his appreciation of how, in general, a book of this sort should be written. Also exceedingly valuable has been the continuous and wise guidance provided by two members of the Oriental Institute faculty of the University of Chicago, namely, Dr. Gustave E. von Grunebaum and Dr. John A. Wilson. Others deserving of gratitude for aid and encouragement are Edward A. Bayne, former Economic Adviser to the Government of Iran; James M. Barker, head of the 1950 International Bank mission to Turkey; and Elizabeth Monroe, Middle East editor of *The Economist*. Last but not least, great thanks are due to my wife for her constructive criticisms and for her laborious assistance with the maps appearing at the end of the volume.

In view of the inevitability of unintentional discrimination, I have not attempted to make this list complete. But I am nonetheless grateful for the assistance freely bestowed by many others not mentioned here.

H. V. C.

Tuscaloosa, Ala.
April 1, 1952

Challenge and Response

in the Middle East

❖

CHAPTER I

Introduction

The most characteristic, and perhaps the most important, manifestation of mid-twentieth-century liberalism is the strong aspiration of American liberals for a world where the grosser economic and social inequalities, as among the geographical regions, will have been removed. The removal process, it is agreed, can be encompassed by a suitable extension of Western technology, methodology, and capital resources to the peoples of underdeveloped countries on a basis of voluntary give-and-take.

There is no want of evidence that such an aspiration may be intellectually justifiable and that the fears entertained by our more conservative elements—for example, that hopes for success would soon be frustrated by the resistances, ignorance, and inertia of the groups being aided—may not be at all warranted. Nineteenth-century concepts have yielded unconditionally to the anthropologists' strong assertion that there are no inherent qualitative mental differences between any given race of people and any other race. Perhaps even more important have been the results of the great increase in friendly personal contacts between Americans on the one hand and natives of underdeveloped countries on the other. It has become apparent that the spiritual and cultural gaps are considerably narrower than had once been supposed.

The net result of these and similar findings has been, almost inevitably, a tendency on the part of liberal Americans to envisage the problem of developing underdeveloped countries as a relatively uncomplicated one, even in spite of the apparent variations in regional and local conditions. These variations, as to their detailed aspects, are conceded to be suitable matter for study by the Orientalist, the philosopher, the theological student, and the historian, but not by the person whose main concern is with the "practical" problem of furnishing technical or financial assistance. For the needs of the latter, it is deemed important only to determine, with the help of anthropologists, the precise historical stage of advancement which a given underdeveloped country has reached. As for the steps of action stemming from such a diagnosis, we have at our command fully documented economic histories of nations and peoples who have passed from the earlier evolutionary stages of development to higher ones. This approach to the problem has, apparently, the virtues of being scientific, practical, and efficient; it is indeed based upon the same sort of method which it is proposed to apply to the solution of those problems that are strictly technical in nature.

To the writer, who has spent upwards of a decade of his adult life in underdeveloped countries in Asia and Latin America, it has seemed that there is one distinct weakness in the manner of approach just described. This is the fact that it completely ignores certain elements which, in the sphere of internal American planning, are never left out of account by planners. Those elements are local public opinion and the factors entering into its composition.

Is the public opinion in underdeveloped countries so rational, regular, and easily predictable—in short, so unlike our own—that universalized principles can be applied in substitution for detailed observations of present-day facts?

In the strong belief that the correct answer to this question is in the negative, and in the earnest hope that American aid programs for at least some of the underdeveloped areas will be executed on the basis of an opposite assumption, the writer offers this study of present and recent planning in the Middle East, in the context of the most noteworthy regional and local variations observable in that part of the world.

The purpose of this study is to determine, if possible, the nature of situations and trends with regard to living standards in the Middle East during the period January 1, 1919, to December 31, 1950. The method employed will be a close examination of all major plans for elevation of standards of living in that region during the period reviewed. Such a scrutiny may be expected to reveal in some detail both the types of condition which it has been sought to remedy and the difficulties ordinarily encountered in connection with the remedial efforts. The result of such a survey should be at least a few important findings touching upon the problems of present-day and near-future planning for the reduction of poverty in that strategically important sector of the world.

One important reservation should be made. Usually a "major plan" is one which involves extremely heavy costs, occupies enormous numbers of people in the labor of fulfillment, and is a prominent feature of the political and economic life of the country or region. But if the study were to be confined to projects having all those aspects, some of its manifest purposes would be defeated. It would be highly improper to leave out of account the small plan or the restricted plan (particularly if it relates to laying a suitable educational or sanitary foundation) which is specifically designed to pave the way for an eventual execution of an integrated plan of great magnitude. In the opinion of many, plans of such a nature constitute the best initial approach to comprehensive integrated planning on a nation-wide or region-wide basis. Sometimes known as "pilot projects," they have the virtue of providing inexpensive tests as to the possibilities for major planning, and of exposing, without too great cost or loss, some of the main obstacles which would have to be confronted in the execution of the more grandiose plans. Because of these virtues, the "pilot project" might well be classified as a somewhat advanced phase in the evolution of rational planning activities. Hence it will also be necessary to review the histories of some schemes which, though modest as to their immediate aims, actually contained large implications.

Before embarking upon a detailed discussion of the various plans which have been selected for consideration, it is necessary to consider briefly the whole complex of underlying conditions in the Middle Eastern region, which may be connected in one way or another with the results of past projects or with the prospects for current ones. The paragraphs which follow constitute an attempt to supply the minimum essential background data in regard to political, social, and economic conditions in the Middle East during the period under review.

HISTORICAL AND POLITICAL BACKGROUND

All of the independent countries of the Middle East are successor nations, either directly or through steps of succession, to the Ottoman Empire or the Persian Empire. The formal existence of the Ottoman Empire, which had been steadily losing territory during the nineteenth and twentieth centuries, was terminated in 1923 upon the conclusion of the Treaty of Lausanne, between Turkey and the Allied Powers of World War I. However, after the Armistice of Mudros of October, 1918, the *de facto* existence of the Ottoman state was at best confined to approximately the area now possessed by the Republic of Turkey. Generally speaking, that is where the Turkish language predominates, and indeed has predominated for many centuries. It consists of a large Asiatic section, known as Anatolia, and a much smaller European section, the two being separated by the Turkish Straits and the Sea of Marmara.

1. *Turkey.* During the period 1918–23, the authority of the Ottoman Sultan, who was at the time little more than a puppet of the victorious Allied Powers, was challenged by Mustafa Kemal Pasha, a Turkish military leader, who organized the so-called Nationalist group. The Turkish Nationalists rapidly built up their strength and popular following and were ultimately able not only to force the Sultan's abdication but also to persuade the Allied Powers to negotiate peace terms with them on the basis of recognition of the Nationalist leadership as the *de jure* and *de facto* Turkish Government. Soon after the conclusion of the Peace of Lausanne

the Nationalist leaders proclaimed the birth of the Republic of Turkey.

2. *The Area Formerly Under League of Nations Mandates.* A large former Ottoman area directly to the south of eastern Anatolia, extending from the old Ottoman-Persian frontier to the Mediterranean Sea, was wholly under Anglo-French military occupation in the era immediately following the Armistice of Mudros. The ultimate fate of this region, largely populated by Arabic-speaking peoples, was determined by a long sequence of secret agreements, open declarations, and international conferences, all involving the great European powers, beginning as early as 1915 and reaching a substantial conclusion in 1920.[1] In the latter year, by virtue of the agreements of the San Remo Conference, held under League of Nations auspices, the area was divided into three separate political units, namely, Syria, Palestine, and Iraq. Syria was placed under French supervisory control, subject to the stipulations of Article 22 of the League of Nations Covenant, whereunder Syria's independence was "provisionally recognized," but with limitations admitting of divergent interpretations as to the degree of authority which France could properly exercise. Palestine was assigned to Great Britain, also under League of Nations mandate, to be developed in whole or part as a "national home" for Jews, but with suitable safeguards to be provided for the established civil and religious rights of the non-Jewish population. Iraq was also assigned to Great Britain, under a League of Nations mandate similar to France's mandate for Syria.

In the early 1920's one consequential change occurred in this political setup. Availing herself of an optional provision (Article 25) in the mandate for Palestine, Great Britain excluded practically all of the large region between the Jordan River and the Iraq frontier from the area reserved as a national homeland for Jews. The excluded area became a separate political unit, known until 1949 as Trans-

[1] The main ones were: (1) the Straits Agreement of March 18, 1915, between Britain, France, and Russia; (2) the Hussein-McMahon correspondence of 1915-16 between the Sherif of Mecca and a representative of the British Government; (3) the Sykes-Picot Agreement of May 16, 1916, between Britain, France, and Russia; (4) the Balfour Declaration (by the British Government) of November 2, 1917.

jordan and now as Jordan, officially "the Hashemite Kingdom of Jordan."

The only other boundary change occurring in the mandated region during the period between wars was the cession in 1939 by France of a small corner of Syria, known as the Sanjaq of Alexandretta, to Turkey. In 1932 the Iraq mandate was terminated by virtue of Iraq's admission into the League of Nations as a sovereign state.

The first alteration of frontiers occurring after the outbreak of World War II involved the Syrian mandated territory. For administrative purposes, France had divided that territory into four sections each having its separate native government, namely, Syria, Lebanon, Latakia (Alawi state), and Jebel Druze. Mainly because of the already existing religious and cultural differences, which became accentuated by the division, Lebanon had shown an increasing tendency to develop and act upon its own separate nationalistic aspirations.[2] Thus, when the mandate was terminated both *de jure* and *de facto* at the end of the war, two new independent states, Syria and Lebanon, came into being. Latakia and Jebel Druze became integral parts of the free republic of Syria.

Soon afterward, in 1946, Great Britain granted full independence to Transjordan. Treaties of 1946 and 1948 reserved for Britain a group of rights in regard to military matters.

It was Palestine, however, which underwent the most drastic change in the era immediately following World War II. Because of the inability of Great Britain, the Jews of Palestine, and the Arabs of that country to come to terms in regard to the future political status of the region, local disorder became rampant after the war. Finally, in 1947, Great Britain requested the United Nations General Assembly to study the situation and make formal recommendations for a satisfactory settlement. The result of the detailed inquiry which followed was the General Assembly Partition Resolution of November 29, 1947. This resolution provided for the division of Palestine into two fully independent states, a Jewish and an Arab

[2] Even before World War I Lebanon (though with more restricted frontiers than its present ones) enjoyed a special political status.

one. The sequel to the resolution was an outbreak of fighting between the Jews and the Arabs of Palestine, followed by Great Britain's announcement of intention to terminate the mandate on May 15, 1948, without regard to the state of affairs which might be prevailing at that time. While Britain was in the very act of carrying out this proclaimed intention, the Jews of Palestine declared their independence and announced to the world the birth of the new state of Israel, with boundaries undefined but generally assumed to enclose at least the area allotted to Jews in the Partition Resolution. On the same day, military forces entered Palestine from the near-by Arab countries (Egypt, Iraq, Transjordan, Syria, and Lebanon), with a view to preventing the consolidation of the new Jewish state. They were resisted by Israel's army, which before long succeeded in gaining the upper hand in this Palestine War. In 1949, through United Nations mediation, armistice agreements were concluded between Israel and the four countries with which she had common frontiers, namely, Egypt, Syria, Lebanon, and Transjordan. These agreements permitted Israel to occupy, pending the conclusion of definitive peace treaties, an area greatly exceeding the half allotted to her by the Partition Resolution. Up to December 31, 1950, no peace treaties had been concluded and the armistice arrangements were still in effect.

By the armistice agreement of 1949 between Israel and Transjordan, the latter was permitted to continue for the time being in occupation of that sizable portion of Palestine over which she had gained military control. Soon after the armistice, the Government of Transjordan changed the name of its state to Jordan, thus virtually proclaiming an intention to annex the territory held on the western side of the river. In 1950 this intention was carried out.

The third part of Palestine, the only one not yet accounted for, is a small strip of seacoast in the southwest corner, bordering upon Egypt. This is known as the Gaza Strip; it is (as of December 31, 1950) occupied by Egypt under the terms of the armistice agreement between that state and Israel.

3. *Egypt.* From the early 1880's until the outbreak of World War

I Egypt was only nominally a part of the Ottoman Empire, being for all practical purposes a British protectorate. Soon after the war had begun, a formal British protectorate was proclaimed. In 1922, however, Great Britain nominally recognized Egypt's independence, though with certain severely restrictive conditions. Since that year, Egypt has made continuous strides toward real independence, which is now virtually complete.[3]

The language of most Egyptians is Arabic, and Egypt is now generally regarded as an Arab state.

4. *Arabia.* The one remaining former Ottoman area to be considered is the great Arabian peninsula, which lies to the south of the former mandated area between the Persian Gulf and the Red Sea, and which is generally considered to be the home of the racially pure Arab and of the least corrupted form of the Arabic language. The whole of this region was, until 1918, nominally part of the Ottoman Empire. At nearly all times, however, the greater part of the peninsula was free from effective Ottoman control. The extent and character of that control, seldom maintained for any appreciable time, varied from period to period.

Up to the end of World War I, Arabia was, generally speaking, a network of independent and semi-independent "shaikhdoms," some of which, particularly along the southern and eastern coastlines, were subject to varying degrees of British protection under the terms of treaties or "truces."[4] Among the Arab rulers of the peninsula rivalries used to be intense and constant and open warfare frequent; and none of those rulers maintained a true government, in the European sense of the word. However, during the period between the two world wars one of the native leaders, Ibn Saud of Nejd, succeeded in subduing the whole of Arabia with two excep-

[3] The 1922 arrangements have been superseded by the more liberal Anglo-Egyptian Treaty of 1936. During World War II the British Government exercised a large measure of control over Egypt, which was an important theater of war. Since 1945 British intervention in Egyptian affairs has been confined to the maintenance of troops in a limited area for protection of the Suez Canal.

[4] The term "truce" is due to the theory that a Moslem state must never enter into a permanent peace with a non-Moslem one. It is, however, permissible to conclude armistices of long duration.

tions: the British-protected coastal areas and the relatively small imamate of Yemen, the latter situated in the southwest corner of the peninsula. Ibn Saud's extensive domains became known as Saudi Arabia. That nation and Yemen are now members of the United Nations.

5. *Iran.* The boundaries of Iran (sometimes known to Westerners as Persia) have remained unchanged throughout the twentieth century; in the nineteenth, there were losses to Russia in the north. From 1907 to 1917 Russia had much political influence in the northern part of the country, and Great Britain was similarly influential in the south. An attempt was made by Britain, though with only short-lived success, to extend her influence throughout the country after the outbreak of the Russian Revolution and to maintain that more or less complete domination after the termination of World War I. In 1941 the country was subjected to an Anglo-Soviet military occupation which lasted until March, 1946. With these qualifications, Iran has throughout modern times been an independent nation.

6. *General.* The historical data contained in the preceding paragraphs are of importance for the evidence they provide that a history of plans involving Middle Eastern living standards during the period 1919 to 1950 is, generally speaking, a history of all such plans during the modern historical era—say, 1700 A.D. to date. Before late 1918 the Middle East consisted practically only of the Persian Empire and part of the Ottoman Empire. In neither of those states were conditions at all suitable for integrated planning of any sort, and in neither was there any persistent official or public sentiment in favor of economic or social welfare projects. Furthermore, the finances of both empires were in highly unsound condition; the political regimes in both were usually inefficient and often corrupt; and the only capital which could have been acquired for major development would have been foreign capital, which, as a rule, flowed only into ventures promising large or sure profits, and unrelated to general living standards.

Thus, when World War I ended, all of the areas which had been under direct Ottoman or Persian control were almost completely undeveloped, as far as high-level attention to the needs of the common man was concerned. Poverty, ignorance, disease, and filth were omnipresent, and almost no conscious efforts had been made to ameliorate such conditions on a thoroughgoing basis.

As for the Ottoman areas not under the Sultan's direct control, these were Egypt, most of Arabia, and part of the small area now occupied by the Lebanese Republic. Arabia, however, was even more backward, economically and socially, than was the main part of the Ottoman Empire; and the only feasible type of planning was that which could reduce this difference in level of advancement. As for the Autonomous Sanjaq of Lebanon, the area was too small and isolated to permit truly major attempts to outdistance the neighboring regions in economic and social welfare projects.

In Egypt, on the other hand, an integrated scheme for river control on a grand scale came into being as early as 1904[5] That plan, however, seems to have been motivated not so much by general considerations of human welfare as by two facts peculiar to Egypt, one of which was particularly obvious, the other particularly alarming. The obvious fact was Egypt's historical and traditional dependence on irrigation from waters of the Nile River for her very survival. The alarming fact was that the population of Egypt was increasing far more rapidly than the means of subsistence. In other words, a dangerous situation existed, and there seemed to be but one way of remedying the worst aspects of that situation. In other respects, conditions in Egypt were hardly more suitable for integrated planning than they were in the areas under direct Ottoman control. Nor did Great Britain's position of dominance in the country affect matters substantially. The British rulers, in order to protect themselves politically, tended to rely upon good relations with the landowning classes, whose interests were as a rule in conflict with those of the majority of the population.

[5] The Garstin proposals of 1904 (*Report on the Basin of the Nile*) were substantially endorsed by Sir Murdoch MacDonald, Adviser to the Egyptian Ministry of Public Works, in his 1920 report entitled *Nile Control*. This general program, which is partly completed, is still unchanged as to essentials.

THE PEOPLE: UNIFYING AND DIVISIVE INFLUENCES

According to the most recent statistics available from authoritative sources, the populations of the independent Middle Eastern countries are approximately as follows:

Iran	18,387,000
Iraq	5,100,000
Israel	1,350,000
Jordan	1,300,000
Lebanon	1,238,000
Saudi Arabia	6,000,000
Syria	3,227,000
Turkey	19,500,000
Egypt	20,439,000
Yemen	4,500,000

The figure for Jordan includes several hundred thousands of Arab war refugees from Israel. Syria and Lebanon have smaller numbers of such refugees, which are not included in the population figures because the governments do not regard them as permanent residents.

1. *Race and Language.* From a linguistic, and also roughly from an ethnic, viewpoint, the present-day Middle East may be divided into four main areas: the Arab states, Turkey, Israel, and Iran. In general, linguistic differences within any one of those sections are not as important as religious and cultural ones, often applying between groups whose native language is one and the same.[6]

As has already been noted, seven of the ten countries, namely, Syria, Lebanon, Iraq, Jordan, Egypt, Saudi Arabia, and Yemen, contain large Arabic-speaking majorities and are customarily regarded as the Middle Eastern portion of the so-called Arab world. It would be a mistake, however, to overstress the importance of the elements of Arab unity. In the first place, the spoken Arabic language has marked regional variations; it is only the literary form of the language, which

---

[6] By far the largest *linguistic* minority in the Near East is the Kurds, whose numbers are approximately as follows: Turkey—1,500,000; Iraq—800,000; Iran—600,000; Syria—250,000. Cf. W. G. Elphinston, "Kurds and the Kurdish Question," *Journal of the Royal Central Asian Society*, 1948, Part I.

Examples of great religious and cultural differences among Arabic-speaking groups within a country are afforded by the Druzes and Alawis of Syria.

is known to all educated Arabs, that is held in common. Also the racial aspects of Arab unity are subject to considerable qualification. Such factors as religious and cultural differences, intermarriage between Arabs and other races over a period of centuries, and wide local variations in the extent of contact with Europe and with the main Ottoman centers have given rise in the course of time to great local differentiations. It is perhaps only in contrast to the other racial and linguistic groups of the Middle East that Arabs can be said to constitute a unity.

Except in the eastern mountain areas where the Kurds live, Turkey contains a highly homogeneous populace, with about 4 per cent of non-Turkish-speaking persons and persons with foreign cultural backgrounds, these divided among numerous small groups. In Iran, although there are some linguistic minorities of indeterminate size in the border regions, homogeneity prevails in a large part of the country. Israel contains a Jewish majority of about 90 per cent, resulting mainly from post-1918 immigration from Europe and from the wholesale flight of Arabs from Jewish-held sectors during the Palestine War of 1948. Practically all Israeli Jews either speak Hebrew or are in the process of learning that language.

The Persian language, though it is Indo-European whereas Arabic is a Semitic tongue, is written in the same script as Arabic.[7] Turkish was also once written in that script, but since the early days of the republic it has been written with the European alphabet, and official efforts have been made to eliminate words of Arabic derivation. Hebrew, which in its modern form is to some extent an artificial language, has its own alphabet.[8]

2. *Political Relations.*   Among the seven Arab nations there is a rudimentary form of political unity, mainly manifested in the Arab League, a sort of regional United Nations established in 1945. This association, however, has assumed in the main a defensive character, that is, an alignment of Arabs against the non-Arab world, particularly the American and European segments thereof. This attitude

[7] Also it has many words of Arabic derivation.

[8] Hebrew is an acquired language, as far as most Israeli Jews are concerned. Many artificial additions have had to be made to the ancient Hebrew to enable it to serve present-day needs.

has it origins in chronic unsatisfactory relations between Arab groups on the one hand and Great Britain and France on the other, in the days when those European nations were in substantial control of the main Arab region, i.e., from 1918 to 1939. It is also probable that the intense antagonism toward Israel now being shown by so many of the politically conscious Middle Eastern Arabs is closely related to the general anti-European feeling.[9] Here it must be recalled that the Jewish position in Palestine has been erected on the foundation of a British political gesture—the Balfour Declaration of 1917. Also a large percentage of the Jews of Israel are of European origin or ancestry.

Positive, internal unity among the Arab nations of the Middle East is by no means so apparent. The relatively easy victory of Israel in the Palestine War, although outnumbered by fifty to one by the Arabs in total population, is certainly attributable in great measure to an absence of adequate cooperative planning of the campaign by the Arab states, which in turn must have been due to insufficient mutual trust. This apparent insufficiency of mutual confidence has, in fact, been in almost continuous evidence during the entire period covered by this study. The program of any one political leader for a thoroughgoing, or at least closer, union of all Middle Eastern Arabs generally meets with uncompromising denunciation by many other leaders; and most programs of that character have clearly implied an assumption of preponderant power by the dominant political groups in the country from which the proposal emanated. Moreover, even plans for the amalgamation of some, but not all, of the countries under a single rule have met with determined opposition, not only in the Arab countries directly involved but in others as well. These issues have led to highly complicated situations, in which it has been practically impossible for outsiders to evaluate the alignments of opposition, particularly as to intensity and degree of permanence. There have, for example, been two separate schemes in recent years for a political union of

[9] These points are best illustrated by the type of material which was offered from 1946 to 1948 by the *Arab News Bulletin*, a biweekly publication of the Arab Office, Washington, D.C., the Arab League's information agency in the United States. The main emphases were anti-Zionist and anti-French.

Iraq, Jordan, Syria, and possibly Lebanon and Palestine. One of these was the Greater Syria project, whereunder King Abdullah of Jordan would have become monarch of the entire region thus united. This scheme met with unrelenting opposition among groups in all of the countries involved other than Jordan; in Syria, however, there has been some indication of support for it on the part of a highly influential faction, at least as a basis for negotiations. There is also the Fertile Crescent Scheme, which originated in Iraq[10] and which differs from the Greater Syria Plan principally in its rejection of the Jordan throne's leadership—this despite the fact that the royal families of Jordan and Iraq are closely related by blood and are apparently well disposed toward one another.[11] As for the governments of Egypt and Saudi Arabia, both have been vigorous in their denunciation of both schemes, even to the point of frequently expressing a willingness to oppose them by force.

Much of this internal dissension in the Arab ranks has stemmed from the personal rivalries among three Arab monarchs, namely, Farouk of Egypt, Abdullah of Jordan, and Ibn Saud of Saudi Arabia. The two other Arab monarchies of the Middle East are Iraq and Yemen. The Iraqi throne is somewhat weakened by the fact that the King is still a minor. As for Yemen, because of the isolation of that country little authentic information is available concerning the present Imam's political attitudes. His late father, however, was known to resent Ibn Saud, against whom he conducted a losing war in 1934. Nor are monarchical rivalries the whole story, insofar as political disunity is concerned. Since the republics of Syria and Lebanon became independent, relations between those neighbors have not infrequently been of a tempestuous character.[12]

The lack of mutual trust among Arab governments in the Middle East has been instanced in other connections. During the between-

[10] The author of the scheme was Nuri es-Said Pasha, who has often been Premier of one or another of Iraq's short-lived cabinets.

[11] King Feisal of Iraq is Abdullah's grandnephew.

[12] For example, in 1947 Syria closed part of the territory adjacent to Lebanon to all foreign travel. And on March 25, 1950, "Lebanon closed its borders to all trade with Syria, thus causing a complete break in economic relations between the two countries." Cf. Middle East Journal (July, 1950, chronology).

wars era those governments embarked unhesitatingly upon bitter tariff wars with one another; indeed, in some instances where the European mandatory powers intervened to prevent or limit such wars, as in Syria in 1935, they met with strong opposition from the native governments involved.[13] Before leaving this general topic, it should be noted that some of the recent friction among Middle Eastern Arabs has been without regard to national lines.[14] Generally speaking, however, nationalism of the nation-state variety has, at least insofar as overt action is concerned, been much more marked than group loyalties transcending national boundaries. The most conspicuous exception has been the strong tendency of the six Arab states represented in the United Nations General Assembly[15] to cast their votes therein as a bloc.

As for intra-regional international relations in which the non-Arab Middle Eastern states have been involved, these have not been too satisfactory on the whole. Turkey's strong tendency, since the establishment of the republic, has been to limit her relationships with her Middle Eastern neighbors and to establish closer ties with the leading Western powers.[16] Turkey also erected heavy tariff barriers against her southern and eastern neighbors, with the result that trade with some of them, most markedly in the case of Syria, has declined to levels well below those prevailing before World War I.[17] Capping the climax was Turkey's annexation in 1939 of the Syrian Sanjaq of Alexandretta (Vilayet of Hatay), ceded to her by France without the consent of any native Syrian government, and probably in violation of the stipulations of the Syria mandate. The Turkish Government stated at that time that, while it had no objection to France's maintaining control over the highly strategic Sanjaq, it strongly objected to a militarily weak independent state occupying that position vis-à-vis Turkey.

[13] Said B. Himadeh, *Economic Organization of Syria* (Beirut, 1936), pp. 252-259.

[14] For example, the Moslem Brotherhood, to be discussed later, is an opposition force of an international character.

[15] Jordan is not a member of the United Nations.

[16] Philip P. Graves, *Briton and Turk* (London, 1941), chaps. 15 and 16.

[17] Himadeh, *op. cit.*, pp. 249, 257; Royal Institute of International Affairs, *The Middle East: A Political and Economic Survey* (London, 1950), p. 411.

Turkey's relations with the seven Arab states are, as of December 31, 1950, correct but somewhat distant. From time to time throughout the past fifteen years there have been numerous bilateral conferences apparently designed to bring about closer relations; but, as far as one can judge by appearances, they have had little result either one way or the other. It is true that, in the Saadabad Pact of 1937, Turkey and Iraq entered into a *rapprochement* containing promise of a future alliance. That agreement, however, has long been dormant, although there are recurrent rumors that the alliance in question may yet come into being. If that happens, it is difficult to see how a conflict could be avoided between such a pact and the Arab League pact, to which Iraq is committed. Among the governing groups in Syria, Turkey seems to be greatly feared.[18]

Relations between Turkey and Iran, on the other hand, seem to be improving. In the days before World War I, the Ottoman and Persian governments tended to keep each other at arm's length, each apparently fearing that the other would be used by the European powers as a pawn against itself.[19] In most of the between-wars period the two strong neighboring rulers, Kemal Ataturk and Reza Shah Pahlevi, followed more or less the same tendency,[20] one manifestation of which was that in each country roads and railways terminated at points at a healthy distance from the frontier between the two states.[21] In 1937, as the general international situation grew more dangerous, this attitude of mutual aloofness (which had already begun to break down somewhat) was abandoned, and the Saadabad Pact (including also Iraq and Afghanistan) was concluded. Political complications caused by the world war made the relations between the two countries somewhat distant again.[22] However, since the end

[18] A. H. Hourani, *Syria and Lebanon, A Political Essay* (London, 1946), pp. 117, 126.

[19] Religious reasons also entered into this mutual wariness. Cf. Graves, *op. cit.*, pp. 58, 65.

[20] There were, however, also tendencies in the opposite direction. Cf. William S. Haas, *Iran* (New York, 1946), p. 155.

[21] Except for an ancient road which was renovated after the conclusion of the Saadabad Pact.

[22] During most of the war Iran was under Anglo-Soviet occupation and Turkey was neutral.

of that war, there have been many symptoms of improvement. Turkey's present plans envisage a fairly rapid extension of her railway system to the Iranian frontier, and corresponding plans exist in Iran.

Relations between Turkey and Israel are at present generally promising. There appears to be a definite desire on both sides to develop at least a close economic *rapprochement*, this point being particularly emphasized by the Turkish Government in its information bulletins.[23] Probable reasons for this desire, on Turkey's part, are her wish to create an anti-Soviet, pro-Western bloc in the Middle East; her chronic difficulties with Syria and, to a lesser extent, the other Arab states; and the prestige consideration underlying an alignment between the two most modern and progressive countries of the region. In the case of Israel, her urgent need for political friends and economic partners in the region is certainly the main consideration. Iran did not recognize Israel until mid-1950; and, although the recognition may be indicative of a new approach, both the government and public opinion in Iran have hitherto appeared to be pro-Arab on the issues of the Palestine War.

Relations between Iran and the Arab states are, on the whole, satisfactory, as far as mutual sentiments and to a lesser extent trade relations are concerned. There is, however, much room for constructive development, particularly in the field of communications and of agreements which would facilitate the development of the Tigris-Euphrates-Karun river system as an integrated whole. A good start was made during the between-wars period toward the breakdown of the religious barrier (to be discussed later) which had theretofore separated Iran from the Arab world. Also a highway was constructed between Baghdad and Teheran, and an Iranian air line instituted a regular service between those two points. There are now periodic rumors that neither Iran nor Iraq would be averse to a restoration of the Saadabad front.

At the time of writing, it is difficult to predict what course Israel-Arab relations will take. There have been recent indications of

[23] *News from Turkey* (New York: Turkish Information Office), II and III (1949 and 1950), *passim.*

CHALLENGE AND RESPONSE IN THE MIDDLE EAST

a possible *rapprochement* between Israel and Jordan.[24] The two states were more or less forced to adopt a common attitude vis-à-vis the United Nations General Assembly Resolution of December, 1949, calling for an internationalization of Jerusalem. Since then several parleys have taken place between Israel's and Jordan's official representatives. Otherwise, however, there have been practically no indications of possible breaches in the status of mutual hostility between Israel and the Arab countries.[25]

3. *Religion.* No discussion of Middle Eastern politics would be complete without some consideration of the religious background.

Islam, because of its enormous numerical following, tends to overshadow all the other religions of the region.[26] It is, however, a decidedly open question whether this religion is a potential political force of first magnitude and, as a corollary proposition, whether there is any near-future likelihood of a large-scale political union of Moslems in the Middle East and elsewhere. Such a union would necessarily be based both on the religion itself and on the cultural patterns which the religion has produced.

On the surface, there is considerable evidence against any such likelihood. Even a cursory examination of the past record reveals instances in which Moslem has waged war against Moslem, with each faction supported by Christian allies. Furthermore, it would be an error to suppose that Islam (the Moslem world) is any freer from schisms and internal differentiations than is Christendom. The following paragraphs contain a brief, sketchy summary in this regard.

There are two major divisions of Islam, manifested by sects known as Sunni and Shia. The Sunni sect is regarded as the orthodox one; it outnumbers the Shia by about two to one in the Middle East as a whole, and by much greater margins in Egypt, Turkey, Saudi Arabia, Syria, Jordan, and Lebanon. These two sects are still further

[24] Albion Ross, "Jordan Seen Ready for Israeli Accord," New York *Times*, March 4, 1950.

[25] "Israel, Iraq Study Population Shift," New York *Times*, July 4, 1950.

[26] By a rough calculation based on figures given by the Royal Institute of International Affairs (*op. cit., passim*), there are about 2,500,000 Christians and Jews in the independent countries of the Middle East other than Israel, of which nearly half are Egyptian Copts. Nearly all of the other inhabitants of those nine countries are Moslems.

subdivided, the subdivisions in some cases giving rise to marked differences in cultural and behavior patterns.

One result is that, in each of three of the independent Moslem countries in the Middle East, there is an official religion which shows great divergencies from the customs, practices, and beliefs outside of the country in question. The three are Iran, Saudi Arabia, and Yemen. Iran is the world's main Shiite country; and there Shiism, whose origins seem to stem less from purely religious causes than from its associations with pre-Islamic Persian history through a royal marriage, has become closely associated with Iranian (Persian) nationalism.[27] That nationalism is based to a large extent on pride in the distinction between Persian culture and traditions on the one hand and Arabic on the other.

The Arabs were, of course, the prime movers in the developments which made the so-called golden age of Islam possible. Theirs was the martial and crusading fervor which, emerging from the wilderness, produced the downfall of great civilized empires and brought Islam to the Atlantic shores. Theirs, too, was the Prophet Mohammed in whose name all Islamic traditions developed; the book containing the inspirational sayings in the form of melodious poetry; the language and beautiful script in which the holy book, the Koran, was written; and, not least important by any means, the tolerance which made possible the circulation of ideas introduced from sources external to their own group.

On the other hand, many of the intellectual foundations of Mohammedanism were laid by Persian scholars, whose influence at the court of the Arab caliphs of Baghdad was considerable and more or less continuous. Also, during most of Islamic history, the Persians have displayed greater mental flexibility than the Arabs, and have been less disposed to adhere to dogma which was difficult to justify in the light of changing conditions.[28] Further, Persian Shiism has been of a much more colorful character than the traditionally

[27] T. W. Arnold, *The Preaching of Islam* (New York, 1913), p. 209; Haas, *op. cit.*, pp. 70-91.
[28] H. A. R. Gibb, *Mohammedanism, An Historical Survey* (London, 1949), p. 123.

austere Sunnism, which outlaws both music and representational art. These bans, to be sure, are not always strictly observed.

Thus, because of the conflicting claims as to whose contribution was the more important, and because Persians and Arabs have always maintained their separate identities, it is not unnatural that mutual jealousies should persist in an era when both groups find themselves in a state of decline.

Yemen is also a Shiite country, but hers is a special form of Shiism which has relatively little in common with the Iranian brand, and which has not produced any strong bonds between the two countries. Saudi Arabia follows the Wahhabi deviation of Sunnism, which stands for a return to the simple monotheism of Mohammed, uncolored by scholasticism, mysticism, or superstition. Wahhabi practices are highly puritanical, and there is a strong tendency to abhor the relative moral laxity of Moslems, both Sunni and Shia, in other lands. The Wahhabi movement has had a strong influence upon trends in modern Mohammedanism in other parts of the Sunni Middle East, particularly in Egypt.

Nor is this the whole story. Turkey, too, is in a class by itself with regard to religion. As a result of Kemal Ataturk's reforms, a wave of atheism, or at best indifference to religion, spread over the country; and these attitudes are still decidedly the preponderant ones among educated Turks, and Turks in the urban centers, under fifty years of age. Religious edifices have been requisitioned by the government for other uses; and, in 1943, this writer lived in a Turkish city of 15,000 inhabitants in which not a single place of Mohammedan worship was open. Since mid-1947, however, there has been some indication of a religious revival, promoted for political ends by the Democratic party, whose 1950 election victory may well be partially attributable to the popularity of such a policy in the rural regions. Manifestations of this revival have been the reestablishment of theological faculties, which had been banned since 1923, and the dispatch of Turkish representatives to the annual pilgrimage to Mecca. It may be added that, among Turks of all classes, a definite distinction is still made between *Moslem* Turks (i.e., Turks of Mohammedan descent) and "minority Turks"; in short, there is still some recognition, perhaps vague in some quarters, of cultural affinity between Turkey and other parts of the so-called "Moslem world." Thus, although the surface indications are mostly to the contrary, there does seem to be an outside possibility that Turkey's nominal membership in the Moslem community of nations might yet become an important political consideration. The other side of the picture is that Turkey's political orientation toward the West seems now, more than ever before, to be the primary trend.

Besides Turkey and Saudi Arabia there are four other Sunni Moslem countries in the Middle East, namely, Syria, Jordan, Egypt, and Iraq, in the last of which the Shia Moslems are believed to outnumber the dominant Sunni group. Among the populations of those countries wide internal differences exist as regards the degree of religiousness. The evidence seems to be that most of the educated people in all those countries take their religion somewhat lightly. Nevertheless there is at least one powerful organization, the Moslem Brotherhood, which at all times makes its presence felt as a militant crusader for religious conservatism and which, it is generally conceded, might at some time in the future prove stronger than the agnostic groups. Here it should be noted that in the rural regions of those four countries even the educated dare not speak or act in opposition to the religious principles generally regarded as orthodox. The Moslem Brotherhood is strongest in Egypt, where it has been responsible for several political assassinations, including that of Prime Minister Nokrashy Pasha in 1948. There are, however, branches in the other three countries which are not without their influence.

Authoritative scholars, generally speaking, incline to the position that Islam is a potentially close political unity. These men fully recognize the strong divisive forces but insist that there is a still stronger underlying oneness which may well manifest itself in the future as a defense against the more unpopular aspects of Western influence upon the Middle East. The arguments advanced, though highly worthy of consideration, are too complex to admit of brief summarization. They are not unrelated to arguments in support of a thesis that Arab unity, despite all the contrary superficial indications, is an important reality. In fact, it is probably impossible to discuss the pros and cons of Arab unity without strong emphasis upon the religious aspect of the question. For, apart from the religion itself, there is the question of shared cultural patterns based wholly or partially upon the Moslem religion. These matters have been particularly well analyzed by Messrs. H. A. R. Gibb (*Modern Trends in Islam*) and A. H. Hourani (*Syria and Lebanon: A Political Essay*).

As intimated, all eight of the nations mentioned in the preceding paragraphs have large Moslem majorities, though in some of them non-Moslem groups have economic influence, as, for example, the Copts in Egypt. This non-Moslem influence is, however, everywnere on the decline, most markedly in the case of Jews. It is in Turkey, surprisingly enough, that the decline has been particularly marked.

The remaining two countries, Israel and Lebanon, have non-Moslem majorities. In Lebanon a bare majority is Christian (as far as can be ascertained from somewhat questionable statistics), with the remainder of the population largely Mohammedan. This raises interesting questions in regard to Lebanon's future. But for Christian separatism, Lebanon would hardly have any excuse for separate existence; yet Moslem influence is strong in Lebanese governmental circles, and the present Prime Minister is a Moslem. The present official Lebanese attitude, which is by no means shared by the whole population, is one of loyalty to the majority points of view of the Arab League. In this connection it should be pointed out that most, but probably not all, Lebanese Christians regard themselves as Arabs from the ethnic standpoint. Nevertheless they are not without their fear of the Moslem Arabs, by whom they are so greatly outnumbered in the Middle East. This fear might conceivably lead in time to a *rapprochement* between Lebanon and Israel. About 90 per cent of Israel's inhabitants are Jewish by religion. But religion seems to be only a minor element in the existing antagonisms between Israel and her neighbors.

This discussion does not by any means exhaust the matter of religious and racial crosscurrents in the Middle East. Syria, for example, has a great and confusing mass of so-called "minority problems," in most of which it is virtually impossible to separate the religious from the other aspects. What is particularly important to note, however, is that in some situations Arabs are aligned against Arabs on religious grounds (e.g., Copts vs. Moslems), while in others Moslems are aligned against Moslems (e.g., Kurds vs. Arabs) on racial grounds or even religious (e.g., Sunnis vs. Shiites).

4. *Political Structure.* With respect to political structure, the ten independent nations of the Middle East are divisible into four groups, namely, absolute monarchies, constitutional monarchies with oligarchic rule, republics with oligarchic rule, and democracies. The two absolute monarchies are Saudi Arabia and Yemen, neither of which shows any symptoms of modern constitutional reform or parliamentary development. The constitutional monarchies are Egypt, Iraq, Jordan, and Iran. These countries have most of the superficial earmarks of parliamentary democracy, that is: elections (often free and secret), legislation by elective representatives, resignations of cabinets following parliamentary defeats, etc. The basic reality, however, is that, up to the present time, no matter how many changes of ministers occurred within a government total political power has always remained vested in a single economic class, namely, the possessors of great wealth, with even this class usually completely dominated by one particular subclass—the large landowners. Moreover, the same situation prevails in Syria and Lebanon, although these nations are republican in their formal structures. This dominance of one group in the populations has resulted mainly from the great influence over the peasantry possessed by the large landowners and, to a lesser extent, the large merchants.[29]

Of the remaining two countries, one, Israel, has a broad and far-reaching democratic political structure. The other, Turkey, may now be regarded as having completed the most important transitional stages from dictatorship to democracy.

5. *Internal Unity.* Four of the ten Middle Eastern countries—Turkey, Israel, Saudi Arabia, and Yemen—possess a high degree of internal unity and coherence, except as to personal and family rivalries in the last-named state. The Turkish Republic, during the

[29] In Syria at present the military has considerable political power; but this seems to be a temporary state of affairs as far as the army command's intentions, and possibly also its abilities, are concerned. Cf. Ross, "Syrian Civil Rule Faces Final Test," New York *Times,* June 6, 1950.

twenty-seven years of its existence, has known no major domestic unrest except on the part of the Kurds in the eastern part of the country. Kurdish unrest seems to be chronic in all countries where Kurds live, and the problem has been less serious in Turkey than in Iraq, Iran, and Syria. Although Turkey's success in handling the internal situation is partly attributable to a highly efficient secret police force, which maintains checks and controls in all parts of the country, it is also probable that the positive elements of serious civil strife have generally been lacking. The founder of the Republic, Kemal Ataturk, was adored by the Turkish people; and his successor, Ismet Inonu, was personally well liked, though his policies led to his somewhat surprising electoral defeat in 1950.

When the Jewish state (later Israel) was no more than a political aspiration on the part of a group of homeless people, it was not difficult to imagine that the project might be wrecked, if not by external factors, by internal disunity. Reasons were that the Jews of Palestine, with their many different national and cultural origins, might become divided, on the basis of such origins, into numerous mutually uncongenial groups; that the extremist Jewish political groups (i.e., the terrorists and expansionists) might in time come to blows with the more moderate elements; and that the religious orthodox Jews would possibly not tolerate a Jewish state organized along secular lines. At present, although Israel is scarcely more than two years old, and it is therefore perhaps too soon to judge, the great preponderance of evidence is that these predictions have been proved to be baseless.

Saudi Arabia and Yemen are exceedingly primitive countries, and it is doubtful that a popular revolt would be possible in either of them, at least for some time to come. It is true that the Imam, Yahya, of Yemen was assassinated a few years ago; but that was apparently a "palace revolution," although the question of Westernization of the country was an issue as between the small groups which opposed each other.

In Egypt there is more or less constant internal unrest, which in recent years has been marked by numerous assassinations of prominent political figures, including two successive Prime Ministers in 1945 and 1948 respectively. It is in Egypt that the Moslem Brotherhood (*Ikhwan al-Muslimin*), a body of fanatical religious conservatives, enjoys its greatest strength, ideologically supported by Al-Azhar University, the world's main center of intellectual Mohammedan orthodoxy.[30] Moreover, Egypt has a considerably larger middle class, both absolutely and relatively, than any other Arab country except Lebanon; and this middle class has many and profound sources of dissatisfaction, not the least of which is the chronic failure of landlord-dominated governments to adhere to their promises of reform. Furthermore, industrialization has advanced farther in Egypt than in other Arab countries, and labor unrest is at times acute. Finally, the lot of the Egyptian peasant is apparently about as bad now as at any other time in Egypt's long history, characterized as that has been by the unhappy lot of the oppressed and exploited cultivator. This last factor has not yet given rise to serious disturbances, but no authorities on Egypt deny the possibility of peasant outbreaks in the foreseeable future.

In Jordan, although there has never been any organized civil strife, sharp disagreements between King Abdullah and other members of the government were frequent, particularly on the question of a united Arab world. The main reason these disputes never went far is that Abdullah always knew how to back down gracefully whenever it was clear that the preponderance of influential opinion was uncompromisingly against him.

The history of Iraq has been characterized by continual troubles involving the various minority groups, including Shiites, Kurds, and Assyrians. Taken all together, the minority groups constitute well over half of the country's population. Some of the troubles, such as the Assyrian affair of 1933, have led to considerable bloodshed.

Syria has had minority difficulties similar to those of Iraq, but their scale has not been so great since Syria became fully independent. Under the French mandate, conflicts between the various racial and

[30] Negatively, the ideals of the Moslem Brotherhood and Al-Azhar are somewhat similar. However, the Brotherhood openly rejects Al-Azhar's "debased clericalism." Cf. Charles Issawi, *Egypt, An Economic and Social Analysis* (London, 1947), pp. 149-173.

religious elements constituted an almost perpetual problem for the mandatory power. The complete political separation of Lebanon from Syria has helped in some measure to lessen it. However, this particular type of unrest has been amply supplanted by troubles due to differences on major political issues, as, for example, the question of whether there should be a political union between Syria and neighboring Arab countries. During 1949 and 1950 the Government of Syria has been completely lacking in stability.[31]

There has been little overt internal strife in Lebanon since that country's attainment of independence. But there are potentially inflammable materials, which from time to time become strongly evident: the mixed Moslem-Christian population, with no decisive preponderance of power on either side; the apparent existence of a large body of informed public opinion out of sympathy with the government but powerless to oppose it; the participation of many Lebanese Moslems in Syrian internal politics;[32] and uncertainties in regard to Lebanon's political and economic future.

Iran, uniquely among the nations of the Middle East, has been (in 1946) the victim of Soviet-inspired civil strife. Since that year there have been no internal outbreaks of a major nature, but all of the available evidence indicates that the elements of serious trouble are present in force. This has been particularly true since the Shah visited the United States in 1950 and, upon his return, declared his intention to take a strong hand against the selfish landowners who were allegedly sabotaging economic reform in Iran.

In summary, if we omit Jordan, where the situation has always been kept under control and where British influence is strong, it appears that five of the ten Middle Eastern governments are confronted with highly difficult, if not dangerous, internal situations. These matters are discussed further in the chapters on the individual countries.

[31] Ross, "Alert Is Ordered for Syrian Army," New York *Times*, May 16, 1950.
[32] "The Syrian National Party, a semi-military organization favoring the incorporation of Lebanon into a Greater Syrian State, had long been proscribed [by the Lebanese Government], and further measures were taken to liquidate it in July, 1949 when its 'leader' Antun Saada, was shot after a secret court-martial for intrigue with the then dictator of Syria." (Royal Institute of International Affairs, *op. cit.*, p. 393.)

SOCIAL AND ECONOMIC BACKGROUND

SOCIAL AND ECONOMIC CONDITIONS IN 1914

The most conspicuous characteristic of the Middle East, up to mid-1914, was its extreme "backwardness" in the matter of social and economic development.[33] Some of the manifestations of this backwardness, which in broad outline were identical for the two Middle Eastern empires, are described by Dr. Millspaugh in regard to Persia as follows:

During the centuries that followed its moment of world supremacy, Persia experienced for longer or shorter periods invasions, civil war, anarchy, famines, epidemics, reigns of terror, and merciless oppression. . . .

The struggles and evolution in France and England, which resulted in the perfecting of national unity and the disappearance of feudalism, had no parallel in Persia. Semi-nomadic tribes, each a closely bound and largely autonomous group and each clannish, warlike, and given to banditry, made up from a fourth to a third of the population. . . . The social system . . . remained free of caste and of hereditary nobility. Nevertheless, the country had a class of grandees, whose privileges and power rested in the main on the ownership of land. . . .

At the base of this system, the millions of peasants, practically bound to the soil, huddled in walled villages for solidarity and security, barely subsisting under conditions of most extreme poverty. Their toil had three simple objects: to exist, to satisfy the demands of the landowners, and to meet the multiplied exactions of an extravagant and rapacious government. Over all, the Moslem clergy exercised an authoritarian influence; and in the towns a fairly numerous and influential middle class had developed, consisting of government officials, army officers, scribes, artisans, merchants, and tradesmen. . . .

Women, closely veiled, lived on an inferior plane, and except for the family intimacies of the *anderun*, moved in a world of their own, secluded, ignorant, and pretty much narrowed down to their biological function. . . .

No one ever closed or bridged the chasm that separated people and government. A deep cleavage persisted, not only in political organization, but, more seriously, in the habits and long memories of the people.[34]

[33] The great Moslem civilization was definitively terminated by the Mongol invasion which occurred in the thirteenth century A.D. As a matter of policy the Mongols destroyed the main irrigation works in Iraq.

[34] Arthur C. Millspaugh, *Americans in Persia* (Washington, 1946), pp. 11-12.

The question which naturally occurs to us is why such a state of affairs persisted in the Middle East, even after immense progress had been made in Europe along social and economic lines. Since the two regions were never wholly out of contact with each other, and since the Middle East had been the center of splendid civilizations in ancient and medieval times, reasons must be sought, first, for the decline, and second, for the failure to follow the West in social and economic advances during the modern era.

These questions are partially answered in *The Middle East: A Political and Economic Survey:*

The natural resources of the Middle East are few and . . . there is inadequate rainfall over much of the area. Equally important is the shortage of industrial raw materials, except oil. Turkey has coal, iron, and chromium; Egypt has iron, as yet unexploited; the Dead Sea is a valuable repository of bromine and potassium salts; and there are deposits of other minerals elsewhere especially in . . . Iran. The overall picture, however, is not favorable. The Middle East in general is deficient in basic materials such as coal and iron, timber (except in parts of Iran), and building stone is lacking in the Nile delta and the lower Tigris and Euphrates.

The economic backwardness of the Middle East has a historical basis as well. The Mongol, late Mamluk, and Ottoman systems did not provide the strongly centralized administration necessary to countries which depend on a highly organized irrigation system for their agriculture. Under such conditions, the irrigation system broke down, settled peasants were forced to become nomadic pastoralists, public security deteriorated, and trade was hampered. A decisive development took place in the sixteenth century when the Cape route to India replaced the Middle Eastern route. From then till the nineteenth century the Middle East became a backwater in the world's trade, while the Great Powers of the West were developing the wealth of India and America and laying the foundation of their industrial and commercial supremacy. During these centuries of comparative stagnation the Middle East peoples lost any economic power they possessed to develop their own resources, and fell still further behind when the West became industrialized.[35]

Not mentioned in the foregoing paragraphs but certainly of great importance in connection with the situation in 1914 were the effects

[35] Royal Institute of International Affairs, *op. cit.*, pp. 62-63.

of the Mohammedan religion, as it had been translated into actual thought and practice, upon the social and economic development of the Middle East. In its early days, that religion had helped materially to produce the Arab golden age, which is generally considered to have represented the highest civilization of the medieval period. One failure of that age, however, was in the matter of generating popular yearnings after wider knowledge. While a brilliant intellectual life was conducted at the highest social levels, the great scholars made little or no attempt to reach the masses.[36] Such an attempt might still have been made in due time but for a development in the ninth century A.D. which served to "freeze" religion and thought in the Middle Eastern segment of the Moslem world. "Most unfortunately for . . . Islam, a Khalifa arose who had a relish for theological discussions and a high opinion of his own infallibility. This was Al-Mamun. It did not matter that he ranged himself on the progressive side; his fatal error was that he invoked the authority of the state in matters of the intellectual and religious life. Thus, by enabling the conservative party to pose as martyrs, he brought the prejudices and passions of the populace still more against the new movement."[37]

Gradually, in both Sunni and Shia branches, the control of higher education passed into the hands of theologians. The result was that both religion and everyday thought became permeated with dogma and stripped of vitality.[38] But, if this fact alone was not sufficient to produce a static society, that result was certainly produced by the nature of the matters taught to students and in turn passed along by them, in still more rigid form, to the unlettered populace.

One patricularly important tenet was that all knowledge comes through special revelation from Allah (God); in the Sunni orthodox interpretation it was even held that good and evil could not be distinguished by the intellect.[39] God's revelations, moreover, had been reserved for a few chosen persons; and only a few specially licensed persons were competent to interpret them. Still further, in the Sunni

[36] Duncan B. Macdonald, *Muslim Theology* (New York, 1903), p. 153.
[37] *Ibid.*, p. 154.
[38] Gibb, *op. cit.*, p. 145.
[39] Macdonald, *op. cit.*, p. 136.

branch, the interpreters (*ulema*) were bound by strict rules of construction.[40] In both the Ottoman and Persian empires, the *ulema* were part of the governmental structure and were used by the rulers for the achievement of their personal ends. However, because of their immediate influence over the masses, the *ulema* were also very powerful in their own right.

To this it should be added that the very word "Islam" means *submission*, that is, submission to the revealed will of an all-powerful Creator who, according to the orthodox tenet, is not even under an obligation to do justice.[41] The good Moslem must, accordingly, seek contentment in those blessings, few or many, as may come his way in the ordinary course of events. Given all these circumstances, the almost inevitable next step in logic is the conclusion that social welfare is not the concern of the government, and that it is improper for individual Moslems to press for social reform.[42] The main end result—and indeed the condition actually in being in the year 1914 —is oppression and exploitation by the ruling class and acceptance of these by the masses in a spirit of fatalism, passivity, and strong conservatism. An additional inevitable result was the general distrust by the people of the region of their respective governments. Although the nineteenth century had produced two strong revival movements in Islam, these had, even by 1914, not yet affected the great majority of people in the two Middle Eastern empires.[43]

In Lebanon, where the majority of the inhabitants were Christians, and whence there had been a considerable amount of emigration to the Western Hemisphere with a resultant interchange of ideas, the reactionary religious influences were not so powerful as in most parts of the Ottoman Empire.

THE IMPACT OF THE WEST

1. *Social and Economic Aspects.* Since 1914 the fact of outstanding importance in regard to the Middle East has been the strong

[40] *Ibid.*, p. 38.

[41] *Ibid.*, p. 136.

[42] R. Levy, *The Sociology of Islam* (London, 1931), p. 283.

[43] The revival movements were the Wahhabi movement in Arabia and the Senussi one in Libya.

and growing influence of the Western world upon its life and thought. In Yemen this influence has been only slight; in Saudi Arabia it has thus far been kept under strict control by King Ibn Saud. As for the other eight nations, all have already adopted Western methods to a greater or lesser extent, and all are clearly interested in proceeding still farther along those lines. In all but Saudi Arabia and Yemen, moreover, there are strong currents of both governmental and intellectual opinion in favor of going ahead with programs of economic Westernization, or "modernization," at a greatly accelerated rate. It is true that fears are held in many quarters, especially among the wealthy groups and the religious Moslem elements, of possible undesirable results of the Westernizing process; but such fears are, as a rule, not in any sense deterrents or brakes upon the widespread impatience for progress, of at least one sort or other, in the direction of Westernism. There are, to be sure, many disagreements as to the precise form which the advances shall assume; but questions of this nature are regarded as problems to be faced only as they arise in some specific shape. The only circumstance under which economic Westernization is definitely rejected by Middle Easterners as a whole is where it is suspected that the development may take place under conditions reminiscent of colonial or economic imperialism on the part of the Western powers. With this one qualification, there is now almost constant pressure on the part of the nine Middle Eastern nations (i.e., all but Yemen) to be furnished with extensive outside assistance, both financial and technical, in the modernized development of their territories.

This urge toward Westernization is not necessarily the same as the urge, now noted in some quarters, to raise Middle Eastern living standards. Certainly the latter consideration is entering into the question more and more. However, there are other reasons why economic Westernization is desired, and it may well be that these others are still the primary ones in most minds. One of them is the feeling that, in the world as it is today, a nation's or group's greatness is determined (or at least judged) by the amount and efficiency of modern machinery which the nation or group has at its disposal. Another, no doubt, is the conviction that cherished values, traditional and cultural, cannot be defended effectively unless the defenders have Western-style mechanical weapons of defense. That these reasons are more important in many minds than the standard of living consideration is evidenced by the fact that many Middle Eastern politicians have strongly advocated Westernization along mechanical lines while at the same time demonstrating that their concern for general living standards was little more than nominal.[44]

Doubtless the most immediate stimuli toward Westernization in the Middle East have been provided by the two world wars and their aftermaths. Both of those wars have furnished Middle Easterners with powerful object lessons as to the immense difficulties experienced by peoples and groups who are not well equipped with modern machines and with the ability to operate them. World War II, moreover, brought a partial demonstration to educated Middle Easterners that Westernization is not solely a matter of machines but rather a far-reaching network of conditions and methods, economic and social, in the absence of which mere machines could hardly be made to function effectively. Most particularly they have been impressed by close observation of the fact that the achievements of the West have been facilitated in large measure by well-developed statistical techniques, channels for efficient and rapid interchanges of information between experts in different fields, and methods of producing large quantities of experts who are not only technically skillful but also honest, cooperative, stable, energetic, and contented with the work for which they have been trained. As a result, it is now widely realized that no modernization program can be truly complete without attention to such nonmechanical matters as education, legal systems, banking, and a host of others.[45]

[44] Ross, "Iran's Parliament Faces Power Test," New York Times, February 11, 1950.

[45] During World War II the activities of the belligerents ruined the normal economic patterns but quickly and efficiently replaced them with patterns almost equally satisfactory. This substitution was mainly due to the efforts of the Middle East Supply Centre, an Anglo-American wartime agency.

The efficient conduct of the more direct Allied war effort in the Middle East could also be observed and admired at close range. This was particularly impressive in view of the widespread belief, in the early stages of the war, in Germany's invincibility.

In Saudi Arabia and Yemen indications are that the rulers' fears
of the results of Westernization outweigh to some extent their
desire for the benefits.[46] Neither of the rulers, however, rejects
Westernization entirely. Both seem to be anxious for it, to the
extent that the foreseeable result appears to them to be surely
beneficial when viewed from all aspects. For the other nations,
generally speaking, haste in achievement seems to be far more important than complete certainty as to ultimate outcomes. Turkey
has been a good example of this in the past. Among the Middle
Eastern nations, Turkey was a pioneer in extensive Westernization;
and so great was the desire to achieve spectacular and statistically
imposing results, particularly in the development of manufacture,
that far too little attention was paid to the details of planning and
the coordination of those details. The same was substantially true of
Iran in the period between wars, and of Egypt to a lesser degree. The
other Middle Eastern areas were under League of Nations mandates
during the between-wars period and underwent limited Westernization on a "safe and sane" basis, as dictated by the mandatory powers.
At present the four Arab nations which were under mandates seem
inclined to follow in the early footsteps of Turkey, Iran, and Egypt.
Israel's position is rather different, since the Jews of Palestine had
already, before the termination of the mandate, accomplished a great
deal on their own in the way of Westernization, and because their
European background has exempted them from the necessity of
having to learn the nature and purposes of Western ways. It is
hardly questionable that Israel's success in altering the face of part
of the Middle East has been a potent stimulus to the other nations,
from the double viewpoint of rivalry and of showing what could be
done with limited resources.

But, although the interest now being taken in Westernization
necessarily strikes the casual observer, a much more important fact

[46] King Ibn Saud of Saudi Arabia is apparently deterred from thoroughgoing
Westernization more because of the disapproval of the Wahhabi shaikhs and
notables than because of his own convictions. It has been authoritatively reported
to this writer that in 1945 Ibn Saud, in defiance of traditional Wahhabi
principles, imported a motion-picture apparatus. This was kept in the royal harem
because all activities in the harem are immune from outside discussion and
criticism.

about the present-day Middle East is the great number of obstacles to any substantial achievement in that direction in the foreseeable future. Even the nations with greatest head starts, with the exception of Israel, have thus far done little more than scratch the surface of the major problems connected with modernization. In none of the nine nations (other than Israel) have the major evils which Westernization can help to remedy, and which were discussed in the section on 1914 social conditions, been alleviated to any great extent. Thus, for those nine the general nature of the job ahead is still nearly as formidable as it was immediately after the termination of World War I. Indeed, according to some observers of the scene, the over-all problem may be greater for the nations which have already embarked upon programs on a large scale than for those whose Westernization to date has been along simpler, less frantic lines. This argument runs that the latter are less likely than the others to have acquired knowledge which will later have to be unlearned, or to feel inclined to throw good money after bad because of pride in showy but worthless achievements.

2. *Cultural and Philosophical Aspects.* In connection with this general topic of the Western impact upon the Middle East, certain aspects which are not of a specifically economic character require brief consideration. This is because those aspects may have an exceedingly important bearing, now or later, upon the question of raising living standards in the region.

The misgivings which two groups, namely, the very wealthy and the very religious, have in regard to Westernization of a thorough-going character have already been mentioned. In addition, however, there are some much more widespread, and it should be added much less easily definable, misgivings which probably affect by far the greater part of the present educated population.

In all the Middle Eastern countries except Saudi Arabia and Yemen the whole complex of folkways in the larger centers has been influenced considerably by contact with European ways and European goods. In the areas near the Mediterranean this influence has been felt, with varying intensity, for centuries; in some cases, notably Egypt and Lebanon, doubt has even been expressed as to whether the countries are properly classifiable as Oriental.

Nevertheless it is now true, as it has never been before, that the increased momentum of Western influences threatens to reduce drastically all the traditional Oriental elements in Middle Eastern culture, including the characteristically Islamic cultural elements. Indeed there are already indications that the impact is beginning to reach the rural areas, which were until recently immune. This trend is a disturbing one to most thoughtful Middle Easterners. And, although there are many and widely divergent reactions to the problem, it seems to be generally agreed among them that, while Western economic and scientific practices should be accepted, acceptance should not imply a complete rejection of local cultures and traditions in favor of imperfectly imitated Western ones.

The fear is now being expressed in some quarters that unless a positive approach to the question is forthcoming soon the matter will be settled by default. In Mr. Hourani's opinion, such an outcome would be tantamount to a total degeneration of the Middle Eastern population into "Levantinism." By this he means a partial connection with two or more cultures but no true identification with any culture at all. The corollary to such a state of affairs, which is even evident to a considerable extent at present, might well be an adoption of all the evil aspects of Western-style nationalism (i.e., intolerance, arrogance, etc.), coupled with an omission of all the virtues thereof. It might also involve a wholehearted acceptance of Western materialism, unbacked by any of the spiritual elements, Western or other, which could soften materialism.[47]

The existence of this problem is a fact of the highest importance in the present-day Middle East. There is, moreover, virtual unanimity among the informed writers on the subject in the assertion that this "soul-sickness" to which the intellectuals of the region confess is fully shared by the masses to the extent that they have been exposed to the European impact. The masses, however, are in a worse position than the intellectuals, since they are unable to diagnose their affliction.[48]

[47] Hourani, op. cit., passim.
[48] Ibid.; Gibb, Modern Trends in Islam (Chicago, 1947), passim; Gustave E. von Grunebaum, "Attempts at Self-Interpretation in Contemporary Islam" (unpublished), Section II, passim.

PRESENT SOCIAL AND ECONOMIC CONDITIONS

The following paragraphs contain discussions of the social and economic conditions of the present day, most of which appear to be traceable in considerable measure to the interaction of the forces noted in the preceding section.

THE PROBLEMS OF AGRICULTURE

Although the estimates on the subject vary, it is universally agreed that, in every Middle Eastern country other than Israel, the rural population constitutes well over 50 per cent of the total settled (i.e., nonnomadic) populace. It is also the consensus that, in Egypt, Iran, Iraq, Jordan, Syria, and Turkey, the agricultural element (including seminomads who devote a substantial portion of their time and effort to cultivation) constitutes 75 per cent or more of the entire population. In other words, a predominantly rural economy prevails in all Middle Eastern countries except Israel. In the latter country the nonrural elements constitute about four-fifths of the populace.

Since there is virtually complete agreement among economists that the future prosperity of the Middle East will depend to a large degree on industrialization with emphasis upon the processing of protective foods such as fruit, dairy products, and eggs,[49] there would seem to be at present a highly uneconomic distribution of most of the populations. However, in the present state of Middle Eastern agriculture, there is no way of altering the general ratio and thereby gaining satisfactory results. Only with greater efficiency of farming methods and facilities would it be possible to transfer appreciable numbers of people from agriculture to industry and commerce and at the same time maintain the supply of primary products for consumption at its present, hardly adequate level.

The most usual authoritative suggestion along remedial lines is to improve and modernize agriculture through the application of whatever capital resources may be available for the purpose. It is argued

[49] The markets for such products would be (1) local, (2) the highly industrialized countries of Europe, (3) other Asiatic countries as their per capita purchasing power increases. Also, cf. Issawi, *op. cit.*, pp. 72 *et seq.*

that, even if the expenditures for this purpose are uneconomic by the criteria generally applied to business transactions, the net result in increased prosperity of the country concerned would more than neutralize the immediate losses. Hence the government of each country should make every effort to gather together the necessary funds, from both domestic and foreign sources, on whatever terms possible, within reasonable limits.[50]

In all of the nine countries expenditures of this nature could produce conditions whereunder greatly increased yields of farm products would be possible. In most of the region summer farming is at present impossible because of the complete lack or dearth of rain. There are also extensive areas where the soil is fertile but cannot be cultivated at all because of insufficiency of water. Yet the available water supplies are still far from exhaustion. In Iran, according to the report by Overseas Consultants, Inc., only one-third of the land which is potentially arable has been cultivated during recent years; and a similar situation obtains in Turkey, Syria, Iraq, and possibly even Saudi Arabia. Some of the areas which are largely unused would not even require additional water; more advanced techniques would be sufficient.[51]

It has been demonstrated that this situation could be largely remedied; but an inclusive remedy will necessitate many costly projects involving such activities as damming, canalization, and so forth; and it will be equally necessary to see that the newly reclaimed land is used for the benefit of the country as a whole, and not merely for the growth of some export item which enriches a few people at the expense of the ordinary farmers. Upon the completion of all such undertakings as could be shown to be economic from the long-range viewpoint, the value of crops produced in the Middle East, as well as the average farm income, could be more than doubled, at a conservative estimate. Additional measures in aid of agriculture, such as controlled seed selection, could make still higher yields possible.[52]

But these theoretical possibilities will not materialize simply through

[50] United Nations, *Final Report of the United Nations Economic Survey Mission for the Middle East* (Lake Success, N.Y., 1949), Part I, pp. 2, 3. Also Alfred Bonné, *The Economic Development of the Middle East* (London, 1945), p. 151.

[51] Bonné, *op. cit., passim.*

[52] *Ibid.*

application of the scientific and engineering procedures. The farmer himself must be dealt with. He must be educated in the modern methods which it is proposed that he should apply. Even before that, he must be given at least some of the fundamentals of a general education, or else the technical lessons will be lost upon him.[53] To what extent are these accomplishments possible?

What is the present condition of the farmer and, in general, the rural population of the Middle East, which constitutes so large a percentage of the general population? There are, to be sure, local and national variations, but it is possible to draw a composite picture which holds good for the entire region, with the exception of Israel.

Everywhere, the real income per capita from farming is exceedingly low. In Egypt, for example, an unskilled farm laborer receives the equivalent of about 22 cents a day for work which is irregular throughout the year. The average annual income for all actual farmers in that country is estimated at $54.75, as against an estimated per capita income of $100 for all Egyptians. While the gap between the average cultivator's income and the average for the entire population is probably wider in Egypt than in most Middle Eastern countries, there is no doubt whatever that in all cases the average cultivator's income is considerably lower than the other figure. In the light of that fact, the United Nations' estimates of per capita incomes for various countries in 1949 are indicative of the Middle Eastern agriculturists' plight in general:[54]

United States	$1,453	Lebanon	125
Canada	870	Egypt	100
France	482	Syria	100
Ireland	420	Iran	85
Israel	389	Iraq	85
Soviet Union	308	Saudi Arabia	40
Turkey	125	Yemen	40

As regards the attitudes of the Middle Eastern governments toward their respective rural communities, relatively little change occurred during the period between 1914 and 1945; for the subsequent period, it is still not at all clear that the greater manifestations

[53] *Palestine Royal Commission Report, July,* 1937 (London, 1937), p. 339.
[54] Will Lissner, "Income per Person in Soviet Held $308," New York *Times,* December 4, 1950.

of concern will soon be translated into widespread action. In Egypt the word *fellah* (cultivator) is used as a term of contempt.[55] In theory, the real concern for farmers should be much greater in Turkey, where the Anatolian peasantry were always identified with the Turkish governing group as against the other Ottoman races, and also in Iraq, where the present agricultural relationships have evolved in large measure from a democratic tribal system. Actually, however, when fully exposed the situations appear to be little different in those countries, although a change for the better may now be in the making in Turkey. Otherwise such differences as may from time to time exist are apparently attributable more to personal policies of governmental leaders than to any general feeling of compassion for the peasantry on the part of the ruling groups.

Although total school enrollments increased in almost all Middle Eastern countries during the between-wars period by a considerably greater percentage than the corresponding increases in population, the peasant was little affected by this progress. Except in Turkey and Lebanon—in both of which primary education is still far from being general—no consequential progress has been made, up to the time of writing, toward reduction of the ignorance and illiteracy of the rural communities. Thus, generally speaking, the Middle Eastern peasant is still in no position to evaluate his hard lot, and to have ideas as to what remedies might be suitable. The resultant situation is that, while the vast majority of small farmers are now overcomplacent rather than unduly turbulent, there is an ever-growing possibility that the rapid spread of modern communications throughout the country districts may result in widespread rural unrest—an unrest, moreover, which, if based upon the present state of education, might well be characterized mainly by irrational hatreds and determination to do all possible damage to oppressors, both real and fancied.[56]

[55] Issawi, *op. cit.*, p. 148.

[56] In connection with the general topic of education it should be particularly noted that female education still lags far behind male education in all the Middle Eastern countries except Israel, and that, although this situation has improved greatly in the upper classes of the populations except in Saudi Arabia and Yemen, the prospects of large-scale education for Moslem peasant women in the near future seem remote everywhere. Cf. Roderic D. Matthews and Matta Akrawi, *Education in Arab Countries of the Near East* (Washington, 1949), *passim*; *Population Census of Egypt, 1937* (Cairo, 1942), pp. 9, 262.

But here we have another vicious circle. For, with ignorance and conservatism as deeply entrenched as they are, it is exceedingly difficult to plan for great educational progress within a short time. Yet unless there is such progress, it is hard to see how any rational pressure for reform, on the part of the persons primarily concerned therewith, can be produced. A solution, therefore, would be possible only if the governments of the countries would take it upon themselves to provide extensive reform, even in the absence of pressure from the interested parties. By the time of writing, all governments in the Middle East, with the probable exception of Yemen, had in principle recognized the necessity for taking such steps; had issued numerous official pronouncements on the subject; and had even taken fairly extensive action ostensibly in the direction of fulfillment.[57] These developments, however, have mainly brought into the open the many and formidable obstructions which will have to be cleared away before any real progress can be achieved.

Most important of all, the small cultivators' difficulties are due in great measure to conditions from which members of the ruling class (i.e., people with decisive influence upon the respective governments) derive profit. In Egypt, Syria, Iraq, Lebanon, and Iran, the governments are dominated by landowners, who depend for their power on the support of an ignorant peasantry and on the lack of interest in rural matters on the part of the remainder of the populace. Since these landowners are mostly absentees and are not accustomed to concerning themselves either with the maintenance of their properties or with the problems of their tenants and laborers, they would probably find it impossible to adapt themselves to a situation in which the cultivation was performed efficiently by educated persons at the actual farmer level, or in which it might become necessary for landlords to keep in close contact with their tenants or laborers, either on their own initiative or through sympathetic deputies. Hence, generally speaking, it is to their advantage to keep basic rural conditions approximately as they now are, though with improvements in the superficial appearances. An additional factor in the situation is that the peasant has no capital and therefore has to borrow money at

[57] United Nations, *op. cit.*, Appendix IV.

exorbitant rates of interest (since the lender's risk is great) in order to finance the growing of his crops. But, as loans to farmers are a recognized and traditional form of investment on the part of the upper classes, and as the latter are the ones who determine the nature of laws and policies, it is not difficult to see how impasses can, and in fact do, develop.[58]

The obstacles might not be so formidable if alternative forms of profitable investment were available to the men of wealth in the Middle East. But there is a traditional fear on the part of the rich men of the types of local investment which are regarded as particularly sound and orthodox in America and Europe. This fear has often been attributed to long centuries of governmental corruption and inefficiency (still by no means at an end), and of governmental stifling of individual enterprise through unscientific taxation. Such explanations are perhaps too simple a dismissal of the matter, in the light of present-day conditions. More relevant may be a general underlying lack of confidence, not infrequently observed behind the bold determined front, in the capacity of the Middle East to advance along Western lines. An additional factor may be that the rates of interest on such investments are so much lower than on agricultural loans (which are sometimes made at rates as high as 200 per cent) that it must seem to the capitalists to be an immense sacrifice to divert their money into those channels. This sentiment has, it is true, begun to diminish to some extent, particularly in Turkey, where the demand for government bonds has increased considerably. But for the most part it is still strong.

The traditional distrust of governments, sometimes even on the part of persons who have influence upon the governments, has additional consequences of importance from the viewpoint of this study. It greatly hinders the establishment of suitable systems of taxation and thereby keeps the governmental revenues which might be used for agricultural assistance at unnecessarily low levels. Hoarding, concealment of resources, and bribery of officials are age-old practices in the Middle East, long regarded as morally legitimate defenses against

[58] Doreen Warriner, *Land and Poverty in the Middle East* (London and New York, 1948), pp. 22, 23.

the tax collector, who often operated on the basis of a contract with the government permitting him to collect and to retain whatever surpluses he could gather over and above the amounts contracted for.[59] Also, with these practices prevailing to such an extreme degree, it has not yet been possible to establish sufficiently far-reaching banking systems in the Middle Eastern countries. In short, it is both difficult to assemble, for any given purpose, the large unused capital resources which are in existence and impossible to increase those resources at anything like the rate of increase regarded as normal in Western countries.

It is a matter of commonplace observation that the farming equipment in the Middle East is of the most primitive, and that, generally speaking, the tillage methods are those which the present farmers' ancestors have applied since time immemorial. Some of the foremost authorities on the subject, however, are inclined to question whether the average farmer in that region would have any wide choice in this matter, even if he were much better educated and had capital funds at his disposal, together with ample water supplies. The holdings are often too small for the use of machinery. Nevertheless the situation could be improved to some extent by (1) a greater abundance of animals for draft and manure purposes; (2) a diminution in the number of destructive animals, particularly of goats; (3) better agricultural implements of a simple nature.

Particularly important are the questions of land tenure and water rights. The typical Middle Eastern cultivator holds the land which he cultivates on a most precarious basis. Some cultivators, indeed, are mere laborers, hired on a seasonal basis in a market where the available labor is plentiful for the tasks which have to be done, and where wages in consequence are at shockingly low levels. A much larger number are small holders of plots which they have the privilege of tilling on their own. Most of these latter, however, have no legal pro-

[59] There are extensive hoards of gold, which have generally been accumulated in the hope of purchasing land as soon as a good opportunity presented itself. Some of the hoards are in the possession of peasants. As a rule, peasants refuse to accept currency other than metallic. Even among better-educated people there continues to be a strong preference for gold and silver over paper. This is particularly true outside of the main cities.

tection against eviction and are thus at the mercy either of the landowner or of the government. This state of affairs has resulted from the vagueness of the Ottoman and Persian land codes and customs, which contained no provision for the rights of persons occupying, but not owning, agricultural land. Further, few clear titles were ever established under those codes, so that conflicts in claims to landownership have generally been settled in favor of the claimants wielding the greatest political power, or, in other words, those whose needs were least. But it has not even been the case that a decision in favor of the poorer farmer was an unmitigated blessing, since he frequently soon felt impelled to sell his holding in order to free himself from hopeless debt, and thereafter to farm it on a tenant basis. The general result has been that most farmers in the Middle East, in order to keep themselves from starvation, have had to submit themselves to the will of one or another wealthy landowner, who, through his power to take away from them their entire means of livelihood and all hope of return on borrowed money, was able to hold them as virtual slaves. Still worse, many of these great landowners, whose own titles were subject to dispute until recently, have succeeded in taking advantage of new land laws to acquire clear ones. In the territories under mandates, the fundamental unfairness of such an outcome was well realized by the mandatory authorities, who, however, failed to find any other way of instituting an efficient land registration system in sufficiently short order. Most of the truly great landowners are absentees, and it is rather generally agreed by experts on the subject that most of them serve no beneficial social purpose.[60] They are speculators rather than farmers or landed nobility. In many cases the landowner is also the moneylender to whom the cultivator must apply for the financing of his crops. He is, in fact, in a position to force the cultivator to borrow from him and from no other moneylender. He can also force the cultivator to vote for him when he stands for a seat in Parliament.

Under such a system, the cultivator has little incentive to do his

[60] Any apparent disagreements among experts on this point have to do not with the necessity or otherwise for land reform but with the question whether such reform should be sudden or gradual. It is often pointed out that rural credit facilities might first have to be improved.

farming efficiently, or to treat the soil in such a manner that it will continue to yield the maximum over a long period of years. This situation is all the more true since there is little rationality in the way the land is divided among individual peasants. The division is nearly always in the form of small holdings, which become even smaller as the populations of the countries increase. Distribution and inheritance are ordinarily governed by traditions with which the absentee landlords, conservative and poorly informed on agricultural matters, are not disposed to interfere.

At the time of abandonment of the Arab areas by the Ottoman authorities there was immense confusion as to the nature of land rights. While the mandatory powers made concerted efforts to remedy at least some of the deficiencies related to land tenure, there is much room for doubt that the general situation has improved greatly since 1918. The problems are now particularly acute in Syria, Iraq, Egypt, Lebanon, and Iran; less so in Turkey and Jordan.[61] But even when land tenure is not an acute problem, the moneylender still is. Agricultural banks have been established; but, in addition to the difficulty of obtaining adequate capital, they have been handicapped by their inability (and sometimes, perhaps, lack of desire) to prevent misuse of the funds. Not only has it been virtually impossible to limit loans to those for strictly agricultural purposes, but also large landowners have borrowed from the banks in order to relend the money to cultivators at much higher interest rates. Little progress has been made in the direction of cooperatives.

The difficulties connected with land tenure are matched by the somewhat similar complications with respect to water rights. The Ottoman customary water laws stipulated that ownership of land did

[61] Turkey was able to take advantage of the revolution following World War I to do away with large-scale ownership of land in great measure. In 1945 a law was passed designed to carry the process still farther. No action was taken under this law until 1950, but the government elected in that year seems to be planning to take action.

In that part of Arab Palestine which has been annexed by Jordan the present preponderance of landownership by small holders is perhaps mainly attributable to the fact that so many of the larger Arab holdings in Palestine were sold to Jews, who were obliged to furnish compensation in the form of land to the evicted tenants. Cf. Royal Institute of International Affairs, *op. cit.*, p. 310.

not convey any rights to the use of water on or in the vicinity of the land. Thus it could, and often did, happen that one person could render another's land useless by depriving him of all possible sources of water. Needless to say, these laws, which still apply in modified form in Turkey, Syria, Lebanon, Iraq, and Jordan, will have to be altered if the projected irrigation schemes are to serve their true purposes. In countries where water is at such a premium the only practicable system is to have all distribution of water in the hands and discretion of the government. In Egypt, the government has had a monopoly of this nature since time immemorial. In Iran, however, the system is the same as in the majority of former Ottoman lands. In all those countries there are political obstacles to revised legislation.[62]

A further obstacle often mentioned to the development of Middle Eastern agriculture is the extensive waste of land and water resources which has taken place over the centuries. Forests, for example, have been destroyed and soil extensively eroded because of the forages of animals and men. It is probable, however, that much of the damage can still be repaired to a considerable extent if reclamation is begun in the near future. Meanwhile there is a great deal of land which with irrigation could be made highly fertile almost immediately but which is not at present being used at all, and in some cases has not been used for centuries.[63]

HEALTH AND SANITATION CONDITIONS

Although there are wide variations as to nature and degree, it can be said of all the nine countries (omitting Israel) that health and sanitation conditions are exceedingly bad, by Western standards. These conditions, moreover, affect such a large percentage of the

[62] Iraq, Syria, Lebanon, and Jordan all have new water laws vesting control in the government. However, in all cases these contain saving clauses of such a nature as to leave the old law substantially in effect. Cf. Warriner, *op. cit.*, pp. 73, 92, 115; *Report by H. M. Government on the Administration of Palestine and Trans-Jordan*, 1938, p. 407; G. F. Walpole, "Land Problems in Transjordan," *Journal of the Royal Central Asian Society*, 1948, Part I, p. 62.

[63] Robert R. Nathan, Oscar Gass, and Daniel Creamer, *Palestine, Problem and Promise* (Washington, 1946), pp. 115-122; E. B. Worthington, *Middle East Science* (London, 1945), pp. 93-98; United Nations, *op. cit.*, p. 2; Bonné, *op. cit.*, p. 151.

population that the economic loss from illness, chronic and otherwise, must be enormous.

The problems presented are divisible into three main categories: treatment of disease, measures for the prevention of specific diseases, and public health measures designed to promote conditions unfavorable to disease. The greatest progress to date has been made in the first category, the least in the third. One good example of the difficulties in the third category is the authoritative estimate that an expenditure of over $750,000,000 would be required in order to provide safe drinking water to the Egyptian population. And, even with this expenditure, part of the populace would not be reached.

It has also been ascertained that in some cases highly disastrous consequences from the health viewpoint have been produced by the introduction of modern equipment and facilities onto the Middle Eastern scene. A case in point is the great increase in schistosomiasis in Egypt, resulting from the institution of perennial irrigation. There is reason to believe that at least half of the rural population of Egypt is afflicted with this serious disease. However, as far as the Middle East as a whole is concerned, malaria is a far more serious problem than schistosomiasis.

In addition to the many other questions which must be answered before the health problem can be solved, there is the speculation as to whether it would even be desirable to reduce the death rate by sanitary measures while other conditions remain as they are. Some believe that the main net results would be increased pressure on the food supply, with illnesses from other causes supplanted by illnesses resulting from undernourishment. Ailments of the latter type are widespread even now, particularly, again, in Egypt. Practically the whole rural population of that country is said to be undernourished to a serious extent.

Illustrative of the foregoing statements, and of the slowness of the progress, is the following report made in 1947 by Mr. Lingeman in regard to health conditions in Turkey:

These facts serve to illustrate the backwardness of peasant conditions: (i) There are not more than 4,590 qualified doctors in the country (one for every 4,000 inhabitants); 1,085 dentists; 475 nurses; 1,635 midwives and 2,197 members of the sanitary services excluding apparently 600 members of the sanitary services and 730 midwives in the villages. (The infantile mortality is appalling.)

(ii) In 1937 there were 8.68 hospital beds in the whole country for every 10,000 inhabitants. The hospitals in Turkey are concentrated in the big towns. Out of 16,354 hospital beds in all (including military hospitals), 7,500 are in Istanbul.

(iii) There is no organization which sets out to teach the most elementary principles of prophylaxy to the peasants . . . and render first-aid to the sick and victims of accidents in the villages.

(iv) In spite of the anti-malarial campaign already in force it is calculated that at least 10 million working days are lost yearly owing to its scourge alone.[64]

NOMADISM

The problem of the wandering tribes and their raids upon the cultivated areas is still a highly important one, though in all parts of the Middle East the nomad populations are dwindling. It has become a trite, though undoubtedly true, remark that the nomad cannot exist alongside the factory, railway, and motorcar. Continuous progress is being made by governments in the task of absorbing nomads into the settled population, and even greater progress in reducing the dangers from raiding.

While there are no accurate statistics in regard to nomadic populations, one 1950 estimate was that nomads and seminomads in Syria amounted to about 500,000 persons.[65] Only Israel, Lebanon, and Egypt are virtually free from this problem. A complete solution will probably require several decades.

COMMUNICATIONS

Any large-scale industrial, agricultural, and power projects in the Middle East will necessarily depend for their effectiveness upon an appropriate extension of communications. At present, road and rail communications are decidedly inadequate, with a particularly marked

[64] E. R. Lingeman, *Turkey: Economic and Social Conditions in Turkey* (London, 1948), p. 148.

[65] Royal Institute of International Affairs, *op. cit.*, p. 384.

paucity of international roads and railways[66] and of all-weather roads from the farms to the main railways and highways. A fair amount of work has already been accomplished toward the remedy of this situation; but it is only in Israel, Lebanon, and western Syria that conditions approach being satisfactory from the viewpoint of agricultural, industrial, and commercial needs. In Turkey road building has lagged far behind some of the other aspects of modernization. As a result, bottlenecks are constantly occurring which lessen considerably the country's effective productiveness. The only reason this same situation does not hold in some of the other countries is that both production and communications have remained at low levels.

OIL

No discussion of the Middle Eastern economy would be complete without some consideration of the petroleum question. As is well known, the region is particularly rich in oil resources, of which the most important known ones are in Iran, Iraq, and Saudi Arabia.[67] The exploitation of these resources is entirely in the hands of American and European firms; the benefit to the region is in the form of governmental revenues from royalties and of local expenditures by the companies and their personnel.[68]

At the time of writing, the bases of royalties were in the process of being drastically revised.[69] The rate prevailing before the revisions has varied from 17 to 34 cents a barrel during the postwar period.[70] The

[66] The main international rail routes are: (1) Europe-Istanbul-Baghdad-Basra; (2) Europe-Istanbul-Beirut-Haifa-Cairo. The latter route is at present disrupted by the technical state of war between Israel and the Arab states.

[67] Kuwait, Bahrein, and Qatar, all British protectorates which are not discussed in this study, are also major oil producers in the Middle East.

[68] Until October, 1950, no royalties were paid to nonproducing countries through which pipe lines passed. In the case of pipe lines completed at or after that time, transit royalties will be paid; but it is not yet possible to calculate the effect which these will have upon the countries concerned. Revenues from this source will clearly not be comparable to export royalties paid to the producing countries. Cf. United Nations, *op. cit.*, Part I, pp. 41, 51.

[69] As to the status of this situation with respect to all three countries at the end of 1950, cf. Ross, "Aramco to Share Oil Profits 50-50," New York *Times*, January 3, 1951; also "Aramco Guarantees Oil Royalty in Deal," New York *Times*, January 5, 1951.

[70] Royalties, in each case, are based on somewhat complicated formulas. During most of 1950 Saudi Arabia was receiving about 34 cents a barrel.

following schedule shows the great increases in oil production which
have occurred during the past four decades in the Middle East:

	Iran	Iraq	Saudi Arabia
	(thousands of barrels a day)		
1910			
1915	9.9		
1920	33.4		
1925	96.0		
1930	125.6	2.5	
1935	156.9	75.1	
1940	180.9	66.2	14.7
1945	352.0	95.7	58.4
1947	425.0	50.0	247.0
1950	654.0	133.8	546.7

For all three countries, oil revenues are coming to constitute a substantial portion of the total governmental income—amounting already
to at least 60 per cent, and probably much more, in the case of Saudi
Arabia. Those countries, too, are guaranteed a low price for oil supplies consumed within the territory; whereas in Palestine, under the
British mandate, petroleum products from the Haifa Refinery were
sold at prices higher than those prevailing in England. Generally
speaking, however, Middle Eastern oil can hardly be regarded as an
integral part of the regional economic life. The local governments
have little or no control over the exploitation and the profits; the oil
fields and refineries are remote from the main centers of population;
and the local personnel requirements of the oil industry are small in
relation to the magnitude of the business.[71] The main power of the
local governments is to halt or curtail the companies' activities if
these are deemed contrary to national interests. Although this is a
costly expedient, it has nevertheless been resorted to twice, first by
Iran in 1932[72] and later by Iraq in 1948. It would not be possible to

[71] The Anglo-Iranian Oil Co. employs about 60,000 Iranians. The Arabian
American Oil Co. employs about 10,000 Saudi Arabians. (Royal Institute of
International Affairs, op. cit., pp. 90, 224.)

[72] In March, 1951, after this chapter had been completed, the Iranian Parliament passed a law nationalizing the country's oil industry. By the end of October,
1951, this had resulted in a complete withdrawal from Iran of the British oil
company's personnel and a virtually complete stoppage of work in the fields and
refinery.

increase local control over Middle Eastern oil unless the Middle Eastern nations could find means of obtaining technical and financial assistance from Western sources, with a view to enabling them to exploit the oil profitably themselves. Such an outcome is unlikely in the near future, since the only source from which assistance could conceivably come would be the foreign oil companies themselves, and it would probably be contrary to their interests to provide it. Turkey, by exception, has control over her own oil output; but no truly major deposits have yet been found in that country.

DENSITY OF POPULATION

With respect to six Middle Eastern countries (the only ones which lend themselves at all readily to such a statistical check), it is proposed to apply a crude test with a view to determining whether over-population is likely to constitute a problem in any of them during the next thirty-five years. The assumption will be that, in all cases, the agricultural population will have been reduced to one-half of the total population. It will also be assumed that the total population of each country will have increased by 100 per cent, or at the high rate of 2 per cent per annum. Finally, assumptions will be made as to the acreage which, *with adequate population*, could reasonably be expected to be cropped in a given year thirty-five years hence. These estimates will be based on an extension of cultivation and irrigation to all areas which are now known to be reclaimable. Under these various assumptions the following figures (based on the most authoritative statistical sources available) are obtained:

	Acreage Theoretically Croppable		Population	
	1948	1983	1948	1983
Egypt	8,800,000	11,500,000	19,528,000	39,056,000
Syria	3,700,000	9,000,000	3,350,000	6,700,000
Iraq	6,000,000	17,000,000	4,950,000	9,900,000
Iran	11,000,000	60,000,000	17,000,000	34,000,000
Turkey	25,000,000	40,000,000	19,500,000	39,000,000
Lebanon	800,000	1,100,000	1,208,000	2,416,000

Thus the maximum size for an average family farm (for five persons) in 1983 would be: Egypt—3 acres; Syria—13 acres; Iraq—17 acres; Iran—18 acres; Turkey—10 acres; Lebanon—4.5 acres.

It seems therefore to be demonstrated, particularly in view of the cautious nature of our assumptions, that Iran, Iraq, and Syria should be able to develop their territories without any fear of overpopulation in the foreseeable future. In Turkey there is no patently decisive evidence one way or the other; but, according to a wide consensus of expert opinion, Turkey is not regarded as being faced with an over-population problem within the next thirty-five years.

In the cases of Egypt and Lebanon, which appear offhand to be confronted with serious overpopulation, the matter is little improved if the same test is performed under the assumption of 1 per cent annual increase in population—probably an unrealistically low estimate—even when the greater productivity of irrigated land is taken into account.

As for the other countries, all that can be said is that, according to present appearances, Israel and Jordan will find it difficult to rid themselves of their serious population problems, complicated as those are by immigration of huge dimensions during recent years. There are no adequate bases for judging Saudi Arabia's and Yemen's prospects.

Generally speaking, the presence in Syria and Lebanon of Arab refugees from the Palestine War does not particularly alter the long-range situation in either of those countries.

PUBLIC FINANCE

The following table shows illustrative figures of per capita governmental expenditures of certain Middle Eastern countries in recent years:

Country	Year	Per Capita Expenditure
Egypt	1946–47	$22
Syria	1946	9
Lebanon	1946	20
Palestine	1946–47	47
Iraq	1945–46	18
Turkey	1947	21
Transjordan	1947–48	16
Iran	1942–43	12

For the year 1947-48 the per capita expenditure of the United States Government was $268.23. In no year since 1933 has it been lower than $50.

.   .   .   .

This concludes the portrayal of the main relevant aspects of the Middle East scene. The picture, it must be frankly admitted, reveals little clear light along the horizon ahead. Too, it is fully apparent that almost any kind of attempt to alter basic conditions in a thorough-going manner would meet with strong, and perhaps insuperable, resistances.

The main problem will, therefore, be to discover those points at which the resistances may be *relatively* low, and where, in consequence, there may be some possibility of establishing "bridgeheads" of fundamental progress.

The chapters which follow, most of them dealing with individual countries of the Middle East, have been written with a view to offering possible clues as to suitable locations for such prospective bridgeheads.

❖

CHAPTER II

Egypt

GENERAL BACKGROUND

Social and economic conditions in present-day Egypt are, to a considerable extent, rooted in extremely ancient history.

Throughout recorded time the outstanding fact about Egypt has been the complete dependence of the population, for its very existence, upon the Nile River. Without irrigation water obtained from that stream no cultivation would be possible, and the settled portions of the country would soon be transformed into desert. Given irrigation, however, Egypt's soil in the vicinity of the Nile is highly fertile, permitting the production of large and valuable crops. Those crops have always been by far the most important source of the country's wealth.

A logical consequence of this condition was the need for an authoritarian form of government, once the rural population had increased beyond the number required for cultivation along the river's banks. Because the water supply of the natural river is limited and subject to marked variations as to annual flood peaks, the distribution of water must be centrally controlled if the land as a whole is to prosper. Central control is, however, a large-scale operation, which cannot be accomplished efficiently except by an authority well provided with funds or having great resources of labor at its command. The only authority of such a nature in ancient times, and even in much later days, was the ruler of the nation.

The control over Egypt's whole water supply was tantamount to potential control over all aspects of Egyptians' lives. In practice, too, the early Egyptian rulers made free use of this power and thereby established important precedents for future ages. Not only did they decree what crops each peasant should grow, but also they required practically the whole population to perform labor on an unpaid basis. While this form of labor may have been necessary for the construction and upkeep of the irrigation works, it was also used extensively for such purposes as the construction of immense tombs to house the rulers after death. The tradition developed that the relationship between ruler and ruled was that of master and slaves.

The long reign of this tradition, interrupted only by periods of chaos and decay, produced in Egypt a social climate somewhat different from that which obtained, at the end of World War I, in most other areas of the Middle East. The tradition of the free, democratic tribal community was virtually nonexistent; and the history of the common agriculturists, who had at all times constituted by far the most numerous element in the Egyptian population, was one of centuries of repression, ill treatment, and extreme poverty, without many offsetting factors. This state of affairs had come to be accepted by most as one which, in view of its long persistence, was irremediable. The rulers and their immediate followers tended to regard their own privileges as based on natural superiority, and to despise the *fellahin*, whose attributes were so far inferior to theirs. The absence of a social welfare philosophy in the Moslem religion has also been a factor in this situation.[1]

It is largely for these reasons that the problem of raising living standards has presented greater difficulties in Egypt than in some of the other Middle Eastern countries. The indifference of the ruling class has, as a rule, been matched by the *fellahin*'s attitude of resignation. The middle classes, as social forces of opposition, have come

[1] Charles Issawi, *Egypt, An Economic and Social Analysis* (London, 1947), pp. 6, 9-11, 149; Earl of Cromer, *Modern Egypt* (New York, 1908), II, 131, 193, 323, 406.

into prominence only during relatively recent times. Though they do not share with the *fellah* his resigned attitude, their handicap is that they are still groping for philosophies suited to their needs. They have consequently been unable to assert themselves effectively. They have gained neither the respect of the ruling group nor the support of the *fellahin*.[2]

There were, however, other aspects to the background picture at the end of the First World War. Although general standards of living had not become an object of important consideration in Egypt, the same could not be said as to economic development and Westernization. In the early nineteenth century Egypt's ruler Mohammed Ali (1811-48) had taken particular interest and considerable action in the matters of founding modern industries and expanding the country's irrigation facilities to the greatest extent possible. Among his successors, Ismail (1863-79) not only went ahead with the irrigation program on a large scale but also inaugurated an ambitious program of public works, with extensive technical and financial assistance from abroad. All this was destined not to improve the lot of the *fellahin* but to increase the wealth and amenities of those who were already well off. To encourage an expansion of cultivation the rulers made large grants of newly irrigated land, free of taxes for a period of years, to persons who would undertake to bring it under crops. The agricultural crop increasingly emphasized was cotton—which particularly lends itself to slave-labor techniques; which was useful mainly from the viewpoint of export profits; and which, if grown by large landowners and exchanged mainly for foreign luxury goods desired by them, reduces the potential food supplies for the peasants. In this manner a new landlord element came into being and assumed the most prominent role in Egyptian society. This was not a new social class but rather a small, already favored group to which the ruler, for facilitation of development and state revenues therefrom, had transferred some of his prerogatives. The new landlords were every bit as zealous as the state had been, and continued to be, in exploiting the *fellahin* to the utmost degree. By the end of the nineteenth century

[2] Issawi, *op. cit.*, pp. 150-151.

the greater part of the cultivated area was in the hands of the large landowners.[3]

Long before that time Ismail had become bankrupt, and the industrial enterprises had collapsed completely. In 1882 Great Britain assumed a virtual protectorate over Egypt, with a particular view to controlling governmental finances and liquidating the country's large debts to foreign governments and nationals. Ismail had had to abdicate.[4] His positive legacy was the new irrigation works, other important public works of a miscellaneous character (including the Suez Canal), the great private estates, and the widespread cultivation of cotton.

During the period from 1882 to 1914 the British protectors concerned themselves actively with the further expansion of the cultivated area and of perennial irrigation. The main reason was that the pressure of population on Egypt's resources was increasing at an alarming rate, and there was a certainty of eventual famine unless drastic remedial measures could be taken.[5] With Egypt's glorious ancient history as an inspirational precedent, and with modern Western technology at hand to improve upon even the best of Egypt's old irrigation systems, the British aspired to control the river in such a way as to make every possible drop of water available for the irrigation of Egyptian soil. In 1904, after a considerable amount of work had already been done, Sir William Garstin, Irrigation Adviser to

[3] *Ibid.*, pp. 14-16; Doreen Warriner, *Land and Poverty in the Middle East* (London, 1948), pp. 48-49.

[4] Ismail abdicated in 1879. He died in 1895.

[5] In 1800, according to the most authoritative estimate, Egypt's population was 2,460,200; by 1882 it had risen to 6,831,131. From 1813 to 1877 the area under cultivation was increased from 3,050,000 acres to 4,743,000 acres. Since the periods from 1800 to 1813 and 1877 to 1882 were troubled eras in which public works were at a virtual standstill, these acreage figures are considered to be applicable, for all practical purposes, to 1800 and 1882 respectively. Furthermore, as indicated in another footnote, the proportion of the area devoted to cotton was greatly increased between 1800 and 1882. Thus, even if the most favorable assumptions are made with regard to other factors, such as improved agricultural methods and conversion from basin to perennial irrigation, it is still unquestionable that the pressure on food resources increased substantially. Cf. W. W. Cleland, *The Population Problem in Egypt* (Lancaster, Pa., 1936), p. 7 *et passim*; Issawi, *op. cit.*, p. 14.

the Egyptian Government, published a plan for achieving the ultimate in possibilities for control of the Nile.[6]

Garstin's *Report on the Basin of the Nile* has continued, even to the present day, to constitute the basic authority in regard to the development of the Nile for Egypt's benefit. At the time of publication, however, it was revolutionary in its implications that Egypt might not be a geographical unity in itself, but rather part of a much larger geographical unity, namely, the entire Nile Valley. Garstin's revelation was that Egypt would in time have to depend on control works erected in upstream countries in order to assure herself of the increased supplies of water which she would eventually be needing. This revelation was destined to produce major political consequences.[7]

None of the proposed upstream works were constructed during the period of the protectorate. Britain did, however, facilitate a considerable increase in the cultivated area by the construction of huge modern dams and barrages on the Egyptian section of the Nile.[8] In this connection she did not interfere with the established practice of converting the newly reclaimed lands into large estates, cultivated mainly for cotton. Although there is much to indicate that Britain was not unmindful of the *fellah's* lot, it was apparently regarded as politically inexpedient to uphold his interests too strongly against those of the landlords. This attitude was due to the fact that the landlords could easily have diverted the other classes' attention from their immediate grievances by making scapegoats of the British protectors, who were transferring large percentages of Egypt's revenues into foreign hands—a fact which even many *fellahin* had strongly protested. In that case the British might have had to face the wrath of a united populace.[9]

Under the circumstances, it was the landlords and not the *fellahin*

[6] "Egypt," *Encyclopaedia Britannica*, 1946 ed., p. 93; "Irrigation," *ibid.*, pp. 685-689.

[7] Sir W. Garstin, *Report on the Basin of the Nile*, Cmd. 2165 of 1904 (London, 1904), *passim*.

[8] A list of these works is to be found under "Reclamation," in the 1930 issue of the *New International Year Book*, 1931, p. 673.

[9] Issawi, *op. cit.*, pp. 34-37; Warriner, *op. cit.*, pp. 49-50.

who benefited from the extension of cultivable land, except in the purely negative sense that the *fellahin* were given a reprieve against mass starvation and such epidemics as might come along in connection therewith. More substantial services rendered by the British to the *fellahin* were the abolition of forced labor and the reduction of taxes. But, in at least one respect, the *fellah* was hurt rather than helped by the new developments. In the process of attempting to convert all land from basin irrigation to perennial, the prevalence of both schistosomiasis and malaria among the peasantry was enormously increased.[10] Furthermore, the extensions and intensification of cultivation, great as they were, did not keep pace with the rapid increase in population. Largely because of the emphasis upon cotton, the financial returns to great estate owners showed a definite ascending trend in proportion to their total holdings.[11] From the *fellah's* viewpoint, however, this meant simply an increase in the rents paid by small tenants but not in the wages of agricultural laborers. There was thus the curious spectacle of a highly profitable agriculture supported by ultramodern engineering works but based upon a peasantry which, in spite of the reforms, continued to exist in the depths of misery.[12]

The structure of social classes was altered during the nineteenth century, and the twentieth up to 1914, by the continuous increase in the numbers of the middle-class elements. This was based partly upon the expansion of Egypt's commerce due to the existence of the Suez Canal, partly on the miscellaneous demands arising directly

[10] Issawi, *op. cit.*, p. 158; Warriner, *op. cit.*, pp. 38, 41-42; E. B. Worthington, *Middle East Science* (London, 1945), p. 45.

[11] According to Hussein Sirry Pasha, Egyptian production of cotton from 1820 to 1930, in bales, has been as follows: 1820—234; 1830—46,669; 1840—48,377; 1850—96,100; 1860—149,050; 1870—491,500; 1880—698,000; 1890—1,040,000; 1900—1,610,000; 1910—1,876,000; 1920—1,509,000; 1930—2,069,000. Cf. "The Evolution of Irrigation in Egypt," *Modern Egypt News Bulletin*, March, 1948, p. 12.

[12] Cleland, *op. cit.*, p. 91; Warriner, *op. cit.*, p. 38; Issawi, *op. cit.*, pp. 64, 74-76.

Mr. Kirk's view that the period of British control constitutes "one of the finer chapters in the history of British imperialism" is possibly true if the magnitude of the problems faced is taken into consideration. Cf. G. E. Kirk, *A Short History of the Middle East* (London, 1948); also Earl of Cromer, *op. cit.*, *passim*.

or indirectly from the various modernization programs, and partly on the increased need for civil servants as the British introduced efficiency into the practices of government. This growth of the middle classes had, as early as the 1880's, produced in Egypt a conspicuous degree of class consciousness, which, however, did not extend to the *fellah* class, at least as a whole. The class consciousness became converted, for the most part, into nationalism and anti-Westernism, since, in spite of all British efforts to prevent this, the grievances against the ruling class were identified with the British occupation. Because of this phenomenon, the main clamor was for freedom from foreign control, rather than for internal reform. Up to 1914 there was little development of manufacturing industries, and hence no urban proletariat of consequence had been introduced into the picture.[13]

During World War I Egypt prospered to some extent because of the requirements of the British armed forces. In the period immediately after the war, the *fellahin* were somewhat better off than they had been for many years.[14] During this era concerted efforts were commenced by the Egyptian Government, which in 1922 was partially freed from British control and ostensibly democratized, to conclude definite arrangements for a substantial furtherance of the training of the Nile and the expansion of cultivation.

Although public attention was closely centered on the discussions of this question, it is significant that the matter of Egyptian living standards did not enter into the high-level conversations to an important extent. Indeed, the general assumption seemed to be that any newly reclaimed land would, in accordance with the now traditional practice, be granted or sold by the state to wealthy men, and that the costs of the projects would be self-liquidating through the receipts from the sales or the increase in the taxable values of the land in question.[15] There appeared to be little realization among the middle classes of the economic implications for themselves of such a pro-

[13] Issawi, *op. cit.*, pp. 34-36.
[14] Alfred Bonné, *The Economic Development of the Middle East* (London, 1945), p. 26.
[15] In his book, *The Training of the Upper Nile*, published in 1939, Mr. F. Newhouse assumes that matters would be handled on such a basis, and does not suggest any possible alternative procedures. See p. 88.

cedure. Those classes were practically without representation in the government and Parliament.[16]

But, from the viewpoint of nationalism, the middle classes assailed all projects for construction of irrigation works outside of Egyptian territory. The belief existed that this would encourage Great Britain, in control in the Sudan, to perpetuate her domination over Egypt by means of her power to cut off the water supply. The Wafd, the political party which professed the greatest devotion to middle-class interests, strongly supported this view while out of power—and was able to produce powerful emotional currents in regard to the matter. Nevertheless, after protracted delays, partially ascribable to the relatively slight interest of most landowners in the prospects afforded by remote-future reclamation,[17] proposals for external extensions of the irrigation works, including constructions in the Sudan and in Ethiopia, were approved in the Egyptian Parliament, in 1932 and 1933, by large majorities. It may be noted in this connection that the Wafd leaders, when in power themselves, had shown themselves favorably disposed toward proposals of the same general nature. The Wafd leaders were, like those of the other parties, largely of the great landowner class.[18]

Because of the outbreak of the Italo-Ethiopian War in 1935 only part of the approved constructions were completed before the commencement of World War II; and much of the reclamation work necessitated thereby has still to be done.[19] There is now a program for constructing the remaining required engineering works over a period of twenty-five years or more.[20] This plan does not call for any alteration of existing practices in regard to the disposition of the reclaimed land. Meanwhile the population has been steadily increasing at a faster rate than food production; the per capita consumption

[16] Issawi, op. cit., p. 170.
[17] Ibid., p. 61.
[18] Oriente Moderno, February, 1932; May, 1932; July, 1932; July, 1933.

As regards the Wafd party, while it is true that its main concern in practice has generally been for landowner interests narrowly conceived, there have been outstanding individual Wafdist leaders whose outlooks have extended much farther. One of those was Saad Zaghlul Pasha.
[19] Warriner, op. cit., p. 45.
[20] National Bank of Egypt Economic Bulletin (1950), III, No. 3, 164-165.

of most staple articles has declined considerably; and it is agreed by most authorities that the standard of living of the average Egyptian *fellah* has never, in any period of history, been substantially lower than it is today. Doubt has, in fact, been expressed whether there can be any real cure for this other than large-scale emigration to the Sudan or Iraq, involving two to five million people.[21] The great constructions facilitate remarkable increases in cultivation, but this advantage seems to be consistently neutralized by (1) the time consumed in making the new works fully effective[22] and (2) the fact that, under existing conditions, the rate of population growth seems to undergo an upward adjustment in harmony with each increase made in the cultivable acreage. The constructions are urgently needed; but they are at best palliatives unless coupled with other measures.[23]

Industrialization on a scale greatly exceeding that undertaken elsewhere in the Arab Middle East came into being in Egypt during the period between wars. This had the result of adding an urban proletariat to the low-income classes. This class, however, has never become sufficiently large to assert itself with any degree of success; and, in the eyes of the more powerful middle classes, proletarian and peasant interests were not at all comparable in importance to the matter of freeing Egypt completely from British influence. Thus, while there was a decided growth of the realization that living standards should receive more official attention, this fact was rendered innocuous by the continuous anti-British agitation, which was extended also to agitation against the non-Egyptians and Egyptian minority persons controlling important commercial and industrial undertakings in the country. Up to 1936, when a treaty was concluded which virtually ended all remaining British control in internal affairs, the government in power showed little or no inclination to prepare or consider far-reaching plans for raising the living standards of the

[21] Birth control has also often been suggested as a possibility, but the obstacles to such a revolutionary development, involving people in the depth of poverty and ignorance, are many and obvious.
[22] See subsection of this chapter entitled "The Decline in Living Standards." Cf. also Warriner, *op. cit.*, p. 46.
[23] *Ibid.*, pp. 3, 36-38; Bonné, *op. cit.*, pp. 25-26; 34; Issawi, *op. cit.*, pp. 44, 48-50, 55, 201-202.

impoverished elements of the populace. Available at all times was the pretext that it was difficult to accomplish anything along such lines as long as Egypt was not free.[24]

The Wafd government, which came into power in 1936, was in a somewhat different position. For one thing, the Wafd party had always professed to be the friend of the common man. For another, those who had agitated for freedom would be anxious to see concrete favorable results, now that a considerable degree of independence had been secured. Under these circumstances, Nahas Pasha, the new Premier, in his Speech from the Throne introduced a radical departure from all previously stated governmental policies by emphasizing the necessity for social welfare measures of a far-reaching nature.[25]

However, because of a rift with the palace, which still has the ultimate controlling hand in Egypt, the Wafd party did not remain in power for long. Its main achievement was that it made a beginning in the matter of plans and projects for raising living standards and that other party governments from that time on have felt obliged to follow the lead thus given. But relatively little was accomplished along these lines before the outbreak of World War II.

During World War II Egypt was the main Allied base in the Middle East. Britain, by a show of force, gained King Farouk's cooperation in making the base an efficient one—which temporarily stopped the more overt manifestations of internal unrest but unquestionably increased the real tensions and made the possibility of an eventual internal crisis much greater. The war had two main effects upon Egypt. While greatly increasing the anti-British sentiment, it also produced a grudging admiration for British accomplishments and imparted to the middle classes a powerful feeling that the only way of coping with the British successfully was to make genuine

[24] Issawi, *op. cit.*, pp. 82-83, 88, 95, 152; Elizabeth Monroe, "British Interests in the Middle East," *Middle East Journal*, April, 1948, p. 138.

[25] *New International Year Book*, 1936, p. 228; *Oriente Moderno*, June, 1936, p. 353.

One should not be confused by previous governmental advocacy of assistance to the *fellahin*. It has been a common practice among Egyptian landowners to press their own interests in the guise of appeals to the government for "assistance to the *fellah*." This was presumably a legacy from the British occupation. Cf. Cleland, *op. cit.*, p. 96.

and unified efforts to Westernize the country. Conspicuous British achievements, moreover, had not been limited to a mere increase in, and diversification of, Egypt's industrialization. The Middle East Supply Centre had deemed it desirable to protect general urban living standards and had given practical demonstration that this protection could be accomplished to a large extent, even in spite of the drastic adverse effects of the curtailment of foreign shipping upon the normal domestic economy. Both the palace and all political parties saw the necessity of taking at least considerable token notice of the new trend in thought. Moreover, there was a desire, at the top political levels, to embark upon activities which, because of their apparent relationship to mass living standards, would promote Egypt's prestige abroad.[26] Foreign criticisms of Egypt's ruling class, centered upon its alleged lack of social conscience, were becoming embarrassing.[27]

It was clear, however, that official concern in the matter of raising living standards might in practice be limited largely to token and minor concern, with emphasis on the spectacular and with a continued appeal to the narrower forms of nationalism to divert public attention from the great gap between the few rich and the many poor. This would, moreover, still be possible because of the continued maintenance of the British foothold in the Sudan. Under the circumstances, one apparently important aspect of the question was whether there would be some men at the top level of the government sufficiently enlightened, in the Western sense, to wish to exert pressure upon their reluctant colleagues to cooperate in meaningful programs.[28]

This question now seems to have an affirmative answer. The present government includes at least two men who were apparently

[26] This aspect of the matter is, for example, reflected in King Farouk's Speech from the Throne of January 16, 1950. Cf. *Egypt News Bulletin*, February, 1950, p. 8.
[27] "Review of the Work of the Middle East Supply Centre," *Department of State Bulletin*, September 30, 1945; Worthington, *op. cit.*, p. 2; Warriner, *op. cit.*, p. 49.
[28] Paul Seabury, "The League of Arab States: Debacle of a Regional Organization," *International Organization*, August, 1949, p. 549; C. L. Sulzberger, "U. S. Seeks Mid-East Reform," New York *Times*, March 19, 1950.

selected for their ministerial posts because of their genuine interest in the advancement of social welfare. This circumstance is perhaps a good measure of the pressures upon the leaders now in power.[29]

It still remains to be seen whether these developments will lead to a truly important breakdown of resistance at the top social level or, on the contrary, to an eventual feeling on the part of the dominant class that yielding should be carried no farther. In the latter event, it is even conceivable that the dominant class would be willing to risk the possibility of a social revolution by violence, because the great landlords, as a group, feel themselves dependent for their wealth and power upon the present irrational economy which perpetuates human misery and prevents efficient national development. Thus, while even their own estates could doubtless become more profitable if labor conditions were better, and labor thereby more efficient, such an argument has little appeal for them, since they fear that the introduction of major improvements would almost inevitably be coupled with the elimination of the absentee landlord as a factor in agricultural production. The main elements underlying this fear are the ignorance of most landlords in regard to the principles of economics and of scientific agriculture; the general belief among them that an Egyptian peasantry shorn of its centuries-old accommodation to static conditions would constitute a blind, uncontrollable force, amenable neither to generous compromise nor to reason; and their feeling of satisfaction, based on long experience, with the benefits to their class achievable from the existing relations of production.[30] Any evaluation of current plans for the elevation of living standards must be made in the light of these factors.[31]

[29] Sulzberger, *loc. cit.*; "School Fight Led by Blind Egyptian," New York *Times*, September 5, 1950.

[30] This problem might be solved by a wholesale transference of landlords' wealth to new manufacturing enterprises. However, since most of them lack the necessary experience for making sound calculations as to profitability of industrial investments, it is unlikely that many would be willing to run the risks involved in such a revolutionary procedure.

As for the feasibility of any scheme for partitioning the estates and pensioning the ex-landlords, the difficulty would probably be in convincing the persons involved that such a step was not merely an opening wedge for further drastic action.

[31] Issawi, *op. cit.*, p. 78; Warriner, *op. cit.*, pp. 48-49.

During World War II there was a beginning of formulation of the major plans for raising Egyptian living standards which are now in effect. It seems probable, however, that for many years to come all such plans will be overshadowed by the great Nile irrigation developments, the expenditures on which cost the Egyptian Government £E43,500,000 from 1919 to 1939.[32] Some of the factors underlying this great relative prominence of river development, and resulting in its capture of people's imaginations, are: the immensity, complexity, and ingenuity of the system of Nile constructions; the great amount of time which will have been required for the completion of the entire development; the large number of countries involved; the exotic character of some of the problems;[33] and the world-wide interest in the Nile as the life-giver of ancient Egypt. When compared with this project, all other developmental schemes which Egypt might advance tend to appear somewhat colorless, however appropriate they may be from the viewpoint of raising the status of the people as a whole. Needless to say, the ideal situation would be a merger of the two types of planning, to the extent that both would primarily serve one central purpose, namely, the elevation of general living standards. Such an outcome, while not wholly out of the question, is not probable for the immediate future.

Up to the present there has been no modification of the complete control by the Egyptian Government over all supplies of water, the construction and management of the feeder irrigation canals including all their control works, and the planning on a nation-wide basis of what crops shall be planted.[34] However, the King, though his estates are by far the largest in Egypt, is now only one of many landowners; indeed, all of Egypt's cultivated land is divided into the private holdings, large and small, of individuals and companies. Except in the case of the large owners with great political power, the ownership rights seem to be partially theoretical, in view of the government's continued dominance over activities, its facilities for forcing issues, and the paucity of legislation favorable to the small

[32] Issawi, *op. cit.*, p. 56.
[33] Some of these, such as the interference of hippopotamuses with the upstream gauges, are discussed by Mr. F. Newhouse. Cf. *op. cit.*, *passim.*
[34] Warriner, *op. cit.*, pp. 48-49.

holders. Nevertheless, all of the more obvious questions as to the rights of ownership, such as eminent domain, rights of way, and expropriation, are definitely regulated by laws of long standing. The small private holdings tend to become still smaller with the passage of time, through inheritance and partition. However, the total area occupied by them is increasing[35] because of the practice of large estate holders of giving their permanent laborers small plots in payment for their work.[36]

The main statistical data in regard to present-day land tenure are brought out in an article published in the April 8, 1950, issue of the New York *Times*, reading in part as follows:

A memorandum by the Minister of National Economy, Mohammed El Vakil Bey . . . put the number of those who work on the land at 5,161,000 and the number of those who have land holdings at 2,661,000. It stated that the number of landless laborers had increased during the decade from 1937 to 1947 much faster than the number with even little property.

The number of landholders with less than one acre was put at 2,000,000 of the total of 2,661,000 landowners. The memorandum then went on to show that 40% of the total arable land was owned by ½% of the total number of landowners.

The present cultivated area of Egypt amounts to about 9000 square miles. About 3000 additional square miles will be cultivable after the planned irrigation and reclamation developments have become effective. Beyond that point there is little prospect of consequential expansion in the cultivable area. There are, to be sure, also possibilities for increasing the productivity of areas already irrigated, through conversion from basin to perennial irrigation. These, however, are insufficient to offer any hints as to the solution of the great problem, particularly as long as landlord profits are so high and their expenditures so unproductive.[37]

[35] From 1905 to 1940 the total area of holdings up to five acres increased from 1,264,034 acres to 1,895,477 acres. Even as an absolute increase, this rise was slightly larger than the increase in the entire cultivated area in Egypt during the same period. Cf. Warriner, *op. cit.*, p. 37.

[36] Issawi, *op. cit.*, p. 14; Warriner, *op. cit.*, p. 36.

[37] *New International Year Book*, 1950, p. 159; *National Bank of Egypt Economic Bulletin* (1950), III, No. 3, 164.

As for possible partial solutions of the problem, the almost unanimous expert opinion is that the breaking up of the great estates into small but viable holdings, together with an alteration of the inheritance laws and a consolidation of holdings which are too small to be economic, would constitute the most important step in the right direction, which the government could take if its members were inclined to face realities.[38] There is, in fact, practical demonstration of the fact that yields are higher by upward of 12 per cent on farms of about five acres than on large estates in Egypt, when all other conditions are equal. Under the circumstances, such a partition-consolidation policy not only would be of considerable immediate benefit to the *fellahin* but also would stimulate the formation of cooperatives and, by redistributing purchasing power, provide an incentive for the establishment of new Egyptian industries. The main reason industrialization has thus far proceeded so slowly is that the internal market is exceedingly restricted. The wealth is mainly concentrated in the hands of persons who spend excessive amounts on foreign luxuries, unproductive services, and foreign securities. By contrast, about 90 per cent of the population belong to the groups chronically afflicted by poverty, illiteracy, and disease.[39]

The following paragraphs describe and discuss the major plans, during the period 1940 to 1950, for elevation of Egyptian living standards.

THE HEALTH IMPROVEMENT SCHEME

Probably not another country in the entire world has so formidable a total health problem as Egypt. Although no accurate statistics on the subject exist, there is a wide area of expert agreement on some of the most prominent aspects of the question. While the greatest chronic menace, perhaps, has been the malaria-bearing mosquito, it has also been authoritatively estimated that, as an average day-to-day

[38] In addition to eliminating the factor of exorbitant landlord profits, this would almost certainly decrease the influence in the government of elements unsympathetic with the *fellahin's* interests.

[39] Issawi, *op. cit.*, pp. 78, 199; Warriner, *op. cit.*, p. 48; United Nations, *Final Report of the United Nations Economic Survey Mission for the Middle East* (Lake Success, N.Y., 1949), Part I, pp. 37, 52-53.

situation, 90 per cent of the population are afflicted with trachoma, 75 per cent with schistosomiasis,[40] and 40 per cent with ancylostoma (hookworm). Moreover, the vast majority of the populace is at all times exposed to conditions which, from the viewpoint of sanitation, might well seem unbelievable to persons unfamiliar with the country. The death rate is the highest in the world.[41] The nutritional standards are among the lowest and are apparently steadily deteriorating.[42]

This state of affairs marks the greatest obvious contrast between Egypt and the Western countries. Thus, in any concerted attempt to raise living standards, the matter of public health must necessarily receive important consideration.

Whether or not the health problem as a whole can be tackled satisfactorily in isolation from such problems as land reform and education is another matter. The consensus of authority is that this cannot be done. Some of the reasons given are: (1) that even the complete elimination of a certain disease germ from a country serves no permanent purpose if the conditions which favored its growth are permitted to endure; (2) that, unless national public health programs are completely integrated as to all possible implications, the net result in a country like Egypt may simply be to lower the death rate while the high birth rate is maintained, thereby increasing the pressure of population upon the food resources and thus augmenting the incidence of the ailments due directly to malnutrition; (3) that, except for demonstration purposes, there is not much use in developing new public health facilities without making provision at the same time for well-qualified personnel in adequate quantities to maintain the facilities, together with general education in regard to uses and

[40] This disease occurs in two forms, one of which is known as bilharziasis. Sometimes, however, the latter term is used incorrectly in reference to both forms. Cf. David L. Belding, *Textbook of Clinical Parasitology* (New York, 1942), pp. 551-588.

[41] In most years since 1905 it has exceeded 26 per 1000, even according to official estimates, which are generally believed to be understatements. Cf. Cleland, *op. cit.*, p. 51; Issawi, *op. cit.*, pp. 44-45.

[42] Worthington, *op. cit.*, pp. 150, 152, 155; Issawi, *op. cit.*, p. 46; Warriner, *op. cit.*, p. 41; United Nations Secretariat, Department of Economic Affairs, *Technical Assistance for Economic Development* (Lake Success, N.Y., 1949), pp. 293, 305.

purposes, on a continuing basis. In summary, hard as it may be for the populace to carry its present burden of disease, there would perhaps be an even more unfortunate situation if hopes were to be raised, only to be lowered thereafter.[43]

The fundamental problem, in short, is how to make a start toward the elimination of ignorance and poverty. And, since that is the case, the most important first step in any integrated public health program would probably be an alteration of the present systems of land tenure. This would enable the *fellahin* to get somewhat better nourishment and, by encouraging them to believe in possibilities of bettering themselves, would also produce a climate more conducive to rudimentary forms of education.

But even this would be no more than a small beginning. It would have to be followed up by a gradual, patient, and uninterrupted process of indoctrinating the *fellahin* in all parts of Egypt with regard to the practices to be followed for maintenance of general sanitation and individual health. For the institution of such indoctrination on a large scale, far-reaching sociological changes at the upper levels of society would be prerequisites. For example, people of the middle classes would have to overcome their present strong distaste for life in the rural regions.[44] Here, however, an additional process of indoctrination is involved, which also could not be completed effectively in a short time.

Nevertheless, to the many Egyptians who had come to believe that Westernization and the raising of living standards were primary essentials for the country, it was unthinkable that immediate direct steps in the nature of large-scale assault on the health problem should be omitted. National dignity demanded this, even though there were no immediate answers at hand to the deeper questions in connection with the matter. The types of project most favored, and ultimately selected, were: (1) those which are ordinarily symptomatic of a highly advanced stage of civilization; (2) those which are particularly conspicuous, or which produce impressive statistical results; (3) those which, viewed superficially, could stand on their own merits as

[43] Worthington, *op. cit.*, pp. 141-181.
[44] *Ibid.*, p. 174; Issawi, *op. cit.*, p. 157.

accomplishments, without dependence upon the success of accompanying measures involving external social and economic factors.

The present intensive activities in certain phases of public health may be regarded as evolutionary developments of a grand plan which was put into effect in 1944. Although this was a five-year plan, some of the original aims were greatly expanded before the termination of the five-year period. For all practical purposes it may be considered that a modified version of the original project is still in effect.

In 1944 the Egyptian Parliament passed a Health Statute embodying the five-year plan. The total cost of the program was then estimated at £E52,000,000. The main projects, and the estimated cost of each, were as follows: (1) a scheme for distribution of pure drinking water to a population of 4,000,000 in cities and towns—£E8,600,-000; (2) health centers for each group of 15,000 in the population—£E5,700,000; (3) universal inoculation against bilharziasis and ancylostoma—£E4,580,000; (4) increase in the number of hospitals in the towns—£E4,000,000; (5) extension of drainage in the towns—£E4,000,000; (6) treatment of tuberculosis and pellagra—£E3,000,-000; (7) drainage of marshes—£E3,500,000.[45]

No complete record is available as to the extent to which the original five-year goals of this plan were considered to have been achieved. It can be stated, however, that, as time went on, four aspects of the program were particularly emphasized, namely, pure water supplies, construction of hospitals, development of health centers, and the campaign against malaria. The last of these has been in part strikingly successful; it was reported in 1945 that one newly imported malaria carrier, *Anopheles Gambiae*, had been completely exterminated throughout the country.[46] It is not yet known whether this can be regarded as a permanent result.

There is now a major project, work on which has been going on since 1947, for expansion in the supplies of pure water to the rural districts. For the delta, five large waterworks, with networks of mains, are planned; the construction contract for at least one of these has

---

[45] Warriner, *op. cit.*, pp. 42-43.

[46] H. van Zile Hyde, "World Health Organization—Progress and Plans," *Department of State Bulletin*, April 4, 1948; Mark F. Boyd, *Malariology* (Philadelphia, 1949), p. 794.

already been placed. The remainder of the scheme envisages the boring of 12,000 wells, to be equipped with hand pumps, and the installation of 2000 power pumps at suitable points where pure water is, or will be made, available. The estimated cost of the entire project is £E21,000,000, and the estimated time required for completion ten years from 1947. According to official reports, the percentage of the rural population supplied with pure water was increased to 40 per cent (from 25 per cent at the beginning) during the first three years of the program.[47]

The present program for hospital construction envisages one 500-bed hospital in each provincial headquarters town and a 100-bed hospital in each district headquarters town or village throughout the country.[48] No estimate is available as to the total cost, but the current annual budgets of the Ministry of Public Health average about £E12,000,000, the larger part of which is available for this aspect of the health program, together with the health centers. Some excellent hospital buildings have already been constructed, and the work is continuing.[49]

The total aim of the health center program remains substantially the same as in 1944. However, as was to be anticipated, this particularly fundamental phase of the total public health campaign has not progressed at all rapidly. According to the United Nations Economic Survey Mission, which made a study of development in Egypt in 1949, eighty village health centers had been completed by the end of 1948, and the construction of thirty additional ones was in progress in 1949. The total number planned is 1200—all in rural villages.[50]

It is too early to judge as to the concrete results, from the human viewpoint, of this large-scale plan for health improvement. The lasting value of the hospitals and the pure water supply systems can hardly be determined until it can be observed whether the main-

[47] United Nations, *op. cit.*, Part I, p. 69.
[48] These were, according to the official census of 1937, 23 provinces and 146 districts.
[49] United Nations, *op. cit.*, Part I, p. 70.
[50] *Ibid.*

tenance is of the same high quality as the construction and installations. The health centers are discussed in a later section of this chapter, "The Village Improvement Scheme."

THE FIVE-YEAR PLAN

The best brief description of the Five-Year Plan, and of its results to date, is contained in the *Final Report of the United Nations Economic Survey Mission for the Middle East*, published December 28, 1949:

In 1946, the Egyptian Government approved a five-year plan. . . . This is a development plan consisting of classes of desirable work, with some named projects, for which funds are regularly provided in the Egyptian Budget. The plan originally included the Aswan electrification project; establishment of an Industrial Bank; electrification of some railway lines; and general improvement of transportation, many health measures, new schools, etc. . . . Certain sections are executed each year, but details are not available. The Palestinian campaign, the cholera epidemic, and the establishment of large separate projects have probably led to some modification of the plan.

The cost was estimated at £E96 million, of which £E46 million was out of General Reserve and £E10 million in each of 5 years from current revenue.

In 1946 £E22 million was allocated out of General Reserve as follows:

(1)	Roads	£E4,000,000
(2)	Reclamation of swamps	2,000,000
(3)	Cairo main drainage	2,000,000
(4)	Schools and hospitals	1,500,000
(5)	Irrigation and drainage	6,000,000
(6)	Pure drinking water supplies . . .	3,250,000
(7)	Agriculture	1,700,000
(8)	Other projects, etc.	2,000,000

Subsequent additional funds voted have been £E7.8 million (general reserve) in 1947; £E4 million in 1946; £E5.2 million in 1948; with reductions in 1948 of £3.6 million. These items are all from General Reserve; current revenue allocations in 1947/48 were £E8.5 million (not fully utilized), 1948/49 £E9.4 million; and in 1949/50 £E12.4 million.[51]

[51] United Nations, *op. cit.*, Part I, p. 70.

This "plan" seems to consist mainly of an allocation of priorities among the developmental ventures which were being contemplated in 1946. As for the monies appropriated, there is clearly an overlap between this plan and the more specific developmental plans, such as the Health Improvement Scheme. The principal feature of interest is the evidence afforded as to the attitude taken by the Egyptian Government vis-à-vis the question of raising living standards, the means chosen for doing this, and the relative emphases upon the various alternative means. The importance assigned to the matter of pure drinking water is perhaps of particular interest.

Actual expenditures on the Five-Year Plan have fallen considerably below the amounts appropriated, partly because of the financial stresses occasioned by the Palestine War, partly because of the difficulties experienced in importing the necessary materials. Egypt has large sterling balances, but much of the equipment needed for the development decided upon is not available from sources within the sterling area. The dollar assets at the government's disposal have been distinctly limited.[52]

For a comparison of the 1946 policy with that of the government in power in 1950, King Farouk's Speech from the Throne, delivered on January 16, 1950, is probably the best indicator. Discussing the question of social and economic progress, which he strongly emphasized in his address, he listed nine proposed lines of progress in the following order: (1) industrialization, (2) the Aswan power scheme, (3) improvement of irrigation and drainage, (4) a gradual extension of free schooling to all levels, (5) an immediate grant of free primary, secondary, and technical schooling in existing institutions, (6) development of the role of Al-Azhar University (the world's leading center of Moslem orthodoxy) in Egyptian education, (7) the building of hospitals and health centers, (8) immediate and drastic steps to lower the cost of living, (9) a social security act to provide pensions for every family which had been deprived of its wage-earning capacity through death, infirmity, or old age.[53]

[52] Ibid., Part I, pp. 52-53.
[53] Egypt News Bulletin, February, 1950, pp. 8-9.

THE VILLAGE IMPROVEMENT SCHEME

The general nature of the Village Improvement Scheme, as embodied in an act of the Egyptian Parliament passed in 1944, is outlined in B. A. Keen's book entitled *The Agricultural Development of the Middle East*:

The country will be divided in accordance with local variations into a number of units which, when the scheme is in full operation, will number about 400, with an average of 15,000 acres. Each unit will have a model demonstration farm, under a resident agronomist, where the results of the work, carried out by the Ministry of Agriculture's crop research stations will be tested and shown; and a veterinary centre for disease prevention, the improvement of animal husbandry, the control of abattoirs, and the conversion of animal waste product to fertilizers.

The key part of this scheme is a Council of Agriculture for each unit, charged with a variety of duties . . . that make for improved standards in agriculture and rural welfare. The Council has machinery, including a link with the local agricultural inspectorate of the Ministry of Agriculture, for interpreting the Ministry's policy to the farmers, and for passing back to the Ministry the views and needs of the area.[54]

In actual practice this scheme has been combined with the health center phase of the Health Improvement Scheme. The merger has greatly facilitated cooperation among government officials working toward similar or mutually complementary goals in rural areas. Mr. Roderic D. Matthews has recently described the resultant situation:

One suggestion which has been tried in Egypt promises an acceleration of improvement in living conditions. This plan provides for a team of workers, with arrangement for adequate housing and wholesome recreation. This team includes a doctor, nurses, social workers, agricultural agents, and teachers. The housing which is provided is of a type acceptable to a group which has had the advantage of living under better conditions in the cities. The general philosophy of this team is to help the villagers move forward as fast as the villagers can be awakened to the need for change. Forcing change before the villagers want it is definitely avoided. Members of these teams are enthusiastic about the plan and hopeful that others will join them or develop other teams to

[54] B. A. Keen, *The Agricultural Development of the Middle East* (London, 1946), p. 44.

work in similar villages. This attitude is in sharp contrast to the situations where teachers feel that they are being punished by being sent to rural areas. Morale is at a low ebb when this feeling prevails.[55]

Mr. C. L. Sulzberger discusses the same situation in the March 19, 1950, issue of the New York *Times*:

Dr. Ahmed Hussein, the able Minister of Social Affairs, . . . is trying to push through gradual reform and shape up a coordinated social welfare program despite the opposition of the wealthy power groups, who wish neither higher taxes nor an educated peasantry. . . .

The leading Wafd party is giving some reluctant support. This correspondent visited one of Dr. Hussein's rural welfare centers in the sordid village of Manawahla, in the district of Monufia.

It was touching to see how earnestly young doctors and social workers were trying to improve local health and sanitation concepts, stock breeding and community spirit. Such centers, which are established for 10% of the villages, are founded on joint contributions by the Government and the peasants themselves.

The basic idea is that each participating fellah shall contribute even a few cents so all will feel part owners and share the responsibility and so will acquire the habit of speaking up with confidence against the wealthy squires who used to dominate them.

The German-educated Dr. Hussein and his assistants have managed to reduce the infant mortality in three years (in these centers) from 10 to 7 a thousand. But Egypt still remains fundamentally feudal, with an average annual income for a fellah of 19 Egyptian pounds (about $54.75) and for a city worker of 53 pounds (about $152.65).[56]

While the program has lagged far behind the original ambitious plans and faces a prospect of increasingly stubborn high-level opposition, there is nevertheless some ground for slight optimism. The scheme is of particular interest in connection with Egypt's decision, announced on November 12, 1950, to participate in the United States Government's Point Four Scheme, which provides for the encouragement of such projects.[57]

[55] Middle East Institute, *Americans and the Middle East: Partners in the Next Decade* (Washington, 1950), p. 5.

[56] Sulzberger, *loc. cit.*

[57] In the latter part of 1951, Dr. Ahmed Hussein resigned as Minister of Social Welfare. According to a reputable press correspondent whom the writer interviewed, the resignation was motivated by externally inspired and damaging interference with the setup of the ministry while Hussein was on vacation.

THE SOCIAL SECURITY SCHEME

Egypt has led all other Arab countries in enacting major social security legislation. The nature and implications of the act passed in June, 1950, are discussed in two contemporaneous articles published in the New York *Times*:

Egypt will announce tomorrow that every worker, whether in agriculture or in the cities, has the right to a Government pension in his old age. Widows left with dependent children and workers permanently incapacitated will also be covered.

. . . The new legislation was prepared by Ahmed Hussein, Minister for Social Affairs, and Menning Friis, Danish social welfare specialist of the UN. Actuarial studies were prepared by an ILO mission.

. . . The maximum pension for an Egyptian worker with a substantial number of family dependents . . . will be $83 a year. This . . . is three-quarters of the legal minimum wage for unskilled urban workers. In rural regions the basic pension will be $31.60 a year. . . .

Great pains have been taken in preparing this legislation not to disturb the age-old system of security based on the family or household group. The pension is reckoned on the basis of the family group, not of the individual. Deductions will be made for earnings from property or work, but not for voluntary contributions of members of the family group or anyone else to the individual's support.

. . . The burden that the pension system will place on the national budget is limited by the death rate. . . . Few Egyptians live to the pensionable age of 65. . . .[58]

The Ministry explained that an estimated 500,000 beneficiaries with another 1,000,000 dependents could be cared for at present at a cost of only some $18,000,000 a year, with the average pension rate around $33.60 annually.[59]

The net effect of this plan would apparently be to increase the total annual income of the impoverished elements, estimated at about

[58] According to the *Population Census of Egypt*, 1937 (Cairo, 1942), there were in 1937, out of a total population of 15,920,694: 578,072 persons from sixty to sixty-nine years of age; 472,843 persons of seventy years and over.

The article quoted is: Albion Ross, "Egypt Will Enact Old-Age Pensions," New York *Times*, June 23, 1950.

[59] "Egypt's Pension Plan Set to Low Standard," New York *Times*, June 24, 1950.

16,000,000, by $18,000,000. Since much of the additional revenue needed for the plan would be in the form of taxes paid by those classes, the over-all gain to them is apparently only slight.[60]

THE UNIVERSAL FREE EDUCATION SCHEME

In his study made for the Middle East Supply Centre in 1944, Dr. H. B. Allen expressed the following views in regard to the problem of extending elementary education in the region covered by this study:

In providing schools to meet the situation already described there appear to be two important ends to be attained: one, an immediate objective; the other, an ultimate goal. The immediate objective is to supply at the earliest moment a reasonable amount of elementary education, however lacking it may be in some of its finer details, for a large and increasing proportion of the population. The ultimate goal is to create rural schools that are adapted as thoroughly as possible to village conditions.

The objective first named appears to be the one that should be the present concern of many of the Middle East countries. Every available means should be employed to achieve this end. The limited resources of villages, together with special taxes exacted from the landlords, combined with appropriations of the Ministry of Education, should be freely drawn upon to provide the necessary grounds, buildings, and equipment. Every possible source of teachers should be thoroughly investigated and fully utilized. The educational requirements for engaging in the teaching profession should be maintained at minimum standards until the supply of instructors can be greatly augmented. The preparation of teachers should be considerably speeded up.[61]

These opinions are of particular interest in view of the intensive campaign for expansion of educational facilities which is now being waged by the Egyptian Ministry of Education. This campaign is based upon a policy announced by the incumbent Wafd government upon its assumption of power in January, 1950. There is some reason to believe, however, that the Minister of Education is now endeavoring to force the issue of universal free education more strongly than most of his colleagues in the government had intended or wished. Farouk,

[60] United Nations, *op. cit.*, Part I, pp. 37, 52.
[61] H. B. Allen, *Rural Education and Welfare in the Middle East* (London, 1946), p. 6.

in his Speech from the Throne, had simply referred to "a gradual extension of free schooling at all levels."[62] The following excerpts from subsequent New York *Times* articles on the subject give the impression that views such as Dr. Allen's quoted above are now being accorded greater weight than those of the Egyptian ruling class, and that the result may be considerable conflict between the Minister of Education on the one hand and his government colleagues and the Parliament on the other:[63]

Egypt's blind Minister of Education, Dr. Taha Hussein Bey, is leading a crusade to stamp out illiteracy and raise the general standard of education. He has issued a new appeal for free education for all Egyptians.[64]

The law [establishing free universal education] is being attacked primarily as representing a backbreaking financial burden for the state. Already the Egyptian budget for education is equal to the total budget of certain years in the Thirties and the flood of children now pouring into the schools is recognized as just the beginning.

There are far too few teachers and classrooms. The number of children taking the primary certificate at the end of their seventh year to enable them to enter the five-year secondary schools rose in one jump from 45,000 to 75,000.

When he was told there were not enough public secondary schools to meet the demand, the Minister of Education ordered the children into private schools, arranging for the state to pay the teachers' salaries. The school directors refused to accept further candidates. Mr. Hussein then announced that no children could be turned away and that a place must be found for everyone who had a primary certificate.

Mr. Hussein was warned that what he proposed to do was impossible and that the state would have to retreat before the financial burden entailed. When he was told that secondary teachers were required to have a basic college education and two years of teacher training he said that such requirements were a luxury for the present and that a basic college education would have to do until the supply of teachers was great enough to permit raising the requirements.

The desire for education has become strong in the large section of

---

[62] *Egypt News Bulletin*, February, 1950, p. 8.

[63] Nevertheless, the program was apparently still in full effect as of November 15, 1951. On November 13, in a public address on the occasion of National Struggle Day, Premier Nahas Pasha referred with pride to this aspect of the Wafd party's education policy.

[64] "Blind Egyptian Asks Free Public Schools," New York *Times*, May 29, 1950.

Egypt's urban population and much of the rural population. Teachers tell of parents accepting privation to the point of hunger and chronic physical weakness to give their children an education.

It has been difficult for critics of the new program of free education to make headway against the emotional impact of Mr. Hussein's pleading. He is a natural orator with exceptional mastery of his case and the spectacle of this famous blind man demanding that the masses of Egypt shall be led out of darkness is virtually irresistible. His passionate demand for free education cost what it may was one of the important factors that swept the Wafd party back into power last January.[65]

In this general connection it may be noted that Egypt's main difficulty in regard to education, between 1919 and 1950, has been the lack of balance between higher education and the earlier stages of learning. The result has been a chronic unemployment among Egyptians with university degrees. A further result has been a discontented intellectual class.[66]

OBSERVATIONS

THE DECLINE IN LIVING STANDARDS

Although the Egyptian Government maintains fuller statistics than any of the other Arab countries, and although the official statistical data have been supplemented by numerous estimates allegedly based on thorough studies of such matters as national income and distribution of working population, it is evident that the available data along these and other lines contain many inconsistencies and inaccuracies.[67]

Nevertheless, the general conclusions reached, and assumptions made, in this chapter regarding the downward trend of living standards and particularly of food consumption due to population pressure appear to be accepted practically universally.[68] Especially interesting in that connection is the following analysis, made in 1936 by

[65] "School Fight Led by Blind Egyptian," New York *Times*, September 5, 1950.
[66] Issawi, *op. cit.*, pp. 180-181; Monroe, *op. cit.*, p. 138.
[67] Issawi, *op. cit.*, p. 74.
[68] The writer has come across many statements on this subject which were not wholly conclusive, but none in the nature of attempts to refute the thesis. Cf. United Nations, *op. cit.*, Part I, pp. 52-53; Issawi, *op. cit.*, p. 49.

Professor Cleland, which, in the light of subsequent developments, now seems to have been exceedingly overoptimistic:

While the cultivable land has been slowly increasing in the past half century, due to irrigation works, the population has increased still more rapidly with the result not only that the land has had to carry more people, but that the average person, on the other hand, has gained, and in the future can gain, little from these developments. The density in 1927 was 1,045 per square mile, or 0.39 of a feddan per head. According to the program of the Irrigation Department for reclaiming waste lands and expanding the areas under perennial irrigation, the maximum which the Nile is capable of watering is 7,100,000 feddans, as compared with 4,900,000 feddans before the system was operated extensively, that is, before 1891. The works necessary to guarantee this improvement will probably not be completed before 1955 at the very earliest. Shortly after that date, at the present slowly declining rate of growth, the population will probably have reached about 17,000,000, and the amount then available per head will be 0.42 of a feddan, a gain in average land wealth of 0.03 of a feddan in 30 years. In 1886 this average was 0.65; and in 1917, 0.42. Thus it would appear that the effort at improving the water supply will not have increased the per capita acreage, but rather only have prevented a greater loss. About all that can be said in this regard is that the crop acreage will have been increased thanks to the perennial irrigation, to a figure slightly higher than in 1917, the rise being from 0.600 to 0.672 of a crop-feddan (crop-acre) per head.[69]

According to present plans, the total perennial irrigation of Egypt's cultivable area will not have been completed before 1975 at the earliest, as against Professor Cleland's supposition that it might be completed by 1955.[70] Further, whereas Cleland envisaged a 17,000,000 population for 1955, Egypt's existing population in 1949 was 20,045,-000 according to official estimates, and 18,000,000[71] by the most conservative unofficial estimates.[72]

[69] Quotation is from Cleland, op. cit., p. 91.

The concept of "crop acreage" is based on counting a one-acre plot as two crop-acres if it is placed under crops twice during a single year.

[70] National Bank of Egypt Economic Bulletin (1950), III, No. 3, 164.

[71] United Nations, op. cit., p. 52.

[72] In March, 1948, Hussein Sirry Pasha wrote: "During the last forty years the population has grown by 63.7 percent while the new lands brought under cultivation have increased only by 6.2 percent." ("The Evolution of Irrigation in Egypt," Modern Egypt News Bulletin, March, 1948, p. 33).

The following statistics of daily money wages of unskilled agricultural laborers shows how, after being at a high level during and immediately following World War I, these wages had finally reached a new low by 1939:[73]

	Delta	Upper and Middle Egypt
1914	2.5 to 3 piasters	2.5 piasters
1920	7 to 8 "	6 "
1928	4.5 "	4 "
1933	2.5 "	2 "
1939	2.5 to 3 "	2 to 2.5 piasters

Regarding the effect of the Second World War on agricultural wages, Miss Doreen Warriner makes the following statement:

During the second world war, money wages doubled, and in 1942 were about 6 piastres per day. But the cost of living rose faster; the price of maize had trebled during the same period, so that real wages fell.

The rise in the cost of living during the war had tragic results. A malaria epidemic . . . caused the death of 100,000 in these provinces (i.e. Qena and Aswan) in 1941–3 as a result of their half-starved condition.

Thus the war, which brought some improvement in prices and incomes to the cultivators in other Middle East countries, worsened the position of the fellaheen, except in so far as there was an expansion of industrial employment.[74]

As late as November 11, 1950, it was being reported that "economic distress among the peasants and workers has increased and virtually nothing has been done to relieve it." This is ascribed in part to "inflation and profiteering." These conditions have obtained ever since the end of World War II.[75]

[73] Issawi, op. cit., p. 80.
[74] Warriner, op. cit., pp. 39-40.
[75] Clifton Daniel, "Potential Revolt Simmers in Egypt," New York Times, November 12, 1950.
The cost of living indexes for food aliments in Egypt have been as follows since 1938: 1939 (June-August)—100; 1940 (average for year)—112; 1941—141; 1942—194; 1943—263; 1944—312; 1945—325; 1946—310; 1947—298; 1948—299; 1949—303. Cf. Statistical Office of the United Nations, Monthly Bulletin of Statistics, December, 1950.
On January 9, 1951, after this chapter had been completed, the following statement appeared in the New York Times:

GENERAL

There now seems to be little doubt that a social conscience has made its appearance in Egypt in some restricted quarters, and that it has even begun to penetrate at the top governmental level. It is equally clear that the manifestations of social conscience are being more and more appreciated by the lower social strata. The lesson of the great contrast between the attitudes of Drs. Ahmed Hussein and Taha Hussein, on the one hand, and those of the great landowners and the great majority of party leaders, on the other, is by no means wholly lost.

The reverse of the coin is that there is still no evidence of any general change of heart, present or prospective, within the ruling group. Indeed, there is a wide consensus of expert opinion that the Wafd party, which came into power in January, 1950, on the basis of promises to make far-reaching improvements in the conditions of the Egyptian people as a whole, has in practice proved neither more efficient nor less corrupt, all things considered, than the general run of its predecessors in power. It seems likely, moreover, that the conscientious efforts toward social reform which are now being made in some quarters will be doomed to either stagnation or failure unless they are soon accompanied by much farther-reaching reforms along other lines, which do not appear to be forthcoming.[76]

It is all very well to attempt to hold peasants' interest in schemes for their improvement by requiring those peasants to pay part of the costs. But if at the same time their incomes are being steadily re-

---

"Egypt's post-war prosperity in terms of national money income, which is at an all-time high, has been accomplished by a ten percent decrease in the average income, according to a study by Mohammed al Rifaat, an economist. . . .

"His conclusion is that over-all industrial and agricultural production is slightly less than before and during part of World War II. . . . He . . . adds that there are indications that the average Egyptian with small savings has been forced to consume them in part or in whole because the high cost of living has reduced real income. . . .

"The figures showed a definite income decrease for the average Egyptian of all classes, except the wealthy. . . . Price increases mean that the value of the Egyptian pound now is about thirty percent of what it was in 1939."

[76] Daniel, *loc. cit.*; also editorial entitled "Suez and Sudan," in November 17, 1950, issue of the New York *Times*.

duced, the application of such a philosophy will obviously have its definite limitations. Further, while it is nearly always possible to single out certain sections of the populace and bring about striking alterations in their status, the greatest difficulties are likely to occur after the early demonstrations have produced a general clamor for more meaningful reform, suggesting to the dominant class that a wholesale upheaval of existing institutions is in the making.[77]

CONCLUSIONS

There are clearly only two possible major first steps to a solution of Egypt's present problem of poverty. One is a planned large-scale emigration. The other is a redistribution of landholdings which would eliminate the absentee landlord[78] and, to the greatest extent possible, divide the available land among the *fellahin* in the form of holdings of about five acres per family. A farm of this size is generally regarded as viable, particularly under conditions of perennial irrigation.

The latter of these two alternatives is undoubtedly to be preferred, since a planned emigration would be in the nature of a treatment of symptoms, rather than of a cure. What is particularly needed is drastically altered attitudes, policies, and direction at the top governmental level. Without those, an emigration policy might fail to achieve the desired results. The landowners would still be on hand, and would be quite capable of creating pressures upon the government, as they have done before, for relief from the "exorbitant labor costs." Thus the outward movement might be stopped before it had

[77] Proposals for land reform, made at high official levels, have not been completely lacking during the postwar period. Also there was, in 1948, an actual distribution of *newly reclaimed* land among small farmers, involving 300-450 families (2000-3000 persons) which had previously been without land of their own.

However, in all cases, either the scheme put into practice has been a small one which did not attack the roots of the problem or the official proposal has been in vague terms, accompanied by too many safeguards for the benefit of large landowners and followed by a long period of silence indicating that the cabinet as a whole had no intention of taking strong action in the matter. Cf. *Modern Egypt News Bulletin*, March, 1948, p. 33; *Encyclopaedia Britannica, Book of the Year*, 1946, p. 279; Ross, "Big Land Holdings in Egypt Assailed," New York *Times*, April 8, 1950.

[78] Issawi, *op. cit.*, p. 73.

served any significant purpose, or even reversed after it had been well begun. Moreover, as far as the development of industry is concerned, it is easily conceivable that an immense numerical diminution of the population might hurt matters more than the increase in per capita spending power would help them. Much would depend on the precise nature of the emigration plan. The formulation would constitute a difficult problem.

The other alternative, by contrast, while having all the advantages already mentioned, has no obvious defects. It could bring into being (1) an increased per capita income for the rural population; (2) an opening for new industries, which in turn would absorb part of the rural surplus and thereby create still more spending power and consequent possibilities for manufactures; (3) improved agricultural yield as a result of greater confidence in the government on the part of farmers; (4) increased general receptivity to health and education matters, which in turn would (5) augment the productivity of the populace. Still further, as new industries became successful, more and more previously idle capital would become available for industrial expansion. Finally, if such a scheme proved not to be a completely satisfactory remedy, an emigration scheme could still be carried out.

In short, such a scheme could set into motion a long chain of favorable developments, with no easily foreseeable automatic stopping-point. This event would be particularly likely in view of the pioneering developments which have already taken place in the fields of health, education, and village improvement.

It is only through such means as these that the present major plans for raising living standards can actually fulfill their purposes.

CHAPTER III

❖

Saudi Arabia and Yemen

SAUDI ARABIA

The history of major planning in Saudi Arabia for the elevation of general living standards differs markedly from that of all the other Middle Eastern countries in at least three important respects.

The first difference is that Saudi Arabia's major planning was begun at a much lower stage of social and economic advancement than that which prevailed at the beginning of planning in other Middle Eastern countries. The second is that Saudi Arabian planning, insofar as the policy decisions are concerned, has been almost entirely the work of one man, King (formerly Sultan) Ibn Saud, carried out over a period of nearly four decades during which he has possessed absolute control over all or part of the present territory of the country.

The third difference is that the successful implementation of the initial planning was already well advanced before any Western or Western-style assistance was offered or sought. Thus, in their original and nuclear aspects—inspirational, ideological, and practical—the planning and execution have been largely Oriental in character. The West, to be sure, entered prominently into the picture in the later stages; but by that time definite patterns had already been established. Even at the present time, despite the firm establishment of a great

85

American oil concession in the northeastern part of the country, there is no clear indication that Western influence will soon acquire a decisive character outside of the limited areas where the Arabian American Oil Company conducts, or will shortly be conducting, regular operations. Those areas, which are sparsely inhabited by Saudi Arabians not connected with the oil company, are well separated from the rest of the nation both by geographical factors and by governmental policy.

The Bedouin Settlement Plan which Ibn Saud inaugurated in the year 1912 must, in any classification, be ranked among the major plans for elevation of living standards in the middle East. The enormous geographical area eventually involved (927,000 square miles), the change which has been produced in thought currents throughout the Arabian peninsula, and the length of time (1912 to the present) during which this plan has been the central core of Ibn Saud's general developmental program—all these elements lead to the conclusion that the scheme has been one of outstanding importance.

In the paragraphs which follow, the Bedouin Settlement Plan is described and discussed. In connection with the discussion, it must always be borne in mind that statistical data in regard to Saudi Arabia are meager and that most of the figures used are rough approximations, based, however, on the most reliable sources available.

The Bedouin Settlement Plan

In 1912, as ruler of Nejd,[1] Ibn Saud seems to have become strongly convinced of the futility of endeavoring to hold sway over any large section of Arabian territory under the conditions then prevailing. The main obstacles, which appeared to be almost hopeless ones, were the chronic impermanence of tribal alliances and the gradual infiltration of foreign political dominance into Arabia. Following the ancient and revered traditions, Arabians recognized no loyalties above their tribal loyalties; in the wars which were constantly breaking out between native rulers of territories, the alliances among the numerous tribes fighting under those rulers were forever fluctuating. By any

[1] Nejd is a region of central and eastern Arabia, never exactly defined as to its extent, which now constitutes not more than one-fifth or one-sixth of the entire kingdom of Saudi Arabia.

Western scale of values, there was no sense of duty and responsibility, either between one tribe and another or between any given tribe and the territorial ruler. Promises were freely broken whenever it was felt that the momentary self-interest of one's own tribe could be served by such a breach. Under the circumstances, it was manifestly impossible for a territorial ruler, whose domains necessarily contained several tribes or parts of tribes, to plan for the future with even a moderate degree of assurance. Moreover, if this situation persisted for long without sharp modification, the great powers would almost certainly take advantage of it to carve up Arabia, as they had already carved up Africa, for partition among themselves. Already Great Britain had acquired extensive political influence along the eastern and southern coasts of the Arabian peninsula. Now, also, the Ottoman authorities were endeavoring to acquire actual, as opposed to nominal, control of all the Arabian territory not yet preempted by the British.

The leading authorities on the subject seem to be agreed that Ibn Saud's concern about this situation was motivated more by personal ambition than by any determination to preserve features of the traditional way of life, though the latter consideration unquestionably entered into the matter. Apparently he was mainly anxious to find some method whereby he could assuredly hold his nuclear territory and his hoped-for territorial acquisitions against all challengers, Arabian and foreign. It was particularly clear to him that military force was not in itself sufficient for such a purpose. The force which was today his might tomorrow be on the side which opposed him.

Ibn Saud concluded that the only suitable remedy would be a gradual abolition of tribalism, which in turn would depend upon a substantial reduction of nomadism. At that time, 80 per cent or more of the population of Nejd was nomadic, most of the rest being small farmers in villages, constantly menaced by Bedouin raids, and merchants and craftsmen in widely scattered trading centers. The situation in the rest of Arabia was, generally speaking, substantially similar.

Having reached this conclusion, Ibn Saud decided to devote the rest of his life to a progressive establishment of agricultural colonies in all parts of his domain, these to be peopled mainly by members of nomadic tribes. The end objective was a large settled population, interested primarily in the maintenance and protection of their plots of land and dependent upon state machinery for the furnishing of that protection. But, if this goal was to be achieved, it was essential that the agricultural colonies should prosper—to such an extent, at least, that the colonists would in time lose their taste for the nomadic life, with all its insecurities and privations.

Any such project was necessarily beset with difficult problems. For one thing, Ibn Saud's revenue for all purposes, personal and governmental, was not much more than about $400,000 a year; his subjects probably numbered at least 200,000.[2] But the hardest task, to all appearances, was to lure people into the adoption of a way of life which they at that time held in contempt.

This last problem was solved by making militant religion the basis upon which the colonies were established. The members of each agricultural settlement were to constitute part of the Wahhabi Ikhwan (Brotherhood). Each colony, in addition to cultivating the soil, was to hold itself in readiness at all times to fight for the puritanical Wahhabi beliefs, in order both to make converts and to prevent the intrusion of other Moslem sects into Wahhabi territory. As a preliminary measure, the Wahhabi faith, which had grown corrupt with the passage of time, was cleansed of its impurities—by Ibn Saud's command, but with more or less complete public approval. Indeed, these moves along religious lines proved highly inspirational to Ibn Saud's subjects, who were apparently in a state of psychological readiness for them. In 1912 the first of the agricultural colonies was established at Artawiya, in Nejd.[3] There, where no cultivation had previously been attempted since ancient times, and where the only

[2] The annual revenue figure is based on Mr. H. St. John Philby's estimate of £100,000 as Ibn Saud's annual revenue in 1917. Mr. Philby was apparently convinced that the 1917 revenue represented more or less normal conditions for that general era. The population figure is little more than a rough guess based on fragmentary data. Cf. Philby, "The Golden Jubilee in Saudi Arabia," *Journal of the Royal Central Asian Society*, April, 1950.

[3] Herr von Mikusch has provided the best account of the beginnings of the Bedouin Settlement Scheme. Cf. Dagobert von Mikusch, *Ibn Saud* (Leipzig, 1942), pp. 134-142. Cf. Also H. St. John Philby, "Ibn Saud," *Encyclopaedia Britannica*, 1942 ed., p. 34 *et seq.*

signs of life were a few old wells for the use of transients, irrigation of a simple form was introduced and a fairly sizable area brought under crops, with the aid of a few rural village dwellers whom Ibn Saud had introduced as teachers. The grants of land to the settlers were in the form of small privately owned holdings. Water rights were determined by Ibn Saud or his representative on a dictatorial basis, with provision for appeals and equitable adjustments on the same basis. As for the fraternal aspects of the colonies, these were centered upon the mosque which was invariably constructed along with the residential dwellings. Similar practices were followed in all subsequent allotments of land under the Bedouin Settlement Plan. And, when Ibn Saud's wealth became greater, money grants were made to colonists to enable them to pursue their cultivation without falling into debt.[4]

The Artawiya beginning was followed by the gradual establishment of similar colonies in other parts of Nejd (and its conquered dependencies) on the same basis. By 1927 there were about a hundred of them; and Artawiya had grown to a town of 10,000 inhabitants. Many difficulties had meanwhile been encountered, not the least of which was the colonists' frequent insistence on placing the ostensible austere religious motive for the colonies higher than Ibn Saud's more immediate motive for instituting them. Later, in 1929, after this same issue had produced overt civil strife, Ibn Saud adopted two new policies. Thereafter he lessened the emphasis upon religion, more or less frankly subordinating it to national considerations; he also gradually worked out plans for a standing army, instead of continuing to depend upon the enthusiasm of the colonists in military matters. He would not have been able to take these steps effectively but for the fact that by that time many of the colonists had become well satisfied with the sedentary, agricultural way of life.

One distinct advantage that Ibn Saud had enjoyed in connection with the execution of this plan was that there were no major internal

[4] Afif I. Tannous, "Land Reform: Key to the Development and Stability of the Arab World," *Middle East Journal*, Winter, 1951, p. 13; Royal Institute of International Affairs, *The Middle East: A Political and Economic Survey* (London, 1950), p. 85.

forces impelling him to go ahead faster than was his wish. In fact, all of the domestic pressures upon him were in the opposite direction. The latter could be dealt with in many cases by those shrewd tactics which Europeans tend to attribute to all Oriental monarchs, and which Ibn Saud actually had at his command. Religious conservatism, for example, could sometimes be reduced by, so to speak, "fixing" the Ulema. This body, which was recognized by the populace as the highest authority on the interpretation of the Koran and the sacred traditions, could be induced to make rulings that, for example, since automobiles and radios were not mentioned in the Koran it must not be assumed that Allah intended to prohibit their use.[5]

In 1925, by virtue of conquest, Ibn Saud had become King of the Hejaz, the seat of the Holy Cities, Mecca and Medina. Until 1932 that kingdom was governed under a constitution which imposed limits upon the ruler's powers; but in that year Ibn Saud annexed the Hejaz to his own domains. These developments gave him full control over the fees from pilgrimages, amounting until 1940 to five to twenty million dollars a year.[6] The great additional income enabled Ibn Saud to make much larger direct expenditures upon national security, as, for example, upon a network of wireless communications in strategic spots throughout the country. By this means he became able to take prompt measures against persons or groups who threatened to interfere with his plans.

The presence of the agricultural colonies, on the one hand, and Ibn Saud's desire for security of rule, on the other, have acted and reacted upon each other in such a way as to produce interesting results. To an increasing extent the colonists looked upon Ibn Saud's government as the principal means of insuring their own security and were consequently more and more disposed to support it. That support, to be sure, meant an end for all time of intratribal solidarity among the settled groups, since that solidarity was inconsistent with a be-

[5] Von Mikusch, op. cit., pp. 140, 315, 316, 336.
[6] Estimates in regard to the receipts from pilgrimages vary widely. Cf. Philby, "The Golden Jubilee in Saudi Arabia," p. 121; Royal Institute of International Affairs, op. cit., p. 84; Raymond F. Mikesell and Hollis B. Chenery, Arabian Oil: America's Stake in the Middle East (Chapel Hill, N.C., 1949), p. 77.

stowal of primary allegiance upon a national ruler belonging to a family other than one's own. Ibn Saud, for his part, recognized the necessity of doing all in his power to make the conditions of the colonists ever more satisfactory. One consequential result of this interaction has been that Bedouin raiding and insecurity of travel from place to place have been largely eliminated, first in the Nejd, later in the whole of present-day Saudi Arabia.[7] This increased security for agriculture and this removal of the greatest economic attraction of nomadism have, as always, raised the volume of new agricultural settlement, even apart from special settlement plans. While it is probable that 50 to 60 per cent of the country's population is still nomadic,[8] the preponderant power is now in the hands of the settled population.

In 1929 Ibn Saud extended the agricultural settlement scheme to the Hejaz; from 1932 on, it has been applied in all parts of Saudi Arabia, the extent of which has been unchanged since that year. According to the plan as it has existed since 1912, no colony shall be regarded as complete until it has at least 2000 settlers. Wahhabism is still an important secondary basis of the colonies. Through the use of religious teachers known as *Mutawwi*, Ibn Saud has succeeded in spreading the Wahhabi faith from Nejd to at least small groups in practically all corners of his huge country. This practice has greatly reduced the scope of the settlement problem outside of the Nejd. In those other regions, for the most part, similar contemptuous ideas had been held by the people in regard to the sedentary life; in addition, the religious background had been less conducive to attempts at unification.

Throughout the period between wars Ibn Saud studied the question of applying Western methods in the execution of his settlement program. At first, however, the Western techniques and equipment introduced into the country were almost entirely for security purposes. Later, as the attainment of internal tranquillity reduced the need for policing, and as it became apparent that external dangers could be averted better by political tactics and negotiations than by

[7] K. S. Twitchell, *Saudi Arabia* (Princeton, 1947), p. 121.
[8] *Ibid.*, p. 108.

the employment of an army which could not hope to overcome major foreign opposition, the primary stress was more and more upon application of Western methods for peaceful purposes, such as the improvement of agriculture and the subsidiary matters of road and rail communications, port development, education at the lower levels, and betterment of health conditions. There is now an Agricultural Administration, whose annual budget approaches $1,000,000 for expenditure on miscellaneous minor agricultural improvements and assistance. While the techniques of cultivation have remained primitive on the whole (mainly characterized by the wooden plow so familiar in the Middle East), more modern practices are gradually being introduced in selected small areas.

In 1938 the Saudi Arabian Minister of Finance submitted to Ibn Saud a plan for an irrigation project of a more elaborate nature than anything theretofore attempted. It was designed to be an integral part of the general colonization scheme, the progress of which had been slowed down somewhat by the world-wide economic depression. The irrigation of 8000 acres in the Kharj district of Nejd, by the pumping of waters from deep pools with Diesel engines, was proposed. The supervision of the work was to be performed by two Iraqi engineers, in accordance with the general policy of obtaining technical help from Middle Eastern sources whenever possible.

The eventual upshot of this proposal, which received Ibn Saud's approval and on which work was begun at once, was the dispatch in 1942, at the King's own request, of a United States Agricultural Mission to Saudi Arabia. This official governmental mission covered 11,000 miles in its study of water and other resources of the country, and its efforts have been followed up by several subsequent trips of foreign experts for the exploration and examination of developmental possibilities, and even for the actual direction of works.

There are no satisfactory estimates as to the amount of land now cultivated or the amount of additional land which could be brought under cultivation. However, in 1947 an official of the United States Department of State expressed the belief that the arable acreage could be increased at least tenfold by the utilization of underground waters alone.[9] The desirability of proceeding as rapidly as practicable with the reclamation program has been emphasized by the food shortages which occurred in Saudi Arabia during World War II, when pilgrimage receipts were inadequate to pay for needed imports of food. Unfortunately, since there are no available criteria for estimating the rates of population growth, past and future, the precise needs of the country in future years are hard to assess.

There is probably little scope for the construction of truly major irrigation works, but an abundance of possibilities for profitable small schemes exists; and it should be noted that most of the present cultivation is on a rain-fed basis. The Kharj project, which has produced a 2000-3000-acre model farm owned by King Ibn Saud, was expanded to cover the near-by area of Khafs Dagra, where similar water conditions obtain.[10] There is, however, one unfortunate aspect of these projects in the Kharj neighborhood. It has been described by Mr. Halford L. Hoskins:

A situation of this nature in more aggravated form exists in the famed Al Kharj oasis in Saudi Arabia. . . . From the horticultural point of view the undertaking has been a distinct success, but in another respect it is probably doomed to eventual failure. The tract is watered from a deep natural reservoir, whose waters are hardly potable. Every irrigation channel is rimmed with alkaline salts. The basin which constitutes the oasis has no outlet to the sea and hence from year to year as new sections of the sandy waste are put to the plow, others are abandoned as no longer productive.[11]

In addition to these larger projects, Ibn Saud is now pursuing a continuous policy of sinking wells in all parts of the country, so as to permit nomads to become farmers. An American-supervised ground-water survey, scheduled to begin early in 1951, should be of assistance in enabling him to accomplish this object with still greater efficiency.

[9] Richard H. Sanger, "Ibn Saud's Program for Arabia," *Middle East Journal*, April, 1947.
[10] Twitchell, *op. cit.*, p. 42.
[11] Halford L. Hoskins, "Point Four with Reference to the Middle East," *Annals of the American Academy of Political and Social Science*, March, 1950, p. 88.

ADDITIONAL NOTES

Oil Developments. The first production of oil on a commercial scale in Saudi Arabia took place in 1936. The subsequent enormous increases in production are indicated in the following schedule, showing average daily production:[12]

Year	Average Daily Output (bbls.)
1936	100
1938	1,400
1941	16,100
1944	21,300
1947	247,000
1950	546,700

The financial implications for Saudi Arabia of these great increases are discussed in the following sections of New York *Times* articles which appeared shortly after the end of 1950:

The Arabian American Oil Company . . . has agreed to share its profits half and half with the Saudi Arabian Government, company officials disclosed here today. . . .

The agreement . . . was said to represent a new departure in the policy of the oil industry in the Near East.

The half-and-half profit-sharing agreement was made retroactive to the beginning of 1950. Estimates indicate that the oil company's payments to the Saudi Arabian Government for the year 1950 will be increased by about $30,000,000 from about $60,000,000 to $64,000,000 under the old agreement, to about $90,000,000 to $94,000,000 under the new agreement. Payments in 1951 will considerably exceed $100,-000,000 at present rates of production.

United States taxes are to be deducted before the net operating income is calculated. . . . The existing concession terms had nearly always excluded the taxing of the concession and earnings. However, the Aramco agreement accepts the principle of taxation.

According to a dispatch from Jedda, King Ibn Saud issued on December 26 a Royal decree stating that any company engaged in prospecting and producing oil or other hydrocarbons was required to pay an income tax of fifty percent of its total receipts after deduction of certain amounts, such as foreign taxes.

[12] Mikesell and Chenery, *op. cit.*, Appendix II, Table 6.

Within the structure of Saudi Arabian legislation, the royalty, there-fore, will apparently become more or less of a hedge against bad times. . . .[13]

Reliable Saudi Arabian trade statistics were not available. Oil income from the Arabian American Oil Company and the Saudi Arabian share of Pacific Western's payments for drilling rights in the Neutral Terri-tory[14] plus pilgrimage expenditures amounted together to something like $100,000,000 in 1949 and $105,000,000 in 1950 provisionally and approximated the volume of her imports. Income was steadily increasing. It was estimated that sixty percent of it was obtained from the Arabian American Oil Company.[15]

The relations between King Ibn Saud and the Arabian American Oil Company have apparently been at all times good. The company has shown a readiness to cooperate with the King in his moderniza-tion plans, while at the same time discreetly refraining from attempts to force the issue. The oil company also has a continuous program for the education and technical training of Saudi Arabians in its employ, who number altogether 10,000-15,000. At present this pro-gram has relatively little effect on the country outside of the area of oil operations.

Possible Implications of the New Wealth. It might normally be supposed that the sharp and enormous rise in Saudi Arabia's wealth would have enabled King Ibn Saud to make greatly accelerated prog-ress in the program for nomad settlement and modernization of agriculture. It seems fairly clear, however, that such progress has not been at all commensurate with the increase in revenue; indeed, there have been continual recent reports, apparently authentic, of "budg-etary difficulties."[16] Several factors seems to enter into this question. In the first place, a class of large landowners is beginning to make its

[13] Albion Ross, "Aramco to Share Oil Profits 50-50," New York *Times*, January 3, 1951.
The last sentence means that no royalty will be paid unless a royalty at the previously stipulated rate would exceed the amount of the new tax.

[14] The Neutral Territory is a small area lying between Saudi Arabia and the small shaikhdom of Kuwait. All the resources of that territory are owned by Saudi Arabia and Kuwait in common.

[15] New York *Times*, January 3, 1951, p. 79.

[16] New York *Times*, May 18, 1950; June 11, 1950.

appearance,[17] apparently as an indirect result of the additional revenue. The increased revenue resulted in increased subsidies paid by Ibn Saud to tribal chiefs for pacification purposes. The rise in the amounts of these subsidies brought wealth to the town merchants, who have invested part of their profits in land purchases. These new landowner-merchants now constitute a class opposed to large-scale agricultural reform. For obvious reasons, their short-range losses would be considerable if the subsidies to tribal chiefs were to be reduced and the money spent on nomad settlement and general rural improvement. The chiefs concur in this opposition, which in both cases often appears in the shape of resistance on religious grounds to all forms of modernization. The true motives are perhaps a mixture of religious and economic ones. To the extent that they are religious, they enjoy the support also of the religious teachers, who constitute Saudi Arabia's most important professional class.[18]

It has also been recently reported that the unproductive expenditures of princes and favorites of the royal house have contributed to the financial difficulties. Still another item in the account has been the $6,000,000 loan which Saudi Arabia in 1949 undertook to make to Syria, presumably for political reasons. It is, of course, true that Saudi Arabia's finances were greatly harmed by World War II, which brought a temporary cessation of the pilgrim traffic before the oil revenues had become large. There would seem, however, to have been ample time and opportunity to recover from that setback.

Mr. H. St. John Philby, whose close familiarity with Saudi Arabia extends back over a period of more than thirty years, comments as follows on these matters:

On the whole the results [achieved by Ibn Saud] have been extremely good, but there is an aspect in which the results have not been so good. . . .
Around [Ibn Saud] . . . everything has changed and inevitably the influence of all this wealth that has come to his country affects his sons

[17] No estimate is available as to the amount of land which has passed into the hands of large landowners. According to the best reports, however, the small landowner is still decidedly preponderant in agriculture. Cf. Tannous, *op. cit.*, p. 13.
[18] Mikesell and Chenery, *op. cit.*, pp. 74, 83, 87, 89.

and relations much more than it has affected Ibn Saud himself, to his great credit.

In 1917, I estimated the total revenue of Saudi Arabia, as it then was, as £100,000 a year. . . . When you consider that the total revenue of the country in 1917 was £100,000 and that in 1949 it was £30,000,000, you must agree with me that it will take a very wise administrator and wise people to make the best of that very sudden, almost too sudden, wealth.[19]

Summary and Conclusions

There has certainly been a great rise in general living standards throughout most of the present area of Saudi Arabia since 1919. But from 1939 to 1950, although the upward trend was continued after wartime interruption, the *general* showing has perhaps been less impressive, when the enormous additions to governmental revenue are considered. While it is regrettable that so few precise data are available regarding the distribution of the greatly increased wealth among the populace, it is nevertheless permissible to make certain assumptions and endeavor to arrive at one or two rough conclusions.

Even if the population has trebled during the last thirty-two years, which is improbable, the agricultural production has certainly increased in far greater measure, since 30 to 40 per cent of the present population, estimated as 6,000,000 altogether, are now engaged in cultivation, as against not more than 5 to 15 per cent of an assumed 2,000,000 total in 1919. Additional facts are that there is no evidence of overcrowding of the presently cultivable land; that the greater part of the present agriculture is on a basis of small ownership, which normally produces higher yields than tenant farming; that the small owners have been the objects of much solicitude on the part of the government; and that practically all of the production is of food crops. Although there is no specific information on the subject, the problem of rural indebtedness seems to exist and possibly to account for some of the land sales which have been made to urban merchants during recent years. However, even with a relatively large total debt burden there can be little doubt that this segment of the population is materially much better off on the whole than it was in

[19] Philby, "The Golden Jubilee in Saudi Arabia."

its former nomadic condition, marked as the latter was by complete insecurity and by a dependence for livelihood on raids upon poor regions and communities. As for the present-day nomads, it may be assumed that in many cases the ordinary tribesmen have shared in the ever-increasing subsidies paid to tribal leaders, the amounts of which seem to be closely correlated to national revenues. This assumption is based upon the observed fact that, in Arab tribal communities which have not yet emerged from a completely nomadic state, the customs and traditions are marked by a high degree of political and economic democracy. Thus, although there may now be a nascent tendency for the tribal leaders to discard their traditional roles, to identify themselves with the large landowner class, and to lose interest in the welfare of their respective tribes, certainly, as far as the Saudi Arabian tribes as a whole are concerned, that stage is not yet well advanced. This considerable elevation of living standards is surely attributable in large measure to Ibn Saud's Bedouin Settlement Plan.

But great dangers lie ahead. For all her sudden acquisition of such a fortune as could hardly have been dreamed of in 1919, the estimated per capita income of Saudi Arabia in 1949 was still no more than $40 per annum.[20] Thus, if the country is to become truly prosperous, a large percentage of the governmental revenues must be used to develop it and to fulfill all the implications of the settlement program. However, if this project is to be carried out, the newly wealthy elements will have to be persuaded to curb their growing desires for imported luxuries, the expenditures on which contribute little to general economic and social advancement. Such persuasion may be difficult, first, because there is no widespread understanding among Saudi Arabians of modern economic principles, second, because the main basis of oppositions within the country continues to be simply "Westernization versus no Westernization," with no permissible intermediate positions or qualifications.

Here Ibn Saud is confronted with a dilemma. If he attempts to alter the prevailing religious convictions and prejudices, the net

[20] Will Lissner, "Income per Person in Soviet Held $308," New York *Times*, December 4, 1950.

result might well be an inundation of the country by Westernism in the form of unbridled materialism, coupled probably with civil strife, a general hatred of the West, and exploitation of the peasantry based upon a drive to make money for unproductive expenditures. But if he leaves religious convictions and prejudices as they are, the development of Saudi Arabia will almost certainly be greatly retarded; the nature of such development, moreover, would probably be based more upon political and tactical considerations than upon the people's needs.

In view of Ibn Saud's advanced age, the solution of this problem may depend upon the degree of statesmanship which Crown Prince Saud will be able to muster after he comes to the throne.

YEMEN

Recently, in an article discussing the relative stages of advancement of the Arab countries, an American newspaper commentator described Egypt as modern feudal, Saudi Arabia as early medieval, and Yemen as Biblical.[21] This classification, while open to objection from the viewpoint of scholarly accuracy, nevertheless affords a good over-all impression of many aspects of the life in those countries.

There is not the slightest evidence that there are, or have been during modern times, any consequential plans for raising living standards in Yemen.

For nearly half a century, up to the time of his assassination in February, 1948, Imam Yahya ruled the country on a basis of thoroughgoing isolationism. The most conspicuous Western penetration into this isolationism was made by Italy, which entered into treaty relations with Yemen in 1926 and thereafter, until 1940, was at all times represented in the country by a few officials, engineers, doctors, and merchants. The Italian treaty paved the way for several other pacts with foreign nations, but these produced even fewer tangible results of consequence.[22]

[21] C. L. Sulzberger, "U. S. Seeks Mid-East Reform; It Is Held Up to King in Egypt," New York Times, March 19, 1950.
[22] Renzo Sertoli Salis, Italia, Europa, Arabia (Milan, 1940), passim; Hugh Scott, "The Yemen in 1937-38," Journal of the Royal Central Asian Society, 1940, Part I, pp. 30-32.

A limited amount of technical assistance was rendered to the Imam from 1927 to 1932 by an American engineer, K. S. Twitchell, on the basis of a philanthropic gesture toward Yahya by another American, Charles R. Crane. Twitchell's work consisted largely of investigations and demonstrations, but also included a partial completion of two modern highways leading from Sana to Hodeida by different routes. Apart from these stretches, the country is still practically devoid of modern transport communications. In 1909 a French engineer, A. J. Beneyton, made preliminary surveys for a proposed railway, but the line was never constructed.[23]

Even since Yahya's death and the accession of the new Imam, Ahmed, there has been little indication of any disposition on the part of the Yemen Government to accelerate its modernization activities appreciably. Also the isolationist policy has been altered but little, in respects other than superficial.

As for the elevation of rural living standards, this problem may not be such a vital one in Yemen as it is in the other Middle Eastern countries. Although accurate information is far from complete, there is considerable evidence that the natural conditions for intensive agriculture on a rain-fed basis are favorable in the most populated parts of the country. While little is known about the status of land tenure, peasant indebtedness, and such matters, there is not, according to the best indications, much dire poverty among Yemenite farmers, who constitute the great majority of the country's population.[24]

In the cities matters are apparently different. Nearly every book or article on Yemen refers in particular to the almost universal addiction of city dwellers of the lower (and by far the most populous) social strata to a drug called Qat. This drug lessens vitality and destroys working efficiency. Moreover, public health conditions in Yemen's cities are extremely bad, as plainly indicated by the nature of the maladies prevailing among Jews who have migrated from Yemen to

[23] K. S. Twitchell, *Saudi Arabia* (Princeton, 1947), pp. 139-140; "Arabia," *Encyclopaedia Britannica*, 1946 ed., p. 172.

[24] *New International Year Book*, 1950, p. 636; Harold Ingrams, "A Journey in the Yemen," *Journal of the Royal Central Asian Society*, 1946, Part I, p. 69.

Israel. These have provided testimony of a gross disregard for general sanitation, and probably for urban social welfare as a whole, in the country from which they emigrated.[25]

SUMMARY AND OBSERVATION

The information available regarding Yemen is too fragmentary to constitute a basis for determining the precise nature of the problem of social and economic development. There is also, however, no reasonable prospect that the rulers will soon provide facilities for major cooperation between Yemen and the advanced countries in efforts along developmental lines.[26]

[25] "Israel Is Struck by a Record Cold," New York *Times*, February 7, 1950.

[26] Although there was a "Free Yemeni" movement which in 1948 challenged Ahmed's right of succession and his reactionary policies, it appears in retrospect that the struggle was largely in the nature of a rivalry between two families, the Rassids (Ahmed's family and also the late Imam Yahya's) and the Wazirs, with modernization as a side issue. Events, moreover, showed that modernization has no widespread appeal either for the masses or for the upper classes.

CHAPTER IV

❖

Jordan

GENERAL BACKGROUND

Jordan (known until 1949 as Transjordan) is, except for Saudi Arabia and Yemen, the least modernized of the independent Middle Eastern countries.[1] Noteworthy advances have, however, been made during the period covered by this study.

Poverty and disorder were the main characteristics of Transjordan in the first days of British mandatory administration. The small urban population was of little consequence, and some of the top-level government officials had been imported from other Arab countries. The small cultivable area, which extended at its widest thirty miles to the east of the Jordan River, was largely organized on a tribal basis, with constant strife between villages, chronic disputes over village boundaries, and inefficient cultivation due to the perpetual menace of raids by the desert nomads who constituted a large (though indeterminate) percentage of Transjordan's population. Raids by one nomadic tribe against another were also frequent. The nomads, moreover, showed no respect for the new international frontiers.[2]

[1] United Nations, *Final Report of the United Nations Economic Survey Mission for the Middle East* (Lake Success, N.Y., 1949), Part I, p. 36.
[2] Great Britain, Colonial Office, *Report by His Britannic Majesty's Government to the Council of the League of Nations on the Administration Under Mandate of Palestine and Transjordan* (London, 1925-39), 1925, p. 62; J. B. Glubb, *The Story of the Arab Legion* (London, 1948), pp. 57-59.

There were two basic obstacles which the British authorities had to surmount before any semblance of order could be introduced. One was the fact that raiding by nomads was not only a well-established and accepted custom, not regarded as criminal, but also an economic necessity in view of the lack of alternative means of livelihood in the country for the persons who participated in raids. Additionally, the nomads were proud of their way of life and contemptuous both of agriculture and of urban occupations.[3]

The second obstacle was the almost universal distrust among the settled populace of any form of organized government. This was, in the main, a consequence of the chronically arbitrary, inefficient, and corrupt quality of the former Ottoman administration in Transjordan. The British were confronted with a general spirit of non-cooperation, manifested especially in the concealment of information needed by the government and in the by-passing of government when making transactions of the types which by law were required to be registered. The main consolation for the British, as they approached these problems, was that the population of Transjordan was relatively small (always well under half a million).

The accomplishments of the British authorities in Transjordan have been highly praised by some competent critics. The small groups of men who have handled the situation were in nearly all cases well chosen for the task; it seems clear that they showed ability, sympathetic understanding of the people of the country, and emotional restraint.[4]

The first great task of the mandatory regime was the reduction of raiding by Transjordan tribes across international frontiers. The second was to discover some means whereby a measure of faith in the government could be established in the towns and villages. By

[3] Great Britain, Colonial Office, op. cit., 1933, p. 245; Eliahu Epstein (now Elath), "The Bedouin of Transjordan: Their Social and Economic Problems," Journal of the Royal Central Asian Society, 1938, Part II.

[4] Glubb, op. cit., passim; Hans Kohn, Nationalism and Imperialism in the Hither East (London, 1932), p. 166; Doreen Warriner, Land and Poverty in the Middle East (London, 1948), p. 77; E. B. Worthington, Middle East Science (London, 1945), p. 14; A. Konikoff, Trans-Jordan, An Economic Survey (Jerusalem, 1943), p. 35.

1926 substantial progress had been made in the control of the raids, and also in the attempts, through the use of a small number of pro-British ex-nomads (about ninety at first), to make the nomads understand the reasons for the control.[5] In the meantime it had been deemed inexpedient to apply the weight of government too forcefully to the solution of the internal problems. Every effort was, however, made to demonstrate to the population the advantages of using governmental services and of making one's due contribution to the efficient maintenance thereof. As for crimes of a grave character in the settled areas, the direct handling of these matters was entrusted to the small native-manned Arab Legion, the members of which had been carefully trained to be fair and consistent in their actions, though severe if the circumstances warranted. Through this method, respect for the authorities was greatly enhanced.[6]

The advances made along these lines by 1926, while certainly not enormous, were deemed sufficient to provide possibilities for major planning toward a much more complete establishment of internal order and a general improvement of living standards. The first intermediate goals set were (1) the introduction of a systematized land registry in the towns and the cultivated area, with a view to eliminating the main source of hostility between villages; (2) the establishment of an effective system of taxation, which would both increase governmental revenues and, by its fairness in application, produce added confidence in the government. An important consideration in this connection was the fact that there was no possibility of settling the nomads, and thereby incidentally protecting the cultivators, until some knowledge could be acquired in regard to the ownership of cultivable land in the country. Accurate information along these lines was not obtainable from the Turkish records, and, although it seemed probable that the state had clear title to much of the land in question and could therefore dispose of it as it willed, complete assurance on the point was what was needed. Indeed any future improvements of great consequence along any lines at all seemed to be more or less

---

[5] Great Britain, Colonial Office, *op. cit.*, 1926, p. 66; Glubb, *op. cit.*, *passim.*
[6] Great Britain, Colonial Office, *op. cit.*, 1924, p. 69; 1926, pp. 66-67.

dependent upon the outcome of whatever scheme might be devised to encompass the two aims mentioned above.

From these considerations the Land Settlement Scheme, unquestionably the most successful of all such schemes applied in the Middle East during modern times,[7] was worked out over a period of two years and then put into effect. This, together with two pilot projects worked out by the United Nations Economic Survey Mission in 1949, represents the sum total of major planning for the elevation of living standards in Jordan.

Before describing the detailed nature of the three plans, and the results to date, certain general observations should be made in regard to Jordan's (or Transjordan's) position during the period from 1920 through 1950:

1. During the whole of that time the country has been beset by financial difficulties. The small population, and the general economic layout, made it impracticable to consider any developmental schemes which might involve heavy expenditure. The local British authorities were under a constant necessity not only of exercising the most rigid economies but also of seeking grants and loans from London in order to pursue their main objectives successfully. The annexation of Arab Palestine in 1949 has made the situation even more difficult, since that area is not a prosperous one and is now crowded with refugees, 280,000 in number, from the Palestine War. There are also 70,000 refugees in the main part of Jordan; the percentage increases of population have been 61 and 18 respectively, and the aggregate population of the combined territory, including refugees, is now about 1,210,000.[8] Jordan has suffered other acutely adverse effects from the Palestine War, notably the loss of Jewish Palestine as a market for agricultural produce and, still more important, the loss of the only convenient transit route for imports by sea, that is, across territory now possessed by Israel.

This situation has led to a belief in some quarters that Jordan may

[7] The writer has been unable to find any criticisms couched in terms other than of the highest praise of the manner in which this project has been executed. Cf. esp. Konikoff, *op. cit.*, p. 35; Worthington, *op. cit.*, p. 14.

[8] United Nations, *op. cit.*, Part I, pp. 18, 23, 36-37; Gene Currivan, "Gaza Arab Exodus to Jordan on Way," New York *Times*, July 22, 1950.

never become self-supporting.[9] The following report appeared in the November 26, 1950, issue of the New York *Times*:

The economic situation in the Kingdom of Jordan has worsened since the union of the areas on the two banks of the Jordan River early this year, an Arab News Agency says, adding that the Government has concluded that fundamental changes must be introduced at once in the national economy to avoid bankruptcy. The balance of trade this year is said to show imports exceeding exports by ten times. . . .

Two British economists who investigated the situation early in the year prophesied that this autumn Jordan would run out of reserves entirely. The figures indicate that for most practical purposes the prophecy is correct.

However, the United Nations Economic Survey Mission (Clapp Mission), which visited Jordan late in 1949 and made extensive investigations, was not pessimistic as to the possibilities for Jordan's future as considered from the long-range economic viewpoint. Fairly substantial possibilities for development—in agriculture, industry, and communications—which could prevent collapse and introduce a limited measure of prosperity, even in the absence of peace with Israel, were pointed out by the Mission.[10] It is probable, moreover, that potential facilities for outside assistance of a suitable nature are more ample at present than they were during most of the period of British control.

2. Truly comprehensive planning for Jordan's economic future would be virtually impossible under present conditions, because Jordan and Israel aspire to use the same sources of water for some of their future irrigation and hydroelectric developments. Before the ambitions of either can be satisfied, an agreement covering all phases of the subject must be concluded between the two nations. This will not be possible, however, until a peace treaty has been negotiated between them.[11]

[9] Albion Ross, "Jordan Seen Ready for Israeli Accord," New York *Times*, March 4, 1950.

[10] United Nations, *op. cit.*, Part I, pp. 37, 45-48.

[11] Comparison between Israel's and Jordan's plans for future exploitation of water resources may be made from examination of: United Nations, *op. cit.*, Part I, pp. 76-78; and James B. Hays, *T.V.A. on the Jordan* (Washington, 1948), *passim*. Israel's present plans are based on the Hays report, to the extent that it will be relevant when Israel's frontiers are definitely settled.

3. In 1949 the Jordan Government advanced one step ahead of most of the Arab governments when it established a Development Board at a high official level. Although it is too early to judge as to the effectiveness of this board, the step must nevertheless be regarded as a potentially important one.

4. There are relatively few individuals of great wealth in Jordan; and, despite the wartime and postwar increases in the numbers of wealthy merchants at Amman, there has been no marked development of class consciousness or continuous domination of the government by a clique concerned only with its own vested interests. Even in the early days of the mandatory regime the large landholder was a comparative rarity, who had some political influence, to be sure, but not at all comparable to that wielded by his counterparts in Syria and Iraq. Subsequent events have not favored an augmentation of this power.[12]

5. To all appearances, many Jordanians have been deeply impressed by the contrast between the improved conditions in their own country, on the one hand, and the chronically unhealthy ones prevailing in some of the neighbor countries. The awareness of this contrast, coupled with the desire to keep clear of the neighbors' plights, has probably influenced Jordan's official attitudes in some instances.[13]

THE LAND SETTLEMENT SCHEME

In 1926 the Government of Transjordan enlisted the services of Sir Ernest Dowson to conduct an inquiry as to ways and means of improving agricultural taxation and of establishing a comprehensive and efficient land register. In the following year Dowson submitted his recommendations, emphasizing particularly that a reliable fiscal survey was an indispensable condition precedent to success. He also laid down the broad, general lines of procedure best calculated, in his opinion, to achieve the government's principal aims. The steps taken by the government in 1927 and 1928 were based almost entirely on Dowson's suggestions. The later steps followed logically from the

[12] I. Chizik, "The Political Parties in Trans-Jordania," *Journal of the Royal Central Asian Society*, 1935, Part I, p. 96; Marcus Machenzie, "Transjordan," *Journal of the Royal Central Asian Society*, 1946, Part III, p. 261; Warriner, *op. cit.*, pp. 22, 77.

[13] Glubb, *op. cit.*, *passim*; Great Britain, Colonial Office, *op. cit.*, 1938, p. 310.

initial ones, plus the experience which had meanwhile been gained. The long-term policy was to convert Transjordan, by slow stages, into a country of small landowners, each having his own permanent plot for cultivation. Most villages had theretofore been organized on the *masha* basis, the main feature of which was periodic partition of tribally held land among the tribe members.

The first official action taken was the passage in 1927 of a Land Demarcation, Survey and Valuation Law. A Survey and Demarcation Commission was then formed, under the supervision of a British officer. In 1928 this commission embarked upon the tasks of demarcating state domains, forests, village boundaries, and the boundaries of internal sections of villages, as occupied by comprehensive family groups, also of assessing the net annual agricultural value of the land within each fiscal block (village, village section, large estate, or uncultivated plot). Demarcation was based on the ascertainment whether rights, private or tribal, had been acquired under any law, written or customary, then or previously in effect. The basis of assessment adopted was the number of kilograms of wheat or *rotls* of grapes annually obtainable from the fiscal block. Also in 1928 a law was passed which virtually outlawed transactions in land until the land in question was duly registered, whether under the Ottoman laws still in effect or under such new system as might later be put into effect.[14]

In 1929 the Survey, Land Registry, and State Domains departments of the government were amalgamated into a single Department of Lands. In the same year the Disposal of Lands Law was passed, providing (1) that the Director of Lands might dispose of any state-owned plot two and one-half acres or less in area, and valued at £P10 or less; (2) that the Executive Council of the Transjordan Government might dispose of any area greater than this; (3) that payment for such plots might be spread over a period of years, but that no further disposal might be made until payment was completed and the new ownership duly registered. The objects of this law were: (1) the disposal of areas which, though uneconomic in isolation, could usefully be annexed to neighboring properties; (2) the facilitation of

[14] Great Britain, Colonial Office, *op. cit.*, 1927, p. 80; 1928, p. 110; 1933, pp. 246-247.

building; and (3) the placing of land, at a reasonable price, in the hands of persons who by their own efforts had rendered it, or intended to render it, productive. A policy subsequently adopted was to cancel land sales, or withhold registration, when it appeared that the purchasers were not respecting the object of the sale.[15]

In 1931 a new tax law was drafted, which substituted a uniform 6 per cent tax on the production values, as assessed in the above-described manner, for the complex network of production, land, and road taxes which had been in force for agricultural lands since Ottoman times. The draft provided that the distribution of the tax among individuals within each fiscal block should be handled by the villagers themselves under the supervision of government officials.[16] The law, as actually passed in March, 1933, contained two modifications which had been forced by the large landholders in Parliament. These were that, except as regarded state domains sold after the passage of the law, the total agricultural tax collected under the new system should not increase the former total by more than £P10,000; and that, in cases in which an individual's tax would be increased by more than 50 per cent, the increase should be effected gradually, according to a set rule, over a period of five years.

The work of demarcation, survey, and valuation over the whole area deemed by the government to be possibly cultivable at any time in the future, amounting to 2,500,000 acres,[17] was completed in 1933. Both the methods which had been applied and the results which had

---

[15] *Ibid.*, 1929, p. 164; 1933, p. 247; 1934, p. 265; 1937, p. 318.

[16] It was clearly intended that the partitions which would later take place should be based on the principle of proportioning each man's share to the tax which he had to pay. The partitions were actually conducted on such a basis. Cf. *ibid.*, 1931, p. 193.

[17] The extent to which cultivation could be increased in the Transjordan section of Jordan, if irrigation works were to be erected, has been a matter of considerable dispute, with resultant wide ranges of estimates. One difficulty is that there will probably never be enough water to reach all the land of cultivable quality. It seems probable, however, that the area now under cultivation could be increased by about 50 percent. For the annexed area across the Jordan River, it is not yet possible to obtain any estimate. Cf. Warriner, *op. cit.*, p. 75; M. G. Ionides, *The Water Resources of Transjordan and Their Development* (London, 1940), p. 233; *New International Year Book*, 1950, p. 286. Cf. also Great Britain, Colonial Office, *op. cit.*, 1933, pp. 246-276.

been achieved not only satisfied the government's purposes but also met with general approval on the part of the persons involved. This success seems to be attributable in part to the suitability of the procedures decided upon but mainly to the fact that the authorities showed a willingness to modify the established procedures to the extent necessary to allay distrust or to clarify the advantages of the reforms in terms which had some relation to the limited horizons of the persons involved. In a number of cases it was found possible to make expedient compromises by interpreting the laws broadly, but without sacrificing fundamental principles. Simple solutions, since they were found to be more acceptable, were usually given preference over those arrived at by complicated reasoning. The government also showed a readiness at all times to make attractive compromises in regard to its own claims. In view of the confused state of such Ottoman records as existed, it would have been virtually impossible to complete the work so satisfactorily in such a short time had not elastic methods been applied, by persons having a good understanding of the mentalities with which they were dealing. Most of the direct contacts with villagers were handled by native officials who had been carefully trained under British direction.[18]

As the stage was set for the next step, a law was now passed providing for the settlement of rights to land, the permanent partition of lands held in common ownership, and the registration of all rights held throughout the cultivable zone. In this connection the following important policies were adopted:

1. The partitions were to be performed on the ground by the villagers, themselves, under the close supervision of a settlement officer whose duty was to prevent gross unfairness or inefficiency. They were to be immediately followed by demarcation and survey of the individual properties.

2. Every effort was to be made to bring landowners into direct contact with the official registrars and to discourage the prevalent practice of dealing with the registrars through intermediaries, such as lawyers and petition writers.

3. No attempt would be made to enforce collection of the registra-

[18] Great Britain, Colonial Offices, *op. cit.*, 1929-1931, 1933, *passim*.

tion fees until some alteration in the legal status of a given plot necessitated recourse to a registrar. This provision meant, in effect, that registration would be virtually complete about ten years after the completion of settlement.

4. In the partitions the settlement officers were to make every effort to insure a division of village lands into fewer and better-shaped plots in place of the many long, narrow strips which each cultivator had usually acquired from any temporary partion under the *masha* system.

In 1933 a Land Settlement Court was established for the arbitration of disputes arising from the various procedures outlined. However, in order to further promote confidence in the administrative authorities, the practice later developed of discouraging resort to the court and encouraging aggrieved villagers, wherever possible, to apply to the survey staff of the Land Registry for inspection and fact-finding—a service made available for a small fee. In the majority of cases the latter process provided satisfactory bases for liquidation of the grievances. As time went on, the Department of Lands was becoming more and more popular; spontaneous resort to its services was increasingly common. An additional, and even more important, consequence of the settlement procedure was that cultivators began to show much greater interest in paying proper attention to their holdings and making necessary improvements. Also they began to co-operate among themselves financially, in order to avoid having to deal with moneylenders.[19]

Two problems of great consequence were still unsettled at the beginning of 1934. One was the separation of rights of ownership as between plots of land and the trees growing on the land. The other was the lack of integration between land ownership and water rights. The former question seems to have been satisfactorily settled by a 1934 addendum to the Land Settlement Law enabling settlement officers to work out arrangements whereby the ownership of land plots and of trees thereon would, as far as possible, coincide. The question of water rights, on the other hand, hung fire until 1947 because of political pressures. In that year a law was passed which provides for a

[19] *Ibid.*, 1934, p. 241; 1935, pp. 288, 290, 301; 1936, p. 326; 1937, p. 315; 1938, p. 326.

settlement and registration of existing water rights, and for assumption of control of water distribution by the government in areas proclaimed by executive decree to be Irrigation Areas.[20] Although this does not automatically abolish the old state of affairs, some limited improvements are being facilitated by the new legislation, simply because quite a number of cultivators have shown themselves willing to trust in the authorities to settle their water disputes fairly and have not been insistent upon a strict observance of the legal technicalities. The way for these reforms had been paved by the approaching completion of the land settlement procedure, which had given such general satisfaction.[21]

An examination should now be made of some major developments which took place while the settlement scheme was unfolding and which would hardly have been possible but for the successes that were being achieved with that project. In 1930 the government, having established clear title to adequate quantities of land for disposal to additional cultivators, issued orders to the Arab Legion to put an end to tribal raiding by nomads. The order was quickly and successfully executed, the last of all raids occurring in July, 1932.[22] The steady encroachments of modern transport upon the desert had already convinced many nomads that there was no profitable future in raiding, and the main immediate need was for official action with which to drive the point home. In general, the method applied was to use or threaten force only in cases where demonstration and persuasion had failed or were impossible because of circumstances. Because the way had been well paved by the favorable impressions conveyed to nomads by their former associates who had joined the Arab Legion, the results exceeded the fondest hopes of the British authorities. These developments are describd by Brigadier Glubb as follows:

"Raiding . . . was abolished in a few months without inflicting a single casualty on the tribes and without putting a single tribesman

[20] G. F. Walpole, "Land Problems in Transjordan," *Journal of the Royal Central Asian Society*, 1948, Part I, p. 62; Great Britain, Colonial Office, *op. cit.*, 1938, p. 407.
[21] F. G. Peake, "Trans-Jordan," *Journal of the Royal Central Asian Society*, 1939, Part III, p. 391; Worthington, *op. cit.*, p. 60; Warriner, *op. cit.*, pp. 77, 80.
[22] Glubb, *op. cit.*, p. 71.

in prison. No subsequent attempt was ever made to revive it, even when the Government was deeply involved elsewhere in internal disturbances or in war. And finally these tribesmen, who had for centuries regarded the Government as their natural enemy, enlisted in their thousands in the Arab Legion, and have ever since been amongst the most loyal and patriotic citizens of Trans-Jordan."[23]

By 1934 the government was in a position to announce that raiding was definitely a thing of the past. In 1948 the commanding officer of the Arab Legion could write that security of life and property was more complete in the Transjordan desert than in the British Isles, though nearly all Transjordanians who roam the desert still carry rifles.[24]

The first attempts to settle the nomads failed.[25] In 1933, however, Transjordan was smitten with near-famine, and the authorities took full advantage of this to reemphasize the advice which they had been giving to nomads to take up cultivation. The moral was not lost; a settlement movement began, which acquired considerable momentum about 1937. The government rendered all possible assistance, including some limited financial help. The policy which evolved was not to settle the nomads on a year-round basis, but rather to encourage them to supplement their pastoral activities by cultivation during part of the year. This system provides distinct advantages, both to the seminomads and to the country as a whole. The former are enabled to hedge their risks, since it is hardly ever the case that pasturage and desert-fringe cultivation fail in the same year. At the same time the

[23] *Ibid.*, p. 113 *et passim*.
[24] *Ibid.*, p. 165.
[25] The first limited tendency of nomads to settle was noted by the government in 1929; this, however, seems to have been more in the nature of land speculation than of genuine settlement. In 1931 a large-scale settlement of one tribe, the Beni Hassan, took place, 5000 title deeds being issued to tribesmen by the government. In the same year a highly ambitious program for the settlement of all nomads on a basis of extensive official assistance was proclaimed, but this was eventually absorbed into the general Land Settlement Scheme, with many of the original frills removed. The great majority of nomads were not yet ready to settle, and the program was also beyond Transjordan's financial means. Cf. Great Britain, Colonial Office, *op. cit.*, 1929, p. 138; 1930, p. 219; 1931, p. 193; also Konikoff, *op. cit.*, p. 55.

country is not deprived of its meat supply, as it would probably be if nomadism ceased completely.

As early as 1939 the government was able to report to the League of Nations Council that there was no section of any nomadic tribe which did not have at least some small plots for cultivation during part of the year. It seems evident from much later reports that this trend has gradually evolved into a new way of life for practically all nomads and that, although there have been drawbacks, this new way of life is, for the most part, proving highly satisfactory to the persons concerned.[26]

In spite of incomplete statistics, it is possible to assert with complete assurance that the increase in Jordan's population from 1918 to 1939 (officially estimated at 45,389 over an original 306,000 during the period 1929-38) was at a considerably slower rate than the tempo of progress during that period. All observers have reported a markedly favorable contrast as to the general appearance of the settled area, the morale of the cultivators, and the material goods which they possessed.[27] Brigadier Glubb went so far as to state, in 1938, that the Jordanian tribesmen (settled and seminomadic) were "probably financially prosperous compared with most Oriental peasants."[28] The same writer has made the following observations in regard to some of the results of nomad settlement:

That this change-over to agriculture was in the nature of a revolution is shown by the fact that ten years later [i.e., in 1948] no such change had taken place in Syria and Iraq. In most cases, the tribes were converted by persuasion. In one or two rare cases, a small amount of pressure was applied: . . . In punishment for their misconduct we sentenced them there and then to take up farming, and awarded them a large tract of land southeast of Amman in which the sentence was to be carried out. . . . Ten years later, I paid a special visit to the section

[26] Great Britain, Colonial Office, *op. cit.*, 1938, p. 318; Glubb, *op. cit.*, pp. 169, 170, 189.

[27] Royal Institute of International Affairs, *The Middle East: A Political and Economic Survey* (London, 1950), p. 425; Konikoff, *op. cit.*, p. 53; B. A. Toukan, *A Short History of Trans-Jordan* (London, 1945), p. 5; B. A. Keen, *The Agricultural Development of the Middle East* (London, 1946), p. 84; Ionides, *op. cit.*, p. 238.

[28] "Economic Situation of the Trans-Jordan Tribes," *Journal of the Royal Central Asian Society*, 1938, Part III, p. 457.

again. As far as the eye could reach the land was ploughed where ten years before had been only desert and thorn bushes. . . . The shaikh of the tribe was supervising the operations of a tractor plough.[29]

Education, though still limited, was being increased at a rapid rate, as indicated by the fact that, during the academic year 1938-39, there were 8512 schools in the country, as compared with 7408 in the preceding year. Infant mortality was steadily declining, as shown by the rates per thousand for the years 1934-38: 1934—242; 1935—211; 1936—201; 1937—203; 1938—181.

As for the subsequent period, probably, in view of all the great difficulties which Jordan has experienced, as mentioned above, general living standards have declined somewhat as compared with 1939. It is perfectly clear, however, that the recession, if any, has by no means brought the country back to anything like the 1918 level. The government, moreover, has done everything possible to protect "old Jordanians" against involvement in the special problems arising from the great influx of refugees and the annexation of Arab Palestine. Most current reports indicate that, up to December 31, 1950, a fair measure of success had been achieved in this attempt. Predictions for the future are, as already indicated, not so optimistic.[30]

Before concluding this section on the Land Settlement Scheme it should be particularly noted that, although a somewhat similar scheme was put into effect in Syria during the between-wars period, the results were by no means so happy as in Jordan. If any single reason for this difference can be regarded as controlling, it is the fact that there was a determination on the part of the Jordanian authorities not to permit the shaikhs of tribes to benefit from the scheme to the extent of becoming large landowners and exploiters. To prevent their becoming so, the authorities concentrated a large part of their efforts on protecting the ordinary tribesmen against transactions or negotiations conducted in secret against their interests, and on making sure that every tribesman was fully informed in regard to the

[29] Glubb, op. cit., p. 170.
[30] United Nations, op. cit., Part I, pp. 19, 46; Michael Clark, "Jordan's Fate Tied to Foreign Capital," New York Times, January 21, 1951; Toukan, op. cit., p. 5.

implications of all actions and transactions having a possible effect on his future welfare. The potential power of the shaikhs was also weakened by the land tax, which made them hesitant about acquiring large quantities of land without definite plans for its utilization.[31]

THE WADI ZERQA PLAN

The primary objective of the United Nations economic survey conducted in Jordan in 1949 was to find means of employment for the Arab refugees from the Palestine War, the great majority of whom were in Jordan's territory. A further consideration, however, was the determination of possibilities for pilot projects which would serve the double purpose of (1) accomplishing a useful object in themselves and (2) providing the necessary experience for the undertaking of more comprehensive planning in the future. Care was also exercised to select schemes which could surely be well integrated with foreseeable future developments. Because of the refugee aspect of the matter, any plans selected had to be prepared in such a way as to insure the maximum employment of human labor and the minimum use of machinery, to the extent that such considerations could be applied economically.

The main points about the Wadi Zerqa Plan, as set forth in the *Final Report of the United Nations Survey Mission to the Middle East*, are as follows:

The Jordan Valley is by far the greatest land asset in Jordan for development under irrigation farming. Rough estimates have led to the belief that some 375,000 dunums [i.e., 93,750 acres] of land in the valley are irrigable. Of this total 188,000 dunums are stated to be under irrigation at present. It is probable that the annually irrigated area is only of the order of 100,000 dunums. . . .

Irrigation is done at present almost entirely from the series of 9 or 10 wadis which flow into the Valley from the east and of which the Wadi

---

[31] Warriner, *op. cit.*, p. 80; Glubb, *op. cit.*, p. 342.
During World War II a fair amount of privately owned land in Jordan found its way into the hands of Syrian speculators. These transactions, however, seem to have been more or less nullified by the refusal of the occupants of plots to recognize the legal rights of the absentees, and the apparent unwillingness of the government to protect the speculators. Cf. Warriner, *op. cit.*, pp. 77, 79.

Zerqa is one. The drainage basin of the Wadi Zerqa is the largest of all the wadis east of the Jordan River. . . . Only small areas on the valley floor are at present irrigated annually by the uncontrolled flow of this wadi. Although water is essential for cultivation in this arid area, there is no storage at present to conserve the higher stream flows and permit the use of that water during the dry season for irrigation and water supply. . . .

It is proposed to develop this watershed area completely as a unit, that is, to construct the necessary roads into the area; to provide water for perennial irrigation through the development of storage; to build the necessary small check dams on principal gullies to minimize siltation and to do all the necessary afforestation work, terracing and planting of fruit trees where this seems to be feasible. A central village is also to be included as part of the development in order to provide adequate housing facilities for construction workers and in the future partially to satisfy the permanent housing requirements in the area.

. . . From the information now available a dam 35 metres high should provide sufficient capacity for the initial operation of the project for a period of about ten years. It seems quite possible that in the future the dam may have to be raised by as much as 10 metres. . . .

In addition to the storage dam, a headworks structure will be required where the wadi enters the Jordan plain. This structure would lead the water into the main irrigation canal and thence into the secondary and tertiary canals. The capacity and plan for these canals will depend on the agricultural programme, which will be fully determined only after some years of research, but will gradually develop from the outset.

It is roughly estimated that by means of storage and regulation the volume of water for irrigation purposes can be approximately doubled as compared with present low flow conditions. . . .

The . . . Wadi Zerqa project is of great importance to the future of this area [i.e., the Jordan Valley]. It has been conceived with the threefold purpose of experiment, demonstration and development. The first aspect will determine how best to use the irrigation supplies of the locality, the crops to grow, the water requirements of the selected crops, the intensity of cultivation which the water resources and other considerations will permit, the best cultivation practices and the economies of fertilizing. As a demonstration it will cover, on the agricultural side, the several aspects of soil and water conservation and land use, and in its various phases will be a guide for the future development of other areas. As a development it will bring more land under cultivation, and will increase production not only on land to be newly cropped but on the area already cultivated. . . . The total irrigable area is not known at present but during an inspection trip through the area it was obvious that a considerable area of land is available for irrigated farming in or within a reasonable distance of the Wadi Zerqa land.[32]

Up to December 31, 1950, no major work had been done on the Wadi Zerqa project. The Jordan Government did, however, have further engineering surveys of Wadi Zerqa conducted in March, 1950, by a British firm.[33] Also Jordan provided all possible facilities to enable the United Nations to proceed with its work relief projects for refugees.[34] However, this program had to be discontinued in November, 1950, because the United Nations had been able to collect only $38,000,000 of the $54,000,000 which had been estimated as necessary. Only $10,000,000 had been expended on work relief, and the balance was transferred to the direct relief account, since the latter form of relief is considerably cheaper and permits maximum conservation of funds. Only 7000 of the refugees had been employed on the short-lived operations, most of which were on Jordanian territory.[35]

It is clear from all reports that Jordan is fully prepared to go ahead with the Wadi Zerqa undertaking as soon as the United Nations or some other body provides the wherewithal. Indeed Jordan alone of the Middle Eastern countries has consistently shown enthusiasm vis-à-vis the Survey Mission's recommendations, and has raised no important objection to any of the conditions laid down or subsequently implied in connection with the relief schemes. Equally noteworthy is the fact that there have been no reports of complaints by the Jordan Government regarding the delays in getting the work started. The former showing is due in part to the fact that, unlike the other nations involved, Jordan is desirous of absorbing the refugees into her own economy on a permanent basis. It is, however, at least equally important that, even after the annexation of Arab Palestine, Jordan is still relatively free from the more blatant forms of nationalism and anti-Westernism.[36]

[32] United Nations, *op. cit.*, Part I, pp. 96-98.
[33] Clark, *op. cit.*
[34] *Ibid.*; Benjamin Shwadran, "Assistance to Arab Refugees," *Middle Eastern Affairs*, January, 1950, p. 2.
[35] Ross, "U. N. Work Relief in Mid-East Fails," New York *Times*, November 15, 1950.
[36] Royal Institute of International Affairs, *op. cit.*, p. 48.

On December 31, 1950, the situation was not well clarified. On December 3, by a unanimous vote, the United Nations General Assembly had endorsed a new program for Arab refugees, which was to be based on their permanent integration into the economies of such countries as would be willing to accept them on that basis. Although it is too early to judge, such a basis is apparently favorable to Jordan and to the Wadi Zerqa Plan. Whether the necessary funds will be forthcoming this time remains to be seen.

THE WADI QILT PLAN

The Wadi Qilt Plan is very similar to the Wadi Zerqa one; the sponsorship, general nature, purposes, and even present status of the two are substantially the same. The main difference is that, whereas Wadi Zerqa is on the eastern side of the Jordan River, Wadi Qilt is on the western territory annexed by Transjordan in 1949. The scope of the present problem to be solved on the western side is considerably greater, in view of the extremely large number of refugees in that area. Otherwise, however, the difficulties are perhaps less than might be supposed. As far as can be determined, a large proportion of the inhabitants of the annexed area have accepted their absorption into Jordan with more or less equanimity.[37] Also general conditions in the two regions were somewhat similar before the annexation. There are few large landowners in the western section, and, as compared with the situations prevailing in most Arab countries, there has

[37] The main currents of opposition seem to be in the ranks of (1) some of the refugee groups, who are being constantly subjected to propaganda which filters into Jordan from outside, and which has been attributed variously to the Communist party, the Arab League, and the Egyptian Government, and (2) some of the educated Moslem and Christian residents of Jerusalem, who resent being identified with a state as "backward" as they consider Jordan to be. Probable reasons why absorption into Jordan appeals to many Palestinian Moslems, including apparently a large percentage of the refugees, are (1) because Jordan, as a rule, has more peaceful and orderly conditions than those they would probably encounter in any other Arab state which they might join; (2) because Jordan, despite its small size, has distinguished itself militarily, through the Arab Legion, above all other Arab states; (3) because, for the peasantry, there is less danger of exploitation if the union is with Jordan. Cf. Clark, *loc. cit.*; *Middle East Journal*, Winter, 1951, p. 72.

been no marked development of an economic class structure there. The land in that section, though mostly of poor quality, is, like Transjordan's, capable of considerable further development. The farming techniques in the west seem to be, on the average, superior to those applied across the river. In respect to irrigation, however, more has been done on the eastern side of the Jordan.[38] The standards of living in the two sections were, in general, about the same before the outbreak of the Palestine War. Land settlement had been begun in Arab Palestine before the annexation but was by no means complete. Also some of the results were not entirely satisfactory. Jordan's successful experience should be helpful here.[39]

GENERAL CONCLUSIONS

Conditions in Jordan, at the time of writing, are probably more propitious for planned improvements in living standards than those in any other country of the Middle East. In Jordan most of the advances made to date have been characterized by a quality and speed permitting full absorption of the benefits by the populace, without any appreciable backsliding or creation of unforeseen and undesirable results. Perhaps even more important, Jordanians of all stripes appear to have been strongly impressed, through demonstration, of the merits of going ahead by slow, steady processes, which begin in the village and are suited to the state of readiness—in short, to the type of progress which most authorities believe should be particularly stressed in underdeveloped countries, and which are probably the quickest and most efficient in the long run.[40] Also, short-range

[38] The present irrigated area on the eastern side of the Jordan is about 65,000 acres, of which most is irrigated by primitive methods. Cf. Konikoff, *op. cit.*, p. 32.

[39] Warriner, *op. cit.*, pp. 21-22; United Nations, *op. cit.*, Part II, p. 11; Robert R. Nathan, Oscar Gass, and Daniel Creamer, *Palestine, Problem and Promise* (Washington, 1946), pp. 184-185.

[40] Prominent among those who have expressed such a view in regard to the nature of suitable developmental progress are Gordon Clapp, Chairman of the United Nations Survey Mission of 1949, and E. B. Worthington, formerly of the Middle East Supply Centre, which operated in the area during World War II. Cf. United Nations, *op. cit.*, pp. viii, 5; Worthington, *op. cit.*, pp. 6-7.

The opinion that this policy has at all times been followed closely in Jordan (Transjordan) since 1920 has been expressed by J. B. Glubb (*op. cit.*, p. 177) and B. A. Toukan (*op. cit.*, p. 2).

prestige considerations, and the more strident forms of nationalism, are not highly important elements in Jordan's case; and no particular distrust of foreign or international assistance has been voiced.[41] Still further, there are in Jordan fewer internal conflicts of interest, present and foreseeable, than in most of the other countries.

It is, therefore, possible to predict that, given adequate and appropriate financial and technical assistance, Jordan will be willing and able to cooperate closely with the foreign or international planners who aim sincerely at improving her living standards. Moreover, because of the nature of the advances thus far made, the country may soon be psychologically ready for development at a considerably enhanced rate.

Four reservations must, however, be made. One is that these conclusions might not hold good were Jordan to be absorbed into a much larger political unit, including also the territories of Syria and Iraq. For, in that event, the Jordanian area might be but a minor part of an immense complex of difficulties and differences.

The second reservation is that, if foreign and international agencies neglect to follow Britain's precedent of sending highly competent and understanding men to assist Jordan in her development, much of the good work accomplished in the past may prove to have been futile.[42] It must be remembered, in this connection, that Jordanians have not always been as well disposed as they are now toward official agencies.

The third reservation is that any *permanent* solution to Jordan's present problems will be dependent on the establishment of peace, within at least the next few years, with Israel.[43]

[41] This is almost certainly due to the happy relations enjoyed by Jordanians with the British officials stationed in the country during the mandatory period. Some of the latter have remained in Jordan in advisory and other capacities since that country achieved independence.

[42] Worthington, *op. cit.*, p. 7.

[43] It is to be noted, however, that Jordan has already moved farther in this direction than have any of the other Arab countries. It is a matter of general knowledge that there have been extensive secret negotiations between the two governments. Cf. Gene Currivan, "Israel Renews Efforts for Peace with Arabs," New York *Times*, October 15, 1950.

The fourth and last reservation is that the nature of the future leadership in Jordan will be an important element in the maintenance or loss of the present favorable status.[44]

[44] This chapter was completed before the assassination of Abdullah in July, 1951. For a few weeks after that occurrence, events in Jordan conveyed the impression that the writer's analyses might no longer be applicable. However, as of November 15, 1951, conditions in the country seemed to be stable once more, even in spite of great financial difficulties.

CHAPTER V

❖

Lebanon

GENERAL BACKGROUND

For a proper evaluation of the history of major planning for the elevation of Lebanese living standards, it is first of all essential to review the complex background conditions which have prevailed in Lebanon during the period covered by this study. There are four central aspects: (1) the relatively advanced social and economic status of a large section of the populace, (2) the great maze of conflicts of interest and sentiment in the country, (3) the character of the government, and (4) the population problem. Each of these will be discussed in turn.

THE ADVANCED SOCIAL AND ECONOMIC STATUS

More than one-half of Lebanon's population is Christian; and the Lebanese Christian community has, over a period of more than a century, maintained a much closer contact with the West than have the great majority of the Middle Eastern people.[1]

Because of this Christian predominance, and because of the relative geographic insulation of Lebanon from the rest of the Ottoman lands but not from the sea, Western institutions were enabled to develop

[1] A. H. Hourani, *Syria and Lebanon, A Political Essay* (London, 1946), *passim.*

considerably earlier and to a much fuller extent than in other parts of the Middle Eastern region. Social and cultural differences from the rest of the empire were accentuated by these developments, even to the point of giving rise to powerful sentiments of political separatism. One result was that part of the area now occupied by the republic of Lebanon achieved local autonomy under a Christian governor, several decades before the final collapse of the Ottoman state. During the period of autonomy, in which French influence was considerable, Westernization proceeded still farther. In addition to the French influence, an important factor was the large-scale emigration of Lebanese Christians to less crowded parts of the world, mainly in the Western Hemisphere. This is discussed more fully later.

During the period of the French mandate these tendencies were carried still farther, particularly in the field of Western-style education, conducted largely under private auspices. Lebanon's educated middle class now comprises a far larger percentage of the total population than any other Arab country's. It should also be noted in this connection that social welfare and social conscience have been taught and applied extensively by such institutions as the American University of Beirut and the French Catholic missions, both of which enjoy great prestige in the country. An additional development of the twentieth century has been the appearance of a European pattern in the agricultural life of the country. About one-half of the rural community now consists of small freeholding peasants, possessing compact plots in lieu of the scattered strips into which Middle Eastern smallholdings are so often divided.[2] These peasants, moreover, are generally considered to be much better informed and more progressive than peasants in other Arab lands. Although, in general, their cultivation techniques and implements are still primitive, they have demonstrated an ability and initiative to achieve far better results from these simple methods than the great majority of Middle Eastern farmers. Yields of crops are in nearly all cases considerably higher in

[2] Royal Institute of International Affairs, *The Middle East: A Political and Economic Survey* (London, 1950), p. 402; Doreen Warriner, *Land and Poverty in the Middle East* (London, 1948), p. 84.

The French mandatory authorities undertook to consolidate scattered farm holdings upon the request of the individuals concerned.

Lebanon than in neighboring Syria. For example, in 1946 Lebanon's barley crop yielded 0.54 ton per acre, as against 0.31 for Syria. For potatoes, the corresponding figures were 3.18 and 1.89 tons respectively.[3]

In Syria, 80.2 per cent of the total acreage was devoted to cereals and 19.8 per cent to other crops. In Lebanon, the respective percentages were 64.7 and 35.3. To some extent these differences are attributable to higher rainfall in Lebanon. Lebanon's superiority is not wholly due to this cause, however.

But, although agriculture occupies about two-thirds of the Lebanese population, the most prominent feature of the Lebanese economy has always been its trading sector.[4] After World War I, when Lebanese merchants could no longer play their former part as import-export traders for a large hinterland, they succeeded in adapting themselves well to new mercantile roles, which in their present form are described as follows by the United States Economic Survey Mission for the Middle East (Clapp Mission of 1949):

Lebanon's financial capacity is remarkable, relatively, although it has not operated hitherto so much to the advantage of the State as to that of private individuals. The Lebanese have proved their ability to turn their little country into an active and efficient centre for exchange, gold dealings, brokerage and trade involving many currencies besides their own, and the movement of goods which may never touch Lebanese territory. In November 1948, the authorities encouraged these activities by removing in practice the remaining restrictions on sales and purchases of exchange.[5]

During the period between wars Lebanon's manufacturing industry underwent a complete change-over from cottage crafts to modernized production. Lebanese workers, moreover, showed themselves much more adaptable to this change than those in other parts of the Middle East, even including Turkey.[6] By contrast with Turkey and

[3] Royal Institute of International Affairs, *op. cit.*, p. 401.

[4] United Nations, *Final Report of the United Nations Economic Survey Mission for the Middle East* (Lake Success, N.Y., 1949), Part II, p. 27; Said B. Himadeh, *Economic Organization of Syria* (Beirut, 1936), pp. 199-200.

[5] United Nations, *op. cit.*, Part I, p. 49.

[6] Alfred Bonné, *The Economic Development of the Middle East* (London, 1945), p. 83.

Iran, industrialization in Lebanon was entirely on a private enterprise basis. Although this development was not extremely large, it covered a wide range of products, including alcohol, arak, biscuits, beer, chocolates, preserves, pastry, cement, hosiery, silk cloth, cotton thread, cotton cloth, matches, soap, brushes, essential oils, eau de cologne, and razor blades. Some illustrative figures for 1938 are 1,558,054 liters of beer, 189,000 pairs of hose, 171,000 tons of cement, and 14,980,000 boxes of matches.[7]

Industrial development advanced still farther during the war. In 1946 the production of matches was 24,635,000 boxes, and of cotton thread 1,710,000 kilograms. On the other hand, the production of cement had dropped to 157,600 tons. Generally speaking, Lebanon's industrial production in 1946 showed a favorable comparison with neighboring Syria's modernized production, particularly if the difference in population is taken into account. Lebanon's production of electric power in that year was 61,450,830 kilowatt-hours as against 47,712,000 kilowatt-hours for Syria.[8]

CONFLICTS OF INTEREST AND SENTIMENT

Since the end of World War I, and to a large extent even before that time, the populace of Lebanon has been exceedingly heterogeneous, with Moslems and highly diverse Christian sects living together, often without even any local segregation. This heterogeneity has produced internal conflicts of interest and sentiment, in which traditional factors continue to play as important a role as do practical problems of the present day. Between Christian groups, conflicts exist as to whether Lebanon should be primarily a Christian state or an Arab state in which religious differences are largely obliterated. There is also a conflict between, on the one hand, the "old Lebanese," that is, persons whose families have always lived in autonomous Lebanese territory, and, on the other, persons who either have been absorbed into Lebanon by virtue of boundary changes or have migrated to Lebanon from other parts of the Middle East. This latter

[7] Ministère des Affaires Etrangères, *Rapports sur la Situation de la Syrie et du Liban*, 1921-1938 (Paris, 1923-39), 1938, p. 25.
[8] Royal Institute of International Affairs, *op. cit.*, p. 404.

dichotomy, which is by no means universally recognized by the two groups in question, tends to override religious lines. There are also, however, decided cultural differences, usually based in the first instance upon religion, even among the most populous Christian sects, namely, Maronites, Greek Orthodox, Greek Catholics, Protestants, and Gregorian Armenians. These are only prominent examples of the innumerable conflicts of interest and sentiment which prevail in the country. One fact of great importance should be noted in this connection: although Lebanon still has a slight Christian majority, the somewhat smaller Moslem community is, on the whole, considerably more unified.[9]

THE CHARACTER OF THE GOVERNMENT

The Lebanese electoral system, which is based on indirect suffrage and proportional representation of the various religious communities, has remained substantially unchanged since 1861. This system would be hard to change because of the virtual impossibility of devising any new one upon which all important elements in the populace would be willing to agree. Partly because of the electoral system and partly because of the greater coherence of the Moslem community, Lebanese governments nearly always represent the social pattern which is most prominent among Lebanese Moslems.[10] That pattern, which forms a sharp contrast with the advanced conditions now so widespread among the Christians, is one of large rural estates owned by city notables who derive their wealth and power from exploitation and domination of the peasantry. By practically unanimous report of expert observers, the peasants living under these conditions are no better off than their counterparts in Syria, Egypt, Iraq, and Iran. The Moslem landowners, moreover, gain enough political support from the wealthy Christian elements, largely mercantile, to ward off challenges leveled at this economic and political pattern.[11]

[9] An excellent discussion of these matters is to be found in *Les Institutions Politiques du Liban*, by Pierre Rondot (Paris, 1947), pp. 22-55. Cf. also Hourani, *op. cit.*, pp. 64, 97.

[10] Hourani, *op. cit.*, pp. 91-92; Rondot, *op. cit.*, pp. 38-40.

[11] Royal Institute of International Affairs, *op. cit.*, p. 415; Hourani, *op. cit.*, p. 184; Afif I. Tannous, "Land Reform: Key to the Development and Stability of the Arab World," *Middle East Journal*, Winter, 1951, p. 12.

The type of government which has resulted is lacking in efficiency and generally unconcerned with the welfare of the people as a whole. It is, however, well protected by a top-heavy bureaucracy consisting in the main of friends, relatives, and favorites of the class in power, as well as persons to whom members of that class are under political obligations.[12] Too, the government has control of security forces out of all proportion to the customary needs of a country of Lebanon's size. The Clapp Mission commented thereon as follows:

Improvement of the budget mechanism might advantageously be accomplished by a revision of the purposes to which expenditure is devoted. This is a question on which hasty judgments would be dangerous; it requires careful study before action is decided upon. But at first sight it is striking that well over one-third of budget expenditure is absorbed by national defence, gendarmerie, police and security, taken together. Further, it appears that the number of public employees has trebled over the last ten years. While making due allowance for the increased tasks assumed by the Government, and for a growing population, it seems probable that numbers could be reduced without loss of efficiency.[13]

Some of the consequences of this situation have been: the failure of the government to supplement adequately the widespread educational activities undertaken by private interests;[14] a persistence of sectarianism in education, with few generally accepted basic concepts as to the purposes of education; and inadequate attention to public health matters. With regard to these matters, the budget figures would not offer a good criterion for judgment. The public health branch, for example, seems to be sufficiently staffed, from the viewpoint of number and competence of persons employed. It has been customary, however, for public health officials to use their offices mainly for the building up of lucrative private practices. There have also been reports of high fees collected by them for services which should have been rendered gratis as part of their official duties.[15]

The French mandatory authorities were unable to provide remedies.

[12] Hourani, op. cit., p. 204; Hans Kohn, Nationalism and Imperialism in the Hither East (London, 1932), p. 203; Gabriel Menassa, Plan de Réconstruction l'Economie Libanaise et de Réforme de l'Etat (Beirut, 1948), pp. 286-288.

[13] United Nations, op. cit., Part I, p. 50.

[14] Rondot, op. cit., p. 23.

[15] Middle East Institute, Americans and the Middle East: Partners in the Next Decade (Washington, 1950), p. 33; Hourani, op. cit., p. 90.

There were two main reasons for this failure: first, the popular suspicions engendered by the French, and generally encouraged by Lebanese governments, because of the appearance which the French gave of favoring the Maronite community as against all others; second, the general dependence of France, throughout the Syria mandated territory, on the support of the great landowners, whose powers she feared.[16] French control did, to be sure, facilitate highway and port construction[17] and a formulation of some first-class irrigation schemes of large scope, though mainly as to their scientific, rather than human, aspects.

THE POPULATION PROBLEM

The upward trend in Lebanon's population is well illustrated by the following official population estimates:

1926	598,000
1935	855,000
1947	1,186,000 (December 31)
1948	1,230,000 (December 31)

The growth of Lebanon's population has been mainly from natural increase, though it was aggravated first by the permanent admission in the 1920's of thousands of Armenian refugees from Turkey and later by the return of Lebanese who had previously left the country. In 1943 there were about 70,000 Armenians in Lebanon;[18] and it must be assumed that nearly all of these had originally been refugees, or their descendants.[19]

The population problem has been a troublesome one for Lebanon ever since 1880. It was about that time that the outward movement of Lebanese began to assume large proportions, which it maintained until 1931. The average annual net emigration during the period 1900-1930 seems to have been about 7000. Since 1930, however, the outward movement has been supplanted by a surplus of returning emigrants often accompanied by their foreign-born children. The

[16] Warriner, op. cit., p. 123.
[17] In 1943 Lebanon had 1425 miles of improved highways.
[18] Rondot, op. cit., p. 32.
[19] Subsequently there has been a large exodus of Armenians from Lebanon to Soviet Armenia. However, it is improbable that this has been of sufficient volume to affect the arguments substantially.

main reason has been the imposition of stricter immigration laws by the countries of destination. The principal ones were Argentina, Brazil, and Uruguay, with the United States next in importance.

In the great majority of cases the emigrants have maintained contact with their relatives who stayed behind. The remittances of emigrants have added considerably to Lebanon's monetary resources. That they continue to constitute an important source of foreign exchange is indicated by the fact that they accounted for 13 per cent of Lebanon's foreign receipts in 1946.[20]

However, welcome as these contributions to the economy must be, they are hardly of adequate amount to constitute a solution to the population problem, particularly in view of the aggravation of this problem by the virtual stoppage of emigration. All of the more facile palliatives have indeed already been put into effect. There is little or no idle cultivable land, and for decades a large percentage of the farming community (estimated now at 40 per cent) has supplemented its farm income by seasonal work in the cities.[21] In most cases in which irrigation could be applied by private initiative, it already has been. Also, as intimated, Lebanese agriculture has been rationalized to the extent which has been possible through purely private initiative, with only limited intervention by the governmental authorities. Still the number of idle workers continues to grow at a faster rate than new industries can be developed with the resources and the type of governmental planning now at hand.[22]

The spending power of Lebanon's poorer classes has declined, both as between 1914 and 1936-39, and as between the latter years and 1948-50. In 1937 the French authorities conducted an exhaustive study in regard to the average real earnings of Syrian and Lebanese workers in handicrafts and manufactures in 1913 and 1937 respectively. Its conclusions were as follows:

The survey which has been made in several regions of Syria and Lebanon gives a sufficient indication of the extent to which the cost of living has risen since the end of the Ottoman era, and enables us to ascer-

[20] For Lebanon's balance-of-payments accounts from 1939 to 1946, inclusive, cf. Royal Institute of International Affairs, *op. cit.*, p. 412.

[21] Menassa, *op. cit.*, p. 11.

[22] United Nations, *op. cit.*, Part I, p. 49.

tain whether the rise in wages has been commensurate with the increase in living costs. . . .

It appears that, to buy the same quantities of primary necessities of equal quality, a laborer had to work: in 1913, . . . twenty-two and one-half days; in 1937, 48 days.[23]

In the report no distinction is made between Syrian and Lebanese workers; it is therefore assumed that no important local differences were found in Lebanon, as compared with the rest of the mandated area. The Lebanese practice of doing factory work for part of the year and agricultural labor for the rest probably does not affect the situation materially, since the old handicrafts were also in many cases supplementary occupations for farmers. Too, in other respects the role of industries in the economy was substantially the same in 1913 as in 1937. As for increased yields from agriculture between 1913 and 1937, it seems most unlikely that these were adequate to offset the increased pressure upon the land.[24]

As for the subsequent period, the cost of living indexes for food aliments (based on June-August, 1939, prices) have been as follows at Beirut since 1939: 1940—114; 1941—not stated; 1942—435; 1943—612; 1944—663; 1945—732; 1946—662; 1947—604; 1948—626; 1949—568; September, 1950—509. Since 1943 there has been an average spread of about 100 points between the indexes for food aliments and those for all commodities, the latter indexes being the lower. The general tendency during that period has been for the spread to lessen.[25]

It is improbable, with such inflation and with the continued rapid increase in population, that the spending power of the poorer classes in general has kept up to its 1939 level. Although no reliable compilations are available, real industrial wages and real wages in commercial houses and government (the two together involving more than 100,000 workers)[26] must have undergone a marked decline, since Lebanon has no trade-union movement competent to maintain

[23] Ministère des Affaires Etrangères, *op. cit.*, 1937, p. 25.
[24] Fouad Saade, *L'Agriculture Richesse Nationale* (Beirut, 1942), p. 27.
[25] Statistical Office of the United Nations, *Monthly Bulletin of Statistics*, December, 1950.
[26] Menassa, *op. cit.*, p. 384(21).

wages at levels commensurate with such great increases in prices. With respect to the present condition of the middle classes of the populace, Mr. Menassa writes:

"Whereas in 1939 there was social harmony, with each of the different classes of the population living within its means and station in life, the war has had the result of greatly reducing the resources and living standards of a large part of the middle class."[27]

There is no reason to believe that the prosperity of the large landowners and merchants has declined, either absolutely or relatively.

THE COUNTRY'S URGENT NEEDS

It is universally agreed that Lebanon's urgent economic needs at present are (1) the development of a much higher degree of industrialization and (2) a maximal intensification of the country's agriculture. Although there are few possibilities for adding to the area now in regular use for farming, it is known that through concerted and centralized efforts much better use could be made of the present acreage. The United Nations Survey Mission for the Middle East summarized this question as follows:

Lebanon's problems of development are not identical with those of neighboring Arab countries. They are more restricted in nature and, though wheat is now and may long remain the most extensively grown crop, they relate more to specialized intensive agriculture under fruit and vegetables than to the wide-scale growing of ordinary field crops or to livestock production. With the developments of the country's water resources attention will concentrate on intensive farming. Increased production of the wheat, which the country needs, is more likely to result in future from an improvement through research in the yield from the existing area than from any extensive increase in the area itself.[28]

Since Lebanon has no known mineral resources of consequence, the main possibilities for profitable future industries must be based upon the processing of the products of an intensified agriculture. But, before any such developments can be greatly extended, the power supply must be increased in large measure. In summary, no problem is more important for Lebanon at this moment than the development of the country's water resources. There has, moreover,

[27] *Ibid.*, p. 22.
[28] United Nations, *op. cit.*, Part II, p. 28.

been a realization of such a need, ever since the beginning of the mandate era. As has already been stated, small private irrigation installations have become fairly widespread, but there is still an area of about 100,000 acres which could be reached either through large, government-sponsored irrigation schemes or simply by alteration of existing water laws or cancellation of existing concessions which militate against the maximal application of potential irrigation facilities.[29]

As for the production of hydroelectric power, the potentialities are enormous:

A simple calculation shows that the potential power from these drops, even when losses are taken into account, amounts to 7,000,000,000 kwh. for rain-fed falls . . . , and the same for snow-fed ones. . . .

Taking into consideration only the power derivable from natural flow, that is, without storage facilities, and from low-lying waters only, the available power can be reckoned at 250,000,000 kwh. . . .

It would not be exaggerating to estimate at 200,000 k.v.a. the hydro-electric power which could be controlled in Lebanon if we proceed to train our principal rivers, e.g. Litani, Awali, Nahr es-Safa, Nahr Ibrahim, Bared. The Litani alone, with training, is capable of commanding 120,000 k.v.a.

Under such conditions, the power produced annually would be increased to 1,500,000,000 kwh. . . .

The capital necessary for this work would amount to about £L140,-000,000 of which half would be used for the purchase of foreign-made equipment.

From the viewpoint of our national budget, the installation of hydro-electric power would create an annual income of about £L9,000,000, which would enable us in ten years to cover the costs of equipment purchased abroad.[30]

In view of such possibilities, even if they are somewhat exaggerated, it seems extraordinary that, after the passage of thirty years since France's assumption of supervisory control over Lebanon, no far-reaching schemes for the exploitation of water resources have been brought to the point of actual utility for the populace. It is indeed possible to add that neither the French nor the Lebanese authorities produced any major integrated plans along such lines, or along any

[29] *Ibid.*, Part II, p. 27; Menassa, *op. cit.*, pp. 556-563.
[30] Menassa, *op. cit.*, pp. 273-274.

other lines designed to raise living standards. The first plan which could conceivably be dignified by those adjectives was the one formulated for the Litani River system by the United Nations Economic Survey Mission for the Middle East (Clapp Mission) in 1949. This one may be regarded as an evolutionary development from previous piecemeal planning, coupled with sporadic attempts at execution, dating from practically the beginning of French control. Involved in these attempts have been: the French mandatory government; the Lebanese Government; and the British authorities (Spears Mission and army), who were in virtual control of Lebanon during the years 1941-45.

The main United Nations recommendation stresses the utilization of the Litani flow for power purposes, while the matter of irrigation from that river's waters is dealt with under several more or less unconnected headings in other parts of the report. Also the Yammouneh irrigation and hydroelectric projects receive separate and special treatment, although Lake Yammouneh is really an integral part of the Litani River system.[31] This writer sees no purpose in such a separation, particularly since even the Clapp report is not altogether consistent on the point, as instanced by the fact that it urges the Lebanese Government to "deal with the watershed as a whole" and also to give consideration to the effects upon irrigation of the proposed Litani power developments.[32] Since all these schemes are clearly interrelated, and since each will eventually be judged according to its contribution to the total Litani River system development, it is deemed advisable, for the purposes of this study, to consider them all as part of a single project of large dimension, which will be referred to hereafter as the Litani-Yammouneh Scheme. The main historical background and current data in regard to that scheme are as follows:

THE LITANI-YAMMOUNEH SCHEME

The Litani is generally classified as one of the seven most important rivers of the Middle East from the economic viewpoint, the others being the Nile, Tigris, Euphrates, Jordan, Orontes, and Karun. Of

[31] Feliks Bochenski and William Diamond, "TVA's in the Middle East," *Middle East Journal*, January, 1950, p. 64.

[32] United Nations, *op. cit.*, Part I, pp. 99-101.

these only two, the Karun and the Litani, run their entire length within the territory of a single nation and can consequently be exploited in all parts by the territorial government without international agreements on the subject. However, as will be seen presently, even the Litani is not without its international implications.

Described in the Clapp report as "Lebanon's major natural resource," the Litani River rises in the north-central part of the country and flows first in a southerly direction between the Lebanon and Anti-Lebanon mountain ranges, forming the fertile Beqaa Valley at a considerable altitude above sea level. It then turns abruptly to the west and descends sharply to the Mediterranean, its mouth being between the ancient cities of Sidon and Tyre.

At present there is no irrigation from the Litani or its subsidiaries, except to a limited extent along the banks. It is proposed to use the flow of this river for the irrigation not only of the southern part of the Beqaa plain but also of a narrow coastal strip crossing the mouth of the stream; the northern part of Beqaa plain would be irrigated mainly from Lake Yammouneh. But even after all conceivable irrigation needs in the Lebanon were adequately served, there would still be an immense surplus of Litani water utilizable either for diversion for irrigation of land in other countries or for the production of hydroelectric power for Lebanon's, and possibly also Israel's and Jordan's, needs.[33]

The potentialities of the Litani River system were first given prominence by Zionist groups shortly after World War I, when the question of the frontier between Palestine and the Syria mandated territory was being negotiated between Britain and France. There was at that time a strong Zionist demand that the section of the Litani which flows from east to west should constitute part of the frontier between Palestine and Syria. This demand was rejected, and Palestine was compensated by the inclusion of all of Lake Huleh, all of Lake Tiberias (Sea of Galilee), and the whole of that stretch of the Jordan River which connects the two lakes in the territory which she received. However, despite this manner of settlement, it was quite customary in subsequent years to include, in Jewish plans for the

[33] Cf. E. B. Worthington, *Middle East Science* (London, 1945), pp. 56-57.

development of Palestine, proposals for use of the Litani as one of the sources of water supply which would be available to the Jewish economy. The assumption apparently was that an agreement could be concluded with Lebanon (or whatever power might be in control of Lebanon) whereby irrigation water could be sold to Palestine. In this connection it was usually intimated that Lebanon had no foreseeable need for more than a relatively small portion of the river's flow for her own purposes. Since the French and Lebanese plans related mainly to flood control and irrigation, the Zionists had a certain amount of documentary evidence for their assertions.[34]

The first project undertaken by the French authorities for the development of Lebanese water resources was a study in regard to a more complete use of the waters of Lake Yammouneh. The studies were begun in 1922, and in 1929, according to a report to the League of Nations, the matter was still being studied. It seems likely that the investigations were delayed by the serious political troubles in the Syria mandate territory in the mid-twenties; but there is no evidence of great official concern, by either French or Lebanese authorities, over the protracted duration of the inquiries and the nonappearance of concrete recommendations. Finally, in 1931, a definite irrigation project for the Yammouneh was approved by the Lebanese Chamber of Deputies, with the cost estimated at 13,000,000 French francs. Not until 1933, however, was a contract awarded for some of the works of construction; and only in 1934 did work actually begin. By December 31, 1936, the collection works and a 2180-meter tunnel leading therefrom were almost finished. Also in 1936, a contract was awarded for the construction of a three-kilometer canal from the exit of the tunnel to the beginning of the actual irrigation system. In the following year a contract was granted for the main and secondary canals within the irrigation area. In 1938 it was officially reported that "the work was being continued slowly by the Lebanese Government."[35] After World War II had broken out, the work was abandoned.[36]

[34] Robert R. Nathan, Oscar Gass, and Daniel Creamer, *Palestine, Problem and Promise* (Washington, 1946), pp. 102-104, 402-403.
[35] Ministère des Affaires Etrangères, *op. cit.*, 1938, p. 159.
[36] Worthington, *op. cit.*, p. 56.

In the meantime, beginning in 1924, the French authorities had undertaken flood control works on the Litani, not involving water storage, which were completed in 1928 to a sufficient extent to avert the most serious dangers of inundation. Three years later the French governmental branch, Régie des Etudes Hydrauliques, worked out a project for the irrigation of 27,500 acres in the South Beqaa through the use of the Litani River and feeder springs. Actual work on this project, however, had not been begun up to December 31, 1950.

Beginning in 1931 the Lebanese Government, with a view to establishing appropriate conditions for the future irrigated area, made a cadastral survey of the Beqaa lands and undertook a consolidation of such farm holdings in the Beqaa as were separated from one another though owned or cultivated by one and the same person. By December 31, 1938, the number of holdings had been reduced from 164,714 to 14,878, and the size of the average holding increased from 0.3673 hectare to 2.2611 hectares (about 5.6 acres). In connection with the same general program the government also repaired old roads and constructed new ones, connecting the villages of the region with the main arteries of transport communications. Further, it dug irrigation and drainage ditches for the future use of individual farmers. These operations, although never completed, had been brought to an advanced stage before the war broke out. The Beqaa is the only part of Lebanon to which a program of this comprehensive nature has ever been applied.[37]

After the British military occupation of Lebanon in 1941 the Yammouneh work was resumed as one of several enterprises conducted jointly by the Spears Mission (British), the British Commonwealth armed forces, and the Lebanese Government for the purpose of increasing food supplies in the Middle East during the emergency period of shortages. However, the commencement of this work was long delayed because of complications which arose in regard to water rights. The legal status of that matter was, and still is, that a decree had been issued in June, 1925, by the French High Commissioner nationalizing the water supply; but, because of political pressures, a

[37] Ministère des Affaires Etrangères, *op. cit.*, 1931, p. 149; 1934, p. 161; 1937, p. 165; 1938, p. 158.

second decree had been issued in 1926 continuing the old state of
affairs in effect "temporarily" for a period of forty years. For all practical purposes, the use of the country's water supplies was thus uncontrolled except by the laws which prohibited trespassing upon private
property, and in some cases by rights based upon "immemorial use."
Finally, however, the Spears Mission succeeded in making satisfactory
practical arrangements, and the operations were begun. But before
the work could be completed, the war had ended. Shortly afterward,
for urgent political reasons, both British and French authorities with-
drew from Lebanon in haste, leaving this and a number of other
projects unfinished. A problem yet to be faced at that time was the
lack of accurate knowledge as to what happens to all the water which
Lake Yammouneh loses through leakage, a large part of which is presumed to reach the Litani eventually. It was not known whether the
leaks could be sealed effectively without adversely affecting springs
already being used for irrigation purposes, and possibly also the future
Litani developments.[38]

Work was later resumed on this project by the Lebanese authorities, and by December 31, 1948, it was estimated that the entire
scheme was about 45 per cent completed.[39] At about the same time
Sir Alexander Gibb and Partners, in the course of their economic investigations in Lebanon, recommended a pursuance of these operations. The work is now at last nearing completion. It is now also
planned by the Lebanese Government to install a hydroelectric station which will utilize a fall of 220 meters from the tunnel already
completed in connection with the Yammouneh irrigation scheme.
The Clapp Mission investigated both irrigation and hydroelectric
schemes and was of the opinion that the effects upon the water
regime of the country should be carefully studied before the taking
of any further action.[40]

The area to be irrigated by the Yammouneh development amounts
to 24,000-30,000 acres. The estimated cost of the irrigation development, from the time work was last resumed by the Lebanese authori-

[38] Worthington, op. cit., p. 56; Warriner, op. cit., p. 92; James B. Hays,
T.V.A. on the Jordan (Washington, 1948), pp. 18-19.
[39] Encyclopaedia Britannica, Book of the Year, 1949, p. 424.
[40] United Nations, op. cit., pp. 84-85.

ties, is about $1,000,000. No cost estimate has yet been made for the hydroelectric project, the completion of which would require three to five years. The power achievable from that project would be about 30,000,000 kilowatt-hours per annum and would in all probability be limited to the period from March to mid-October, since the irrigation development will apparently require storage of all the water accumulating during the winter months.[41]

Another Litani project is the Qasmieh Irrigation Scheme, which was begun during the Second World War and later abandoned by the Spears Mission, armed forces, and Lebanese authorities. Work was later resumed by the Lebanese Government. The studies are complete; operations are well advanced and should be completed shortly. The purpose of this scheme is the irrigation of the coastal plain from Sidon to a point ten kilometers south of Tyre. The area involved amounts to about 11,000 acres in all, of which about two-thirds would be watered by the Litani and the rest by artesian wells. The estimated cost, from the time work was last resumed by the Lebanese authorities, is $900,000. This project, like the Yammouneh one, has required tunneling, which was completed by the South African Army.[42]

The South Beqaa irrigation project was finally undertaken by the Lebanese Government after it had become fully independent. Extensive drainage works are necessary in connection with this scheme, since the French-constructed flood control system is not adequate for an introduction of maximal irrigation. The work on the drainage project has reached an advanced stage, and flooding now appears to be under much better control; but the irrigation works have apparently not yet been commenced. The area to be irrigated is 27,500 acres, and the time required for completion would be about two or three more years. The estimated cost, excluding the old French structures, is $1,200,000. No major structures are required.[43]

With regard to the South Beqaa project, the Clapp Mission recom-

[41] Ibid.; Menassa, op. cit., p. 279.
[42] United Nations, op. cit., Part I, p. 84, and Part II, p. 71; Worthington, op. cit., p. 57; S. F. Newcombe, "A Forecast of Arab Unity," Journal of the Royal Central Asian Society, 1944, Part II, p. 162.
[43] United Nations, op. cit., Part I, p. 84; Part II, p. 71.

mended that further studies be undertaken, and was insistent on the point that subsoil water and water rights should be included in the study. The examination of water rights would appear to be of particular importance, since large estates predominate in the Beqaa,[44] and the owners of such estates are seldom willing to make sacrificial concessions for the benefit of the entire farming community.[45] Thus, if advance precautions are not taken with regard to this matter, the project may, like the Yammouneh one, be greatly delayed in execution or even brought to a complete halt.

With these four projects completed it would still be possible to utilize the Litani for production of large amounts of hydroelectric power, and possibly also for additional irrigation. The Clapp Mission was clearly convinced that the former purpose should be given priority, in view of the facts that *Lebanese* irrigation possibilities from the Litani will have been substantially taken care of by the schemes already mentioned and that the general nature of the Litani flow offers unique possibilities for immense power production. Another consideration, perhaps, is that the Hays Plan, which constitutes the main basis of current official thinking in regard to the future irrigation of Israel, does not contemplate a diversion of the Litani for that purpose. Thus, as far as the long-range requirements of the Lebanese and Israeli economies are concerned, it seems likely that, as industrialization of these two small, densely populated countries progresses, the aggregate need for power produced by the Litani will be much greater than the aggregate need for the river's waters for further irrigation.

The Clapp report cautions, however, that with the possible exception of the partially completed projects already mentioned no works involving the Litani should be begun without an extensive preliminary survey of all conceivable aspects of the matter. Such a survey would require at least a year and would cost about $240,000.

[44] Tannous, *loc. cit.*

[45] It often happens that great estate owners are more concerned with the general maintenance of vested rights than with the possibilities of eventually augmenting the value of their properties. It is estimated that the irrigation projects now under consideration would double or treble the value of lands in the Beqaa region, and quintuple the values in the coastal regions. (Menassa, *op. cit.*, p. 283.)

Because of the great potential value of the Litani to Lebanon, and because of the danger that the potentialities might not be utilized to the full if work were to be commenced on the basis of present knowledge, the Mission recommended strongly that this investigation enterprise be given the top position among Lebanon's developmental schemes. The Mission also listed it as one of the four projects particularly recommended as providing future possibilities of work relief for Arab refugees from the Palestine War, of whom there are 100,000 in Lebanon. The costs of these projects were to have been defrayed to a large extent by the United Nations, provided that adequate contributions could be obtained from member countries. The Litani survey was the only such scheme recommended for Lebanon.

The Clapp Mission's estimate, when added to the estimate given for the Yammouneh-to-Litani drop, reveals that a total annual production of possibly 780,000,000 kilowatt-hours, delivered at load centers in Lebanon, could be achieved by appropriate utilization of the Litani-Yammouneh water system. Or, alternatively, a diversion could be made at the southern bend of the stream, connecting it with the near-by Hasbani River, the northernmost tributary of the Jordan River. If that should be done, the 550-meter fall to the Dead Sea could probably be utilized for the production of an even larger total amount of power, part of which, however, would be for the use of Israel or Jordan, not Lebanon. In such event, Lebanon's loss of potential power would be in the neighborhood of 200,000,000 kilowatt-hours per annum.

Both the engineering and the political aspects of this question are exceedingly complex. They are, moreover, closely interrelated, in view of proposals which are now being considered sympathetically by the Israeli Government, viz., use of the Jordan River system (beginning, if possible, with the Lebanon headwaters of the Hasbani), together with an artificial salt-water channel from the Mediterranean Sea to the Jordan Valley, for the production of hydroelectric power.[46] This Mediterranean-Dead Sea project also has its inspirational and prestige aspects, and it is possible that the Israeli Government would

[46] Hays, op. cit., passim; W. C. Lowdermilk, Palestine, Land of Promise (New York, 1944), passim.

be loath to abandon it definitively.[47] The question whether this scheme could be effectively combined with plans for total utilization of the Litani River system, resulting in a production far greater than that of either program taken alone, has apparently not yet been studied.

The Clapp report contains the following strong recommendation in regard to the Litani scheme:

"The study and development . . . should only be the responsibility of qualified personnel experienced in dealing with problems of this magnitude and complexity.

"A study of the whole Litani River system and its watershed requires the special ability of many technicians. It requires the effort of a co-ordinated team of specialists, including geologists, hydraulic, civil, mechanical, electrical and architectural engineers, economists, cost estimators, construction engineers and specialists in the financing of such projects."[48]

Lebanon has also numerous other untapped possibilities for the production of hydroelectric power. One estimate, already mentioned, is that a total of 1,500,000,000 kilowatt-hours per annum could be produced.[49] This may be somewhat exaggerated, but there seems in any case to be little room for doubt that, if the proposal to divert part of the Litani's flow into the Jordan River system were to be adopted, the resultant loss of power to Lebanon could be neutralized by developments from other sources.[50] At present the production of hydroelectric power is very small, the largest installation being of 4000-kilowatt capacity.[51]

Yet, in spite of all these possibilities, and the increasingly urgent

[47] W. C. Lowdermilk, who has done the most to popularize the "Jordan Valley Authority" concept, the main feature of which is the Mediterranean-Dead Sea project, has consistently been rendered great homage by Zionist organizations and by the government and people of Israel. In March, 1950, he was appointed adviser to the Israeli Government and on December 31 was still serving in that capacity.

[48] United Nations, op. cit., Part I, pp. 99-101; Part II, p. 40.

[49] Menassa, op. cit., p. 274.

[50] As to these possibilities, cf. United Nations, op. cit., Part I, pp. 85-86; Menassa op. cit., pp. 270-280; Bochenski and Diamond, op. cit., p. 64.

[51] United Nations, op. cit., Part II, p. 40.

need for their exploitation, indications are that the present rate of progress is no more rapid than was the average tempo of such activities during the era of the French mandate. Up to December 31, 1950, there was no evidence that any important preparations had been made by the Lebanese Government to implement the main Clapp recommendation, published on December 28, 1949. There were two possible immediate reasons for this. One was the great delay by the United Nations in producing the necessary funds—which, however, was more probably the effect than the cause of Lebanese attitudes. The other was the fact that popular political currents had meanwhile arisen in some parts of the Middle East, which militated against the taking of action recommended in the Clapp report. Thus, in Lebanon, where the Mission had gained great favor, and where advice had been particularly desired in regard to the proposed Litani developments, the belief seemed to gain ground after the Mission's departure that there were ulterior political motives, inspired by the United States Government, behind the Clapp proposals.[52] Beirut became, in a sense, the main center in the Middle East of unofficial resistance to implementation of the recommendations. The chief ostensible issue was whether or not there should be a definite understanding that all Arab refugees from Israel should in time be permitted to return to their former homes in Israeli territory. The Lebanese governmental authorities became involved in this question, even to the extent of refusing transit privileges for relief food supplies destined to Arab refugees in Jordanian territory. During the latter part of 1950 there were indications of a somewhat more tolerant governmental attitude both in regard to the refugee situation and in regard to the general principle of cooperation with the United Nations in connection with its Middle East works programs. However, by the time this altered policy had been adopted, the chances that the United Nations would be able to finance the Clapp programs had become forlorn. A United

[52] Developments of this nature stem in large measure from a widespread anti-Western sentiment among the Lebanese people, based on suspicions as to French motives during the mandate period, to which reference has already been made. The ruling class has profited from such sentiments, which tend to distract attention from internal conditions; and much of its power is now based on its ability to use this xenophobia for its own ends.

Nations Assembly Resolution of December 3, 1950, had the effect of terminating those programs in favor of an attempt to solve the Arab refugee problem on a revised basis.[53]

SUMMARY AND CONCLUSIONS

The history of the Litani-Yammouneh projects is particularly instructive, not only because those projects offer the best hope of laying the foundations of improved living standards in Lebanon, but also because the fact has been consistently recognized by practically all parties concerned with the improvement of those standards. The lessons from this history are emphasized by the fact that the need for execution of these works has been acute and increasing. They are further emphasized by the testimony furnished by the Clapp Mission as to the reality of some of the most impressive possibilities.

There may well have been some unavoidable budgetary difficulties. Also, it would probably be unfair to assign to Lebanon all of the blame for the long sequence of external and internal political troubles experienced. There seems, finally, to be little doubt that some of the engineering problems connected with the Litani-Yammouneh projects have been particularly ticklish ones.

Yet, even after all these points have been conceded, it still seems hardly conceivable that much greater progress could not have been made on these projects, had most of the successive Lebanese governments been truly determined to solve the country's central and obvious economic problem. It also seems hardly questionable, in view of the large educated and Westernized sector of the Lebanese populace, that the government could at almost any time have gained widespread public backing for a determined effort to achieve major concrete results. Under such circumstances, the necessary finances could probably somehow have been provided. The Clapp report contained some simple suggestions regarding the possibilities of budgetary savings. They are the same ones which have been repeated

[53] Albion Ross, "Refugee Relief Clogs Beirut," New York *Times*, February 21, 1950; Ross, "Syria Is Warned on Balking U.N. Aid," New York *Times*, June 7, 1950; "Displaced Arabs Protest U.N. Unit," New York *Times*, May 12, 1950; "Relief for Arab Refugees," New York *Times*, December 26, 1950.

time and again by authorities on the politics and economics of Lebanon.

Even if these judgments were not warranted before the visit of the Clapp Mission to Lebanon, the latest developments surely provide all but complete substantiation. The cost of proceeding with the Clapp recommendations was not great, and the Lebanese budget would surely have stood for a small beginning of efforts on this much-publicized program, which the Lebanese authorities professed to favor strongly.[54] Here it is of little importance whether the attitudes regarding the refugee problem, and the suspicions regarding the Clapp Mission's motives, were justified or not. It is still difficult, if not impossible, to understand why this had to interfere with the modest beginnings upon an enterprise of such great promise to the country.

The unavoidable conclusion is that the prospects for major planning for elevation of Lebanese living standards will not be favorable until Lebanon has governments which are more representative of educated Lebanese as a whole. At present it is hard to see how such a state of affairs might be brought about. Perhaps, however, the privileged class will before long be overcome by the sheer numerical weight of the nonprivileged educated classes.[55]

[54] As to the status of Lebanon's governmental finances in the latter part of 1949, cf. United Nations, *op. cit.*, Part I, pp. 48-51.

[55] One suggestion which has been made, and put into effect by the American University of Beirut, is that educational institutions should attempt to concentrate on altering the social outlook of landowners' sons. To date the university's experiments along that line have produced disappointing results.

❖

CHAPTER VI

Syria

GENERAL BACKGROUND

Nearly all authorities on the subject are agreed that, next to Iraq, Syria is the richest of the independent Arab states in respect of unexploited developmental potentialities. The present cultivated area is estimated at 5,750,000 acres, the cultivable waste at 8,500,000 acres. In addition, there are cultivated regions in which the yields could be increased by the introduction of irrigation facilities. The population is estimated at 3,350,000, as of June 30, 1948. Syria has had an additional apparent advantage over most of the other Arab regions in that assimilation to Western ways was already well begun by 1919 in the larger centers of population.[1]

Yet, in spite of these apparent advantages, Syria's development since the end of World War I has been a slow and much-interrupted process. Up to the time of writing, the advances have not been particularly impressive, except possibly in the matter of highway construction.[2] Nor is the outlook for the immediate future any more favorable.

The reasons are mainly political. At no time since the separation of

[1] A. H. Hourani, *Syria and Lebanon, A Political Essay* (London, 1946), *passim*.
[2] United Nations, *Final Report of the United Nations Economic Survey Mission for the Middle East* (Lake Success, N.Y., December 1, 1949), Part II, p. 41.

Syria from the Ottoman Empire has the internal situation been sufficiently stable and tranquil to provide any reasonable assurance of uninterrupted progress along economic and social lines. In the summary given below of the various political disturbances from 1919 to the present, the geographical area covered is that now occupied by the republic of Syria, with the addition, until 1939, of the now Turkish province of Hatay (Sanjaq of Alexandretta). Although Lebanon was part of the Syria mandated territory under French supervision, a fairly clearcut distinction has always been made between Lebanon and the rest of that territory, sometimes referred to as Syria proper. In a still narrower sense, the term "Syria" has often been used to refer only to the state of Syria, which was a separate administrative area under the French mandate. In this study, however, the Latakia and Jebel Druze regions are also considered to have been parts of Syria at all times from 1918 on.[3]

In 1920 Syria was for a few months the center of an independent Arab kingdom under the rule of the Meccan Arab leader, Feisal.[4] But in the same year, at the Conference of San Remo on League of Nations mandates, an international decision was made to place Syria under French mandate. One of France's initial acts after the conference was to dethrone Feisal and expel him from the country, and thereafter, at least until 1936, to administer the country on a basis which has generally been regarded as a disguised form of direct rule.[5] The expulsion of Feisal was an unpopular move, but it was by no means the only reason for many Syrians' dissatisfaction with France. French administrative measures were not infrequently arbi-

[3] The mandatory power made several successive changes in the political organization of the mandated area outside of Lebanon. In general, however, the pattern was one of three semiautonomous regions, namely, the state of Syria, Latakia (sometimes known as the Alawi state), and Jebel Druze. The Sanjaq of Alexandretta, though having a special political status, was usually a part of the state of Syria.

[4] This was one of a long series of developments resulting from the negotiations in 1915 and 1916 between a British official emissary, Sir Henry McMahon, and the Sherif of Mecca, Hussein. The purpose of the negotiations was to foment an Arab revolt against the Ottoman state. Feisal, who later became King of Iraq, was Hussein's son. He was also the brother of Abdullah, King of the Hashemite state of Jordan.

[5] Hourani, *op. cit.*, p. 170.

trarily conceived and tactlessly executed. Tensions were acute during the period from 1920 to 1925.[6]

In 1925 there was virtually open warfare between French and Syrians. The trouble began in the Jebel Druze administrative area, apparently as a result of unwanted economic and social reforms imposed upon that backward region by the highest-ranking French representative there. The spirit of revolt soon spread over the whole of Syria, and the French experienced the utmost difficulty in finally restoring order after many months of fighting.[7]

From 1926 to 1936, not only was there constant and increasing agitation for independence, mainly on the part of the Sunni Moslem Arabs of Syria; there was also much tension between that majority group and some of the racial and religious minorities. At times some of the minority groups, as, for example, the Alawis of the Latakia region, were inclined to give full support to France in her conflicts with the majority. This gave rise to frequent charges, some of which were perhaps justified, that France was discriminating in favor of the minorities.[8] Under these circumstances it was hardly possible to make accurate predictions as to what Syria's future political status and frontiers would be; even the question whether or not Lebanon would constitute a part of the future independent Syria remained unanswered until 1936. In such a state of affairs there was not much purpose in attempting to execute large-scale, long-term developmental schemes affecting great areas which might later be partitioned politically. Many such schemes were planned in considerable detail, as far as the engineering aspects were concerned.[9] Also a fair amount of piecemeal uncoordinated progress was made in the direction of further actual Westernization. But all attempts to do away with the major deficiencies were balked either at their inception or at early

[6] Ibid., pp. 172, 176; Arnold J. Toynbee, The Islamic World Since the Peace Settlement (London, 1927), passim.

[7] Toynbee, op. cit., p. 413.

[8] Hourani, op. cit., pp. 64, 140-142, 185, 267; Hourani, Minorities in the Arab World (London, 1947), p. 81.

[9] Ministère des Affaires Etrangères, Rapports sur la Situation de la Syrie et du Liban, 1922-1938 (Paris, 1923-39), 1928, p. 124; 1930, p. 65; 1932, p. 58; 1934, p. 64.

stages of execution. The failure along such lines had led to serious results by 1937:

"Judging from statistics of real wages, Syria seems to have been a country in which there was an exceptionally severe fall in standards of living. Figures quoted in *International Labor Review* (April 1939) show that real wages in 1937 were only about half of their 1913 level."[10]

In view of an estimated population increase of more than one-third in the ten-year period 1939-48, together with the continued absence of reforms and political stability during the postwar years, it seems likely that living standards have declined to an even lower level since the outbreak of World War II.[11]

The land-tenure problem offers an illustration of the difficulties during the between-wars period. The mandatory power could find no satisfactory solution for that problem which would not give offense to the shaikhs and large landowners upon whom France was relying for support. In 1929 the Government of Latakia, composed mainly of Alawis, adopted a policy of forcing large landowners to give up their holdings, and of dividing such holdings among the villagers on a basis of individual ownership and payment of a purchase price in ten installments. However, this practice was abandoned after having been applied to one small group of villages. The reason seems to have been that the mandatory power did not regard it as politically expedient. In general, while the mandate was in effect, the policy was followed of settling all rights by granting titles of individual ownership, but not in such a manner as to promote agrarian welfare as a whole. The process has never been completed.[12]

In 1936, under strong pressure from nationalists, the French authorities concluded a treaty with Syria, in which that country was

[10] Colin Clark, *The Conditions of Economic Progress* (London, 1940), p. 151 n.

[11] Ministère des Affaires Etrangères, *op. cit.*, 1938, pp. 220-221; Royal Institute of International Affairs, *The Middle East: A Political and Economic Survey* (London, 1950), p. 394.

[12] Doreen Warriner, *Land and Poverty in the Middle East* (London, 1948), pp. 22-23, 93, 134; Ministère des Affaires Etrangères, *op. cit.*, 1922-23, pp. 29-31; 1926, pp. 166-169; 1927, pp. 129-136; 1929, pp. 42-44; *et passim*; Said B. Himadeh, *Economic Organization of Syria* (Beirut, 1936), pp. 51-69.

granted a substantial degree of immediate real independence, with political separation from Lebanon. This treaty, however, was never ratified by the French Parliament. Thus, although the mandatory authorities did in any case concede a far greater measure of self-rule from 1936 on, there were many unsolved problems of great consequence, and many tensions. Added to the difficulties which already existed was the public sentiment which began to turn against the principal nationalist leaders after the failure of the latter to produce a binding agreement with France. Also the minority troubles were particularly acute from 1936 to 1939, and matters were further complicated by the civil war in Palestine. Damascus became a center of underground support for the Palestine Arabs, from which secret missions were dispatched to Transjordan and probably to Iraq. As the Zionists were identified with European domination in the Middle East, the most visible result of this activity was a deepening of the anti-French feeling in Syria. As far as economic and social development was concerned, the mandatory power was virtually paralyzed by the political situation, while Syrians were far too much engrossed in politics to be greatly interested in large-scale economic planning.[13]

After the fall of France in June, 1940, the conflict between the Vichy and Free French groups became an important factor in Syrian politics. It continued to be so even after the beginning of British military occupation in the spring of 1941. Syrians particularly resented the fact that the Free French faction, not yet organized as a government and backed only by British power, nevertheless asserted its prerogatives under a mandate from a moribund organization. During the period from 1941 to 1946 Syria was really under triple control. The British had, to be sure, proclaimed her independence, at the beginning of the occupation. However, the mandate had not been legally terminated; in the resultant situation, both Syrians and Free French had reason to be particularly sensitive on issues involving prestige. In the struggle for power which took place between them there developed a tendency for British and Syrians to combine in verbal opposition to the Free French. Partly because of this *rapprochement*,

[13] Hourani, *Syria and Lebanon*, pp. 106-108, 215-226; John Bagot Glubb, *The Story of the Arab Legion* (London, 1948), p. 241.

the British occupation authorities found it possible to proceed with one developmental project of great importance, based mainly on wartime needs but having considerable bearing upon living standards in Syria.[14] This was the scheme for development of the Jezireh wastelands through mechanized cultivation. However, as far as most of the activities of the Syrian Government during that era were concerned, political considerations greatly overshadowed economic and social ones. The determination to achieve complete freedom from French control was the paramount element in official policy, as well as in public opinion. There was little desire to embark upon great undertakings before the attainment of that goal.

The withdrawal of British and French officials took place early in 1946, and the League of Nations mandate was terminated. But complete independence did not produce an end of the chronic political unrest.

The government soon formulated a developmental program, of which the main features were the modernization and expansion of irrigation on the Euphrates, the importation of many types of machinery and tools in order to promote increased industrialization, and the construction of a modern port at Latakia. In the outcome, the main activity was the development of new privately owned industrial enterprises under heavy tariff protection. This, like Reza Shah's much larger program in Iran, seemed not to be directly aimed at raising living standards. Continued support was given to industries which showed little indication of becoming economic propositions, and the general effect of the tariff was to reduce, instead of elevating, living standards by raising the cost of living (particularly for clothing) of a great majority of the population.[15] One aspect of this matter is discussed in the *Final Report* of the United Nations Economic Survey Mission (Clapp Mission), which visited Syria in 1949:

"Money wages in industry are low, it is true, but so is the individual worker's output. Strikers in the Aleppo cotton mills have been de-

[14] Also a considerable number of minor projects were carried out by the Middle East Supply Centre and the British Ninth Army, Cf. Hourani, *Syria and Lebanon*, p. 255; Warriner, *op. cit.*, p. 2.

[15] *New International Year Book*, 1947, p. 642; Arab Office, *Arab News Bulletin* (Washington, December 31, 1947); United Nations, *op. cit.*, Part I, p. 42.

manding that no individual worker should be required to tend more than one loom, as against three at present (and an average of forty in the U.S.A.). In terms of production costs, factory labor is dear in Syria. Also, the workers, organized in unions, can press their demands in an effective manner."[16]

At the same time Syria's financial policies were rapidly leading toward a situation in which, unless other conditions should be particularly favorable, developmental activities would have to be slowed down or even halted because of shortage of foreign exchange. Especially important among such policies was the maintenance of only minor exchange and import restrictions, which in time were abandoned altogether. This policy was motivated by a desire to protect the long-established exchange-brokerage business, which is conducted on a world-wide basis by Syrians. It is highly doubtful that the interests of the exchange brokers correspond at all closely with the general welfare of the Syrian people, or, for that matter, with any long-term Syrian interests other than their own.[17]

In the outcome, other conditions have been by no means favorable. The deterioration in Syria's foreign relations was to produce grave results, beginning in 1948, both for her internal peace and stability and for her economy. In the latter connection, it may be noted that in 1949 military expenditures amounted to £S90,000,000, which, as far as can be determined from incomplete statistics, seems to account for about 40 per cent of the total governmental expenditure for that year. No reduction in military costs was anticipated for 1950.[18]

Also the political situation which has developed has had indirect effects upon the country's economy, both by causing Syria to be a poor risk for foreign lending and by producing a general climate unfavorable to economic development, whether with or without foreign assistance. The main constituent elements in this situation are outlined in the following paragraphs:

Relations between Syria and Lebanon have never been satisfactory since the two states became fully independent. Until 1950 the two

[16] United Nations, *op. cit.*, Part I, pp. 42-43.
[17] *Ibid.*, pp. 35-36, 40-41.
[18] *Ibid.*, p. 39.

nations were joined in a customs union; but this failed to produce
the desired results of mutual benefit, because each party had been
fully convinced that the agreement was an unfair one to itself and
had tried to evade the spirit of the pact. This conflict was possibly
the inevitable result of an attempt to create economic unity between
two immature nations, both of which had just won, and were
determined to protect, their political sovereignty. It proved difficult in
practice to make suitable distinctions between the legitimate exercise
of sovereignty, on the one hand, and sabotaging of the economic
arrangement, on the other, particularly since there was a strong element of fundamental distrust between the two parties. Neither was
convinced that the other's government could be depended upon to
conduct its end of the arrangement in a mature and responsible manner. Also Syrians apparently feared that the union would be tantamount to domination by the Lebanese, in view of the greater
advancement of the latter in knowledge and understanding of economic matters; and there is a chronic fear among Lebanese Christians
of domination by Moslem Syria, which is not only much larger than
Lebanon but also morally supported to a considerable extent by the
rest of the Moslem Middle East.[19]

Another source of trouble between these two nations has been
fresh conflicts in Syria between Moslem and Christian groups; on at
least one occasion the Syrian Government seems to have taken drastic
action against Christians, forcing many of them to seek refuge in
already crowded Lebanon.[20]

Finally, in March, 1950, the customs union was terminated, despite
the opinion of most unbiased experts that the two nations are
dependent on each other economically. It should be noted, however,
that, during this whole period of ill-disguised mutual antagonism, the

[19] V. H. W. Dowson, "The Lebanon, 1948-1949," *Journal of the Royal Central
Asian Society*, 1950, Part I, p. 75; W. B. Fisher, "Population Problems of the
Middle East," *Journal of the Royal Central Asian Society*, 1949, Part III, p. 209;
"Breakdown of Syrian-Lebanese Customs Union," *Middle East Journal*, July, 1950;
United Nations, *op. cit.*, Part I, pp. 39-42; Albion Ross, "Arab Reversion to
Merger Plans Seen," New York *Times*, May 18, 1950; Royal Institute of Inter-
national Affairs, *op. cit.*, p. 409.

[20] George Kirk, "Independent Syria and Lebanon," *Journal of the Royal Central
Asian Society*, 1948, Part II, p. 262.

two countries were at all times making an effort to display a front indicative of solidarity for the benefit of the outer world. The reason was that both of them, in the absence of good relations with each other and with their other neighbors, were dependent on the Arab League for their security.

Cordial relations between Syria and Turkey have been impossible in view of the widespread distrust by Syrians of Turkey's intentions for the future vis-à-vis Syrian territory.[21] The present crucial questions, however, have resulted largely from Syria's futile participation in the war conducted by the Arab League against Israel in 1948. The outcome of that war revealed to politically conscious Syrians not only the weakness of their country as compared with neighboring Israel from the viewpoint of modernization and internal strength but also an unfavorable comparison between Syria and the other Arab states, none of which had emerged from the struggle with such complete discomfiture. To cite only the most embarrassing comparison, Transjordan, generally looked upon as an extremely "backward" country, had fought well with small forces and gained much territory. By contrast Syria, the Arab state which had always been regarded as particularly promising and which showed by no means uncommon manifestations of truly progressive thought, could look back mainly upon an inadequate contribution to the Arab war effort, after having issued many strong pronouncements on the subject, followed by a large share in the untoward results of the war, including the influx of 75,000 unwanted refugees.[22] From that situation, and from the personal rivalries of government leaders, which have tended to overshadow ideological issues at the top political level, the crisis of 1949 arose. It is not yet at an end.

After the Palestine War some widely divergent thought currents had come into being, among Syria's politically conscious elements, with regard to the question of finding a solution for the country's

[21] Hourani, *Syria and Lebanon*, p. 276.
[22] United Nations, *op. cit.*, Part I, p. 23.
    Other ill effects of the war upon Syria have been: severance of road and rail communications with Egypt; the political necessity for abnormally large military expenditures; loss of prestige and sympathy in the West; the encouragement given to personal rivals of the government leaders in power.

pressing difficulties. In some circles a strong feeling has developed that Syria, confined within her present frontiers, will never be capable of acquiring adequate internal strength. The corollary to such a belief is advocacy of a political union or confederation with neighboring Arab states. Others, however, favor a concentration on the development of military strength on a national basis, as a condition precedent both to economic and social development and to the conclusion of agreements with foreign nations on terms satisfactory to Syria.[23] Still others would like to see an immediate beginning of elaborate and spectacular programs of economic development, worked out on the same bases as those on which Turkey's and Iran's programs were originally worked out—that is, without financial assistance from outside and with only a minimum of technical aid, supplied under controlled conditions, from foreign countries and foreign nationals.[24] Under the conditions which have generally existed, and which now exist, governmental policies in regard to developmental projects are constantly changing, and projects are being long postponed, owing to the struggles among the rival leaders for personal prestige and power.[25]

Strong differences of opinion at high political levels in regard to these matters, together with frequent changes in public opinion, produced three coups d'état during 1949. Ever since the first of these, the dominant power in the government has ostensibly been the army, which, however, has completely failed to bring about the active support of a substantial segment of the landowner class, still in the ascendancy in cabinets and parliaments, or to prevent suppressed groups within that class from resorting to underground terroristic activities on a large scale.[26] It has become abundantly clear, moreover, that even within the army there is no solidarity of opinion; it also seems clear that the army is permeated with jealousies and

[23] This was apparently the belief held by Husni Zaim, who held dictatorial powers for several months in 1949.

[24] Ross, "Syria to Finance Own Development," New York *Times*, March 5, 1950.

[25] Elizabeth Monroe, "British Interests in the Middle East," *Middle East Journal*, April, 1948, p. 138.

[26] "Syria Accuses 21 of Terrorist Acts," New York *Times*, November 13, 1950.

rivalries of a personal character, as is the landlord class.[27] During most of 1950 a Constituent Assembly was in session for the purpose of drawing up a new constitution. Because of the great and bitter divisions of opinion among the populace, including a rift on the question raised by the powerful Moslem Brotherhood of including a provision whereby Islam would be Syria's state religion, immense difficulties were experienced in arriving at an agreement. Finally, on September 5, 1950, a revised constitution was adopted by a large majority in the Assembly;[28] but, to judge by subsequent indications, it has failed to produce any material improvement in the general state of affairs. The government in power on December 31, 1950, showed few signs of stability, competence, or widespread support.

In the meantime—and, in fact, ever since the outbreak of the Palestine War—developmental progress has been slight, both as to activities and as to planning at the cabinet level. Work on the leading current project, improvement of the port of Latakia, continued during the early part of 1950, with the foreign exchange costs being financed by Syria's one foreign loan, a dollar loan of $6,000,000 from Saudi Arabia. When Saudi Arabia was unable to continue paying the promised installments on this loan, the Latakia operation had to be abandoned for an indefinite period.[29]

After the departure from Syria of the Clapp Mission in December, 1949, predominant public sentiment in Syria turned strongly against the acceptance of any United Nations or other Western assistance for public works. The government announced definitely that Syria would carry out her own development program with her own resources, presumably with the exception of the Saudi Arabian loan. This pronouncement was, in fact, merely a restoration of a policy which had been in effect from time to time ever since 1946, one result of which had been that, up to that time, Syria and Yemen were the only

[27] "Assassin Murders Syrian General," New York Times, October 31, 1950.

[28] Article 22 of the constitution made mandatory the passage within two years of a law limiting (but not retroactively) the total amount of land which a person might legally acquire by purchase or foreclosure. Up to September 15, 1951, no legislation along such lines had been passed.

[29] United Nations, op. cit., Part I, p. 43; Ross, "Ibn Saud Hard Put on Loan to Syria," New York Times, June 11, 1950.

Middle Eastern countries which had had little or no contact with the facilities of the International Bank or the Export-Import Bank. Underlying such policies is the continually recurrent anti-Westernism of the politically conscious masses in Syria. This is a heritage from the days of the French mandate. It is kept alive by the fact that, in the current and chronic state of governmental paralysis and confusion among the populace, anti-Westernism (and the closely related anti-Zionism) is practically the only dependable basis whereupon political leaders can be more or less sure of gaining a certain measure of united support, at least momentarily. There are no alternative explanations which would be at all adequate.[30]

In September, 1950, there was a reversal of the policy of self-sufficiency. Syria entered into an agreement with the United Nations Relief and Work Administration, involving financial and technical assistance by the United Nations for public works designed to give employment to refugees in Syria. However, Syria had not carried out any of the planning requested by the Clapp Mission. In addition, it soon became clear that, in the then status of the matter, even the combined resources of Syria and the United Nations would not be adequate for the financing of any major project. Also, during the autumn of 1950 an International Bank mission visited Syria. Its report had not been made public before the end of the year.

Besides the results already noted, the above-mentioned situations have had their repercussions in Syrian attitudes vis-à-vis the central international question, namely, Soviet-American relations. Predominant public opinion seems to blame Syria's present woes largely on the United States, ostensibly because of America's present support of Israel and her advocacy of slow processes in the developmental projects which she supports with her dollars. The idea of seeking political and economic support from the Soviet Union has become decidedly popular in many quarters.[31]

It is not easy to predict what turn the situation will take next. It is,

[30] New York *Times*, June 7, 1950; Royal Institute of International Affairs, *op. cit.*, pp. 48-49.
[31] New York *Times*, June 7, 1950; June 30, 1950; July 2, 1950.

however, unlikely at this stage that the politically conscious public
will be satisfied with any solution other than one which would constitute a drastic alteration both of the status quo and of previous
states of affairs. Until this is forthcoming, there is no great probability
that much progress will be made in the formulation or execution of
serious major plans for raising the general standard of living in Syria.

The following paragraphs contain descriptions and histories of the
major plans for raising living standards which have been formulated
or put into effect in Syria during the 1919-50 period.[32]

THE GHAB VALLEY SCHEME

The Ghab Valley Scheme, which has a colorful history and which
has nearly always been regarded by experts as the project most
appropriate for the initiation of a campaign to elevate Syrian living
standards, involves the reclamation for irrigated agriculture of 85,000
acres of swampland situated in the heart of an otherwise densely
populated region. There are also possibilities for the generation of
hydroelectric power, as part of the development. The broad outlines
of each successive proposal for this undertaking have been approximately the same.

In some remote period a volcanic flow filled up the channel of the
Orontes River below Karkour. Subsequently a great lake was formed.
Then . . . sedimentation from the Orontes and erosion from the adjacent
mountains filled the lake. . . . When the river resumed its flow its
gradient was flat and it did not create a channel with a capacity adequate
for the discharge of the flood waters. Thus . . . the fertile lands became
a swamp.

The proposals for reclamation included a canal system for draining
the swampy area below Acharne, a tunnel at Kfeir for assisting in the
disposal of flood waters and regulating works from the Orontes River
to the tunnel. To assist in the control of floods the plan included a dam
at Acharne to form a reservoir with sufficient capacity to store excessive

[32] One matter which is not discussed in this chapter is the agreement concluded
in March, 1949, between the Syrian Government and Mr. James W. Men-Hall,
a Syro-American oil concessionaire. Although this agreement provides for a special
fund to be devoted to the raising of Syrian living standards, there is no evidence
of the existence of any plan as to methods to be used. Cf. *Oil Forum*, March 11,
1949.

flood waters and then release as required. . . . Headworks and canals would be required for irrigation.[33]

The Ghab Valley Scheme has been the subject of as many as three major humanitarian projects with broad international implications. These are briefly described in the following paragraphs:

ARMENIAN REFUGEES

During the entire period between the two world wars the League of Nations was actively occupied in efforts to find solutions, complete or partial, for the problem of Armenian refugees from Turkey. In Syria, where this question was particularly acute, one of the League Assembly's early policies was to arrange for the settlement of as many refugees as possible on the land, and to support the execution of the Ghab Valley Scheme for that purpose. Such a settlement, it was believed, would have several possibly useful results. It would reduce the pressure of Armenians upon urban occupations, in which they were tending to make competition difficult for Syrians. It would help to create a nuclear group of experienced Armenian agriculturists, which would be of value if the League's project for an Armenian National Home in Erivan, U.S.S.R., should ever materialize. Finally, the Ghab Scheme would also be helpful to Syrian agriculture.[34]

In 1925 the French mandatory government definitely announced that the Ghab Valley Scheme would be considered seriously, on a basis of partial financing by the League of Nations, and that a portion of the reclaimed land would be allotted to Armenians, if the scheme materialized. It was apparently anticipated that these Armenian settlers, socially more advanced than Arab peasants, would provide a demonstration of the region's possibilities and thereby pave the way for a larger-scale planned settlement of native farmers in the valley on small privately owned holdings. However, in the sequel, few of the Armenians in the shelter camps in Syrian cities were at all interested in settling on farms. They preferred to take their chances on urban

[33] United Nations, *op. cit.*, Part I, pp. 101-102.
[34] *League of Nations Assembly Records*, 1925, C. V. pp. 19, 94; Ministère des Affaires Etrangères, *op. cit.*, 1926, pp. 100-106; 1927, pp. 65-69; 1934, pp. 54-56; 1938, pp. 50-51.

employment, however unpromising. As the essential preliminary conditions for the undertaking were lacking, it was abandoned.[35]

ASSYRIANS

In 1935 the League of Nations and the French mandatory power were concerned with a new group of refugees, namely, the Assyrians. That small Christian community had twice, since the beginning of World War I, been forced to emigrate from its original homeland in Anatolia; it was now in serious conflict with the Arab majority in the country of refuge, Iraq. By 1935, 6000 Assyrians had already made their way into Syria from Iraq, and both these and many who had remained behind were pressing for a permanent compact settlement of the whole group in Syria. As a result of this pressure, new arrangements were made for execution of the Ghab Scheme, with Assyrians as the immediate beneficiaries. Thirty-seven and one-half per cent of the reclaimed area was to be allotted to that group.

The expenses of this venture were to be defrayed on a proportional basis by the League of Nations, Great Britain, Iraq, and Syria. Settlement was to be open to all Assyrians, whether in Iraq or Syria at the time, possibly up to the number of 25,000, who wished to take advantage of the opportunity. As far as possible, the costs were to be self-liquidating. Assyrians were to render suitable assistance in all of the construction activities, particularly the erection of their own dwelling houses, both temporary and permanent. Also they were to be required to pay in installments for the land which would be furnished to them, on the basis of individual plots, by the League of Nations committee in charge of the settlement. During the period of settlement, and for a time thereafter until satisfactory alternative arrangements could be made, the Assyrian settlement area would be semi-autonomous, under the general supervision of the French High Commissioner of Syria, but directly administered by the League committee and not subject to any Syrian authorities. Just as in the case of the previous plan for Armenian settlement, the possible exemplary benefits to Arab peasants from this undertaking were being borne in mind.

[35] Himadeh, op. cit., pp. 23-25.

This plan also collapsed. In 1936 the High Commissioner of Syria made a strong request to the League of Nations Council that the scheme be abandoned forthwith. There were two important reasons for this request. The first was that the nationalistic feeling among the Arab majority in Syria had risen to a point of intransigent opposition to any form of apparent favoritism vis-à-vis minority groups, and particularly such groups as had not been long established in Syria. Because of this prevailing spirit, not only did it now seem unlikely that the Ghab Scheme would fulfill its purpose of providing a safe haven for Assyrians but also the authorities in charge of the project could not gain control of some plots that were privately owned, as the Moslem owners were unwilling to sell at any reasonable price.[36] The second reason was that the cost estimates on which the plans were based had been found to be much too low, in that insufficient provision had been made for malaria control measures. The League Council, having no means at its disposal for surmounting these difficulties, voted to abandon the Ghab plans and to endeavor to settle Assyrians on the less central Khabur River, where the complications were fewer.

ARAB REFUGEES

In 1946, after the withdrawal of the British and French officials from Syria, the government gave fairly high priority to the Ghab Scheme among the various plans then being considered for the development of agriculture. However, it was not until 1949, after a third group of refugees had fled to Syria, that the project once again assumed great prominence. In the fall of that year the Clapp Mission, after its study both of the question of long-range Syrian development and of the possibilities of work relief for the Arab war refugees from Palestine, strongly recommended that the Ghab Scheme be undertaken at the earliest possible date, and accorded preference over other major undertakings. The Mission considered that the scheme had

[36] Although more than half of the Ghab Valley lands were state domain, it was necessary also to purchase some private land in order to arrange for a settlement of Assyrians on the basis desired. For political reasons, the entire settlement was to be on the left bank of the river in the state of Latakia. The river served as a boundary between that state and the state of Syria. Cf. Ministère des Affaires Etrangères, *op. cit.*, 1925, p. 34; 1935, p. 59.

great potential value not only as to direct results and furnishing a model for planned settlement but also for acquainting Syrians with some of the problems which would have to be confronted in connection with future planning of agricultural improvements on a larger scale. The Mission also recommended, however, that a thorough study of all previous Ghab plans by French engineers and others should first be made, as a partial basis for the formulation of a completely integrated program. The estimated cost of the entire project, as envisaged in the Clapp report, was $16,460,000. The initial costs were to be defrayed by the United Nations, but the final apportionment was left open. The time required for completion was estimated at five years.[37]

The report provides some information as to the elements which should be taken into consideration in the formulation of the integrated plan for the Ghab Valley:

It is proposed to develop this valley completely as a unit. This will require construction of the necessary roads into the area, the provision of drainage works and canals, construction of a dam, if studies indicate it essential, to provide a reservoir for flood control storage during the periods of high stream flow and water for irrigation during periods of low flow, and if possible provide an additional source of the generation of hydroelectric power. A central village is also to be included as part of the development in order to provide adequate housing facilities for construction workers and in the future to partially satisfy the permanent housing requirements in the area. . . .

It will be necessary to determine by experiments the crops best suited and most profitable under the conditions which prevail. Possibilities may well prove to be long staple cotton, sugar-cane and oilseeds, all of which are needed for the development and expansion of Syria's industries. Fruit growing is unlikely to be a major activity. The place of mixed farming in the economy of the area requires consideration.

For this purpose it will be necessary to set up a small temporary experimental station for field investigations. An area of 100 acres should suffice and sufficient information should be obtained in a period of five years to meet the needs of the area. No expensive buildings need be provided. Syria does not at present possess a suitably qualified agronomist to conduct these investigations. It is recommended that a first-class agronomist be recruited from abroad for general agronomical research in Syria and a man of lower grade who will also have to be obtained

[37] United Nations, *op. cit.*, Part I, pp. 101-103 *et passim*.

from an outside country placed in charge of the Ghab experimental station under his control.[38]

Mainly because of the disturbed conditions in Syria described in the earlier part of this chapter, little or no progress has thus far been made in the formulation of plans along the lines recommended by the Clapp Mission. Also the Syrian Government, on at least one recent occasion, expressed the intention of financing the project by the sale of state-owned land in the Ghab Valley at the highest prices obtainable.[39] It is of interest, in this general connection, to note one pointed criticism of the Clapp proposals which has been made publicly by an Arab-American officer of the United States Department of Commerce:

Thinking has not progressed from the technical to the human aspects of this project. . . .
Who will own the land of the Ghab swamp? At present the land is mostly state domain, but partly owned by absentee landlords. Will it be state domain after development, or will it be held by absentee landlords? Who will benefit from it? Other questions arise as soon as the project is completed. How will you settle the people in this swampy area after you make it healthy for them to live there? Will it be the nuclear type of village, in which they have lived for thousands of years, will it be the line village, or will it be farmsteads as we have in this country? These human questions are as important as the technical ones.[40]

These questions are particularly pertinent in view of the experience which the French had, of providing irrigation facilities farther south along the Orontes and then seeing the water wasted because of the irrational state of water rights at the time.[41]
It should be added that little consideration seems to have been given to the possible effect upon Turkish interests of this proposed training of the Orontes waters. Since 1939 the lower flow of the Orontes has been in Turkish territory.[42]

[38] *Ibid.*, p. 102.
[39] Ross, "Syria to Finance Own Development," New York *Times*, March 5, 1950.
[40] Middle East Institute, *Americans and the Middle East: Partners in the Next Decade* (Washington, 1950), p. 39.
[41] Warriner, *op. cit.*, pp. 88-92.
[42] E. B. Worthington, *Middle East Science* (London, 1945), p. 57.

THE JEZIREH SCHEME

The Jezireh is a triangle-shaped province in the northeastern part of Syria, adjacent to the Turkish and Iraqi frontiers.

The cultivable area of the Jezireh is estimated at 2,500,000 acres, of which not more than 800,000 are now under cultivation,[43] even after large-scale wartime development. It is a region which offers decided potential advantages over nearly all other cultivable wastelands in the Middle East, not only because of its great extent and the absence of established and legalized precedents, but also because of the relative accessibility of important markets and because most of the idle land (i.e., possibly 1,250,000 to 1,500,000 acres) could apparently be utilized profitably for agriculture on a rain-fed basis. With additional agricultural machinery, and with people on hand to put such machinery to maximum advantage, the waste areas could be developed with comparatively small expenditure as against the cost of reclaiming an equal amount of land dependent upon irrigation for fertility. The additional absorptive capacity of the rain-fed area has been estimated at 200,000 persons in mechanized agriculture.[44]

A rich granary in Roman times, the Jezireh was almost entirely uncultivated during the modern era up to 1918, and was inhabited largely by nomads. The decade following the end of World War I saw an influx of Turkish minority groups, particularly Kurds and Christians, who came across the frontier to escape persecution and forced assimilation. During this same period, as well as later, there was some migration to the Jezireh of minority persons from other parts of Syria. A gradual but continuous reduction of nomadism in the province also took place, mainly because of official pressure, both direct and indirect. Other developments of the between-wars era were (1) land speculation in the Jezireh on the part of wealthy residents of Syrian cities and (2) the adoption by the League of Nations in 1937

[43] This estimate does not take into account the great cotton boom which occurred in 1950 and which, on November 15, 1951, appeared to be subsiding in great measure.

[44] United Nations, *op. cit.*, Part I, p. 89; Part II, pp. 26-27; Warriner, *op. cit.*, p. 132.

of a formal program for the permanent settlement along the Upper Khabur River of Assyrian refugees from Iraq.[45]

According to the best estimates available, there were in 1939 about 103,000 settled residents of the Jezireh. About 40,000 were Kurds and 30,000 Christians, most of the remainder being Moslem Arabs. There were also about 47,000 nomads spending all or a large part of their time in the Jezireh.[46]

By 1939, largely owing to the settlers' own enterprise, there were many villages and a few urban communities in the region. Also the mandatory government had established substantial control over the nomads, thereby increasing the settlers' security, and had built roads (though of poor quality) concerning the Jezireh with the main centers of population in Syria. However, except for the Assyrian settlement project, to be discussed later, all of these activities had been on a completely uncoordinated, haphazard basis. There had been no official attempt either to make systematic provision for large-scale cultivation of the Jezireh or to solve the increasingly acute problems connected with land rights. The latter question has not, even to this day, been taken up officially.

The reasons for these omissions were, in the main, political. Because of the predominance of the minority groups in the settled population of this border province, Moslem Arab nationalists feared the alienation of the Jezireh from Syria, whether through assumption by France of complete control or through Turkish intervention brought about by border troubles. The nationalists were consequently desirous of introducing an assimilation program, for the purpose of ending all distinctions between the minority groups in the Jezireh and the main body of Syrians. Such proposals, however, were strongly opposed, not only by Christians, but also by most of the Moslem Kurdish community. Perhaps the best solution would have been a permanent autonomous or special political status for the Jezireh. But it would have been most difficult to find any suitable basis for such a status.

[45] Eliahu Epstein (now Elath), "Al Jezireh," *Journal of the Royal Central Asian Society*, 1940, p. 68 *et seq.*; Hourani, *Minorities in the Arab World*, pp. 80-81.
[46] Hourani, *Syria and Lebanon*, p. 140; Epstein, *op. cit.*, p. 70; Ministère des Affaires Etrangères, *op. cit.*, 1937, p. 4; 1938, p. 220.

The various minority groups were united only in their common defensive attitude vis-à-vis the majority. Moreover, all of these groups taken together were outnumbered by Moslem Arabs, if the nomadic population was included in the calculations. In view of all these circumstances, any French-sponsored plan for the Jezireh which threatened to affect the existing distribution of population and of privileges was likely to produce trouble both for France and for the inhabitants of the region. Consequently the policy most frequently followed by the mandatory power was to permit events to shape themselves and at the same time to make every possible effort to maintain order. During the period from 1937 to 1939, after a substantial degree of real control had been transferred from French to Syrian hands, there were such serious disturbances in the province that France was forced to resume direct control temporarily.[47]

The Assyrian Settlement Scheme of 1937, though serving for a limited time as a good example of planned rural settlement,[48] must be regarded as representing a supplementary, rather than central, aspect of Jezireh development because it was based upon irrigated cultivation, for which some possibilities exist in the province. Instituted along both banks of the Upper Khabur River, it consisted mainly of a reorganization, under League of Nations direction, of the already existing provisional settlement of Assyrian refugees, with a view to putting that on a paying basis and also making suitable arrangements for health and education. The scheme was applied only to the 9000 Assyrians who were actually in Syria. The district of settlement was not accorded any special political status.[49]

[47] Hourani, *Syria and Lebanon, passim*; Hourani, *Minorities in the Arab World*, pp. 80-81.

[48] Up to 1941 the Assyrian Settlement Scheme was highly successful in that the colonists, many of whom were at the start unaccustomed to cultivation, became well adapted to the new conditions and also got along well with their non-Assyrian neighbors. During the war, however, their economy was seriously disrupted by the departure of many Assyrians to serve in the Iraq levies. There has never been any adequate subsequent adjustment, and the conditions of the colony have deteriorated greatly. Since the termination of the mandate, no official international inspection has taken place. Cf. Hourani, *Minorities in the Arab World*, p. 81; Worthington, *op. cit.*, p. 5.

[49] Bayard Dodge, "The Settlement of the Assyrians on the Khabur," *Journal of the Royal Asian Society*, 1940, Part III, pp. 301 *et seq.*; Warriner, *op. cit.*, p. 97.

In 1942 the first definite scheme was adopted for a large-scale increase in the cultivated area of the Jezireh. In that year the Middle East Supply Centre (an Anglo-American wartime organization)[50] and the Syrian Office des Céréales Panifiables (O.C.P.) made the joint decision to introduce large amounts of machinery for cultivation of the rain-fed areas of the Jezireh, as one of the means of helping to alleviate the war-caused food shortages in the Middle East. The main planning for the effective use of the machinery was done by the M.E.S.C. According to all reports, considerable difficulties were experienced in connection with this project, mainly because of the unfamiliarity of Syrians with mechanical techniques but also because of the confusion in regard to land rights and the prevalence of the traditional but irrational method of strip farming.[51] Because of the urgency of the program, the M.E.S.C. found it inexpedient to attempt to settle these matters immediately in ways calculated to bring about a permanent improvement in the living standards of the cultivators. Postwar reports of M.E.S.C. officials, however, show that the way was at all times left open for eventual efforts in that direction.[52] It now seems likely that, had the war lasted a year or two longer, effective steps along that line might have been possible; by 1945 the M.E.S.C. had become generally recognized as an efficient and useful general economic planning board for the Middle East as a whole. But, because of the strong wish of the Syrian Government in 1945 to end all official foreign-directed activities in the country, there was no possibility for an arrangement which might permit the uninterrupted continuance of this important development.

In its endeavors both to expand cultivation in the Jezireh and to rationalize existing cultivation with a view to meeting the greatly increased demand for food in the Middle East, the M.E.S.C. acted through the instrumentalities of the national and local governments

[50] As far as Syria was concerned, the administration of the Middle East Supply Centre was British. However, the equipment imported for the projects was mainly American.

[51] B. A. Keen, *The Agricultural Development of the Middle East* (London, 1946), p. 14; Warriner, *op. cit.*, p. 2.

[52] The principal published reports written by such officials were: E. B. Worthington, *Middle East Science* (London, 1945); Doreen Warriner, *Land and Poverty in the Middle East* (London, 1948); B. A. Keen, *The Agricultural Development of the Middle East* (London, 1946).

and of the large landholders of the Jezireh.[53] Because the prevailing high prices of food suggested the possibilities of large profits, the landholders were reasonably cooperative. Also, because the war situation was curtailing normal occupational facilities to a large extent, it proved possible to recruit a fairly substantial additional labor force for the expanded cultivation.

The statistics which are available, though fragmentary, give some idea as to the accomplishments of the M.E.S.C. in the Jezireh. It is known that, before the outbreak of World War II, the quantity of agricultural machinery in Syria was negligible.[54] According to a United Nations survey made in late 1949, there were at that time 600-700 tractors and 350 combine harvesters in the country. About 400 of the tractors, and all of the combine harvesters, were located in the Jezireh. A large fraction of these totals must represent wartime importation. During the period immediately following the war, importation was greatly restricted by the short supplies abroad, and in 1948 and 1949 the Syrian demand was small because of the unexportable wheat surpluses. The existence of these surpluses, incidentally, must not be taken to indicate that the Syrian populace as a whole was particularly well nourished during those years. The problem of distributing surplus food among those who need it has yet to be solved in Syria.[55]

Statistics are also available for the cultivated acreage of the Jezireh in 1943 and 1946—543,600 and 783,000 respectively. The difference can be safely assumed to represent the approximate expansion in cultivation due to the efforts of the Middle East Supply Centre.[56]

During the years 1946-49 there was apparently little, if any, increase in the sown area of the Jezireh. Moreover, some of the advantages brought by the M.E.S.C. were disappearing. For example, the facilities

[53] Since there was no Lend-Lease agreement between the United States and Syria, the supply of equipment was necessarily mainly on a cash-purchase basis.

[54] Some German agricultural machinery was introduced into Syria before World War I, but it was never put to any useful purpose. Syrians were not yet ready to use such machinery effectively. Cf. Himadeh, *op. cit.*, p. 90.

[55] United Nations, *op. cit.*, Part II, p. 25; Maan Zilfo Madina, "A T.V.A. in Syria" (unpublished Master's thesis, University of Chicago, December, 1949), p. 87.

[56] Warriner, *op. cit.*, p. 81; United Nations, *op. cit.*, Part II, p. 26.

for repair and servicing of tractors have been inadequate, and there is
no indication of any official intention to remedy that situation.[57]
Nevertheless, in 1950 it was reported that "the province of Djezireh
enjoyed something on the order of a Western United States land
boom as moneyed men from Aleppo and Damascus rushed to break
new land to plant cotton."[58] No statistical details are yet available, but
Mr. Afif I. Tannous has supplied the following information in regard
to this development:

On the surface, this appears to be the beginning of a sound development. Upon closer examination, however, we encounter a different
reality. The tractor has been put on that fertile soil mostly by speculators
and absentee owners. Concern about the ultimate exploitation of this
great national resource is not uppermost in their minds. Furthermore,
they put the new land under cultivation through an understanding with
the local tribal chief. He guarantees them "protection" of the crop in
return for a portion of the produce. Nowhere does the peasant figure in
this deal other than as a laborer or a sharecropper.[59]

According to all expert foreign observers, the Jezireh offers by far
the most important possibilities for the raising of living standards in
Syria.[60] But, although at the time of writing the construction of
better roads to that province was being heavily stressed in Syrian
developmental thinking, in other respects there is no evidence that any
government, since the acquisition of independence, has ever given
high priority to the matter of Jezireh planning. The most likely
reason for the reluctance is that the government, dominated as it is by
the landlord class but pledged to efforts to raise living standards, has
not wished to become involved in the questions of land tenure which
would necessarily arise in connection with any state-sponsored scheme
for promoting general agrarian welfare in an area controlled principally
by large landholders.[61] As for the troubles caused by the conflicts
between racial and religious groups in the Jezireh, present indications
are that these have been declining in importance, at least since 1947.

[57] United Nations, op. cit., Part II, pp. 25-27.
[58] New York Times, January 3, 1951, p. 79.
[59] Afif I. Tannous, "Land Reform: Key to the Development and Stability of the
Arab World," Middle East Journal, Winter, 1951, p. 11.
[60] Warriner, op. cit., p. 132; United Nations, op. cit., Part II, pp. 25-27.
[61] Warriner, op. cit., p. 96.

The Clapp Mission, in its report of December, 1949, expressed the strong belief that the Syrian Government should, without further delay, prepare an integrated plan for the development of the Jezireh and that, immediately upon completion of the planning, the scheme should be put into effect. It is of interest in that connection to note that neither the Clapp Mission nor any of the other recent expert observers seemed to have any doubt that an adequate transfer of population could be made from other parts of Syria for the realization of such a scheme, and that it would be possible to train the new settlers to use the machinery which would be necessary. Apparently the results of the Anglo-Syrian wartime venture were such as to provide evidence that these problems are soluble ones.

The Clapp report does refer—perhaps too casually—to the difficulties which would inevitably occur in connection with land rights, and expressed the opinion that the time for settlement of these matters is now. An immediate cadastral survey is strongly recommended in the report.

According to estimates made by the Syrian Government in 1948, which the Clapp Mission seemed to find sufficiently conservative, the total development of the Jezireh land suitable for rain-fed cultivation, together with the construction of the necessary roads, could be completed in five years at a cost of about $19,000,000.[62]

The absence of substantial action on these recommendations suggests the conclusion that, unless some drastic political change occurs, there is no near-future likelihood of any major planned economic developments involving the Jezireh.

[62] United Nations, *op. cit.*, Part I, p. 89.

CHAPTER VII

❖

Iraq

Iraq's large program of national development was still in a relatively early stage of advancement on December 31, 1950. Hence any evaluation of the status and prospects, to the extent that general living standards are involved, must be based largely upon a thorough consideration of the pertinent background conditions.

GENERAL BACKGROUND

In the years from 1919 to 1932 Iraq was first under British military occupation for a brief period, then subject to British mandatory rule, under which the Iraqi governments were accorded a large share of administrative responsibility. Since 1932 Iraq has been independent.

For reasons which are discussed below, and which were set forth in clear detail in the British *Special Report on the Progress of Iraq, 1920-1931*, conditions during the earlier period were at no time propitious for major planning for the advancement of the people as a whole.[1] As for the years from 1932 to 1945, world-wide economic depression and later world warfare, superimposed on political immaturity, created additional obstacles, both to planning and to a

---

[1] *Special Report by His Majesty's Government in the United Kingdom of Great Britain and Northern Ireland to the Council of the League of Nations on the Progress of Iraq During the Period 1920-1931* (hereinafter referred to as *Progress Report*) (London, 1931), *passim.*

removal of the major hindrances thereto. The period following the end of World War II has been marked by an apparent determination on the part of Iraqis to make up for lost time.

The *need* for major planning seems to have been fully recognized by politically conscious Iraqis at an early date. European social ideologies were rapidly becoming popular as early as 1920. There was not, however, any adequate recognition of the importance of individual adaptation to those ideologies, in the matter of personal attitudes and relationships, as opposed to mere advocacy. This difficulty persists, though in slightly reduced degree.[2]

In the following paragraphs, summaries are given of specific situations, other than strictly temporary ones, which have adversely affected planning for the standard of living in Iraq.

THE HETEROGENEOUS POPULACE

The Iraqi populace was, and still is, far from homogeneous. The ruling class, composed largely of Sunni Moslem Arabs resident in or near the country's few large towns,[3] has found itself opposed, to a greater or lesser extent, by: (1) the Shia Moslem community, which outnumbers the Sunni element by a small margin, even when non-Arabs are included in the latter;[4] (2) the Kurdish racial minority, armed and often martially inclined, amounting to between 15 and 20 per cent of the total Iraqi population, which in 1948 was estimated at 4,950,000; (3) much smaller, but wealthy and powerful, communities of Christians and (until recently) Jews, with group interests often at variance with those of the dominant minority; (4) powerful Arab tribal leaders, no longer nomadic in most cases but still distrustful of the urban elements in the populace, against whom they have had to

[2] Ernest Main, *Iraq: From Mandate to Independence* (London, 1935), pp. 215-216, 235.

[3] Their power was originally based on the fact that it was a Sunni Arab group which first concerned itself with the establishment of an independent Iraq. This group, which had the support of the British mandatory power, was headed by Feisal, former King of Syria. Feisal became King of Iraq in 1921. His immediate followers were ardent Arab nationalists from various parts of the Arab world.

[4] Royal Institute of International Affairs, *The Middle East: A Political and Economic Survey* (London, 1950), p. 240.

struggle in order to retain their local political and economic power. The importance of these oppositions, taken as a whole, is unquestionably declining; in 1947, for example, a Shiite, Salih Jabr, became Prime Minister of the country. Nevertheless the reality of the divisions is still a force to be reckoned with.

FORCES OF RESISTANCE TO SOCIAL PROGRESS

Although education was greatly extended in Iraq during the period 1919-45, and although members of formerly uneducated families are admitted to government positions at all levels, the beneficial results of this development have been limited by two main factors. The first was the fact that the older generation of town-dwelling Iraqis was uncompromisingly opposed to any social change which might cause the immediate interests of the family group to be subordinated to the interests of the larger and more comprehensive groups, such as the national government. This older generation succeeded, moreover, in having its way, at least to the extent that younger Iraqi officials, however well educated and however much they might at heart deplore the situation, have tended to be unduly mindful of their relatives' petitions and whims, and hence to perpetuate a state of affairs which conflicted sharply with the general good of the country. The second factor was the undesirable new psychological attitudes which developed to a great degree among the newly educated class (often known as the "effendi class"). The members of this group began to regard themselves as an aristocracy, with many and strict limitations upon the activities in which they could with dignity engage. Engineering and technical occupations were excluded because they were associated with manual labor, which was regarded as degrading. As for work which necessitated residence outside of the large towns, that was considered both degrading and distasteful. Perhaps worst of all, the members of this group, while in principle solicitous as to the general standard of living of the entire populace, in practice attached undue importance to their own living standards, these being based on exalted ideas rather than on ascertained financial capacities. It seems probable that this latter trait, still much in evidence,[5] had its origins during the period of great prosperity which Iraq enjoyed during the early years of the mandate. However that may be, it has been an element in the prevention of any widespread development of a true social conscience in the higher social brackets. It has also hindered the establishment of satisfactory relations between urban and rural elements.[6]

THE DOMINANCE OF VESTED INTERESTS

Both under the mandate and thereafter, the Iraqi cabinets and legislatures have been controlled by large absentee landowners residing in the large towns. These officials, apart from watching after their own personal and class interests, have had to be somewhat conciliatory toward the effendi class, and also toward the Arab shaikhs, many of whom, as large landowners themselves, have been partially absorbed into the ruling class. But the government leaders have been under no corresponding necessity to consider the interests of the common agriculturists who now constitute the great mass of the Iraqi populace and whose conditions, nearly always forlorn since the end of the Arab golden age, have, as will later be seen, been deteriorating since the end of the mandate.[7] In short, the government's policies have tended to be based upon vested interests and short-term political expediency rather than upon the long-range needs of Iraq taken as a whole.[8]

EXTREME ARAB NATIONALISM

Extreme Arab nationalism at top governmental levels, with its scapegoat psychology and its eagerly grasped implications that opportunities for all Arabs will be greatly increased when the alleged foreign strangleholds are reduced, has perhaps been a necessary corollary to the situations described in the last three paragraphs. This national-

[5] "Land Reform Tops Iraq Development," New York Times, December 10, 1950.

[6] Main, op. cit., pp. 169, 234-236; Progress Report, p. 241.

[7] Progress Report, pp. 238-240; Main, op. cit., p. 26; Doreen Warriner, Land and Poverty in the Middle East (London, 1948), pp. 106, 113.

[8] Alfred Bonné, The Economic Development of the Middle East (London, 1945), pp. 36, 38; Warriner, op. cit., p. 119; Albion Ross, "Development Is Main Iraqi Issue," New York Times, January 22, 1950; Main, op. cit., p. 182.

ism has produced extensive damage in that it has diverted attention
from vital economic and social issues and focused it upon exaggerated
political oppositions which have hampered economic and social progress. Some of the results have been: (1) unwillingness to allot adequate funds to government departments which were under strong
British influence, even when such British influence was unquestionably beneficial and not at all motivated by British self-interest;[9] (2)
sustained hostility of the non-Arab elements in the populace, especially the large Kurdish group;[10] (3) virtual expatriation of the Jewish
community, which has traditionally played an important and essential
role in the Iraqi economy, without any apparent plans for filling the
vacuum thus created;[11] (4) a chronic and morbid distrust, on the
part of the politically conscious populace in general, of the motives of
Western governments and firms.[12]

THE LAND-TENURE QUESTION

Perhaps the most unfortunate development in Iraq has been the
direction which the official settlement of land tenure assumed. In the
days of the mandate the British had enforced their view that it would
not be desirable, generally speaking, to settle land titles permanently
until a thorough investigation had been made in regard to the existing legal status of land occupancy. This whole matter was exceedingly
complicated because of the confused state of the records which the
Ottoman authorities had maintained, the shifting nature of the
cultivation in Iraq, and the continual tribal migration of seminomads.
The British authorities wished, before taking action of a permanently
binding nature, to study the political and economic implications for
the future of any new principles which might be introduced. Their

[9] This situation applied even after the termination of the mandate, as there
were still numerous British officials in Iraqi government departments. These were
under long-term contracts which could not legally be terminated. Cf. Main,
op. cit., pp. 42, 183, 205.
[10] The present outlook, as regards Arab-Kurd relations, is unclear. In some
respects there has been an improvement during recent years.
[11] "Israel, Iraq Study Population Shift," New York *Times*, July 4, 1950.
[12] "Neutrality Backed in Iraq," New York *Times*, July 3, 1950; Elizabeth
Monroe, "British Interests in the Middle East," *Middle East Journal*, April, 1948,
p. 140.

clear inclination, however, was to envisage land settlement in terms of individual holdings of some sort or other. From the evolutionary viewpoint, some system of collective ownership of land might have been more compatible with the inclinations of the Iraqi rural communities, most of which still had the tribal form of organization, coupled with a dearth of understanding of the full implications of Western-style individualism. The predominance of irrigated cultivation also enters into this question.[13]

Nevertheless, it was the Western point of view in regard to land settlement which ultimately won out—not because the British reached a decision to put it into effect, but because both the absentee landlords of the cities and the tribal shaikhs in the area of cultivation saw distinct advantages in it from the standpoint of their own private interests. The privileges and powers of the landlords were being menaced by the increases in educational facilities and the consequent gradual reduction of their class's monopoly on learning. Only through a complete legalization of their *de facto* control over a large segment of the peasantry could this growing menace to their position be met. The shaikhs, for their part, feared the growing encroachments of the central government upon the tribal domains, where they were accustomed to rule without outside interference.[14] It was important to them to acquire a legal status which the government would be obliged to recognize and respect.

From 1932 on, the Iraqi authorities proceeded to settle titles on a basis of individual ownership. The result was a highly irrational one, though it has conceivably strengthened the government politically for the time being. Many a tribal shaikh whose previous role, at least in customary law, had been that of trustee and administrator of cooperatively farmed lands held in common by the tribe, was enabled by the settlement to acquire sole ownership of large tracts.[15]

This situation arose partly through the registration of great areas of tribally held lands in the names of tribal leaders and partly through subsequent credit operations whereunder lands settled in

[13] Warriner, *op. cit.*, pp. 21, 109.
[14] Main, *op. cit.*, p. 26.
[15] Warriner, *op. cit.*, p. 104.

favor of ordinary tribesmen passed legally into the shaikh's hands in default of debt payments. The latter process had been made possible by the growth of the export market for Iraqi grain, which had introduced the element of money into the tribal economy and a consequent growing preference among shaikhs for individual gains, as against attention to the tribes' needs. Other factors contributing to the final result were: (1) the ignorance and illiteracy of the ordinary tribesman; (2) the world-wide agricultural depression, which prevented peasants from repaying the debts which they had contracted; and (3) the great expansion of pump irrigation in Iraq from 1919 on, due partly to the temporary relative prosperity of the *fellahin* and partly to the shaikhs' loss of interest in performing the traditional tribal function of providing flow irrigation facilities for their respective communities. At the end of World War I there were only a scattered few motor-driven irrigation pumps in Iraq. By 1944 there were about 3000, and over one-half of Iraq's irrigated land derived its water by this means. The small farmers' dependence on pumps gave rise to extensive credit operations in addition to the ordinary advances for crop expenses. In many of the cases of default and foreclosure the pump owner was a tribal shaikh. In perhaps even more cases city merchants and other town dwellers were enabled to acquire possession of large rural domains by substantially the same process. The end result has been that a very large proportion of the cultivated land in Iraq is in the hands either of shaikhs who have ceased to perform any essential agricultural function or of urban residents whose participation in agriculture is confined to speculation and exploitation (by remote control) of the human material.[16]

Except as to education, there is now little difference between the shaikhs and the urban absentee landlords. Moreover, even this difference is being gradually erased as more and more shaikhs send their

[16] An excellent discussion of most of the matters contained in this paragraph is to be found in *Land and Poverty in the Middle East*, by Doreen Warriner, pp. 99-119.

The statements made here in regard to the conditions of agriculturists are, in general, not applicable to the northern rain-fed cultivated area, where small landowners are quite common and the general situation is somewhat better. That area, however, comprises only about 25 per cent of the total acreage annually under crops. (*Ibid.*, pp. 9, 108.)

sons to the cities for schooling. In such cases the son seldom returns permanently to the tribal area.[17] Later, when his father dies and he succeeds as shaikh, he is hardly distinguishable from any other urban absentee landowner. The result, insofar as the ordinary members of the formerly democratic tribe are concerned, was described as follows by Miss Doreen Warriner in 1948:

In the regions of pump irrigation the tribal system has entirely ceased to function. The land is mainly the property of the pump owners, with the cultivators taking a meagre share of the crop, varying from 1/7 to 1/14 or 1/21 of the total. The position of the share-tenant in Iraq is much worse than of his counterpart in Syria.

In districts of flood irrigation the tribal system has disintegrated, but its superstructure, the sheikhs and sirkals, remains. Most of the political functions of the tribe have now been transferred to the State, and the only economic function now performed by the tribal authorities is the control of irrigation, digging of canals, and repairing of breaches, which is done by the cultivators under the direction of the sirkal who has become a kind of farm bailiff acting for the sheikh. Under this system the sheikh and sirkal take together up to 80 percent of the crop, leaving the cultivator some 20–30 percent.[18]

In 1943 the government in power made all these matters still worse by adopting a policy of selling state-owned lands at auction to individuals for the alleged purpose of stopping the growing inflation. At that time more than half of the potentially cultivable land in Iraq was still owned by the state, and there was still the possibility that the above-described state of affairs could be alleviated by sound governmental policies applied to these state domains in connection with projects for irrigation or large-scale mechanization. Instead, the power of the absentee landowner classes has been still further consolidated, though there are no authoritative estimates as to the amount of land which they acquired as a result of these sales. The objectionable practice seems to have been terminated by 1946.[19]

SHORTAGE OF AGRICULTURAL MAN POWER

For the work necessary to develop the country up to its possibilities, Iraq has always suffered from an acute shortage of agricultural man

[17] *Progress Report*, p. 236.
[18] Warriner, *op. cit.*, pp. 106-107.
[19] *Ibid.*, pp. 116, 118.

power. Apparently this situation would not be relieved in large measure by settlement of the remainder of the nomadic population.

With a potential crop acreage amounting to at least 17,000,000 acres and probably a great deal more, as against 6,000,000-7,000,000 cropped annually under existing conditions, it has long been clear that a systematic and efficient exploitation of all the untapped agricultural wealth (by far the greater part of which would be produced under irrigated conditions), together with an equitable distribution of the wealth among the populace, could result in abundance for a population greatly exceeding the present one. According to at least one estimate, Iraq is the only Middle Eastern country which can plausibly envisage the possibility of a general standard of living comparable to Western standards. Here, of course, Iraq's oil resources must also be taken into consideration.[20]

Because of the existence of a great network of ancient canals, a large part of the most fertile land not being used can be reached and utilized through an application of relatively simple irrigation procedures either by the government or by large landholders acting on their own initiative. The land in this category must be regarded, for all practical purposes, as part of the presently cultivable area. But, in view of the labor shortage, it has proved impossible to place more than a small part of this total area under crops in any given year. As is almost inevitable in such circumstances if the peasantry are not emotionally tied to certain fixed locations, the regular practice has been followed of shifting the cultivation from the lands which at any given time are providing decreasing yields to those which are momentarily more promising. This practice is enormously wasteful, preventing as it does any devotion of attention to achieving the best possible results from each plot of land, and also resulting in a general rise in the costs of cultivation as the better and more easily irrigable lands deteriorate. It is only in spite of the existing farming practices that Iraq's inherent fertility nearly always produces a substantial export surplus. In 1946, for example, 255,416 tons of barley and 19,040 tons of "other grains, pulses, and flour" were exported. Iraq's

[20] Ross, "Iraq Seeks Expert for Drainage Plan," New York *Times*, October 31, 1950.

date production, based on a grove of 6,000,000 trees, is the largest in the world.[21]

Iraq's urgent need has always been a sufficient increase of farm population to work the whole of the presently cultivable area with such techniques and implements as are practicable, and her long-term requirement is a rate of population increase consonant with the expansions in that area occurring after the first condition has been met.[22] Clearly the optimum rate of increase would be lowered by the introduction of machinery, the development of mechanical skills in agriculture, and improvements in the education and health of the average cultivator.

STANDARDS OF LIVING

The *Progress Report* of the British mandatory power, published in 1931, contained the following statement: "The high prices obtainable for grain in the post-war years certainly enabled the fallah to buy for the first time such things as cigarettes, tea, sugar, and shoes. These luxuries have now become necessities and the fallah feels the fall in grain prices greatly. He has plenty of food, but no money to buy anything."[23]

However, the *Final Report of the United Nations Economic Survey Mission for the Middle East*, published in December, 1949, stated that "the use of money is confined to a relatively small proportion of the population."[24] In view of the general loss by the *fellahin* of their defenses against exploitation by the landlords, it is safe to assume that, both during the period immediately preceding World War II and during the present era, the general conditions of life have been far below those obtaining in the early days of the

[21] Warriner, *op. cit.*, p. 102; *Progress Report*, p. 198; E. B. Worthington, *Middle East Science* (London, 1945), p. 50; B. A. Keen, *The Agricultural Development of the Middle East* (London, 1946), pp. 30, 86; Royal Institute of International Affairs, *op. cit.*, p. 267.

[22] Ahmed Sousa, *Irrigation in Iraq, Its History and Development* (Baghdad, 1945), p. 50; J'afar Pasha el Askeri, "Five Years' Progress in Iraq," *Journal of the Royal Central Asian Society*, 1927, Part I, p. 65.

[23] *Progress Report*, p. 239.

[24] *Final Report of the United Nations Economic Survey Mission for the Middle East* (Lake Success, N.Y., 1949), Part I, p. 44.

mandate. Those conditions are probably worse, on the whole, than in the days of the Ottoman Empire, when a large part of the rural income was distributed equitably within tribal communities. As for a comparison between present-day conditions and 1939 conditions, there is certainly not the slightest evidence that the situation has been improving for the peasantry as a whole.[25]

There is, moreover, reason to believe that the productive efficiency of the Iraqi *fellah* is very low, even as judged by Middle Eastern standards. One consequence of the shifting, extensive, and wasteful cultivation has been the retention by the *fellahin* in general of character traits which are particularly inimical to attempts to raise their status. Those traits are rootlessness, lack of interest in their work, slackening of efforts when guaranteed a fixed daily wage, ignorance, poor health conditions, and general inertia. Furthermore, "every kind of device and implement is primitive in the extreme, and most of them, including the plough, have been unchanged in the course of several millennia."[26]

Since 1918 Iraq's cropped area in the irrigation zone has been increasing by about 130,000 to 140,00 acres annually.[27] From 1930 to 1948 the total increase amounted to about 95 per cent of the previous area, while at the same time the country's population increase,

---

[25] It is true that, from 1945 on, there have been several agrarian reform projects. However, in the stages in which these now are, there is no likelihood that their results are adequate to offset further deterioration in the general living standards of cultivators in the greater part of the irrigated zone. Cf. "Land Reform Tops Iraqi Development," New York *Times*, December 10, 1950; Afif I. Tannous, "Land Reform: Key to the Development and Stability of the Arab World," *Middle East Journal*, Winter, 1951, p. 16.

As for the living standards of urban workers, these seem to have followed, in general, the same trends as those of cultivators during the period 1919-50. The early mandate era was one of great prosperity, in which all participated to a greater or lesser extent because of the free spending which then took place. This state of affairs was never restored. As for the post-World War II era, the cost of living has been at all times excessively high, particularly for food and clothing. Cost of living indexes at Baghdad for all items have been: 1939—100; 1945—584; 1946—567; 1947—601; 1948—673; 1949—540; 1950—507. Cf. Royal Institute of International Affairs, *op. cit.*, p. 264.

[26] United Nations, *op. cit.*, Part I, p. 43; Keen, *op. cit.*, p. 29; Royal Institute of International Affairs, *op. cit.*, p. 258.

[27] Sousa, *op. cit.*, p. 49; Warriner, *op. cit.*, p. 99.

according to official estimates, was 75 per cent. Offhand, this might seem to indicate that the Iraqi peasant was at least improving somewhat in efficiency. Due allowance must, however, be made for possible errors in the statistical data, for the continuous change-over from nomadism to settled agriculture, and for the probability that in some cases greater acreages are being cultivated with lessened intensity. If this is done, the probable proper conclusion would seem to be that the per capita productive capacity of the *fellahin* has altered but little since 1918.[28]

There is here a distinctly vicious circle, wherein the continued low status of the *fellahin* and the continuance of wasteful methods of cultivation are reciprocally both cause and effect. For example, after great difficulties had been experienced from 1925 to 1930 in the matter of introducing some of the *fellahin* to modern practices including the use of machinery, the hopes of substantial accomplishments along these lines apparently faded away. One result was that, more than ever before, the landlords' understanding of and belief in the country's future possibilities were outweighed by their clear perception of the short-range benefit to themselves as individuals from a continance of cultivation on the traditional bases.[29]

EARLY DEVELOPMENTAL ACTIVITIES

GENERAL DEVELOPMENT

Although until 1945 no major planning for improved standards of living occurred, there was no lack of developmental enterprise in the earlier years. Extension of road and rail communications[30] and of navigation facilities, including particularly the development of the port of Basra, was carried out, though not on a basis of integrated consideration of long-range needs. River control is discussed under a separate heading.

[28] United Nations, *op. cit.*, Part II, p. 32.

[29] This sentiment on the part of landlords was necessarily closely reflected in governmental policies.

[30] In 1940 Iraq's railway system was at last linked up with Syria, Turkey, and all of Europe. Cf. P. W. Ireland, "The Baghdad Railway," *Journal of the Royal Central Asian Society*, 1941, Part III.

The great petroleum developments of the between-wars period, while providing a considerable increase in governmental revenue (exceeding £2,000,000 in fiscal 1944-45), did not have the stimulating effect on economic progress for which both British and Iraqis had hoped. Although the official policy of each successive government was to impound the oil revenues in special funds for public works expenditures, in practice these moneys were often applied to the solution of ordinary budget difficulties caused at first by the depression and later by the disinclination of department heads to see their bureaus cut off from this source of income. Further, until recently, the Iraqi governments were disinclined to obtain sizable foreign loans by pledging future oil revenues as security. Thus, although the so-called "capital works budgets" were never discontinued, the various "year plans" which were based upon them were usually of relatively small scope and not even wholly confined to economic and social developmental activities.[31]

Industrial development, even to this day, has been on a small scale despite the great amount of official attention devoted to it. The capital needed for it proved to be unavailable, mainly because it was politically inexpedient to adopt measures restricting the flow of surplus private funds into foreign investments, speculative land purchases, and loans to peasants at extremely high interest rates. Even though some cabinet officials might have been glad to establish such restrictions, they were not in a position to press the issue since their power depended on the support of persons habitually using their surplus funds so. In 1945 there were ninety-six manufacturing establishments in Iraq, all of which would have been classifiable as minor in nature. Agriculture was, and still is, all-important.

RIVER CONTROL

As for planning in the matter of river control and development, the first scheme was drawn up even before the British occupation of Iraq. This plan, however, was apparently not based upon any official

[31] Monroe, *op. cit.*, p. 140; *Oriente Moderno*, October, 1936, p. 579; "Iraq," *Encyclopaedia Britannica*, 1946 ed., p. 591; Fritz Grobba, *Irak* (Berlin, 1941), p. 90; United Nations, *op. cit.*, Part I, p. 44.

urge to improve the general position of the common man in the country. Probably the main circumstance giving rise to the Ottoman Government's interest was the fact that lucrative export markets had appeared for some of Iraq's agricultural products.

In 1908 the Ottoman Government employed Sir William Will-cocks, a British irrigation engineer, to examine the Tigris-Euphrates system and to make recommendations regarding large-scale control measures. The first result was the publication in 1911 of Willcocks' report, entitled *The Irrigation of Mesopotamia*. The second was the completion, in 1913, under Willcocks' direction, of the first great modern control structure on either river, namely, the Hindiya Bar-rage on the Euphrates. Before the period of Willcocks' activities the irrigation system of Iraq had been in extremely poor—indeed, steadily deteriorating—condition for many centuries. Quite a number of the ancient canals were used for irrigation by crude or makeshift methods, but no new works of any consequence had been constructed, and most of the old structures and ditches were no more than degenerate monuments of a glorious past.[32]

The pioneering work begun by Willcocks was continued by the British authorities during and after World War I, until 1932. Most of the British activities, however, were in the nature of repair and improvement of existing works, the development of canals rather than the rivers themselves, and the compilation of records in regard to the rivers' behavior. During most of the 1932-39 period, when the Iraqi Government was completely independent insofar as economic proj-ects were concerned, Iraq was in the throes of economic depression and budgetary difficulties. A further problem was the instability of governments and the tendency for each new cabinet to alter the irrigation and river-control plans made or begun by its predecessor. The probable main reason for this latter tendency was the great difficulty experienced by every successive cabinet in keeping the loudly critical "effendi class" pacified while at the same time main-taining order and guarding the interests of the landlord classes, upon whose support the cabinets were absolutely dependent. With these

[32] *Progress Report*, p. 178; M. G. Ionides, *The Regime of the Rivers Euphrates and Tigris* (London, 1937), *passim*; Main, *op. cit.*, p. 15.

conditions prevailing, the best chances of staying in power for any length of time seemed to lie in offering programs which were spectacular and different. Also, however, personal vanity and strong personal rivalries within the ruling clique were elements in the situation.[33]

From 1939 to 1945 the war stood in the way of river development. Only one large-scale undertaking was completed on either of Iraq's main rivers between the end of World War I and December 31, 1950. That was the Kut Barrage, on the Tigris River to the South of Baghdad, finished in 1939. It, like the Hindiya Barrage, is not comparable in magnitude to some of the projected works now under consideration. During practically the whole of the period the intention was officially held to complete the Lake Habbaniya project, commenced before World War I by Sir William Willcocks. This involved the use of a large lake (and possibly also a near-by depression) as a flood escape and storage reservoir for the Euphrates River. Despite its relatively modest cost, the project was continually postponed;[34] although actual work on it was at last commenced after the end of World War II, it had not yet been completed by the time of writing. At that time there were no additional partially completed major works on either river or on the tributaries of either.

Particularly significant in these early programs and activities with respect to river control and water-resources development is the fact that, while much attention was being paid to the matter of increasing the croppable acreage, little consideration was given to the restoration of the soil which had deteriorated through neglect or misuse. In the United Nations Survey Mission's *Final Report* the following statement appears:

"The area of salt-deteriorated land apparently exceeds one million

[33] *Progress Report*, pp. 180-182, 191; Ross, "Development Is Main Iraqi Issue," New York *Times*, January 22, 1950.
[34] Work on this project was first stopped by the outbreak of World War I. In December, 1939, a second attempt was made to get ahead with the scheme when a construction contract was signed between the Iraqi Government and a British firm, which made some further progress. This program was, however, forestalled by the outbreak of the pro-German revolt in Iraq in 1941. Cf. V. H. Dowson, "Iraq in 1946," *Journal of the Royal Central Asian Society*, 1946, Part III, p. 252.

acres. . . . Drainage is the principal treatment necessary for the reclamation. The main salts in the soil are highly soluble and if they
are leached out into a suitable drainage system which will dispose of
the saline water, reclamation is comparatively easy and rapid. Nothing has been done so far in the development of soil drainage in the
country."[35]

THE DUJAYLA PLAN

When World War II came to an end, there was a general realization in Iraq that the steps previously taken in the direction of
realizing Iraq's great agricultural possibilities had been woefully inadequate. Moreover, the results of the research and investigation during the war by the Middle East Supply Centre and other wartime
organizations had been such as to redouble the emphases upon the
country's potentialities for future richness.[36] Consequently a strong
popular clamor had begun for constructive activities on a large scale,
and especially for such activities as would surely bring an elevation of
living standards.

It seems clear also that the roots of this sentiment penetrated more
deeply in Iraq than in most other Middle Eastern countries. Unlike
their counterparts in such countries as Egypt, Syria, Lebanon, and
Iran, even the landowning classes in Iraq had arrived at the belief
that a general elevation of rural living standards was essential from
the viewpoint of their own direct interests. There seemed to be not
much choice for them but to see their future returns from agriculture
soon dwindling or, alternatively, to make every possible effort to raise
the efficiency of the cultivators. In theory, a large-scale immigration
program might have produced a solution; but public sentiment was
strongly against that idea because it had been urged by Zionists and
their supporters as a means of reducing the Arab population of
Palestine and thereby removing the main obstacle to the creation of
a Jewish state in that country.[37]

[35] United Nations, op. cit., Part II, p. 31.
[36] Harold Beeley, "The Middle East in 1939 and 1944," Journal of the Royal
Central Asian Society, 1945, Part I, p. 12.
[37] "Mr. Hoover's Plan," Arab News Bulletin (Washington, January 1, 1946);
Bonné, op. cit., p. 143; Warriner, op. cit., p. 4.

The official policy was adopted in 1945 of taking all practicable steps to convert Iraq into a country largely cultivated with mechanized equipment.[38] Comprised in the policy was a gradual building up, in as large a segment of the rural populace as possible, of the skills and attitudes essential to the success of such a program. This did not, however, involve any breaking up of great private estates, or any training program involving peasants established on those estates as sharecroppers. In other words, it would appear that, greatly as a peasant populace of more substantial quality is desired, there is still no disposition among large landowners to sacrifice any part of their present position of political and economic power, as far as their existing rural communities are concerned. Under the circumstances, the progress is bound to be slow, as the amount of uncommitted rural man power available is distinctly limited.

The first definite step in implementation of this policy and the subsequent developments which have occurred up to the end of 1950 along the same lines have recently been described by Mr. Afif I. Tannous[39] as follows:

In 1945, the Iraqi Parliament passed a bill (Law No. 23) authorizing the Government to distribute state domains among landless peasants or tribesmen on the basis of small private ownership. It was a small beginning as the application of the law was restricted to one specific area, the Dujayla lands, in the Kut Liwa south of Baghdad. Some 180,000 acres were put under irrigation and divided into plots of about 60 acres each for distribution to farming families. After a probationary period of ten years, the farmer can acquire complete ownership of the land. At the beginning of 1947 about 400 cultivators were settled on the project land. Possibly an equal number has been settled since that time. In 1946 another project, the Hawjah Settlement Scheme, was finished. It involved the distribution of some 200,000 acres of irrigated land among members of the 'Ubayd tribe.

In June and July 1950 the Government issued decrees by means of which the application of Law 23 . . . was extended to additional areas of state domain: in the provinces of Hilla and Kerbela in the south, in

[38] United Nations, *op. cit.*, Part II, p. 33.
[39] Mr. Tannous, an Arab-American, is an official of the United States Department of Commerce. In the latter part of 1949 he was associated with the United Nations Survey Mission (Clapp Mission) as an adviser.

Diyala in central Iraq, in Sulaimaniya and at the Hawjah irrigation project in the north.

It may be argued that all of these measures do not amount to much as yet. This is true.[40]

Further information concerning the Dujayla scheme is contained in an article published in the November 5, 1950, issue of the New York *Times*:

The plots granted to families are not for small-holder farming. They average 62 acres. In the rich delta area of the Tigris and Euphrates, this could mean a comfortable surplus when developed as a commercial undertaking in the manner of American farms. But they are not large enough to permit the owner to let someone else work the land as a tenant.

The vital elements of the Dujeila program provide that a settler must work for ten years in the field under Government instructions to learn how to use the land advantageously. If he disobeys instructions he receives two warnings and then is expelled from the holding. . . .

The Government provides land, an adequate supply of irrigation water, salaries and housing for the project staff. The settlers have to build their own houses and barns under rules laid down for sanitary construction. Loans are advanced according to the decision of the director, but they are never generous.

The Dujeila plan fulfilled one of the chief requirements of the pilot project by exposing a major blunder. Proper drainage was not provided, and in part of the land salting resulted in its becoming useless.[41]

If it is really a purpose of this and the other settlement projects to create a class of small landowners in Iraq, the results will be dependent in great measure upon the success which will have been achieved by the end of the probationary periods in the establishment of efficient cooperatives, or at the least a farther-reaching system of agricultural credit facilities than Iraq now possesses.[42] At the time of writing the prospects along such lines could not be classified as particularly

[40] Tannous, *op. cit.*, pp. 16-17.

[41] Ross, "Agrarian Reform Expanded by Iraq," New York *Times*, November 5, 1950.

[42] Like most other agricultural banks in the Middle East, Iraq's Agricultural and Industrial Bank has accomplished relatively little in improving the position of the farming community. The moneylender, making loans to farmers at exorbitant interest rates, is still a prominent feature of the Iraq scene. Cf. Royal Institute of International Affairs, *op. cit.*, p. 261.

good. In 1949 Dr. Seton Lloyd made the statement that, even though the Dujayla scheme had been in effect for four years, "the mechanism of assignment has so far proved imperfect, and the co-operative organizations which would be indispensable to success are only now under discussion."[43] As for agricultural credit, although the Iraqi Government has been concerning itself more closely with financial reform during 1950 than was the case previously, there is no evidence that the Agricultural Bank has been an object of important top-level attention. Conceivably, however, the great landlords of Iraq possess different assumptions as to what would constitute "success" of these projects. Under the existing circumstances, it is easy to envisage the prospect of the eventual taking over of these new communities by absentee landlords in the guise of moneylenders. Many landlords would undoubtedly welcome the possibility of gaining control over peasant groups having some experience in mechanized cultivation.[44]

In 1949 there were about 500 tractors in Iraq, as compared to 142 in 1942.[45]

THE HAIGH PLAN

In 1946 the Iraqi Government established an *ad hoc* Irrigation Development Commission under the presidency of Mr. F. F. Haigh, a British engineer. In 1949, after more than two years of studies and surveys, this group drew up a partially coordinated scheme for development and conservation of Iraq's water resources, divided into a program for an initial period of ten years and a subsequent one of indefinite length. It is believed that a completion of the entire long-range program would possibly take as long as fifty years.[46]

The total estimated cost of the long-term program is I.D. 91,515,-000, or about $256,000,000 at the present rate of exchange. Divided into categories, the various expenditures would be: flood control and

[43] *Ibid.*, p. 261.

It is understood that some cooperatives were later established, but the details are not available. Cf. New York *Times*, November 5, 1950.

[44] Keen, *op. cit.*, p. 37.

[45] United Nations, *op. cit.*, Part II, p. 33; Royal Institute of International Affairs, *op. cit.*, p. 258.

[46] United Nations, *op. cit.*, Part I, p. 74.

storage—$62,650,000; irrigation development—$98,728,000; drainage—$66,864,000; power—$17,780,000; navigation—$10,220,000.[47]

Although the details of the program are too lengthy to be set forth in full, the main points of interest are as follows: The flood prevention aspects of the Haigh Plan, which are accorded heavy priority, are designed to remove all further possibility of excessive flood damage in Iraq. Heavy inundations from both rivers have been frequent in the past and have caused losses amounting to untold millions of dinars.[48] But, because of fairly strong public opinion against flood prevention schemes which were uncombined with storage facilities for irrigation, awkward and unsatisfactory methods are still in use for disposing of the overflow. The embankments of the rivers are breached at points selected in advance, and the flow is thereby diverted over cultivated lands where the crops are sacrificed in order to prevent greater losses elsewhere. This method has not even the advantage of always sparing the lands and towns in favor of which the sacrifice is made.[49]

Although water engineers in Iraq have been inclined to recommend scientific flood prevention works even without added advantages,[50] the discoveries of recent years have apparently demonstrated the wisdom (or perhaps the good fortune) of waiting until some suitable sites for multi-purpose works could be located. Four sites on the Tigris River system have now been shown to be adaptable to such combined uses. One of these, the Bekhme site on the Greater Zab, a tributary of the Tigris, became known even before the Haigh Commission's study had begun; during the period immediately following the end of World War II it was generally assumed that works in that locality would be given top priority in Iraq's future development. The commission, however, succeeded in devising an even more promising scheme, namely, that of making use of Wadi Tharthar for the pur-

---

[47] Ibid.

[48] The most recent heavy floods were on the Tigris in May, 1950. It was reported that 4000 houses and 16 factories collapsed; that more than 18,000,000 square yards of cultivated land had been covered by water; that houses and stores on both banks of the river in Baghdad were flooded; and that the damage amounted to hundreds of thousands of dollars. Cf. New York *Times*, May 18 and 19, 1950.

[49] Ionides, *op. cit.*, pp. 7-9.

[50] *Ibid.*, p. 8.

poses mentioned. The two other sites on which multi-purpose dams could be constructed are the "Gibraltar site" on the Diyala River, which flows into the Tigris just below Baghdad, and one on the Lesser Zab River, a northern tributary of the Tigris. The Haigh Commission strongly recommends a prompt beginning of the Diyala undertaking but has reserved judgment with respect to the other sites on tributaries. The commission also strongly recommended the multipurpose Habbaniya project on the Euphrates which had been hanging fire for so many years, but with the reservation that the subsidiary irrigation works be constructed gradually over a long period. However, the Iraqi Government apparently wishes to go ahead with the full scheme as soon as possible. The Diyala and Habbaniya projects do not compare with the Wadi Tharthar one in magnitude. Apart from the Habbaniya scheme and the Wadi Tharthar project, which is described in a later section, no definite decisions appear to have been made by the Iraqi Government on the various alternatives.[51]

The Haigh Plan makes one particularly important departure from previous proposals in that it provides for the development of an extensive drainage system, the total estimated cost of which would be about two-thirds of the amount allotted to irrigation development in the proposals. The most immediate Haigh proposal with respect to drainage calls for a trial program on a small scale in one or another of the areas where the soil deterioration has been particularly great from waterlogging and salinity resulting from overirrigation—due in some cases to natural causes, but more frequently to individual human negligence. The question of adopting such a program, together with the selection of an appropriate site, is now under consideration by the government. The areas principally affected by the conditions mentioned are the lands along the Hillah Branch of the Euphrates River, extensive stretches along the main Euphrates and Tigris banks, and, as a very recent development, parts of the immense date groves which have long derived their water from the Shatt-el-Arab River by tidal irrigation. According to the Haigh Commission, it will not be possible to draw up a precise plan for drainage until there has been an opportunity for observation of results on the trial scheme. The cost

[51] United Nations, *op. cit.*, Part I, pp. 71-72; Part II, p. 32.

of an effective trial scheme is estimated at I.D. 3,000,000 for complete restoration, over a period of ten years, of the area or areas selected. Experimental findings would, however, be possible long before the lapse of the ten years.[52]

The question of hydroelectric power for Iraq is not a pressing one. Through her agreements with international oil interests Iraq is assured of abundant supplies of cheap fuel for irrigation and industrial purposes.[53]

It should be particularly noted that the Haigh proposals are based more on technical considerations, as judged from the engineering viewpoint, than on economic and social needs.

The estimated cost of the first ten-year stage of the Haigh program is I.D. 20,000,000 ($56,000,000). The Iraqi Government will probably not adhere precisely to the Haigh priorities but will certainly be guided to some extent by the commission's recommendations as it formulates its over-all National Development Plan.

THE WADI THARTHAR SCHEME

Although an integral part of the Haigh Plan, the Wadi Tharthar project deserves special consideration on its own, both because of the major nature of its implications and because work on it is about to commence without regard to its integration with other schemes, in "year plans" or otherwise.

Wadi Tharthar is an old, usually dry, river bed which runs for a considerable distance in the north-south direction in the center of Iraq, more or less parallel to both Tigris and Euphrates. To the north-west of Baghdad it terminates in a huge depression which, if the maximal possibilities are ever exploited, can serve not only for Tigris flood prevention but also for supplementary supply to both the Tigris and the Euphrates.[54]

The capacity of the depression is enormous, in fact "adequate to

[52] Ibid., Part I, p. 73.

[53] Cf. Agreement between the Iraqi Government and the Iraq Petroleum Co., Ltd., printed as Appendix L (2) of the 1920-31 Progress Report, p. 319.

[54] Ionides, op. cit., pp. 144-145; Feliks Bochenski and William Diamond, "T.V.A.'s in the Middle East," Middle East Journal, January, 1950, p. 80.

control almost any conceivable high water peak."[55] In addition, it
may eventually make possible the irrigation of 3,500,000 acres of
land which are at present either not cultivable or not perennially
irrigable.[56] This, when added to the 1,000,000-1,500,000 acres of
perennial irrigation now in prospect from the Habbaniya scheme,
would more than double the present irrigated cropped area. This may
well become by far the largest water-control scheme ever yet undertaken in the Middle East.

Arrangements have already been made (in June, 1950) for a loan
of $12,800,000 to the Iraqi Government by the International Bank
for the defrayment of the foreign exchange costs of the first (flood
control) stage of the project. This represents the first loan ever
granted by the bank to any Middle Eastern country. There follows a
description by the bank of the undertakings to which the loan is
directly related:[57]

The project . . . will involve a total capital cost equivalent to about
$29,000,000. . . . The loan is secured by an assignment of oil royalties
and the loan arrangements provide that Iraq will set aside from these
royalties sufficient funds to meet the domestic costs of the project.
The . . . project calls for the construction of a dam across the Tigris
River at a point about 50 miles above Baghdad, which will direct excess
flood waters into an uninhabited and barren depression, known as the
Wadi Tharthar. . . . It is expected that the project will result in improvements in health and sanitation and in increased agricultural production, both by protecting against floods and by preventing dust storms
from the Wadi Tharthar. It will also enable the Government to save
substantial sums now spent on levee maintenance and control and flood
relief measures for the population. . . . The dam is being so constructed
as to permit, at a later stage, the storage of water for irrigation.

The Wadi Tharthar Flood Control Project will be located in the area
from the Tigris River above Samarra extending in a south-westerly

[55] United Nations, *op. cit.*, Part I, p. 71.
[56] This is according to an estimate made by the American-educated Director
General of Irrigation, Abdul Emir al-Uzri. Cf. Ross, "Iraq's Land Plans Behind
Loan Plea," New York *Times*, January 9, 1950.
[57] The first two paragraphs are from the *Fifth Annual Report* of the International Bank for the year 1949-50 (p. 30). The last is from the International
Bank's "WB—Loan No. 261RQ (W.T. Flood Control Project)—Loan Agreement—June 15, 1950," p. 32.

direction for a distance of about 61 kilometres to the Wadi Tharthar depression, about 65 kilometres north-west of Baghdad. A dam will be constructed in the Tigris River near Samarra, together with the necessary connecting levees, an inlet channel with regulator and undersluices . . . so as to divert water . . . into the Wadi Tharthar depression.

This initial stage will require five years for completion, after which the government intends to proceed with the irrigation aspects of the scheme. No estimate has yet been made as to the time which will be required for completion of the entire project.[58] The total cost is now estimated at $50,000,000.[59] For such a major undertaking this amount is not great.

THE NATIONAL DEVELOPMENT PLAN

In April, 1950, the Iraqi Parliament established a Middle Eastern precedent by passing a law which provided unequivocally for the expenditure of all future oil revenues for developmental purposes. It also provided for the establishment of a Development Board to exercise uncontrolled supervision over all day-to-day aspects of economic and social development for a period of five years. This board was to consist of the Prime Minister as ex-officio chairman, the Minister of Finance, and six nonpolitical specialists, two of whom were to be non-Iraqis and one of whom was to be designated as general manager of short-range planning and operations.[60] The plans for each year must have the advance approval of Parliament.[61]

[58] The present plan is to wait until the Wadi Tharthar depression has been filled over a period of years to a fifty-meter height, and then to take up the question of financing of the irrigation project. Cf. Ross, "Iraq's Land Plans Behind Loan Plea," New York Times, January 9, 1950.

[59] This is based on an upward revision of the Director General of Irrigation's January, 1950, estimate of $34,000,000. The revision is in the same ratio as that of the Director General's January estimate for the Wadi Tharthar Flood Control Project to the later International Bank estimate for that stage. (Ibid.)

[60] The appointee to the position of general manager was Arshad al Umary, former Premier of Iraq (in 1946) and former Mayor of Baghdad. Mr. Umary had had engineering training in Turkey but had spent most of his adult life in Iraq in political or administrative positions in the national or municipal government. At one time he had been Director General of Irrigation. Cf. "Land Reform Tops Iraq Development," New York Times, December 10, 1950.

[61] Ibid.; Ross, "Iraq Seeks Expert for Drainage Plan," New York Times, October 31, 1950; Middle East Journal, Winter, 1951, p. 79.

The establishment of such a board had been demanded by the International Bank as a condition precedent to the granting of a loan for the Wadi Tharthar project; and the bank, by subsequently making such a loan, at least implied its satisfaction with the working of the law, as well as the intentions and ability of the government to facilitate efficient operations on the part of the board. The bank had also demanded of Iraq a general overhauling of her financial system and structure and seems to have been satisfied that adequate initial progress had been made in that direction by June, 1950, the month in which the Wadi Tharthar loan was granted.[62]

There had, as a matter of fact, been full agreement in political circles for over three years as to the urgent necessity of economic and social development under the aegis of a small board which could operate more or less independently. In 1949, when Iraq's neighbor, Iran, seemed to be making excellent progress with her Seven-Year Plan ostensibly directed by a Plan Organization not responsible to any of the regular government departments, the necessity of producing an analogous situation in Iraq, in connection with a Ten-Year Plan which had existed in vague shape since 1946, assumed even greater importance in the eyes both of leading citizens and of the populace in general. But, because of strong disagreements as to what the nature and powers of such a board should be, the debates on the subject not only seemed often to reach dead ends but also prevented the government and Parliament from devoting much attention to the content of developmental planning. Indeed, even after the establishment of the board had been approved, the question of the actual persons to be appointed to it continued to occupy major attention throughout the remainder of 1950. Appointments had, in fact, not been completed by December 31, 1950.[63]

It was the legal duty of the Development Board to present a list of projects to the Parliament in time for inclusion in the 1951-52 budget. However, in order to assist the board in this matter, the government

[62] Dorothea Seelye Franck and Peter G. Franck, "The Middle East Economy in 1949," *Middle East Journal*, April, 1950, p. 241; Ross, "Iraq Acts to Keep Capital at Home," New York *Times*, January 14, 1950.
[63] Ross, "Development Aim Is Main Iraqi Issue," New York *Times*, January 22, 1950.

requested the International Bank to conduct a general survey of economic and social conditions in Iraq, similar to the one which the bank had conducted in Turkey in the summer of 1950. At the end of the year the arrival of such a mission was expected within a month or two.

With the matter in its present indefinite status, it is impossible to predict whether development will proceed in accordance with the obviously bright theoretical possibilities. One argument might be that, in view of the final establishment of any sort of Developmental Board after all the strong disagreements on the subject, there is apparently at least a determination among Iraqi leaders to achieve unity and get ahead with the work, even at substantial sacrifices of self-interest. On the other hand, it may be observed that the nature of the debates was not always indicative of a determination even to put aside either trivialities or single-class interests. Most of the government leaders, for example, have been unwilling to have a board of which anyone other than the Prime Minister would be chairman. Their view has been that, since agriculture is the only important economic activity in Iraq (except for oil, which is foreign-controlled), any relinquishment by the government of day-to-day control over agricultural development would be tantamount to relinquishing all control in the country. The landowning shaikhs, however, have held to the view that, whereas the constitutionally established government is responsible to a Parliament in which the shaikh class is well represented, the urban ruling class could easily act outside of governmental responsibilities if the cabinet in power were to assume, so to speak, a dual personality as both government and independent development board. The shaikhs' apparent fear was that the urban landowners, desirous both of raising peasant living standards and of maintaining their own powers, intended to attempt the former at the expense of the shaikhs alone.[64]

In the end, it was the urban ruling class which maintained the key position of control, with the safeguards mentioned. It seems clear, from the main argument advanced by government leaders, that this control will be exercised at least to the point of preventing activities

[64] *Ibid.*; Franck and Franck, *op. cit.*, p. 241.

in conflict with urban landowner interests. Those leaders have, by strong implication, acknowledged that their power is derived in the main from the relationships which they have established vis-à-vis the agricultural life of the country. Clearly their present intention is to preserve those relationships in their existing form.

Because it provides for a definite earmarking of *all* oil royalties to development *without limitation as to time*, Iraq's National Development Plan seems to have greater theoretical possibilities for the future than Iran's Seven-Year Plan. The royalty for 1950 is believed to have amounted to about $17,000,000. It is authoritatively estimated, however, that, because of new pipe-line developments under way, this income will have risen to at least $56,000,000, before 1960.[65]

GENERAL OBSERVATIONS

In any attempt to evaluate the prospects for success of Iraq's National Development Plan, the assumption must first of all be made that no action will be taken by Syria, Turkey, or Iran which would lessen Iraq's water supplies from the Tigris-Euphrates river system. Here it must be noted that, in spite of the international character of that system, there have been no important measures for coordination of the plans of the four countries involved. In fact, it has not even proved possible to arrange for an efficient interchange of information among them in regard to the rivers' movements. The main blame for this situation probably does not rest with Iraq, since her demonstrated concern for the basin as a whole has been far greater than those of the other three countries.[66]

Once this assumption has been made, two considerations in particular must be regarded as of first rank in connection with the weighing of future possibilities. One is the clear fact that the more obviously promising aspects of the planning in its present status are by

[65] As of November 15, 1951, owing to subsequent developments, the prospects were considerably better than this. There was a probability that the annual income would amount to at least $150,000,000 before 1955. Cf. Ross, "Iraq's Oil Income Held Due for Rise," New York *Times*, January 6, 1950.

[66] Numerous authoritative statements have been made in regard to the extent of the cooperation, which seems to vary from year to year but never to be particularly satisfactory. Cf. Worthington, *op. cit.*, pp. 30, 50, 53.

no means conclusive indicators. Far more favorable symptoms could have been observed in connection with the evolution of Iran's Seven-Year Plan, to be discussed in a later chapter. Iran, in her planning, which involved even larger expenditures for the first few years, reached the advanced preliminary stages even more rapidly; showed herself completely amenable to foreign expert advice at a much later stage of planning; and had the additional advantage over Iraq that the monarch of the country was an extremely active supporter of the Seven-Year Plan, even in the detailed form approved by American experts. It was only after the plan had been put into actual execution that insuperable and decisive obstacles became apparent. Since political and economic conditions are similar in the two countries, this comparison must not be overlooked.

The other important element to be considered is the fact that, while there is much awareness in Iraq of the logical connection between increased rural living standards on the one hand and the prosperity of the wealthy classes on the other, apparently few of the landowners are willing to see cultivators' living standards raised to the detriment of their own immediate economic and political interests. These latter depend upon a continuance of shifting, extensive, and wasteful cultivation.

For this reason, coupled with the great difficulty of suddenly abandoning habitual lines of thinking in regard to such matters,[67] it seems extremely likely that future increases in Iraq's cropped and croppable areas will continue to be at least as rapid as the increases

[67] This type of habitual thinking may be the hardest of all types to change. Perhaps the best, and certainly the most cogent, examples of protracted difficulty in changing from an expansionist mentality to an advocacy of making the most of small compact areas are to be found in some of the present-day attitudes both in the United States and in the Soviet Union. In the case of Americans, the mentality is most often manifested in the fears expressed that the United States is in danger of overcrowding, now that there is no longer a frontier of civilization. Letters to newspaper editors often contain an obvious major premise to the effect that the admission of immigrants, no matter on what basis, necessarily makes it more difficult for those already in the United States to find housing, employment, etc. In Russia there seems to be a fairly general feeling, even in spite of greatly improved facilities for intensification of activities, that the only true road to greater prosperity is the way of expansionism.

in population and the improvements in techniques and efficiency. Probably, unless some unforeseen change occurs with respect to the immigration policy, the rate of Iraq's population increase will be no more than 2 per cent per annum over a long period,[68] and consequently the present population of around 5,000,000 will be no more than doubled by 1985. But it is equally probable that, before that time, the great Wadi Tharthar irrigation scheme will have become fully effective. There is still a marked tendency, even in preliminary planning, to envisage development of the country in terms of new large-scale irrigation systems which would bring immense amounts of new land within range of water supplies.[69] The intention is, for example, to go ahead in the near future with the irrigation aspects of the Habbaniya project.[70] On the other hand, there has been little alacrity about undertaking the proposed drainage projects, the necessity for which has been a matter of common knowledge for at least two decades. The newly irrigated land exerts much more attraction than rehabilitated old land, even without close regard to calculations of comparative costs. Moreover, the possibility would always exist that, if it proved momentarily profitable, landlords would commence cultivation on restored land before the drainage was complete. The result would be an acceleration in the demand for newly irrigated land.

If present indications are any criterion, it can be predicted that most of the land benefiting from the extension of irrigation will, through one means or another, fall into the hands of great landlords.

All this certainly suggests that there is no near-future prospect of any substantial improvement in the chronic condition of rural labor shortage. Under the circumstances, it is hard to believe that the wasteful use of land will cease in the foreseeable future. A corollary conclusion is that the development of mechanical skills and advanced

[68] A greater rate of natural increase than this, sustained over several decades, is most unusual.

[69] Every recent published official statement has accorded large irrigation plans a high priority. Cf., for example, "Land Reform Tops Iraq Development," New York Times, December 10, 1950; Ross, "Iraq's Land Plans Behind Loan Plea," New York Times, January 9, 1950; Middle East Journal, Winter, 1951, p. 79.

[70] United Nations, op. cit., Part I, p. 71.

techniques among agriculturists will be a slow process, at least for some time to come.

It has been observed, however, that the desire of landowners to utilize such skills and techniques is already strong. Also, by the time a sufficiently sizable number of graduates from the government-sponsored projects such as Dujayla are available, important economic consequences will follow, even if those graduates do not succeed in retaining private possession of plots of land. If the market conditions are free, the competitive pressure among landowners for employment of the small supply of competent cultivators could easily result in high agricultural wages and relative prosperity of a small portion of the farming community. Observation of this prosperity might, in turn, arouse ambitions for emulation on the part of the ordinary cultivators, and also promote some degree of enlightenment and resentment with respect to the matter of exploitation of tenants by landowners. In such an event, the net outcome might well be both improvement in general efficiency and strong pressure upon the government by the rural populace to create conditions enabling more cultivators to take advantage of the high demand for competent hands. This situation should result in a gradual development of generally higher rural living standards.

Much must depend upon the future policies adopted by the government. At present the government has a monopoly on imports and distribution of farm machinery.[71] This monopoly could be used to promote living standards, but it could also be used for facilitation of a continued exploitation of the peasantry. The latter result could be produced by limiting the possession of agricultural machinery to a small number of favored landowners, thereby conferring on that group the power to employ the more competent cultivators on their own terms.

However, such a policy might not be politically possible, as it might tend to disrupt the rather broad area of harmony which now prevails among and within the landlord classes, and thereby undermine the main sources of support upon which Iraqi governments have always had to depend.

[71] *Ibid.*, Part II, p. 33.

In summary, while Iraq's prospects from the National Development Plan are at present considerably obscured, there is nevertheless a fairly good possibility that favorable results will be forthcoming in ways which are not at present anticipated by the Iraqi planners. Under the circumstances, the great irrigation schemes may prove in retrospect to have been successful, even if their most immediate result is to bring into being an excess of immediately cultivable land, thus promoting a continuance of wasteful practices.

CHAPTER VIII

❖

Israel

GENERAL BACKGROUND

Although the independent state of Israel did not come into being until May 15, 1948, the Jews of Palestine had begun to enjoy a *de facto* quasi-national existence long before that date.

Even before World War I the foundations were being laid, both by international Zionist bodies and by Jewish immigrant groups in Palestine, for the building up of a large, compact Jewish Palestine community.[1] According to the hopes and plans of those Zionist elements whose views were to predominate, the projected community would be based on well-defined philosophical principles[2] and would possess, to the degree rendered possible by prevailing circumstances, the attributes of a nation-state or, at the least, of an *imperium in imperio*—a broadly autonomous political entity under the Ottoman Government or its successor in the Palestine area.

On November 2, 1917, the British Foreign Office, by issuing the

[1] Christians also contributed to the building up of the Zionist idea. With regard to Christian-sponsored proposals made as early as 1840 and 1841, cf. *Palestine Royal Commission Report* (hereinafter referred to as *Peel Report*) (London, 1937), p. 14; Robert R. Nathan, Oscar Gass, and Daniel Creamer, *Palestine, Problem and Promise* (Washington, 1946), p. 39.

[2] As to the nature of those principles in broad outline, cf. Nathan, Gass, and Creamer, *op. cit.*, p. 85; see also the section of this chapter on the Histadrut Plan.

famous Balfour Declaration in which British official support was promised for the establishment of a Jewish National Home in Palestine, made it possible for Zionists to accelerate their planning and to redouble their efforts to promote Jewish immigration into Palestine. In 1920 British civil rule was inaugurated in Palestine. In the same year, at the Conference of San Remo, arrangements were made to place the country under a League of Nations mandate, with Great Britain as the mandatory power. The most prominent, if not the most important, basis of the mandate was the support of such activities as might facilitate a rapid realization of the Jewish National Home in its broader aspects.[3] Although the mandate could not be put into effect formally before the conclusion of a peace treaty with Turkey, it was nevertheless possible to apply its main provisions immediately, in view of the virtual certainty that Turkish rule over Palestine would not be restored. It was generally assumed that the interests of resident Jews, and to a lesser extent those of world Jewry, would thenceforth be Britain's primary considerations in Palestine.

The difficulty in this regard was that, at the beginning of 1920, the Jews of Palestine numbered only 65,000, out of a total population of 648,000, largely Arabs. Even by 1939 the Jewish population was still only about 30 per cent of the total. During World War II the ratio did not change materially. Both elements in the population were increasing rapidly, and the total was approaching the 2,000,000 mark.

The presumption, from the Balfour Declaration and the mandate, was that national political and administrative institutions would soon be set up in Palestine, and that these institutions would be largely controlled by the inhabitants of the country, with Jews having at least a prominent role therein. But the dilemma in which the British found themselves was a serious one. Most of the politically

---

[3] The Balfour Declaration was made a part of the preamble of the mandate. Article 6 of the mandate read: "The administration of Palestine, while insuring that the rights and position of other sections of the population are not prejudiced, shall facilitate Jewish immigration, under suitable conditions, and shall encourage, in cooperation with the Jewish Agency referred to in Article 4, settlement by Jews on the land, including state lands and waste lands not required for public service."

conscious Arabs were wholly unwilling to approve of any special political status for Jews, beyond what would be their normal rights as individual citizens of a country governed by majority rule.[4] Such an idea was in distinct conflict with the most fundamental tenet of Zionism, namely, that the Jewish community of Palestine should enjoy a life designed according to Jewish patterns, and without any necessity for conforming with alien ideas along social, economic, philosophical, and cultural lines. This, too, was apparently the intent both of the Balfour Declaration and of the mandate. But, even if the Arabs had wished to facilitate such an outcome, it is highly doubtful that they would have been able to do so effectively while at the same time retaining potential dominance as a compact majority. The social, cultural, and in particular the economic gaps between the two groups were far too wide; and the enthusiasm and impatience of Zionists for a rapid development of the National Home could not have tolerated a postponement of projects to the distant date when those gaps between Arabs and Jews would have been substantially closed, or when the Jews would be the majority in the population. In the meantime, any necessity for thoroughgoing cooperation between Jews and Arabs would unquestionably have slowed down the tempo of Jewish progress.

Although the mandatory power never succeeded in solving this problem, the Palestine Jews themselves effected a partial solution by establishing quasi-governmental institutions of their own and subjecting the Jewish community to the rulings and actions of these institutions, even in respect of such matters as taxation and conscription. An elective legislative body, the General Assembly of Knesseth Israel, came into being in this manner. It had its own executive council, known as Vaad Leumi, which enforced the Assembly's rulings and also was given supervisory powers over Jewish education, public health, and welfare activities. These two bodies were accorded official recognition by the mandatory power. In purely Jewish localities, local governments set up by the residents and approved by the General Assembly received official recognition in some cases and in others functioned successfully without such

---

[4] Nathan, Gass, and Creamer, *op. cit.*, p. 75; *Peel Report*, p. 371.

recognition. All this was, in a sense, tantamount to Jewish democratic self-rule in a broad field of activities.[5]

The following information in regard to other quasi-public institutions of the Jewish National Home in the preindependence era is contained in *Palestine, Problem and Promise*, an economic study prepared by Messrs. Nathan, Gass, and Creamer, and published by the Public Affairs Press:

The Vaad Leumi is the one Jewish national institution controlled entirely by Palestinians. Because of the peculiar problems connected with the establishment of the Jewish National Home, several other institutions supported by world Jewry have, however, performed many quasi-governmental functions in Palestine. . . .

The most important quasi-public institution in Palestine is the Jewish Agency for Palestine. Until 1929 the World Zionist Organization served as "the appropriate Jewish Agency" which Article 4 of the Mandate gave the status of ". . . a public body for the purpose of cooperating and advising with the Administration of Palestine in such economic, social and other matters as may affect the establishment of the Jewish national home and . . . to assist and take part in the development of the country." In 1929 the Zionist Organization relinquished this official status to a Jewish Agency for Palestine, which included representatives of non-Zionist Jews. The Jewish Agency has an Executive, with a membership designated according to an agreement among the various world Jewish organizations interested in the development of Palestine. This executive functions as the spokesman for the Jewish interest in Palestine in all relations with the Mandatory Administration and other governments. . . .

The Jewish Agency has the greatest financial resources of any quasi-public institution in Palestine. Its range of activities comprehends the whole field of investment and social services, except for land purchase and amelioration, health services, and general education; these functions have been taken over by other bodies. In 1943–44 the Jewish Agency had a total income (apart from borrowing) of £P2,812,000 compared with £P11,514,000 for the Government of Palestine.

Second in resources and scope and oldest among Jewish Palestinian institutions is the Jewish National Fund. It was founded by the World Zionist Congress in 1901 and charged with the task of buying land in Palestine. . . . In addition to land purchase, the J.N.F. engages in soil amelioration, afforestation, and irrigation. . . . In 1943–44 its receipts were £P1,851,000.

[5] *Peel Report*, pp. 48, 346, 352; Nathan, Gass, and Creamer, *op. cit.*, pp. 353-354.

206 CHALLENGE AND RESPONSE IN THE MIDDLE EAST

The third most important world Jewish organization operating in Palestine is the Hadassah Medical Organization supported chiefly by Hadassah, the American women's Zionist organization. . . . In the days before the Palestinian Jewish community was sufficiently well established to provide its own medical services, the work of the Hadassah was more important than that of any other health institution in raising the whole level of Jewish life in Palestine. . . . Hadassah's work is [now] becoming more specialized. . . .

Other important Jewish national institutions include the Wizo (Women's International Zionist Organization), which operates over almost the whole range of Zionist activities. . . . The Hebrew University had receipts (1923–44) of £P1,897,000. Other funds, largely of an emergency character, had receipts (1929–44) of £P3,054,000; the greatest constructive activity of these emergency funds has been the Youth Aliyah—the rescue of Jewish children in Europe and their training in Palestine.

The total receipts of these Jewish national institutions in the years from October 1, 1917, through September 30, 1944, were £P35,620,000. This compares with £P104,039,000, received by the Government of Palestine from July 1, 1920 through March 31, 1944. . . . In 1943–44 Jewish national receipts were, for the first time, more than half as large as Government receipts.[6]

Owing to this wide range of quasi-public activities conducted by and for the Jewish community during the mandate era, it is feasible to regard Jewish national developmental planning and performance as having been continuous since the end of World War I. However, two main differences between the mandate era and the post-independence period should be borne in mind. The first is that the state of Israel occupies only a part (71 per cent) of the territory formerly under mandate. The second is that in the mandate era the Jewish quasi-public institutions had no power whatever in matters directly affecting Arab interests. As the geographical separation between Jews and Arabs was far from complete, this was an important limitation. In cases in which it was desired to advance Jewish interests through projects extending over Arab-inhabited regions, the Jewish bodies could do no more than petition the mandatory government. The latter, moreover, even in spite of the provisions of the

[6] Nathan, Gass, and Creamer, *op. cit.*, pp. 355-357.

mandate, imposed restrictions upon Jewish immigration and later
upon land purchases by Jews.

But, in actual practice, all of the major planning by the mandatory power for raising living standards was based to a large extent
upon preliminary Jewish planning, whether by quasi-public agencies
or by private bodies supported by those agencies. The Government of
Palestine, under the British High Commissioner, did not undertake
any major projects for the sole purpose of raising Arab living standards.[7] A considerable amount of piecemeal assistance was rendered
to Arabs, but the British apparently felt that any large-scale developmental activities undertaken should be of substantial benefit to
both communities. When such possibilities existed, the Jewish community was nearly always ahead of the government, in having its
own proposals ready for consideration. This promptness was only
natural. The Jews were filled with enthusiasm for the development
of the National Home. The government's ardor was apparently
dampened by the political problems connected with nearly every
project which might be contemplated.[8] Furthermore, the Jewish
community was well supplied both with funds and with talented
personnel, as well as competent nonlocal Jewish assistance, for
planning purposes. The government was somewhat handicapped
along these lines, particularly in view of the large expenditures which
it had to make for security purposes.[9]

On May 15, 1948, Jewish Palestine became the independent state
of Israel. Because of the politically and economically fortunate fact
that there are few non-Jews in the territory of the new state, subsequent planning has been unhampered by the former difficulties

[7] The British Government and the Government of Palestine were responsible
for numerous surveys of social and economic situations, but these did not lead
to the formulation of any new major plans of a specific character for raising living
standards. This statement is amply confirmed by sources which are neither Jewish
nor demonstrably pro-Jewish. Cf. Peel Report, pp. 218-219, 224, 254, 313, 337,
339, 363; Doreen Warriner, Land and Poverty in the Middle East (London,
1948), p. 134; E. B. Worthington, Middle East Science (London, 1945), p. 104.
[8] It was exceedingly difficult to produce any far-reaching proposals, along social
and economic lines, which would be acceptable to both Jewish and Arab communities. Cf. Peel Report, pp. 224, 262.
[9] Nathan, Gass, and Creamer, op. cit., pp. 63-65; Peel Report, p. 337.

connected with forced associations with other communities and administrations.

Equally formidable, however, are those problems which have arisen from the damages caused by the 1948 war, the reduced area of the country, the boycotts imposed by neighboring states, the loss of such profitable resources as part of the Dead Sea salts, and the greatly accelerated rate of immigration of Jews from other parts of the world. The presence of these adverse situations has resulted in at least a temporary deterioration in the general living standards of the Israel populace.

In 1936 the Jewish per capita income in Palestine was reckoned to be forty-four local pounds (£P or I£).[10] In 1949 the Statistical Office of the United Nations estimated I£109.50 as the per capita income figure for Israel.[11] But, since the cost of living indexes in 1949 and 1950 were well in excess of three times those prevailing just before World War II,[12] it must be concluded that the real average income of Jews in Palestine (Israel) has declined fairly substantially, in spite of the much greater contributions which their community has been receiving from abroad.

Israel's per capita income in 1949 was, nevertheless, far greater than that of any other country in the Middle East. Lebanon and Turkey are ranked next, each with the equivalent of I£44.65. This would be much lower than the Israel figure even if all donations were deducted from the latter. Thus it seems clear that, in spite of the many difficulties and obstacles, the net developmental progress in Jewish Palestine (Israel) has been much greater than that in any of the other countries considered in this study.

Hence there is apparently some justification for the praise which the total Jewish accomplishment has won from the great majority of unbiased observers. Almost universal has been the commendation, not only for the great initiative and perseverance demonstrated, but

[10] Nathan, Gass, and Creamer, *op. cit.*, p. 150.

[11] Or $389, converted at the rate of $4.00 per pound until mid-September and $2.80 per pound thereafter.

[12] Statistical Office of the United Nations, *Monthly Bulletin of Statistics*, December, 1950.

also for special achievements along such lines as agriculture, industrial development, health, education, and social welfare.[13] Particular feats, such as the conversion of highly saline soil into fertile
farmland, have been singled out for praise. It is true that these
laudatory judgments have often been qualified with the observation
that, because of the dependence on external subsidies, Israel's (Jewish Palestine's) development has been on an "uneconomic" basis.[14]
This, however, would seem to be a moral question rather than an
economic one.

The following paragraphs contain descriptions of the major
plans, 1919 to 1950, for raising standards of living in Palestine (later
Israel).

THE HISTADRUT PLAN

The Histadrut project must be regarded as a major plan, not only
for the Middle East, but also from the viewpoint of the world as a
whole. While serving primarily as the main conveyor of the ideals
of Zionism, it also has much wider implications.

During the first decade of the present century the Zionist movement began to take a decisive turn. This came as a result of search-
ing for ways and means of ending the traditional limitations upon
Jews as to the vocational and other activities in which they might
engage. In the course of centuries, many of these limitations had
become fixed through force of habit and inertia, even where there
were no official restrictions. The fear had, therefore, developed
among some groups of Zionists that, unless strong positive measures
were taken to impel the Jews to move in the opposite direction, any
Jewish National Home would be little more than a new, though self-
imposed, ghetto.[15]

In the solution, the "religion of labor" became the nuclear

[13] *Peel Report*, pp. 45, 47, 118, 124, 311-313; Said B. Himadeh, *Economic
Organization of Palestine* (Beirut, 1938), p. 288; James B. Hays, *T.V.A. on the
Jordan* (Washington, 1948), p. 82; Worthington, *op. cit.*, pp. 140, 175; Warriner,
op. cit., p. 71.
[14] Warriner, *op. cit.*, pp. 70-71.
[15] Nathan, Gass, and Creamer, *op. cit.*, pp. 281-283.

motivating force of practical Zionism,[16] in spite of opposition from
some Zionist quarters.[17] This meant that, in the building of their
hoped-for homeland in Palestine, Jews should participate actively
and fervently in all phases of the developmental processes, even including the necessary manual labor, which should not be regarded as
menial but ennobling. Thus, in the final result, the structure would
be a Jewish one in every detail; and the cultural pattern which would
emerge from this peaceful struggle would be that of a free Jewish
culture. Only in such a way, it was felt, could Jews be relieved of their
age-old dependence upon non-Jews for their daily needs—dependence
on services which they were incapable of performing for themselves,
and dependence on outside demands for a limited number of specialized, and often despised, skills which Jews have tended to
monopolize. Only with the success of such endeavors would it
ever become possible to declare that the ghetto, and with it the
ghetto mentality, was a thing of the past.[18]

Labor, however, can be degrading, if the workers are forced into
competition with persons maintaining very low living standards,
as has always been the case with Arab laborers in Palestine. It was,
therefore, deemed necessary to establish Zionist labor organizations
in order to safeguard Palestinian Jewish workers against possible
exploitation and degradation. The first such organization, called
the Agricultural Workers' Federation, came into being in 1911;
others soon followed. But it was not until 1920 that a single organization was created to serve the needs of all branches of Jewish labor in
all parts of Palestine. The new body was named Histadrut, or the
General Federation of Jewish Labor.[19]

[16] There has usually been a rather wide intellectual gap between the practical
Zionism of the Jews who played direct roles in the development of the National
Home and the absentee Zionism of those who largely confined their activities
to moral and financial support of the project, maintaining little or no direct
contact with Palestine. The latter often have a tendency to regard the National
Home as a worthy object of charitable contribution, but unimportant from
the ideological viewpoint.

[17] Among the opponents of this emphasis are the two large orthodox Jewish
organizations which have espoused Zionism, namely, Mizrachi and Agudas Israel.
Cf. Nathan, Gass, and Creamer, op. cit., pp. 83-84.

[18] Ibid., pp. 281-283.

[19] Ibid., p. 287.

Before the establishment of Histadrut, steps had already been taken to exclude cheap Arab labor, as far as possible, from work on Jewish projects. During the whole period of the mandate there was a virtually complete separation of the two labor forces.

During the thirty years of its existence, Histadrut's activities have been in the nature of an ever-unfolding plan, the central purpose of which has been to take any feasible action, no matter what kind, which would substantially advance the enlightened interests of Jewish workers.[20] Probably the most conspicuous manifestation of this policy has been the extensive investment of Histadrut's own capital in large business enterprises which were deemed capable of promoting the reasonable interests of the community of workers. For example, when building was a major activity in the country, Histadrut established its own construction companies,[21] with a view to assuring that wages and conditions of work would be satisfactory and that at the same time the enterprises would be conducted in an economic manner. Also, where it has appeared that it would be impossible to execute an essential developmental project successfully, owing to the high ratio which wages bore to other costs of production, Histadrut has taken steps to reduce the other costs in order to protect wages and workers' amenities. It was in line with this idea that, when internal transportation costs were keeping the prices of most Palestinian products at a high level, Histadrut entered into the transportation business. Eventually it acquired control of nearly all Jewish transport in Palestine. Outside of the field of investments, Histadrut has concerned itself directly and extensively with such matters as the general education, vocational training, health, and cultural development of Jewish workers.[22]

Unlike most trade-unions, Histadrut has concerned itself with

[20] An informative work in regard to Histadrut is Gerhard Muenzer's *Labor Enterprise in Palestine* (New York, 1947). Some of the data in that book are brought up to date in an article by Victor G. Reuther entitled "The World's Most Successful Trade Union," published in the September, 1950, issue of the *United Nations World*.

[21] The most important one is Solel Boneh, which in 1947 had assets valued at £P2,500,000 ($10,000,000). Cf. Muenzer, *op. cit.*, p. 34.

[22] *Ibid.*, p. 43.

agricultural workers as well as industrial and white-collar workers. An even more significant difference is that Histadrut, instead of attempting to protect already established workers by supporting restrictions upon immigration, has given positive encouragement to all Jews who have wished to proceed to Palestine from their countries of residence in order to perform labor in the building up of the National Home. When such labor immigrants arrived in Palestine, Histadrut invariably undertook to find such employment for them as would be beneficial both to the workers and to the National Home as a whole. The theory was that the two sets of interests were inextricably tied together. This, too, was the theory held by most Zionists in Palestine. Thus, the Jewish political bodies felt the need, above all else, of a large and satisfied working group to perform the many tasks necessary for bringing the Home to full flower, while Histadrut was aware that Jewish labor could not conceivably prosper except in harmony with the development of the National Home.[23]

Accordingly Histadrut supported all enterprises that were both constructive and economic and opposed those which, though containing possibilities of monetary profit, served no good purpose from the viewpoints of development and of the working community's major legitimate interests. As time went on, this policy greatly augmented Histadrut's power in Jewish affairs. Private entrepreneurs whose projects were deemed to promote worthy ends from the viewpoints mentioned could apply to the Histadrut for loans, share funds, or sponsorship and anticipate a sympathetic attitude.[24] In this way Histadrut's network of investments was forever being extended. The organization came to be by far the largest employer in Palestine.[25]

Although Histadrut was not responsible for the original establishment of cooperative and communal agricultural settlements in Jewish Palestine, it has done more than any other body to promote

[23] In theory, the two groups were tied together by their common allegiance to the "religion of labor." In practice, they might easily have become divided on questions relating to security, cost accounting, etc. Perhaps the main reason this did not happen was that the shared distrust of British policies vis-à-vis the Jewish National Home served to keep the bond intact.

[24] Muenzer, op. cit., p. 37.

[25] Histadrut's total investments in Palestine were estimated in 1947 at about £P20,000,000 ($80,000,000). Cf. ibid., p. 13.

the growth, increase in number, and economic functioning of such settlements. The trade-union found it convenient and useful to settle immigrants in the rural regions, in order to develop the country's long-neglected agriculture; and this was done by the establishment of new cooperative or communal farms, financed by the Jewish Agency but to a large extent controlled by Histadrut. These developments, in turn, led to an increase in the scope and volume of Histadrut's other enterprises, particularly along the lines of transport and distribution. And, as Histadrut's enterprises grew, additional economies became possible because of their large scale and the controlled rationalization. In the eventual result, Histadrut became a factor of outstanding importance in the life of every Palestinian Jew. As trade-union, employer, banker, educator, producer, and customer, its activities were encountered in nearly all quarters. It controlled the largest Jewish political party (Mapai) and the Hebrew newspaper of largest circulation (Davar).[26]

In no sense a part of the government, and completely lacking quasi-governmental legal powers, Histadrut has pursued its economic objectives with the full moral support both of the quasi-government of Jewish Palestine and of the later independent government of the state of Israel. In the present Knesseth (Parliament), more than half of the members are also members of Histadrut; and the Mapai party has the largest representation in the coalition cabinet. This large representation, however, has not led to Histadrut's control of the government, in any sense similar to the Communist party's control of the Soviet Government. The democratic processes have remained completely intact, and there is even another important political party (Mapam) composed entirely of Histadrut members. Nor has Histadrut ever attempted to put an end to private capitalism or to other trade-unions in Jewish Palestine or Israel. In the case of farmers, it has regarded owner-cultivators of small private plots as agricultural workers and has accepted large numbers of them as members of its organization.[27] The total membership today is

[26] Ibid., p. 50.

[27] Smallholders were not, however, eligible for admission into Histadrut if they were employers of labor.

330,000 or 58 per cent of all the persons gainfully employed in Israel. In addition to its numerous other enterprises, large and small, Histadrut possesses a widespread medical organization (Kupat Cholim), with 13 hospitals and 550 clinics serving more than 600,000 persons.

It is indeed hard to resist the conclusion that Histadrut is, in a sense, the most important vehicle today for fulfillment of Marxian objectives. This seems to be accomplished, however, through an adaptation of Marxian ideals and methods to the facts of experience rather than through "foolish consistency" and unyielding adherence to dogma. Unquestionably its greatest single accomplishment has been the great expansion in the number of cooperative and communal agricultural settlements and the success achieved by those settlements, with Histadrut assistance, in the application of the most modern agricultural methods. The progress in this domain has won the applause of both friends and foes of political Zionism and is regarded as an object lesson for the other countries of the Middle East.[28] Moreover, in addition to their agricultural activities, some of the settlements engage in manufactures based on agricultural raw materials. Finally, the settlements in general play an important constructive role in the culture of the new Jewish nation.

All of this seems to harmonize with the hopes which many outsiders had for Soviet communism, in the days before the widespread disillusionment had set in. Obviously, however, the success of any such planning would always be dependent on the prior existence of a "religion of labor." Other possibly necessary ingredients are widespread sympathy on the part of the nonunion population and perhaps also a certain minimum degree of social advancement among the great majority of union members. Whether the last-mentioned ingredient is indeed an essential one will probably soon be determined, since the state of Israel contains 150,000 Arabs, and large numbers of Oriental Jewish immigrants accustomed to extremely low living standards are being admitted into the country. It should be noted, however, that Histadrut enjoyed a certain amount of success

[28] Warriner, *op. cit.*, p. 72.

under the mandate in organizing Arab labor along lines consistent with its principles.[29]

The funds for Histadrut's many activities are derived from four sources: (1) union dues, (2) contributions from Zionists outside of Israel, (3) profits from Histadrut's business enterprises, and (4) *ad hoc* fees paid for medical services by nonmembers.[30]

THE RUTENBERG PLAN

From the earliest days of the National Home, the Jews of Palestine have been deeply concerned with two major economic problems, namely, irrigation and power. The reasons are clear to anyone familiar with the country. Palestine's agricultural output was extremely meager in Ottoman days, even as compared with other sections of the Middle East.[31] Moreover, the prospects for substantial improvement were not at all bright, in view of the extensive areas of wasteland—desert, marsh, and barren hills—in a country not much larger than the state of New Jersey. Further, the water supply available for irrigation projects was apparently limited; and there were few visible potential raw materials, and little available fuel, for manufacturing industries. Under the circumstances, the possibility of establishing a real Jewish National Home, which could accommodate all Jews who might at any time in the future wish to go to Palestine, seemed to be somewhat slim unless scientific inquiry should uncover previously unnoted resources.

The leading pioneer investigator of these matters was Pinhas Rutenberg, who prepared a report as early as 1920 on *The Water Resources of Palestine*. From this report it appeared that the irrigation and power possibilities of the country were by no means as limited as had been supposed, particularly if the unadjudicated frontier from Syria could be settled so as to include the Litani

[29] Nathan, Gass, and Creamer, *op. cit.*, p. 297.

[30] Union dues amount to 7½ per cent of wages. Histadrut's budget for 1951 is I£16,000,000, of which I£3,600,000 will be contributed by American Zionists, and possibly smaller amounts by Zionists in other countries.

As of November 15, 1951, Histadrut's over-all position seemed to have weakened considerably, owing to a severe economic crisis which many attributed to the inflexibility of the organization's policies.

[31] *Peel Report*, p. 6.

River, or at least one bank thereof, within Palestinian territory. Fair prospects existed of both irrigation and hydroelectric developments of importance.[32]

After Zionists had failed to gain the inclusion of any part of the Litani,[33] Rutenberg worked out a proposal for the exploitation of the water resources of Palestine's only perennial rivers, namely, the Jordan, the Yarmuk (a Jordan tributary), and the Yarkon. All three of the rivers offered limited irrigation possibilities, which have been greatly expanded by subsequent research. The Jordan and the Yarmuk had, in addition, distinct possibilities for development of a fairly large supply of hydroelectric power.

The result of this proposal was the so-called Rutenberg Concession, granted by the Government of Palestine in 1926 to the Palestine Electric Corporation, a firm organized by Rutenberg and financed by both Jewish and British interests. The awarding of a concession was in accordance with a standard practice of those days—one which tended to limit the scope of developmental activities to those commercially profitable according to customary business criteria. However, to promote the welfare aspects of this particular enterprise the High Commissioner for Palestine imposed limitations upon the concessionaire in the matter of profits and of rates to be charged.[34] There was also a general understanding that the concessionaire company would at all times be headed by persons more interested in the development of the Jewish National Home than in the company's balance sheet.[35]

The Rutenberg Concession gave sole rights to the Palestine Electric Corporation for a period of seventy years, to exploit the Jordan and Yarmuk rivers in Palestine and Transjordan for irrigation and power,

[32] This report has never been published. Cf. Nathan, Gass, and Creamer, op. cit., p. 643.

[33] As to present possibilities for using the Litani for Israel's benefit, see the chapter on Lebanon. Cf. also Nathan, Gass, and Creamer, op. cit., p. 408; Worthington, op. cit., p. 57.

[34] This was not a very serious limitation. By the terms of the contract, the High Commissioner was not entitled, during the first twenty-one years of the concession, to demand a revision of rates more frequently than once every seven years.

[35] Leonard Stein, in The Islamic World Since the Peace Settlement, edited by Arnold J. Toynbee (London, 1927), pp. 381-382.

and also a monopoly in the supply of electricity to Palestine outside of the Jerusalem area, as well as to the whole of Transjordan. The High Commissioner reserved the power to purchase the company at the end of the thirty-seventh year of the concession and at ten-year intervals thereafter.

The main importance of this concession lies in the fact that it was the first endeavor made in the Middle East to develop the resources of a seemingly unpromising area, with official control exercised as to the distribution of benefits. It must therefore be regarded as a pilot project of the first magnitude. The concession was also responsible for the first consequential hydroelectric development in the Middle East; even at the present time, it is the largest in the whole region.[36]

However, as matters now stand, it is questionable whether the Rutenberg Concession has been truly beneficial to Palestine. It has probably served a useful purpose from the point of view of demonstration, but beyond that the issue is by no means clear. From the irrigation standpoint, the accomplishments were exceedingly limited, as the company has been unable to supply water at attractive rates, even in a small area where irrigation was relatively simple. As for the hydroelectric aspect, the construction program was discontinued after one of the two planned stations had been erected and put into operation. Although this station was used until 1948 for transmission of electricity to all major centers except Jerusalem, it became evident at an early date that compared with alternative sources of power it was not as economical as had been anticipated. Later, when an expansion of Palestine's power supply became necessary, the Palestine Electric Corporation decided to install steam plants in lieu of erecting a second hydroelectric plant.[37]

As for the fulfillment of the original purposes of the concession, there seems to be little doubt that the emphasis upon the welfare aspect tended to decline, probably owing to the admission of non-Zionist interests into the concessionaire company's organization. Mr. Nathan, in fact, expresses the opinion that the company has, as a

[36] The plant at Tel-Or, at the confluence of the Yarmuk and Jordan rivers, has an average output of 60,000,000 kwh. per annum when it is functioning. This plant was completed and put into operation in 1932.

[37] Nathan, Gass, and Creamer, *op. cit.*, pp. 168, 178; Himadeh, *op. cit.*, p. 53.

rule, been more concerned with investors' gains than with the development of Palestine.[38]

Further drawbacks have been (1) the international antagonisms produced by the Rutenberg Concession[39] and (2) the fact that both the concession and the hydroelectric plant have been obstacles in the way of further development of the Jordan River system for irrigation and power.[40] These two factors are related to each other. Transjordan's consent to the program was originally given in 1921 by the then British High Commissioner for Palestine and Transjordan.[41] That official, however, was Sir Herbert Samuel, a Jew, who was accused of being unduly partial to Jewish, as against Arab, interests. The concession was, moreover, awarded without the extension of open invitations for tenders.[42] Later, when the Government of Transjordan was making its own irrigation plans involving the use of Jordan and Yarmuk waters, it was confronted with the fact that these could not be executed except with the consent of a private company partially controlled by Jews and more interested, both sentimentally and commercially, in Palestine than in Transjordan. It is also the case, however, that full exploitation even of Palestine's water resources would probably have necessitated the demolition of the Rutenberg hydroelectric plant and the termination of the concession. The Hays report of 1948, discussed later, seems to make that point clear.

In the Palestine War of 1948, and even since the conclusion of the armistices, the Rutenberg plant and its surrounding area have been important bones of contention between Israel and Jordan. Part of the essential equipment was removed by the Jordanian forces, and the plant could probably not be operated in any case in view of the close proximity of upstream waters and territory in unfriendly hands.

[38] Nathan, Gass, and Creamer, op. cit., p. 182; Worthington, op. cit., p. 53.
[39] Norman Bentwich, "Palestine's Progress," Journal of the Royal Central Asian Society, 1935, Part I, p. 79; M. G. Ionides, "The Perspective of Water Development in Palestine and Transjordan," Journal of the Royal Central Asian Society, 1946, Part III, pp. 273, 276.
[40] Peel Report, p. 363; Hays, op. cit., p. 22.
[41] This was a preliminary agreement between the High Commissioner and Rutenberg, dated September 21, 1921. Cf. Stein, op. cit., p. 381.
[42] Ibid., p. 382.

Syria, as the Arab state in whose territory the Yarmuk begins its flow, could become a factor of great importance in this situation.[43] Besides, the whole matter is in a highly confused state at present because of the invalidation in large measure of both Jewish Palestine's and Transjordan's economic planning, as a result of the recent territorial changes. Israeli interests have apparently gained complete control of the Palestine Electric Corporation.[44]

THE HULEH SCHEME

Lake Huleh and the adjacent marshes constitute part of the upper Jordan River system, which has its sources in the hill country of southern Syria and Lebanon and terminates in the Dead Sea. It has long been known that, by drainage of the lake and marshes, a considerable extension could be made to Palestine's cultivated area. The area thus reclaimed, plus a large additional area immediately to the north, could be placed under irrigation. This whole program could be accomplished in a single integrated scheme.

The importance of the Huleh reclamation proposals consists of two elements. In the first place, the Huleh area was the only truly sizable one in Palestine where development of this nature seemed to be feasible without undue expense and without extensive additional investigations. Secondly, since a large part of the area either was owned by the state or could apparently be purchased by the state at low cost, it seemed to afford an excellent possibility for promoting better relations between Jews and Arabs by making the two communities coparticipants in the benefits of reclamation and irrigation works, on the basis of a rationalized agriculture.

The original concession for draining the lake and swamps and improving part of the adjacent land area was granted in 1914 by the Ottoman Government to a Syrian company; in 1918 the concession was confirmed by Great Britain.[45] This company, however, showed

[43] Syria has already undertaken one irrigation scheme and has in contemplation other economic projects, involving the Yarmuk. Cf. United Nations, *Final Report of the United Nations Economic Survey Mission for the Middle East* (Lake Success, N.Y., 1949), Part I, pp. 90-91.
[44] "Pact Adjudged Area to Israel," New York *Times*, September 16, 1950.
[45] The name of this company, after 1918, was the Syro-Ottoman Agricultural Company. Cf. Himadeh, *op. cit.*, p. 116.

little initiative in getting ahead with the work, in spite of the fact that the importance of the project was being frequently stressed in official reports and Jewish quasi-official pronouncements. Finally, in 1934, with the approval of the mandatory power, the concession was purchased for £P192,000 by the Palestine Land Development Company, a Jewish concern. As a condition precedent to its approval, the Government of Palestine stipulated that 15,772 dunums[46] of the reclaimed land should be reserved for the use of Arabs. The total concession area amounted to 56,940 dunums, of which 16,919 were lake, 21,453 swamp, and 18,568 land.[47]

As the scheme was subsequently worked out, after a survey had been made by a British engineering firm,[48] it was proposed to bring under controlled irrigation an additional large quantity of land (partly irrigated already by inferior methods) immediately to the north of the concession area, making the total improved area about 100,000 dunums.[49] The government would pay approximately £P225,000 toward the cost of the work, and the company would pay the rest. The total cost of the entire project, including the cost of the concession and interest on capital during construction, was estimated at £P1,300,000; it was further estimated that about five years would be required for completion.[50]

This proposal, however, met with strong Arab objections, based ostensibly upon Arab unwillingness to approve of the large-scale establishment of Jewish settlements in that region.[51] Nevertheless, after long delays the mandatory power decided to proceed with the project; but meanwhile World War II had forced an indefinite postponement of actual operations. After the war, and until the termination of the mandate in 1948, the uncertainty of Palestine's

[46] A dunum is one-quarter of an acre.

[47] Peel Report, pp. 257-259; Himadeh, op. cit., p. 116.

[48] Rendel, Palmer, and Tritton.

[49] Malaria control was also to constitute part of the program.

[50] Peel Report, pp. 257-259; Himadeh, op. cit., p. 116; Nathan, Gass, and Creamer, op. cit., pp. 409-410.

[51] "The Palestine Land Transfers Regulation," Journal of the Royal Central Asian Society, 1940, Part II, p. 199; Peel Report, p. 88; New International Year Book, 1934, p. 541.

political future made it impracticable to undertake the work. The final details were never completely worked out.

The Government of Israel is now considering the implementation of the Huleh Scheme. However, there may now be some international complications, since it has been learned that successful implementation in the most economical manner might necessitate a diversion of the flow of the Yarmuk River into the Sea of Galilee.[52] This could probably not be made without an agreement with Jordan, in view of the division of sovereignty over the lower flow of the Yarmuk and over the lower Jordan River into which it runs. And, even if such a diversion proves to be unnecessary, the question might be raised whether Israel was legally entitled to cause substantial alterations in the flow of the lower Jordan River, which might be to the state of Jordan's disadvantage.[53] During the mandatory period these obstacles would not have been so important, since Great Britain had control of both Palestine and Transjordan governments.

Apparently a good opportunity was lost by the Government of Palestine and by the Jewish and Arab communities of that country. It was fully recognized that the Jewish company, which had some support from the Jewish Agency, was making a wholly uneconomic commitment, insofar as any clearly perceivable commercial interests were concerned, and that, for this reason, at least the government and the Arab community were in effect being offered major benefits at a much lower cost than would normally have been possible.[54]

THE HAYS PLAN: T.V.A. ON THE JORDAN

In the early 1940's the Jewish quasi-government[55] decided to have a comprehensive survey made of Palestine's water resources by a

[52] United Nations, *op. cit.*, Part I, pp. 19, 44.

[53] See chapter on regional planning.

[54] As for the company's motives, it should be borne in mind that many Jewish transactions of that era were made mainly for the purpose of increasing the area of Jewish settlement in Palestine, without too much regard for the cost. Also cf. "Another 'Emek' in the Making," *Life in Israel*, December, 1950, pp. 4-7.

[55] The Commission on Palestine Surveys took the initiative in this matter. The expenses were defrayed by the Palestine Foundation (Keren Hayesod) of America.

prominent American engineer, Mr. James B. Hays.[56] Permission was obtained from the Government of Palestine, and the survey was conducted over a period of years (1943-46). The result was a detailed plan for the integrated utilization of the water resources which were, or might become, available to Palestine. The plan was published in 1948, in the form of a brightly colored pamphlet entitled *T.V.A. on the Jordan*. It was given extensive publicity, particularly in the United States. Clearly the Jewish aim was to capture people's imaginations by the ingenuity of the proposals, which, if carried out, would change the whole face of the country.

The Hays report was, in a sense, an expert confirmation of assertions which Zionists had been making for some time. Included in the plan, for example, was a great hydroelectric project which involved a diversion of salt water from the Mediterranean into the Dead Sea. This, together with the concept of a "Jordan Valley Authority" along T.V.A. lines, had been suggested four years previously by an American agricultural specialist, W. C. Lowdermilk, in his book *Palestine, Land of Promise*, which had been even more widely circulated. As for the elaborate irrigation aspects of the Hays Plan, it had long been an article of faith among Zionist leaders that Palestine could be rendered abundantly fruitful by the exploitation of untapped sources of irrigation water.[57]

Although little challenged from the engineering viewpoint,[58] the Hays Plan was, even in the last days of the mandate, open to the serious objection that it contained overoptimistic assumptions as to the exploitability by Palestine of water originating outside of that country, and of water diverted into Palestine to the possible detriment of Transjordan. Major works in connection with the scheme were to be constructed in Lebanon, though, curiously enough, the Litani River was not involved. One of the diversion channels was to pass through Syrian territory. Most of the normal flow of the lower Jordan

[56] Hays, *op. cit.*, pp. v-xviii.

[57] *Ibid.*, pp. vii, 61-66; W. C. Lowdermilk, *Palestine, Land of Promise* (New York, 1944), *passim*.

[58] For technical criticism of the plan, cf. E. C. Willatts, "Some Geographical Aspects in the Palestine Problem," *Geographical Journal*, April, 1947.

was to be diverted upstream. Free use by Palestine of water flowing into the country from neighboring territories was taken for granted. And, finally, it was planned to introduce salt water into the lower extremity of the Jordan River, which in that area served as the frontier between Palestine and Transjordan.

But those difficulties were negligible as compared with the ones which arose after the birth of the state of Israel. Large areas which were to have been benefited by the Hays scheme were wholly outside of Israeli territory. When the Clapp Mission inquired into the matter in the latter part of 1949, it reached the conclusion that not more than 15 per cent of the plan could properly be put into effect without international agreements.[59]

The present attitude of the Israeli Government and of Zionists seems to be that the Hays Plan, partly because of its great popular appeal at home and abroad and partly because of the valuable scientific data contained in Mr. Hays' report, is still to be regarded as the general foundation upon which workable programs for irrigation and production of power in Israel are to be developed, in the light of existing and near-future conditions.

But, in view of developments in 1950,[60] there can no longer be the slightest doubt that the full cooperation of Israel's neighbors would be a condition precedent to the implementation of any such scheme. It is presumed, therefore, that Israel intends, after peace treaties have been concluded, to take the initiative in sponsoring proposals for a Jordan Valley Authority on an international basis. The advancement of such a project would almost certainly be greatly delayed, even then, by the necessity for each of the other states (i.e., Jordan, Syria, and Lebanon) to formulate in precise terms the bases of its special national interests in the matter, and by the necessity which would thereafter arise of coordinating the four national interests for the general benefit of all. Not only would it be exceedingly difficult, in the atmosphere of political stresses and strains in the

[59] United Nations, op. cit., Part II, p. 45; Israel Office of Information, Irrigation Schemes for Israel, IM26 (New York, April, 1949), p. 2.

[60] Since the issuance of the Clapp report in December, 1949, Jordan has annexed a large segment of Palestine, and there is a growing tendency among other nations to accept the annexation as a fait accompli.

Arab world, to arrive at a basic agreement even moderately satisfactory to all four parties; also, as has been amply demonstrated in
the case of Iraq, where the complications are not nearly so great,
there would be many knotty questions in regard to the nature and
powers of the control board to be established. Whereas the Three-
Year Plan for 1951-53 (discussed in detail later) envisions an addition
of only 150,000 acres to the irrigated area of Israel, the Hays Plan
contemplated an addition of 600,000-750,000 irrigated acres for the
whole Palestine area. Whereas there are no hydroelectric projects of
great consequence under immediate consideration,[61] the Hays Plan
called for an additional hydroelectric capacity of 600,000,000 kilowatt-hours per year.

The Huleh Scheme is included in the over-all Hays Plan as
"Stage 6." But, if the matter is handled in this way, a diversion of
the international Yarmuk River into the Sea of Galilee will be necessary in order to maintain the level of that lake at the height of its
outlet into the Jordan River.[62]

The total estimated construction cost of the Hays program, as
originally formulated, was £P63,000,000. This estimate was based on
1941 cost and foreign-exchange levels.[63] In 1949 the local pound was
devaluated from a $4.00 to a $2.80 equivalent.

[61] United Nations, *op. cit.*, Part II, pp. 43-46.
Doubtless the most logical substitute for the Mediterranean-Dead Sea hydroelectric scheme, which may no longer be feasible since Jordan has complete control of the lower waters and land areas involved in the project, would be a
utilization of the 1300-foot drop from the Gulf of Aqaba to the Dead Sea via the
Arraba depression. The Arraba depression constitutes part of the frontier region
between Israel and Jordan. Cf. E. Boyko and E. J. Mayer, *The Negev: Facts,
Hopes and Plans* (Tel Aviv, 1950), p. 28.

[62] In January, 1951, after this chapter had been completed, the Israel Government decided to undertake the Huleh project as a separate venture. In March and
April the conduct of actual work on it gave rise to serious border difficulties
between Israel and Syria because the work was being done in a zone which, by
the terms of the armistice agreement between the two countries, had been
demilitarized pending the conclusion of a definitive peace treaty. Syria interpreted
this demilitarized status to mean that Israel's *de jure* sovereignty over the territory
had not yet been established. Cf. New York *Times*, January 21, 1951; January 22,
1951; April 26, 1951. Also cf. Hays, *op. cit.*, pp. 54-55, 71-76.

[63] Hays, *op. cit.*, p. 1.

THE THREE-YEAR PLAN

In April, 1949, Prime Minister David Ben-Gurion announced a Four-Year Plan, of which the stated purpose was to provide room and employment for a doubled Jewish population by the end of 1953.[64] Although this plan was never elaborated in full detail, a start was made on numerous projects based on the aims then proclaimed by the Israeli Government. The main ones announced were:[65]

1. Increased cultivation, with a doubling of the grain-growing area.
2. Development of new industries based on skill and deftness.
3. An intensified housing program.
4. Development of a chemical-manufacturing industry.
5. Extension of the diamond-polishing industry.
6. Rehabilitation of the citrus groves, which had been heavily damaged during the Palestine War.
7. Improvement of the roads to the Dead Sea, where important raw materials are available for chemical industries.

Since more than a year elapsed before detailed specifications for this program could be worked out, the planning was ultimately adjusted to a three-year basis, with the terminal date, that is, December 31, 1953, remaining the same. In this connection it was assumed that the work accomplished during 1950 would be sufficient to make realization of the originally stated purpose possible.

The resultant Three-Year Plan which has been formulated in terms of American dollars, involves an expenditure of $1,500,000,000 on development and immigration during the three calendar years in question. The main proclaimed objectives are:[66]

1. To bring 600,000 immigrants into Israel.
2. To create full employment.
3. To narrow the present large deficit in the balance of trade.
4. To bring Israel closer to self-sufficiency in food.

[64] The estimated population on December 31, 1948, was 867,000, of whom 759,000 were Jews and 108,000 non-Jews (mostly Arabs).
[65] New International Year Book, 1950, p. 277.
[66] "U.S. Jews Pledge Billion to Israel," New York Times, September 7, 1950.

The principal contents of the Three-Year Plan are:[67]

1. The establishment of an additional 40,000 farms, and an increase of the cultivated area by 150,000 irrigated acres and 2,000,000 unirrigated acres.[68]

2. Enlargement of the widespread economic control system which has already been instituted and rigidly enforced.

3. An extension of rationing to all essential supplies.

4. A more effective regulation of prices, wages, and profits.

5. Allocations of raw materials to be proportioned to the amount of finished product delivered by the purchasers.

6. Employment of 95 per cent of Israel's potential work force during the first year of the plan, and full employment in the second.

[67] Irving Spiegel, "3-Year Aid Needs of Israel Outlined," New York *Times,* October 28, 1950; "Ben Gurion Insists on More Migrants," New York *Times,* September 4, 1950.

[68] Before the Palestine War of 1948, the whole cultivated area of Palestine amounted to 2,160,000 acres. The planned increase in Israel's present acreage could be made possible only by the proposed cultivation of the Negev—the largely barren southern area comprising about 3800 square miles.

While there are theoretical possibilities that a large percentage of the Negev land (perhaps amounting to well over 50 per cent of the total area) could eventually be cultivated, it would be decidedly premature at the present juncture to regard even a remote approach to such an outcome as at all likely. One aspect of this complex problem is that, although many ingenious suggestions have been made, there are not even any adequate known sources of drinking water in that area. The farther south one goes, the more saline the underground water becomes. One proposal has been to enclose salt-water wells in a vacuum and distill the water by sun treatment. The extent to which irrigation would be necessary as a condition precedent to cultivation is not yet known.

Unquestionably enormous efforts are being made by the Israel authorities to find solutions for the various aspects of the Negev problem. However, in a letter to the writer dated April 18, 1951, the Israel Office of Information, New York, stated that, as far as present knowledge is concerned, the potentially cultivable area of the Negev is 182,000 acres.

It seems probable that the insertion of this item into the Three-Year Plan was more for purposes of inspiration and morale-building than because of any real hopes on the part of the Israeli authorities that such an extension will be possible.

Cf. Warriner, *op. cit.,* p. 10; "Sun Called to New Job," New York *Times,* July 3, 1950; Nathan, Gass, and Creamer, *op. cit.,* p. 126; Sydney Gruson, "Israeli 'Islands' Absorb Settlers," New York *Times,* February 6, 1951; *Peel Report,* p. 254; Boyko and Mayer, *op. cit.,* pp. 19, 29.

7. Import of $196,000,000 of working capital.
8. Construction of 320,000 dwelling units.
9. Ratio of export to import to be increased from 14 per cent in 1949 to 49 per cent in 1953.

According to the breakdown presented by the Minister of Finance, Mr. Eliezer Kaplan, the expenditures under the plan are to be divided as follows:[69]

Housing and public works	$600,000,000
Agriculture, citriculture, and irrigation	340,000,000
Maintenance of immigrants in camps, re-settlement of immigrants, and social services	290,000,000
Development of adequate transportation	80,000,000
Balance for miscellaneous enterprises	190,000,000

The Israeli Government discussed the details of this plan with American Zionist leaders at a conference held in Jerusalem in September, 1950. The government's proposals were unanimously approved by the American delegates. A month later, in Washington, D.C., Mr. Kaplan presented a report on the subject to a 280-man steering committee of the National Planning Conference for Israel and Jewish Rehabilitation. At that meeting there were 1200 delegates representing forty-four American Jewish organizations.[70]

It is anticipated that two-thirds of the cost of the program, or $1,000,000,000, will be defrayed from sources within the United States. Commercial loans and share investments from American sources, other than government investments, were to be included in the $1,000,000,000 total. It is believed, however, that the greatest reliance will have to be placed on straight contributions from abroad, and on foreign purchases of government bonds. Because the union-protected wages are so high in Israel (particularly so, in view of the artificially maintained high exchange value of the Israel pound), there does not seem to be much outside confidence in the profit-

[69] Spiegel, *loc. cit.*
[70] *Ibid.*

ability of investment.[71] However, the possibility of extensive investment by American Jews on a predominantly sentimental basis
remains.[72]

The Three-Year Plan was to be formally put into effect on January
1, 1951. Shortly after that date, it was to be the most important
beneficiary of a fund-raising campaign in the United States by the
United Palestine Appeal. The latter is the main subsidiary of the
United Jewish Appeal, the consolidated organ for Jewish philan-
thropies. Campaigns toward the same end are to be conducted by
other Zionist bodies, such as Hadassah and Histadrut. Also a campaign to sell Israel Government bonds was to be instituted on May
1, 1951.

A scheme on the ambitious scale of the Three-Year Plan is
regarded by the Israeli authorities as essential for reasons other than
economic. From the economic viewpoint alone, for example, it
would have been highly desirable to restrict immigration temporarily.
For, whatever Israel's ultimate absorptive capacity may be, there was
no possibility of efficiently absorbing the great numbers planned for,
at the rate at which it was proposed to admit them.[73] It was believed
essential, however, that population should be provided for some of
the strategically situated but thinly inhabited regions of the country.
An important contributory element was the fact that the principle
of free admission of Jews into the National Homeland had long been
proclaimed as one of the basic conditions of Zionism. There was,
in consequence, the fear that restrictive measures would be interpreted by world Jewry, whose financial help is so greatly needed,
as an abandonment of Zionism in favor of autarchy.[74]

[71] Nevertheless, there are some indications to the contrary. Kaiser-Frazer has
established an automobile assembly plant in Israel, apparently with the idea of
facilitating the sale of American-style cars in all the soft-currency countries. (Cf.
Hadassah Newsletter, December, 1950, p. 1.) Also the large amounts and the
nature of the recent Export-Import Bank loans to Israel, totaling $135,000,000
in 1949 and 1950, would seem to indicate confidence in the country's industrial
future.
[72] United Nations, *op. cit.*, Part I, pp. 55, 56, 58.
[73] Total immigration from May 1, 1948, to December 31, 1949, was 341,969
persons. Cf. *Statistical Bulletin of Israel*, May/July, 1950.
[74] Moshe Brilliant, "Israel Sets Sights High," New York *Times*, September 10,
1950.

Any forecasting of the possible extent to which the Three-Year Plan will have advanced Israel economically must be done in the light of the country's long-range requirements. Here it will have to be assumed that the funds anticipated will be actually forthcoming.

Doubtless Israel's most important long-range economic need is to develop industries in which labor and raw-material costs will be only minor elements in the price of the finished product. Great expansion along this line seems to be a distinct possibility in view of the large proportion of the population having an educational and environmental background conducive to the .acquisition of high skills. If this end can be achieved to a large degree, Israel can possibly emulate Switzerland in the matter of supporting a sizable population with a high standard of living, in spite of limited natural resources. Since the raw materials for such industries are not bulky, large stocks could be maintained against future shortages of imported materials. High wages, too, would be possible, since the industries in question would be based on skills which were both scarce and in great demand on the world market. Also of interest in the comparison between Israel and Switzerland is the fact that Israel's future possibilities in the matter of attracting tourists are considerable.

But one factor which will militate against such a solution—at least for the time being—is the difficulty, as a result of the Arab states' policies vis-à-vis oil and water resources, in producing or obtaining adequate supplies of power at a sufficiently low unit cost. Still another is the fact that most of the immigrants now being admitted are from countries in Asia and North Africa.[75] In general, the customary standards of living of such immigrants are similar to

[75] In an article published in the December 26, 1950, issue of the New York Times, Mr. Sydney Gruson stated: "In the first eight months of 1950 more than 100,000 Jews from Africa and Asia were brought to Israel, compared with 60,000 from Europe—an almost complete reversal of the ratio in the preceding eighteen months. The source of the African and Asian movement was mainly Yemen, Morocco, Algeria, Tunisia, and Libya and immigrants as a whole are unskilled and illiterate, possessing only the clothes on their backs. . . . On the whole the process of turning their primitive capabilities to modern industrial needs has been slow and industrious."

those of non-Jewish natives of the countries of origin. Hence their adjustment to a quasi-European economic and social environment will present, if it has not already presented, difficult problems requiring special solutions. The large influx of Jews of these types may also have a marked effect upon future cultural trends in Israel.[76]

From the politico-economic viewpoint, Israel's most important long-range need is the development of agriculture to the highest point possible by the employment of the most modern implements and techniques. Here there are two important obstacles. The first is the necessity, already mentioned, of international agreements as a condition precedent to rational extension of irrigation over a wide area.[77] The second is the fact that, although many Zionists have long assumed that the immense southern wastes (the Negev) can be made cultivable, ways and means of producing this result have not yet been discovered, except for relatively small stretches in that arid region.[78] Artificial rain might prove to be a partial answer, but it is also possible that this could not be produced without depriving other Middle Eastern areas of the water which they need and to which they are entitled. In general, the problem throughout the Middle East is not so much a shortage of good soil as a deficiency in the total supply of water, even with the utmost in modern engineering developments.[79]

In view of these circumstances, there is much room for doubt that the Three-Year Plan will advance the Israeli economy to the extent anticipated or hoped for by the planners. It may, however, become possible, toward the close of the three-year period, to formulate a more promising plan for the ensuing years. An important

[76] United Nations, op. cit., Part I, p. 55; Alfred E. Kahn, "Palestine: A Problem in Economic Evaluation," Quarterly Journal of Economics, September, 1944, p. 558; "Influx from West Sought by Israel," New York Times, January 15, 1951.

[77] In 1949 the total irrigated area was about 75,000 acres, most of which was irrigated by means of wells. The increase during 1950 is not yet known but was certainly less than 25,000 acres. Cf. United Nations, op. cit., Part II, p. 19.

[78] See footnote 68.

[79] Commission on Palestine Surveys, Map Showing the Proposed Integrated Irrigation and Hydro-Electric Development of Palestine, October, 1945. (This is issued with James B. Hays' T.V.A. on the Jordan. Cf. also Warriner, op. cit., p. 56.)

factor in this connection is the probability that most of the prospective immigrants into Israel will already have been admitted by the end of 1953.[80]

PROSPECTS FOR THE FUTURE

Probably the most objective expert appraisal of Israel's present prospects along developmental lines is that which was made by the Clapp Mission in the latter part of 1949: "There are forces which cannot be measured in figures, and these forces sometimes decide issues in apparent defiance of reason. Israel has accomplished astonishing things already. It would be as rash to predict that it will not succeed as that it cannot fail. Much depends on the extent of help from abroad."[81]

It has already been pointed out that Israel's per capita income, despite the recent setbacks, is still high by Middle East standards. Probably, also, in view of the activities of Histadrut described earlier, the distribution of national income is far more equitable than in the rest of the region.

But, important as these advances are, it would still be premature to regard the National Home experiment as an assured success.

In the absence of war, it may be assumed that, once solutions have been found for the immediate problems, long-range planning will have at least a fair chance of producing the spectacular results hoped for. Meanwhile there are two vital questions, which so far have no clear answers. One is how soon the rate of increase in production can be augmented faster than the rate of increase in the population. The other is to what extent contributions from world Jewry can be depended upon to bridge the gap which now exists, and which will almost certainly continue to exist until the immigration begins to dwindle considerably. Some of the relevant figures may be noted here:

The latest official estimate of Israel's total population is 1,354,000 (of whom 1,184,000 are Jews), as of November, 1950. Between July 1, 1948, and November 1, 1950, the Jewish population increase was

[80] American Zionist Council, *Israel After Two Years*, April 23, 1950.
[81] United Nations, *op. cit.*, Part I, p. 55.

528,000, of which 480,000 is ascribable to immigration and the rest to natural increase. On November 1, 1950, the total number of Jewish immigrants not yet absorbed into the working population amounted to 115,575.[82]

The Three-Year Plan, 1951-53, calls for a total supply of $1,000,-000,000 in three years from American sources alone. Even if 75 per cent of the American remittance in those years is in forms other than gratuitous, an annual straight donation of $84,000,0000 would still be necessary. But if only 50 per cent is in the form of loans and investments, as seems more likely, the donation required will be $167,000,000 annually. During the eleven months' period from October, 1948, through August, 1949, donations from all countries amounted to $144,000,000.[83] This last figure was almost equal to the total of all receipts from world Jewry funds for the twenty-five years 1920-44.[84]

In view of the many uncertainties implicit in these statistics, there is apparently not much to be added at this time to the statement made in the Clapp report. Peace with the neighboring countries would, of course, greatly improve the situation; but to say that is probably to put the cart before the horse. The Arab states' inducement to agree to peace terms will probably be much greater if it appears to them that Israel will in any case survive economically.[85]

[82] New York *Times*, December 1, 1950.
[83] United Nations, *op. cit.*, Part I, p. 58.
[84] Nathan, Gass, and Creamer, *op. cit.*, p. 3.
[85] As of December 1, 1951, Israel was scheduled to receive economic aid from the United States Government in the amount of $65,000,000, mainly in the form of grants, during the American fiscal year 1951-52. However, this favorable aspect of the situation may be at least offset by the general deterioration of Israel's economy since the completion of this chapter.

CHAPTER IX

❖

Iran

GENERAL BACKGROUND

PERSIA AND TURKEY: PARALLELS

In connection with this chapter on Iran, and the one on Turkey which follows, it is of particular interest to note some of the close parallels between the two countries with respect to the political, economic, and historical backgrounds and earlier trends.

Both countries, up to the end of World War I, had continued to be remnants of great Moslem empires. In both, all previous technological modernization of consequence had been in the nature of projects undertaken by Europeans in their own interests, whether commercial or strategic. The total progress which had been made along such lines was extremely slight. A third similarity was that, after World War I, the European powers and their nationals seemed to assume that it would be possible for them to carry on, both in Persia and in Turkey, in their accustomed roles as seekers of their own ends without regard to the countries' best interests.[1]

As for the political backgrounds, Persia's revolution had occurred

[1] Good accounts of foreign activities in Persia, both before and during the period immediately following World War I, are to be found in *Iran*, by William S. Haas (New York, 1946), pp. 57, 131, 139-140.

in 1906, Turkey's in 1908; in each case a written constitution along Western lines had been the result. Some reservations should, however, be made in regard to this apparent parallelism. Throughout the long history of the Ottoman Empire, Constantinople and Anatolia had at all times been exposed to some measure of Western intellectual influence; the 1908 constitution was by no means the first experiment in Western-style reform. In Persia, by contrast, the events of 1906 were in the nature of a complete novelty. In one respect, though, Persians were better prepared than were Turks for the change. The traditional occupational limitations which Turks had imposed upon themselves militated against any wholehearted acceptance of Western ideas, whether political, economic, or social. Persians had no such basic inhibitions, although there were, of course, many cultural and social obstacles.

The two countries were also similar in that both had small populations in relation to the total acreage which could be made cultivable, given proper irrigation facilities and adequate mechanization. This situation has not altered substantially.[2]

Finally, Mustafa Kemal (Ataturk) in Turkey had his counterpart in the Persian, Reza Pahlevi (later Reza Shah). However, important as are the many similarities between these two leaders, the tactics which they applied, and the circumstances which brought them to the forefront of affairs, the differences in their methods and results, as indicated in these two chapters, are of even greater importance.

REZA SHAH'S MODERNIZATION CAMPAIGN

Reza Pahlevi, as leader of the Russian-trained Persian Cossack Brigade, headed a march against Teheran in 1921 in protest against the submission of the then government to British influence. Pahlevi became Minister of War in the cabinet which resulted from this

[2] According to the best available statistics, the present cultivated area of Iran is 41,500,000 acres, as against 82,500,000 acres of wasteland which could be brought under cultivation through the introduction of irrigation water or machinery. Sixty-five per cent of the present cultivation is on a rain-fed basis. Cf. Overseas Consultants, Inc., *Report on Seven Year Development Plan for the Plan Organization of the Imperial Government of Iran* (New York, 1949), III, 9, 125. Cf. Also E. B. Worthington, *Middle East Science* (London, 1945), p. 182.

crisis, and was from that time until 1941 the dominant political figure in the country. In 1925 he became titular as well as actual head of the government. But, unlike Mustafa Kemal, he did not proclaim a republic. He took the traditional title of Shahinshah (or Shah), which has religious significance in addition to its political import. He ruled with a strong hand.

Pahlevi apparently had no initial intention of dispensing wholly with strong foreign influence, as long as that influence was not British or Russian. In 1922 Dr. Arthur Millspaugh, an American recommended by the Department of State, was appointed by the Persian Government as Financial Adviser, with virtually complete control in the field of governmental revenues and expenditures. Also an American Advisory Commission was employed to assist in administrative reforms. Pahlevi's aim was to eliminate corruption, inefficiency, and waste through the use of these mediums, and thereby to bring into being a general situation more favorable to his proposed campaign to modernize Persia in a large-scale manner and in as short order as possible. As to his main objectives, Pahlevi had the strong backing of the intellectual elements in the Persian populace. According to all authorities on the subject, a state of psychological readiness for drastic change existed. In politically conscious circles, there was a general sentiment of impatience with (1) the highhanded tactics of foreigners, particularly the British and the Russians, and (2) the backward local conditions which made it possible for such tactics to succeed and to assume great importance in Persian affairs.

The era which followed, with all its austerity and its hardships for the great majority of the populace, can hardly be regarded as one in which the general Persian standard of living was a paramount official consideration. A close examination of Pahlevi's policies, as manifested in practice, leads to the inevitable conclusion that the only direct object of importance was to increase Persia's power to resist encroachments and to make Persia respectable in the eyes of her own citizens and of the outside world. To achieve this power and this respectability, she must have modern manufacturing industries, a thriving commerce, efficient and secure communications, well-ordered cities, honest and competent officials, and improved educational facilities—all of these to be completely under Persian control as soon as practicable. To put it differently, the central purpose was to eliminate the most obvious causes of shame, without too much regard to whether the population as a whole benefited or was harmed by the process. In this respect there was a considerable difference, as to official attitudes, between Persia's development and Turkey's. Pahlevi, in spite of his own humble birth, never attempted to introduce Western-style philosophical concepts, such as, for example, the equality of all Persians. Moreover, his tolerance of some established institutions which militated against egalitarianism was in partial contrast to Kemal's relentless uprooting of such institutions.[3]

Pahlevi had, by 1925, acquired a strong conviction that widespread modern communications were Persia's foremost basic need. His central project was the construction of a cross-country railway line which would in time be the nucleus of a great network of railways and highways. As his plans evolved, with the help of extensive advice on the part of foreign engineers, the main question was whether to construct an east-west line, which could be readily connected with the Iraqi and Indian railways, or a north-south line, which would not have the same international implications but which would serve a valuable purpose from the viewpoint of national self-sufficiency. He finally chose the latter, probably because of his wish to take any and all practicable steps as soon as possible to reduce Persia's dependence upon foreign countries. His later decisions as to branch lines refute the idea, sometimes expressed, that he objected to the establish-

[3] Among the established institutions which Pahlevi continued to tolerate were: the widespread existence of large privately held estates, including the extensive crown lands which were, for all practical purposes, his own property; and the theoretical predominance of the Moslem religion in the affairs of the state. The latter situation, however, was modified considerably. The extensive Waqf possessions, i.e., religious sanctuaries and the investments from the sanctuaries' profits, were placed under state administration, with the clergy retained as mere subordinate administrative officials of the government. There followed a great decline in the influence of the clergy during the period of Pahlevi's rule. However, it perpetuated the possibilities both of a future revival of the clergy's influence and of the use of religion by the state as a pretext for failure to remedy inequalities. Cf. Haas, *op. cit.*, p. 157.

ment of any connections at all with neighboring countries. He simply did not accord them priority in his plans.

The Trans-Iranian Railway, built by foreign engineers and, to a large extent, foreign workmen, was Pahlevi's foremost single accomplishment along developmental lines. Completed in 1938 at a cost variously estimated at between £30,000,000 and £40,000,000, it has been regarded as an engineering feat of the highest skill. Although numerous manufacturing industries sprang up in Persia during the between-wars period, the railway network always assumed first importance in the planning activities, followed closely by the road construction activities. In this emphasis upon internal thoroughfares Pahlevi differed somewhat from Kemal. Possibly the only reason is that Persia's communications were in a less developed state than Turkey's at the beginning of the postwar era and hence offered a seemingly greater challenge.

In 1927 a clash occurred between Pahlevi (now the Shah) and Millspaugh, which resulted in the latter's departure from Persia. From that time on, the powers of foreigners in the country were greatly reduced, and matters were handled according to the Shah's own desires. Foreign advisers and technicians were still engaged, but always with the distinct understanding that they were employees, pure and simple, of the Persian authorities, whose word was at all times final. Just as in Turkey, the practice was followed of distributing the contracts of employment among foreigners of many nationalities. The construction of the railway was a highly international undertaking, both as to the contracting firms and as to the skilled labor employed.

Freed from Millspaugh's authority and veto power in financial matters, the Shah made his own arrangements for the financing and execution of the modernization program begun in 1925. As was also the case in Turkey at the time, foreign loans were rejected and the policy was adopted of financing all development from the country's own budget. Persia, to be sure, was in a somewhat better position than Turkey to handle matters this way, since she was receiving, during a good part of the between-wars period, fairly large oil royalties from the Anglo-Iranian (once Anglo-Persian) Oil Company.[4] These, however, were not nearly adequate to finance a total program of the magnitude upon which the Shah was determined. Despite this fact, the Shah never abandoned the policy of complete avoidance of external borrowing.

For the financing of railway construction, the Shah established a special fund comprised of the revenue from a tax on sugar and tea; road construction expenses were defrayed in a similar manner from a newly instituted road tax collected in the form of a customs surcharge. The former tax resulted in a distinct reduction of general living standards, since sugar and tea were for most Persians the only items of everyday use for which they had to pay cash.[5] And, although improvements in agriculture were an integral part of the Shah's general program, this aspect received, for the most part, only token emphasis—wholly insufficient to neutralize the detrimental effects of the taxes.[6] Also some of the heavily protected manufacturing industries which were instituted had the result of raising the costs of necessities far above those which would have prevailed had duty-free imports been permitted. The general consequence was that, by the time of the outbreak of World War II, the economic position of the average Iranian (as Persians were now called) was considerably and chronically worse than it had been in 1925. There was, moreover, no evidence of any intention on the Shah's part to take direct action to improve this situation. The taxes which he had

[4] The oil royalties amounted to £327,523 in 1925. From that year on, there was a general upward trend. The figure for 1938 was £3,545,313. A table of annual royalties is contained in *Iran, An Economic Study*, by Raj Narain Gupta (Allahabad, India, 1947), p. 101.

[5] The government today has a monopoly, which is tantamount to taxation on the sale of sugar and tea.

For information regarding the mode of living, economy, and expenditures of Iranian peasants, cf. Josephine Vogt, A *Study of Home and Family Life in Rural Iran* (New York, 1950), pp. 2-4.

[6] Donald N. Wilber, *Iran, Past and Present* (Princeton, 1948), p. 99.

Another important aspect of this matter is the fact that the great majority of peasants, because of the absence of credit facilities, find themselves under pressure of necessity to sell their surplus produce at the times when it is most plentiful Hence they are usually unable to take advantage of price fluctuations in the places of consumption, or even of new markets opened through extensions of communications.

imposed were, generally speaking, the types which were easiest to collect with large resultant yields. The difficulties being encountered by the present government in collecting income tax and land tax afford testimony as to Reza Shah Pahlevi's wisdom from the purely technical viewpoint. The official propaganda to the effect that Iranians were taxed for their own benefit seems to have been most effective in those cases where the benefits were least.

Education, on a modernized basis, was widely extended during Reza Shah's reign; in general, it was well received. However, owing to inadequate facilities and personnel, much of the progress was not as great as it appeared on the surface to be. As for public health, considerable gains were achieved in the large cities, but the general situation in the rural regions remained much the same as ever. Progress was made in many other fields having some relation to living standards.[7] Emphasis, however, was on spectacular achievements instead of thoroughness in solution of problems. In some cases the net result, from the viewpoint of the persons concerned, was deterioration rather than improvement. Virtually no attention was given to such fundamental questions as rationalization of land and water rights.

In 1941, because of Reza Shah's pro-German activities, Britain and Russia invaded Iran and began a military occupation, with division of the country into a British and a Russian zone, which was to last until early in 1946. Reza Shah was forced to abdicate in favor of his son, the present Shah.

Up to that time, with the exception of the Khuzistan Scheme (discussed later), there had been no major planning in Iran for the elevation of living standards of the population in general. There were, moreover, in 1941, apparently few ideas as to how the great developmental progress which had been made could be applied to the betterment of the whole populace. For many years the government had been in the nature of a quasi-totalitarian dictatorship; criticisms of the Shah's objectives, or apparent objectives, were not permissible. Unquestionably many of the innovations had potential value for the

[7] One example is the status of women. Cf. Haas, *op. cit.*, pp. 153, 182.

future of all Persians, but proposals for realizing these values were yet to appear.[8]

Although, generally speaking, the abdication was a source of relief to most politically conscious Iranians, it is questionable whether the succeeding situation constituted any marked improvement. The occupation, to be sure, gave rise to further development of rail and road communications, also to further industrialization. Politically, however, the new state of affairs had certain unfortunate aspects. In the British zone of occupation the new liberties suddenly granted to the populace were not coordinated either with strong leadership or with inner disciplines. The result was, to a considerable extent, chaos and corruption. In the Soviet zone conditions were under somewhat better control because of the strength of the Tudeh party, which at that time was favored, but apparently not controlled, by the Soviet Communist party. The Tudeh party advocated for Iran an institution of certain Marxist principles, as adapted to specific Iranian needs. Land reform was among the foremost of its proclaimed objectives. The Tudeh following gradually spread in the British zone as well, until it was numerically the largest claimed by any party. But conditions in that zone remained unstable.

In 1943 the young Shah reinstated Dr. Millspaugh, the American who had controlled Persian finances during part of the twenties, as Administrator General of the Finances of Iran, with the same broad powers which he had previously enjoyed. Millspaugh, however, resigned in 1945 as a result of serious disagreements with the Shah.[9]

When World War II ended, the general standard of living was decidedly in the forefront of Iranian thinking at the politically conscious levels. Tudeh followers, because of the Communist influence,

[8] Most of the more recent authoritative writers on Iran are of the opinion that Reza Shah's reforms and activities were, on the whole, well conceived as to their relationships to a fully modernized social and economic structure. They are equally agreed that the existing structure in Iran is decidedly unbalanced, owing in large measure to the lingering effects of Reza Shah's policies, coupled with his failure to cope with the vested interests of landed proprietors. Cf. Haas, *op. cit., passim;* Wilber, *op. cit., passim;* L. P. Elwell-Sutton, *Modern Iran* (London, 1938), *passim.*

[9] A. C. Millspaugh, "Dr. Millspaugh's Stand Given," New York *Times,* October 10, 1950.

had been schooled to think along such lines. Apart from the Tudeh, the preponderance of political influence had reverted to the large landowners, who had retained their great estates throughout the period of Reza Shah's reforms and whose power lay in their ability to control the peasant vote.[10] This group, and their educated supporters, must now of necessity at least give the appearance of being as much concerned as were the Tudeh with the elevation of living standards. Meanwhile the growth of corruption, of inefficient administration, and of the gap between rich and poor was making ever clearer the need of drastic reform of a sweeping and thoroughgoing nature. The situation was, in fact, similar in some respects to the one which had prevailed before the late Shah's assumption of power. The sequel can best be related in connection with the discussion of Iran's Seven-Year Plan, which has outstanding political as well as economic importance.

The paragraphs which follow describe the three major plans which Persia (Iran) has had, between the end of World War I and December 31, 1950, for the elevation of general living standards.

THE KHUZISTAN SCHEME

During the period from 1935 to 1945 a series of attempts were made, in the southern province of Khuzistan, to couple the introduction of modern irrigation and modernized agricultural methods with new settlements of peasants on government-owned wastelands.

For formulation of the original plan an Agricultural Corporation of Khuzistan was established by the state-controlled Bank for Agriculture. The proposals which developed were on a grand scale, providing for one large dam on the Karun River and one on the Karkeh, which would supplement a dam already constructed by the Department of Agriculture but not in use. The precise acreage to be brought under

---

[10] Reza Shah had resorted on several occasions to the punitive confiscation of estates of landholders whom he regarded as dangerous, or who opposed his policies. When the present Shah acceded to the throne with the blessing of Great Britain and the Soviet Union, he undertook to return those confiscated lands to their rightful owners. Cf. Royal Institute of International Affairs, *The Middle East: A Political and Economic Survey* (London, 1950), p. 222.

cultivation was apparently not determined. Each of the proposed new dams would have yielded 70 to 100 cubic meters per second.

However, since Reza Shah was not disposed to divert such large funds from his other enterprises for this purpose, and since it was doubtful whether enough peasants could be induced to settle, the corporation's proposals were watered down considerably. In its revised form, the scheme envisaged a bringing of 175,000-250,000 acres of uncultivated state land under the plow; a voluntary, but assisted, transfer of peasants from other regions; an introduction of agricultural machinery; a construction of houses for the new settlers; and a surpervision of the settlement to prevent the lodging of persons and animals in the same buildings.

By the time of Reza Shah's abdication, a total of about 37,500 acres were actually being cultivated; and the British Army at once assumed charge of the irrigation development aspects of the project, with a view of going ahead with the work and thereby helping to combat the wartime shortages of food in the middle East. At a cost of a million pounds, British engineers brought irrigation water to a sizeable additional area. Meanwhile, about 100 tractors had been imported, or nearly half of the total which Iran now has.

By 1946 the Khuzistan program had been balked to a great extent by a series of gross miscalculations, first by the Iranian authorities and later by the British military authorities:

1. One of Reza Shah's main objects, with respect to this scheme, had been to provide for a large-scale cultivation of sugar cane on the lands in question. But the attempts at this cultivation failed, although Khuzistan had in the remote past been a rich sugar-growing region. This failure is not necessarily permanent. Wheat and barley are now grown in the area.

2. The Iranian authorities were unable to devise means for the transfer to this region of a sufficiently large number of peasants.

3. The majority of those peasants who had been induced to settle could not adapt themselves satisfactorily to the modern techniques of agriculture.

4. The personnel available for assisting the peasants with this adjustment were neither numerically sufficient nor of adequate com-

petence. The established credit facilities were also wholly inadequate.

5. The British Army engineers failed to take measures which would prevent the soil from becoming excessively saline after the construction of irrigation works. Two years after the completion of the British project the soil to which it extended had become so saline as to be completely useless.[11]

Studies of future possibilities for this project are to be conducted as part of the execution of the government's Seven-Year Plan.

THE SEVEN-YEAR PLAN

The Soviet adventure of 1945-46 in Azerbaijan resulted in a large falling off in the Tudeh party's membership and ultimately in an official outlawing of that party. This meant that the power of the great landowners in the government was no longer seriously challenged. Members of the landowner group, in their high official capacities, now took a major step, possibly with a view to preventing any new challenge to their position from arising in the near future. With the aim of putting into effect an integrated plan for the development and modernization of all phases of Iranian economic and social life, but with a general retention of existing basic social structures, the government engaged the American engineering firm of Morrison-Knudsen Company to make a survey of the entire Iranian economy. The survey was made in 1947, and in the following year a national seven-year plan was enacted into law by the Majlis (Parliament).[12] Among the stated objectives, high rank was given to the raising of Iranian standards of living; but the precise intentions of the framers of the bill, with respect to priorities of objects, were left ambiguous by the wording. The government thereupon requested the International Bank to examine the possibility of a substantial loan to Iran for the execution of the plan. The bank, after its examination, expressed the view that additional surveys were necessary and suggested that these might be conducted by an

[11] W. B. Fisher, "Population Problems of the Middle East," *Journal of the Royal Central Asian Society*, 1948, Part III, pp. 212, 219; B. A. Keen, *The Agricultural Development of the Middle East* (London, 1946), pp. 45-46.

[12] The originator of the Seven-Year Plan was Mosharreff Nafici. See New York *Times*, September 8, 1950.

organization composed of representatives of several different foreign engineering firms. This advice was accepted, and a contract for a single integrated survey was concluded between the Iranian Government and Overseas Consultants, Inc., a group consisting of members of eleven American engineering firms. The survey was completed in August, 1949, and a five-volume report issued. An agreement was then concluded between the government and Overseas Consultants, whereunder the latter would stay on in Iran to provide continuous advice in regard to actual operations under the program. Parliamentary approval had already been given to a proposal to establish a Plan Organization, composed entirely of Iranians, which would work out the day-to-day details of the program, and generally supervise its execution, without political interference except as to changes of major policies. The plan was to be financed from Iran's own resources to the greatest extent possible. During the last six years all oil royalties were to be assigned to a fund to be created for the sole purpose of execution of the plan.[13] The consensus of expert opinion was that a large percentage of the total expenditure could be defrayed by Iran from her own resources.

The contract concluded between the Iranian Government and Overseas Consultants on February 1, 1949, had provided that the following matters should be covered in the report to be prepared by the consultants:

1. A thorough analysis of the industrial plants, both governmental and private, including manufacturing, transportation, communication, ports, highways, and mines, whether actually existing or contemplated.
2. A thorough study of the agricultural and irrigation conditions of the country as presently operating and their possibilities of extension and improvement.
3. Consideration of ways and means for increasing the production of minerals.
4. A study of social institutions and services, including education, health, housing, water supply, sanitation, and similar matters.

[13] There was, however, no stipulation to the effect that these moneys could not be transferred to the general governmental funds.

5. A review of the presently established allocation of the over-all appropriations to the several elements of the Seven-Year Plan by categories.[14]

Some of the outstanding conclusions of the report finally issued were as follows:[15]

Farm management is faulty as a result of the lack of agricultural information, the illiteracy of the peasants and the absentee landlord system.[16] Decisions which affect production are divided often among the landlord's agent, the men who furnish animals for plowing and a group of several peasants who provide the labor. As a result, land, labor and the various forms of capital are poorly integrated. The laborer's share is usually inadequate and opportunities for becoming independent owner-operators are almost entirely lacking. . . . [I, 25]

A state of emergency exists. The port of Khorram-shahr is practically blocked, and Bandar Shahpur is unable efficiently to cope with the vessels diverted from Khorram-shahr. Bushire and Bandar Abbas are practically idle, but the former could be used to some extent under present conditions. . . . [I, 40]

The situation with respect to taxation, both direct and indirect, is long due for a thorough overhauling. The return from direct taxes should be increased to permit the reduction of indirect taxes and to fill any gaps in budgetary receipts due to the assignment of revenues to carry out the Plan. The very large proportion of total revenues, over 85%, which now comes from indirect taxes tends to increase unduly the cost of living, and too much of the burden falls on those least able to bear it. . . . [I, 61]

There is need for legislation to help the peasants acquire untilled and neglected land. The fact that the state is a large landowner should mean that a start can be made with state lands. . . .[17] [I, 62]

[14] Overseas Consultants, Inc., op. cit., I, 1.

[15] Ibid. (volumes and pages as indicated).

[16] At least two-thirds, and probably a great deal more, of the cultivated land in Iran is in large estates. Land registration has been begun and is fairly far advanced. However, it has not been coupled with any alterations in the de facto state of affairs. Cf. Haas, op. cit., p. 196; "Agricultural and Industrial Activity and Manpower in Iran," International Labor Review, May, 1949, p. 551.

[17] In this connection the opinion has not infrequently been expressed that in his present condition the average Iranian peasant would not be capable of working a property of his own. Cf. "Agricultural and Industrial Activity and Manpower in Iran," International Labor Review, May, 1949, p. 552.

The majority of landowners . . . have quieted their inner doubts by the belief that two great social forces will prevent any . . . social catastrophe, and they frankly and openly admit that they plan to make full use of these instruments: religion and patriotism. Their position appears to be both socially unacceptable and historically naive. . . . [II, 125]

Estimates place the rural population at about 78% of the total population. With the type of equipment available, these workers were able to produce only about two-thirds of an adequate diet for the people of the nation. . . . [III, 9]

Because loans from the agricultural bank have been made without adequate regulations or supervision, persons connected with agriculture have been able to borrow funds to be used for almost any purpose. . . . [III, 10]

One is never sure of the Government—it may change at any time. Policies are seldom continued for a very long period. Ministries may change several times in one year. The attitude prevails among the people that the Government is their worst enemy. . . . [III, 20]

From available statistics it appears that over 65% of the land at present cultivated depends on rainfall alone. . . . The urgent need for irrigation is manifest. . . . [III, 125, 128]

The system of land tenure in Iran has undergone little change over the centuries. To say that it is archaic is an understatement. However, this system is now so embedded in custom and in the life of the people that it cannot wisely be changed overnight. To attempt this might bring famine, chaos in agricultural relationships, and in the long run would not benefit the peasant.
It is generally conceded, however, that there is a pressing need to work toward the gradual emancipation of the peasant from the present type of feudal control by the generally absentee landowner. . . . It would be futile if the agricultural aid under the Plan merely enriched the land-owner and increased his power. . . . [V, 239]

Overseas Consultants made highly detailed suggestions as to methods of attempting to remedy the situations. They also recommended that the funds for the Seven-Year Plan, which had already been earmarked to a considerable extent by the wording of the enabling act, should be allocated as follows: public health—$46,600,-000; education—$31,000,000; agriculture—$101,700,000; water resources—$57,400,000; meteorology—$1,100,000; surveying and mapping—$10,000,000; town improvement and housing—$85,300,000; transportation—$155,300,000; communications—$15,800,000; industry and mining—$68,300,000; electric power—$31,400,000; petroleum—$23,400,000; statistical organization—$3,800,000; distribution—$400,000; unallocated—$18,500,000.

As to the feasibility of the plan and of the execution of the recommendations made in the report, Overseas Consultants made the following statement: "During our study . . . we have been met many times with the hesitant opinion that what works well in some of the western countries may not work at all well in Iran. We have repeatedly been told that Iranian customs and temperament will not permit certain types of administrative procedure which we believe are essential to the success of the Plan.

"We have taken the position that if Iran is resolute in its determination to achieve the aims of the Seven Year Plan, it must adopt methods which have been tried and proved elsewhere. . . . We have accepted no counsels of despair."[18]

The Seven-Year Plan, in the detailed form in which it was approved by Overseas Consultants, was enormously popular in Iran, where it became the topic of central interest among the politically conscious groups. Calling for an expenditure of $650,000,000 over a seven-year period, it was by far the most completely integrated scheme for the development of a nation as a whole which the Middle East had yet known. Moreover, the chances of success, and of wholehearted cooperation on the part of Iranians of nearly all classes, seemed to be enhanced by the fact that Overseas Consultants had refrained from suggesting any truly drastic remedies of the existing land-tenure and taxation situations. The Majlis, as well as the cabinet, was dominated by large landowners and prosperous merchants, who, for most practical purposes, constitute a single social class.

There were further developments in 1949. A new cabinet took office, headed by Mohammed Saed. This government, although containing a majority of perennial politicians from the landlord class, some widely reputed as corrupt or incompetent, nevertheless pro-

[18] Overseas Consultants, Inc., *op. cit.*, I, 54.

claimed a reform program, even including a noncommittal advocacy of land reform. It was by this time generally understood that the Shah would not approve any cabinet unless it declared itself in such a sense. The Shah, it began to appear, was opposed to the use of the Seven-Year Plan as a mere instrument of the dominant social class. Meanwhile, at the request of the Shah, a Majlis committee had established an Anti-Corruption Board, the duty of which would be to conduct an inquiry and submit a report listing all present or former government officials found to be unfit for office by reason of incompetence or dishonesty.

Probably the most important event of late 1949, however, was the Shah's journey to the United States, ostensibly to cement good relations and to study American technological practices. The Shah interviewed President Truman and assured him of his determination to achieve the proclaimed goals of the Seven-Year Plan. Before leaving, the Shah and the President issued a joint statement, in which they expressed shared sentiments in regard to the future of Iran. The need for raising the standard of living in Iran was particularly emphasized in the statement. The President gave assurance that "applications by the Iranian Government to the International Bank for economically justifiable loans to be used in the furtherance of the program will receive the support of the United States."

In February, 1950, the Shah made a strong speech in Teheran reiterating his determination to put an end to bribery and corruption and to establish social justice. However, the difficulties in the way of doing this were becoming increasingly apparent. Although, as far as public pronouncements were concerned, there was unanimity of opinion among Iranians that strong reforms were in order, this sentiment was by no means being translated into practice in all quarters. Reports being received from the province of Azerbaijan indicated the existence of corruption and repression on a grand scale, pervading the entire official hierarchy and resulting in a large-scale exodus from the province to other parts of Iran. In Teheran, at the same time, the big business community had succeeded, in spite of opposition by the cabinet and the National Bank, in creating a situation of artificial scarcities of merchandise, with enormous profits to themselves and an enormous rise in the cost of living. These artificial situations, superimposed on an economic recession due mainly to serious crop failures, threatened Iran with a major economic depression. At the same time it was generally known that a large part of Iran's private capital was in hiding in foreign countries. Also, in accordance with what had become a well-established practice, most of the wealthier Iranians were not paying their income taxes and land taxes, and the publication in the Official Journal of the names of the delinquents had in no way improved this situation.

As the first half of 1950 advanced, economic conditions deteriorated still further, resulting in the closure of many factories and handicraft establishments. No official steps were being taken to improve the worsening general situation, and public sentiment was displaying more and more impatience for action. Meanwhile, the revenues earmarked for the Seven-Year Plan were being diverted for essential ordinary governmental expenditures, and an urgent need for foreign aid was beginning to appear. This would probably not have been the case had the Majlis been willing to accept a new oil agreement concluded with the Anglo-Iranian Oil Company, which would have doubled the government's revenue from royalties. The Majlis' stand, however, was that no agreement would be acceptable other than one which awarded to Iran at least 50 per cent of the annual profits of the Anglo-Iranian Oil Company.[19] This was considerably higher than what the company had offered. The Majlis' stand had the support of Iranian public opinion.[20] Clearly the strong hope was that an American or international loan of substantial character (probably in the neighborhood of the $250,000,000 previously sought from the International Bank) would be forthcoming. Its effect would be to strengthen Iran's bargaining power in the oil negotiations and at the same time to permit a full-scale continuance of the Seven-Year Plan expenditures.

During May and June the immediate need for at least limited

[19] The British Government has the controlling financial interest in the Anglo-Iranian Oil Co.

[20] Iran was holding out for a royalty which, at the 1948 rate of production, would yield a revenue of about $98,000,000 per annum, as against $25,000,000 at the present royalty rate. Cf. New York *Times*, July 19, 1950.

foreign financial aid became acute. At that time the theory was widely held among Iranians, including the landlords, that the receipt of the desired *large-scale aid* would depend on the establishment of a strong government, capable of taking a positive stand against the chronic and growing corruption and inefficiency. When, in June, Dr. Henry Grady was appointed as American Ambassador to Iran, this theory seemed to find confirmation. Grady, an outstanding economist, had in the past headed several American missions abroad, in all of which an economic objective had been the main one. On this occasion, moreover, Grady was accompanied by a group of other American economic experts, who proposed to remain in the country for a three-month period, presumably to inquire into current conditions. It was strongly felt by most Iranians that an effort must now be made to show Iran capable of efficient cooperation with the United States in the utilization of the expected aid.[21]

On June 27 the Shah, apparently influenced by the considerations just mentioned, appointed as Prime Minister General Ali Razmara, Chief of Staff of the Iranian Army. Razmara was fairly generally regarded as the person most likely to be able to establish more orderly and stable conditions in the country. There had been the feeling, however, that this appointment, which might conflict to some extent with normal parliamentary procedure, should be delayed until necessary as a last resort. Razmara, on assuming office, declared that he would retain his position as Chief of Staff, thereby implying that he would not hesitate to use force on a dictatorial basis should circumstances make this necessary for the attainment of objectives. Razmara also made a clean sweep of those discredited politicians who had comprised the majority in all cabinets since the late Shah's abdication. Some of his appointments were of men with unchallenged reputations for competence.

On July 15 Razmara declared publicly that foreign aid within one month was absolutely necessary. But it was not forthcoming within that time; by mid-September it had become apparent that there were great differences between the ideas of the American economists and those of the average Iranian as to the amount of credit which would

[21] New York *Times*, February 15, 1950; June 27, 1950; September 5, 1950.

be sufficient. The former felt that more than $25,000,000 would be unjustifiable.

Knowledge of this conclusion led to a great increase in the anti-American sentiment which was rapidly coming into being among all classes of Iranians. The belief was apparently growing that the United States' only interest in the country was to control Iranian politics at the top level, without even paying adequately for that privilege. Accusations were made against Razmara to the effect that he was a tool of the "imperialist powers," America and Britain, and these charges seemed to be accomplishing results in the undermining of his position. As a rule, he was opposed both by the majority of landowners and also by the now clandestine Tudeh party, which was believed to be wholly under Communist domination. As time went on, the religious leaders (mullahs), seeking to reestablish their former influence in Iranian affairs, were also participating to an increasing extent in the chorus of disapproval. As for Razmara's following among politically conscious Iranians not affiliated with any of the groups just mentioned, this seemed to depend on the lengths to which he would be prepared to go in the matters of uprooting corruption and pressing the requests for large external aid. In mid-August the report of the Anti-Corruption Committee had been released to the public; on the basis thereof 400 high and medium-level officials of the government had soon been removed from office. Many others listed by the committee had, however, been passed over in this purge, including at least three members of Razmara's cabinet. This discrepancy created a difficult situation, particularly since there were widespread doubts as to whether the Anti-Corruption Committee had performed its duties in good faith. In late September and early October Razmara and his ministers were exposed to a flood of embarrassing questions put to them by deputies in the Majlis.

To meet the public demand for strong action of a less ambiguous character, Razmara, on September 30, gave orders for the confiscation of property of all tax delinquents, and at the same time authorized Teheran Radio to broadcast the names of the delinquents to the nation. Among these delinquents were the great majority of the wealthy and highly placed persons in the country. Razmara had given abundant warning that these steps would be taken, but it had apparently not been believed that he would dare to implement the warnings.

There is, however, no evidence that this move strengthened Razmara's hand to any definite degree by placing preponderant public sentiment on his side. His opponents, too, had arguments with which to impress the public. The strong general anti-American feeling made it possible to attack the government on the ground of its support of Overseas Consultants and to place emphasis on the high salaries being paid to the American engineers, even though the Seven-Year Plan was at a standstill and no American financial aid had been received for its resumption. The members of Overseas Consultants were at the same time publicly expressing their own views, which were highly critical of the Iranian officials associated with the Seven-Year Plan, and of their failure to provide the conditions which had been agreed upon as essential to successful execution. Several of the members, moreover, had either left for the United States or were preparing to do so.

At this stage Razmara must have made some important concessions to the vested interests. Suddenly, and for only a short period of time, he seemed to enjoy great popularity among the Majlis deputies. Not only was he given a large vote of confidence (on the question of retaining a cabinet minister listed as unfit by the Anti-Corruption Committee); also he was cheered by the assembled deputies when, on October 10, he announced the decision of the Export-Import Bank to grant to Iran a loan of $25,000,000.

During the weeks which followed, up to the end of the year, anti-Western feeling rose to new heights in Iran. On November 4 a new trade pact was concluded with the Soviet Union, which had the effect not only of dispelling some of the prevailing gloom in regard to the economic picture but also of suggesting an unfavorable contrast between Russia and the United States as sources of assistance. Later in November an official ban was placed on the relaying of American governmental broadcasts to Iran. The joint American-Iranian official announcement, made on October 19, that

Iran would be the first beneficiary of the American Point Four program had apparently not had any important favorable effect on general public sentiment in the country. The amount earmarked for the Iran program was only $500,000, which contrasted strongly with the amounts of financial aid that had been hoped for. Further, public opinion continued to oppose the ratification of the oil agreement with the Anglo-Iranian Oil Company, despite the fact that it would result in the immediate receipt by Iran of about £30,000,000 ($84,-000,000) in back payments.[22] Premier Razmara took the bold step of declaring himself in favor of ratification, but without visible results except in the negative sense that his government managed to continue in power even after the announcement.

One of the contributing factors to the strong anti-Westernism which still prevailed at the end of the year was the fact that the $25,000,000 Export-Import Bank loan promised in October had not yet been granted. The reason was that, under Iranian law, the acceptance of the loan required the approval of the Majlis, and Razmara had presumably not considered it politically expedient to ask the Majlis for such acceptance in view of the prevailing atmosphere. It is clear, however, that Iranian public sentiment was placing the blame entirely upon the United States; and, possibly because the loan was to have been relatively small and earmarked mainly for purchase of agricultural equipment, the government may well have feared that any action or announcements on the subject would antagonize rather than pacify the politically conscious elements of the populace in their then turbulent state of mind. The feeling against Great Britain was at the same time running equally high. On December 26 Finance Minister Gholam Hussein Fohruhar had found it expedient to withdraw from the Majlis a bill for ratification of the government's agreement with the Anglo-Iranian Oil Company. As he did so, he announced that new negotiations would be instituted on the basis of a demand for higher royalties than those provided for in the agreement. This decision on the part of the Finance Minister came at the end of a week of popular demonstra-

[22] The royalty for 1950 was about $45,000,000.

tions, headed by students, demanding cancellation of all oil agree-ments with foreigners and nationalization of Iran's oil industry.

On January 8, 1951, the Iranian Government formally announced that its contract with Overseas Consultants, Inc., had been terminated as of January 1. The reason given by Mr. Mohammed Nakhaie, Managing Director of the Plan Organization, was that there had been a fundamental disagreement between the Organization and the foreign consultants as to the priorities to be accorded among the various types of projects, namely, agricultural, social welfare, and industrial projects. The Plan Organization's stand had been that the country's most pressing need was for "more and better factories, foundries, and other industrial projects." This was clearly an ad-mission that the Seven-Year Plan had been stripped, by interpreta-tions and developments, of the features which had given both Iranians and Americans particular grounds for encouragement. There was also reason to believe that the Shah and Premier Razmara were no longer disposed to press for retention of their earlier ideas.

Thus, even though general economic conditions had improved somewhat by the end of 1950, all indications pointed not to a lessening of tensions but rather to a heightening thereof. The Shah's and Razmara's attempts in the direction of reforms seemed com-pletely balked. The Majlis had not, during the entire year, passed a single important bill. No annual budget had been approved for the fiscal year March, 1950-March, 1951, and all governmental activities had been conducted on a basis of month-to-month stopgap author-izations. The cost of living index (based on the 1939 level as 100) was the highest in the Middle East in 1950, being at all times in excess of 600.

It was difficult at the time to envisage what sort of action the United States Government could possibly take to lessen the anti-Western feeling and promote a cooperative attitude on the part of the Iranians. Any alteration of the basis of the Export-Import Bank loan might have been interpreted as tacit approval of the altered basis of the Seven-Year Plan, and would possibly also have established a precedent for granting such loans for political reasons without even a formal show of economic justification. As for the extension of

financial aid in any other manner at the time, this might have
established an extremely bad precedent, since it might well have
conveyed to many Iranians the idea that the best way of getting
assistance is to indulge first in unfriendly activities.

As for the Seven-Year Plan, one particularly prominent fact was
that there was no longer any great faith among Iranians in the
possibility that the plan would be guided in the direction of increased
general living standards rather than in that of profit or prestige for
wealthy persons. Moreover, the interest generated in some quarters in
struggling for rational reform and development had apparently been
supplanted by the more customary attitudes of resignation and
inertia.[23]

THE N.E.F. VILLAGE BETTERMENT SCHEME

To many competent observers during recent years it has become
evident that any thoroughgoing attempt to improve living standards
in the Middle East must include direct attention to the needs of
the rural villages which constitute the homes of the great majority of
the population.

In 1943 Dr. Harold B. Allen of the Near East Foundation, a
private American organization, conducted a survey of the basic
problems of village life in Iran. In 1946, at the request of the
Iranian Government, the Foundation began actual operations to
improve the conditions of villagers in the Veramin district, eighteen
miles southeast of Teheran. The activities have covered all the main
phases of the villagers' lives, with particular emphasis upon (1) the
improvement of animals, (2) diverse and better crops, (3) village

[23] Edward Sykes, "Some Economic Problems of Persia," *Journal of the Royal
Central Asian Society*, 1949, Part III, p. 268.

Important subsequent developments, up to April 15, 1951, affecting the Seven-
Year Plan were: (1) the assassination of Premier Razmara on March 7; (2) the
passage by the Majlis, later in March, of an act providing for the nationalization
of Iranian oil; (3) the Shah's announcement, in January, 1951, of his decision to
sell a large part of the crown lands to the tenant-cultivators of those lands at
moderate prices with easy payment terms. This decision apparently relates mainly
to those lands which were (a) confiscated from landholders by Reza Shah and
(b) not returned by the present Shah to the original possessors, because no one
had succeeded in presenting a valid claim. See footnote 10. Cf. also Royal Institute of International Affairs, *op. cit.*, p. 222; New York *Times*, January 29, 1951.

schools, (4) courses for training some of the villagers as teachers, (5) improvement of sanitation in all its aspects. One feature of the program has been instruction in hygiene and agriculture in connection with the teaching of the three R's to adults.

"The work began . . . in five villages and has now been extended to include 35. The Ministries of Agriculture, Education, and Health have cooperated in the conduct of this project."[24]

"When a project is agreed upon by the Government and the representative of the Foundation, it is operated, under supervision, by men and women who are themselves villagers in outlook."[25]

"Landlords were generally pleased with the work of the Foundation, but very hesitant to spend money on this type of activity. The villagers, however, are increasingly happy to participate in the improvement of the environs."[26]

In an address given on June 29, 1950, to the American Newspaper Guild, President Truman made the following statements in regard to the Foundation's Iran program:

"The foundation met a water shortage by drilling deep wells. It overcame water-borne diseases with an inexpensive water filter. It sprayed homes with D.D.T. It sprayed crops with insecticides. It helped to organize schools in each of 35 villages.

"Today, only four years later, the village people are at work in new carpentry shops, vegetable gardens and orchards. And, most startling of all, the yield of grain in this area has tripled."[27]

Examples of some of the other specific activities of the Near East Foundation in connection with the Veramin project are: (1) the maintenance of a small demonstration farm, with experimental plots for vegetables and fruits; (2) miscellaneous sanitary measures, such as the drainage of stagnant pools; (3) the furnishing of instruction in regard to poultry breeding. The last-named activity has some particularly important implications, because by old tradition all matters connected with poultry breeding and raising are regarded as a monopoly of peasant women in Iran. Since the Near East

[24] Overseas Consultants, Inc., *op. cit.*, I, 43.
[25] B. A. Keen, *op. cit.*, p. 40.
[26] Overseas Consultants, Inc., *op. cit.*, II, 45.
[27] New York *Times*, June 30, 1950.

Foundation's most vexatious problem has been that of overcoming peasant conservatism with respect to the status of women, this ingenious means of approaching the female members of the community may well lead to beneficial results far surpassing the more immediate ones. Possibly related is the Foundation's recent decision to introduce the longest-delayed of all its planned programs, namely, courses of instruction in homemaking.

Early in 1950, in order to conduct an important experiment, the Near East Foundation rented the entire village of Mamazan, in the Veramin district. Its purpose was to evaluate the practicability of giving peasants a larger share of the product of their labor than is at present customary in Iran, while at the same time instructing the peasants in the prudent disposition of any increased income which might result. This experiment shows great promise. In an exceptionally bad crop year the Foundation was able, from its share of the crop, to pay the rent and to have a small surplus besides. All surpluses will be used for renovation of the village. It is proposed eventually to rebuild every peasant dwelling.

According to the present plans of the Iranian and United States governments, the key project for the first year of the Point Four program for Iran instituted in October, 1950, will be an extension to other parts of the country of precisely the same sort of village schemes as those now conducted by the Near East Foundation. Already a center for this work has been established in the city of Isfahan, and it is proposed that this center shall cover eighty villages in the vicinity. Similar centers are then to be set up in nine other parts of the country, with similar extension to near-by villages. It is hoped in this manner to produce effects in all regions of Iran.

As of December 31, 1950, the Near East Foundation scheme could be regarded as a highly successful pilot project of small magnitude.

OBSERVATION

Iran is of particular importance in the Middle East at present because it is the scene of two widely different types of important experiment. One is the grand-scale, highly integrated plan covering all phases of the national economy and social structure. The other is the plan for training the "grass roots," to the degree of their ascertained amenability to training. Both schemes, because of the intensity which has characterized the preparatory efforts, must be regarded as pioneer experiments for the Middle East (other than Israel).

In both of these efforts the American role has been of outstanding importance. It should be clear, moreover, in view of the facts and developments mentioned in the preceding paragraphs, that a final failure in either line of planning would reflect most unfavorably upon the United States Government and the American people, particularly because of the government's strongly implied interest in the rendering of adequate financial assistance to Iran.

Thus it would seem unfortunate that there has been no sustained attempt on the part of the United States Government to tie together, on a policy basis, the closely related implications of these two highly important types of planning. Until this attempt is made, there will probably be no way of knowing how Iran's total needs could best be served, given the prevailing political and psychological climates and the amount of money available.

CHAPTER X

❖

Turkey

GENERAL BACKGROUND

From the standpoint of programs for raising living standards, Turkey's post-1918 history may be divided into two distinct periods. The later of these may be considered to have commenced on March 12, 1947, with President Truman's enunciation of the doctrine which has come to bear his name.[1] This presidential declaration inaugurated a period not only of cordial political relations between the United States and Turkey but also of large-scale cooperation between the two countries in attempts to modernize Turkey economically in a thoroughgoing manner.

Turkey's eager acceptance of this offered cooperation, which contrasts so strongly with the policy of economic self-sufficiency followed during most of the between-wars period, is probably attributable in largest measure to political circumstances. The fear of Russian expansionism is traditional and chronic among Turks. During the

[1] The main feature of the Truman Doctrine was the new American foreign policy of "containment" of totalitarian forms of government by means of military and economic aid to nations threatened with subjugation, or limitation of sovereignty, by totalitarian states. In the same speech in which he proclaimed the doctrine, Truman proposed that the first recipients of aid of this nature should be Turkey and Greece. On May 22, 1947, the United States Congress authorized a grant of military aid to Turkey in the amount of $100,000,000.

time between the end of World War II and the Truman declaration this fear had been greatly enhanced by Soviet pronouncements, official and semiofficial, indicative of designs against Turkey's sovereignty and territorial integrity. Traditionally skilled in the conduct of international relations,[2] the Turkish Government welcomed the new American doctrine of "containment," and with it both the immediate military aid offered and the implications of future active American concern in the basic aspects of Turkish social and economic development along Western lines.

The subsequent rapid intensification of the cooperative activities is apparently ascribable to the relative maturity of Turkish official attitudes, as compared both with Turkish attitudes of the between-wars period and with the attitudes currently prevailing in most of the other independent countries of the Middle East. Because Turkey's independence had been maintained for nearly a quarter of a century in spite of continuously trying circumstances; because Turkey's military power was considerable; and because the internal political situation was such as to leave little doubt of internal unity vis-à-vis any foreign attempts to gain control[3]—because of all this, there was in Turkey a widespread spirit of self-confidence, as contrasted with the morbid fears of all foreign influence still being manifested in the Arab states and Iran. Still further, however, modernization in Turkey had been carried to a point far exceeding developments in any of the other Middle Eastern countries, apart from Palestine; it had reached the evolutionary stage where a limited desire exists in official quarters for assessment and evaluation of the real, as opposed to the superficially viewed, results. Also there was a fairly well-advanced

[2] The long survival of the Ottoman Empire, which, throughout the nineteenth and early twentieth centuries, seemed always on the verge of collapse, is attributable in large measure to skillful Turkish diplomacy. The maintenance of Turkish neutrality during most of World War II was similarly a diplomatic feat of considerable magnitude.

[3] Except as regards the Kurds of eastern Turkey, there has never been, since 1923, the slightest evidence of any possibility of a consequential alliance between an opposition group in Turkey and a foreign power, even were Turkey to be invaded. The Turkish Government, moreover, has shown itself fully capable of dealing effectively with threats from the Kurdish quarter. As for the Communist movement, there is no reason to believe that it has ever made much headway in Turkey.

realization that, if modernization is to serve as a source of a great national power, it must be instituted on a thoroughly rational basis. The continuous compromise between development of basic social and economic strength, on the one hand, and immediate military considerations, on the other, had served in general to defeat the long-range objectives in both spheres. The answer decided upon was to accept extensive American assistance on the voluntary basis proposed by the United States.

Since the adoption of this policy has introduced some striking changes in developmental trends, it is desirable to examine briefly the previous general history of Turkish planning with respect to living standards, and also the status of progress as of March 12, 1947.

TURKISH LIVING STANDARDS AFTER WORLD WAR I

During almost the whole of the earlier period the matter of general living standards had played an important role in Turkish official thinking and policy making. After the establishment of the Turkish Republic on October 29, 1923, and even before that date to the extent that the Nationalists exercised *de facto* control in large parts of the country, the basic political program of Mustafa Kemal called for a betterment of the prevailing conditions of *all Turks*, whatever their status in life. The most powerful officials, moreover, have not usually been men whose special interests militated against the execution of an egalitarian program.[4] This fact was reflected both in the Constitution of the Turkish Republic and in the land policy adopted. The great estates which had been a characteristic feature of Anatolia and Thrace during Ottoman days were mostly subdivided into small plots to be owned and cultivated by individual peasants. The execution of this policy was made easier by the fact that the great estates were, for the most part, identified in the public mind with the Sultan's regime. During the years from 1918 to 1923 that government had

[4] When first established in 1920, the Nationalists' political organization, called the Grand National Assembly, consisted mainly of "clerics of a reactionary mentality," who, however, were subservient to the will of Mustafa Kemal. In 1923 and 1924 Kemal conducted a successful campaign to shatter the potential power of persons of that persuasion. Cf. Philip Graves, *Briton and Turk* (London, 1941), pp. 203, 211-213.

steadily declined in public esteem because of its unprotesting submission to the will of the victorious Allied Powers.

It is also noteworthy, however, that the policies pursued were,
from about 1924 on, subject to a theory which generally opposed
direct assaults upon immediate causes of low living standards. Mustafa Kemal (later known as Ataturk), who ruled the country with a
strong hand from 1923 until his death in 1938, clearly demonstrated
by his actions that his most immediate concern was to develop among
all classes of Turks a progressive mentality, as opposed to the then
prevalent reactionary attitudes to which he attributed the main ills
of the country. His belief was that, with a complete change-over in
this respect, the tangible benefits achievable by Western methods
would follow in time almost as a matter of course.

Ataturk's method of promoting this change-over was to attack all
such practices as seemed to him to be particularly characteristic of
the traditional way of life which had been Turkey's for so many centuries. At the same time, by decree, he forced the entire population
to conform outwardly to certain Western ways, while also making
sure that they were exposed to others to the greatest extent possible.
Presumably he felt that the loss of old attachments, by leaving the
populace anchorless, would result in a general groping for new cultural ties. The possibilities in the latter direction would be suggested
by the widespread superficial appearances of Westernization. These
would arouse first curiosity and later a desire for complete assimilation.

The specific aspects of this program are well known. The abolition
of the fez served the double purpose of promoting the use of Western-
style headgear and of making it difficult for Moslems to pray in the
prescribed manner. The introduction of the Latin alphabet produced
a cultural gap between Turkey and the neighboring Oriental countries. The discouragement of Oriental music was designed to produce
a spiritual vacuum which would have to be filled. Ataturk sought to
advance this process by requiring the singing of Western-style march-
ing songs by Turkish soldiers. Since troops were stationed in many
parts of Turkey, and since the soldiers were of peasant families, this
form of Westernization could reach virtually the entire population.

The disproportionate concentration of the Turkish Government on urban industrialization can probably be regarded as an aspect of this same broad program. Although the desire for immediate productive gains and the desire for prestige in Western eyes were certainly important factors in the situation, it seems likely that the main element was Ataturk's wish to widen the exposure to Western ways of life.

Ataturk did not, however, in the manner of his contemporary Reza Shah in Iran, pursue his industrialization policies at the direct expense of the great peasant masses. When confronted with rising costs, the government still refrained from altering the taxation system along lines particularly burdensome to the rural community. Once the burden had become too great to be borne by the ordinary national budget, resort was had to foreign loans, in preference to squeezing out by harsh means all that could possibly be obtained from local sources. This is not to say that all of the measures taken in connection with the industrial program, once it was under way, were of benefit to the peasants. Some, indeed, such as the large-scale subsidization of industries which did not show or promise business profits, were decidedly harmful. But these were measures which had been more or less forced into being by new situations; they were not the fulfillment of previously made plans. Also there is much evidence that, whenever it appeared clearly that the plight of the peasants was deteriorating, the government took at least limited action to remedy the situation.[5]

Under the circumstances, it is necessary, even in spite of the government's general neglect of the rural masses, to regard some of the plans put into effect under Ataturk's leadership as major plans advanced in good faith for the purpose of elevating Turkish living standards. Included in this category are: the Chester Concession Plan, the First Five-Year Plan, and the Four-Year Agricultural Plan of 1937. These will be discussed in detail later in this chapter.

Between the time of Ataturk's death in 1938 and March 12, 1947, the government's developmental policies were, generally speaking,

[5] In 1924, for example, the government distributed seeds, cattle, and agricultural implements among peasants, at a cost of $3,000,000.

those of Ataturk continued in effect. During this whole period, and indeed for three years more, Turkey was under the somewhat similar rule of Ataturk's chosen successor, Ismet Inonu.[6] Less dynamic than his predecessor, and possibly less conscious of ultimate economic and social goals, Inonu nevertheless produced no major changes in the general character of the lines of action followed, prior to March, 1947. Activities were considerably limited by the war and by the continued shortage thereafter of essential materials obtainable only from foreign sources.

LIVING STANDARDS—1947

It is now pertinent to consider the over-all status of social and economic development in Turkey, as of March 12, 1947.

At that time there was universal expert agreement that Turkey's greatest immediate needs, in the economic and social sphere, were: (1) far greater direct attention to the problems of agriculture and of individual agriculturists; (2) better communications and transport facilities, including more adequate port and grain storage facilities; and (3) greater development of industries more directly related than the existing ones to the pressing necessities of the Turkish people as a whole. In connection with the third point, the manufacture of small agricultural implements was often suggested.

When these needs were analyzed as to their relative positions of priority, it was abundantly clear that the most immediately important one was the expansion of communications and transport facilities. Because these were so inadequately developed, most peasants were still wholly dependent on near-by markets and had no incentive for producing in excess of strictly local needs. Also, trade in all types of commodities was being harmed by transport bottlenecks, subjecting the movement of goods to long delays and causing large-scale spoilage of perishable items. As long as such conditions persisted, there was clearly not much opportunity for raising general standards of living substantially, otherwise than on a permanently subsidized basis.

[6] During the latter part of the period of Inonu's leadership Turkey gradually acquired democratic institutions. The May, 1950, elections put a definite end to the dictatorship (if, indeed, it still existed). As candidate for reelection to the presidency, Inonu was defeated by his Democratic party opponent, Celal Bayar.

As a rule, moreover, the peasant's family was adequately nourished. Thus, although in most other respects his condition did not differ much from that of peasants in other Middle Eastern countries, there was not the same urgent need for remedial action of a more direct character than improvement of trade channels. Action of the other type would, however, be both possible and rational, if suitably co-ordinated with a program for expansion of communications and transport mediums.

The major plans formulated after March 12, 1947, were based partially on the considerations just mentioned, partially upon the common immediate defense needs of Turkey and the West, and partially upon political commitments which had to be made in order to obtain the funds appropriated by the United States Congress. Another probable element was tactful consideration of Turkish sensibilities in regard to some of the developmental activities already undertaken.[7] It has become clear, however, that far-reaching economic and social programs along basic lines will probably be achieved even in spite of the limiting factors.

The following paragraphs contain descriptions and discussions of the major plans for raising living standards in Turkey during the period 1919 to 1950.

MAJOR DEVELOPMENT PLANS—1919-50

THE CHESTER CONCESSION PLAN

When, in 1922, the Turkish Nationalists finally assured themselves of complete control of Anatolia and the Constantinople area, the *de facto* government of Mustafa Kemal was confronted with reconstruction and development problems of immense magnitude. Ambi-

[7] E.C.A., for example, has authorized aid in the amount of $1,000,000 for the Karabuk Iron and Steel Works. Recent expert criticisms of those works suggest that this aid may be of doubtful intrinsic value, in view of the uneconomic location of the works and the unfavorable prospects of adequate managerial competence in the foreseeable future. Cf. Max Weston Thornburg, Graham Spry, and George Soule, *Turkey, An Economic Appraisal* (New York, 1949), pp. 109-111; E. R. Lingeman, *Turkey: Economic and Social Conditions in Turkey* (London, 1948), pp. 85-86; Economic Cooperation Administration, *Turkey—Country Data Book* (Washington, March, 1950), Table XIV-1.

tious to convert Turkey by rapid strides into a modern nation, Kemal could hardly have discerned any visible means ready at hand for accomplishing such an object. Under Ottoman rule there had been no modern manufacturing industries in the country, and the mining, utility, and railway enterprises had been, for the most part, under foreign control and operation—in many cases by nationals of the countries with which Turkey was still technically at war. The native inhabitants of Turkey had practically no experience in the handling of such matters. But to entrust to foreigners the main tasks connected with rehabilitation and progress could be tantamount to losing, through economic subjugation, the greater part of what had been gained by military and political tactics.

The economy of the area was in a state of complete disruption, owing to the effects both of World War I and of the Turco-Greek War which had followed shortly afterward. Not only had the latter produced enormous destruction; it had possibly had even more drastic results in the uprooting of populations and the upsetting of customary ways of life. A sequel which was already in the making was the expulsion from Turkey (except Constantinople) of all inhabitants of the country who were of the Greek Orthodox religion. These persons, as traders, mechanics, craftsmen, and competent agriculturists, had played a most useful role in the national economy. The same had been substantially true of the Armenian inhabitants, whose numbers had been enormously reduced by deportations, massacres, and flight from the country. The Turks, for their part, had always limited themselves to a few selected callings (the army, government service, and farming).

The approach to this problem decided upon by Kemal is highly illustrative of the evolution which was to occur in his political and economic thinking. As matters stood in 1922 and 1923, he apparently dismissed any idea that the essential tasks could be performed without extensive aid from foreign sources. Moreover, for want of suitable alternatives, he was disposed to follow—for the time being and for some time to come—the established Ottoman practice of granting developmental and operational concessions to foreign firms. His primary precaution was to select the concessionaires on a basis calculated to restrict the influence of foreign *governments* in Turkish affairs. But at the same time he was eager for major accomplishments in the development of industries and public works and the improvement of all phases of agriculture. A logical solution was to grant the most important concessions to American firms. The United States had not been at war with Turkey, and American policies at the time were opposed to political imperialism outside of the Western Hemisphere.

Among the many concession seekers who had come to Turkey in 1922, probably the most prominent was the so-called "Chester group," composed of Americans and Canadians, with important roles being played by Admiral Colby Chester and members of his family. This group, organized as the Ottoman-American Development Company, succeeded in April, 1923, in obtaining ratification by the Grand National Assembly of two far-reaching long-term concessions. The first empowered the company to construct and operate a great railway network, with exclusive rights of exploiting all mineral resources within a distance of 20 kilometers on each side of the projected line. This concession also conferred a right to construct and operate ports at certain sites. The second concession gave the Ottoman-American Development Company the right to sell, manufacture, and repair agricultural equipment and to lease land for the establishment of model farms. The capital required for all these projects was estimated at over $300,000,000.[8]

In the sequel, however, it soon became apparent that the Chester group had taken upon itself a commitment which it had not the resources to discharge. Far from having $300,000,000 at its disposal, it was not even able to obtain adequate backing for the public flotation in the United States of a mere million-dollar stock issue. There was also dissension within the group; some of the more prominent associates, including General Goethals, withdrew their support. Both projects collapsed, and the concessions were canceled in December, 1923.[9]

[8] "Turkey," *Foreign Relations of the United States,* 1923, *passim; New International Year Book,* 1923, pp. 753-754.
[9] *New International Year Book,* 1923, p. 754; "Turkey," *Foreign Relations of the United States,* 1923, *passim.*

The great scope of these concessions is partially indicated by the agreed stipulations as to the specific routes of the railway lines (totaling 2400 miles) to be constructed. The network was to have comprised a main line, running from Samsun to Van by way of Havza—Amasya—Zile—Sivas—Harput—Diyarbekir—Bitlis, and the following seven branch lines:

1. To Ankara.
2. To Erzurum and the Persian frontier.
3. To Yumurtalik (on the Gulf of Iskenderun).[10]
4. To Mosul, Kirkuk, and Sulaimaniya (all of which are now in Iraq but were at that time claimed by Turkey).[11]
5. From the Ankara branch line to Kayseri and Ulukisla.
6. From the Erzurum branch line to a Black Sea port.
7. A cross-connection between the main line and the Ankara branch.

The ports to be constructed and operated by the concessionaires were to have been situated at Samsun, Yumurtalik, and the Black Sea terminus of the branch railway line from Erzurum.

THE FIRST FIVE-YEAR PLAN

It may well have been the failure of the above-mentioned arrangements which caused Kemal soon to adopt the policy of developing the country without any further resort to foreign capital, except for a few minor concessions granted. The new policy even went so far as to exclude all loans from foreign sources, both public and private. Further, strenuous efforts were instituted to "buy out" such foreign firms as were already established under old arrangements with the Ottoman Government, still legally valid. Until 1930 the whole recon-

[10] Yumurtalik, which cannot be located on any ordinary maps of present-day Turkey, is a small village which it was apparently proposed to convert into a major port.

[11] In view of the subsequent oil developments in the Mosul-Kirkuk region, the importance of this aspect of the concession, with the rights of mineral exploitation on each side of the railway line, would have been great, had the concession continued in effect. There would have been an American interest in supporting Turkey's claim against Britain's (as mandatory power for Iraq) to the area containing the oil fields.

struction and modernization program, which included railway building and some limited industrialization in the later years, was pursued
within the resources of Turkey's meager budget. Quite a number of
foreign specialists, technicians, and advisers were employed; but all
were paid employees of the Turkish Government, lacking the power
to give orders. These advisers were of numerous nationalities.

There is no doubt that, if the means of accomplishment are borne
in mind, the results which Turkey had achieved by 1930 were extraordinary. Particularly important was the fact that order had been established and maintained and war damage repaired. But national
finances were on the verge of collapse; and the prospects of going
ahead with industrial development, which had hardly been begun,
seemed dismal indeed.

In 1930 the Turkish Government took two important steps. It accepted one foreign loan,[12] and it engaged the services of a group of
American engineers and economists to survey the entire economy
and draw up a detailed integrated plan for the most efficient furtherance thereof. The result was the so-called Hines-Dorr-Kemmerer Plan
—which, however, soon gave way to the Soviet type of planning, that
is, intensive concentration on a few specific types of development.
This change was instituted apparently because the Soviet Union, in
its simply formulated developmental programs, was at the time
achieving the very types of result which Kemal most desired for Turkey, and based upon a similar social and economic background. The
Soviet plans, too, were being implemented without foreign capital.
Kemal no longer expected to keep to that extreme; but he did hope
to confine foreign investments to governmental loans and to keep
those down to an irreducible minimum, with the fewest possible
strings attached, and as scattered as possible among the various foreign countries having capital for export.

In 1934 Turkey's own Five-Year Plan was put into effect. It was
partially financed by two Soviet loans, together amounting to $18,-
000,000, and additional loans from Britain, France, and Germany.
The main original objective was to institute or develop the following

[12] A loan of $10,000,000 from the Swedish Match Co., in exchange for a match
monopoly granted to that company's American subsidiary.

manufacturing industries: (1) cotton textiles; (2) hemp products (sacks, ropes, etc.); (3) iron foundries; (4) coke; (5) copper refining; (6) paper; (7) rayon; (8) porcelain; (9) chemicals (caustic soda, vitriol, sulphur compounds, etc.); (10) distillation of rose oil; (11) electric power plants. However, no five-year production goals were announced.

A limited attempt was made to coordinate this industrial development program with agricultural and mineral development, as, for example, by promoting textile industries with a view to expanding the markets for Turkish raw cotton. But, on the whole, there was neither any true integration of Turkey's needs and possibilities nor any close adherence to the purposes originally stated. Work upon the project went ahead vigorously for the entire five-year period; but it is impossible to determine whether the results were equivalent to those intended by the government. Although most of the secondary evidence is to the contrary, perhaps the mere fact that diversified modern industrialization had been instituted at all was in itself a triumph. An additional result was that the accomplishments were sufficiently spectacular to sustain the faith in "year plans."

The industrialization under the Five-Year Plan was carried out under state auspices. The distribution of finances was handled mainly by a government organization known as the Sumer Bank, which constituted in a sense a board of development. One difficulty encountered was the overlap of powers, as between the Sumer Bank and the regularly constituted government departments. The latter sought to further their own favorite projects, with little regard to the economy as a whole. This problem was later multiplied when other banks were entrusted with the high-level promotion of various phases of national development.

This "statism" brought further difficulties in its train. Without the profit criterion as a semiautomatic regulator, the practice grew up of awarding heavy subsidies indiscriminately to uneconomic industries. Also a number of manufacturing plants were not at all well located, from the purely economic viewpoint. Managers of plants were salaried government officials, owing their positions to seniority rather than ability. They were, moreover, hampered by excessive regulations, which often prevented them from making quick decisions when necessary. Further, experienced men were often lured away from their positions as industrial executives by the higher pay and greater prestige obtainable in other types of government employ.

It must be added, however, that, until recently, statism was probably unavoidable in Turkey, especially in view of the determination to restrict the entry of foreign capital and foreign managerial skills within such narrow limits. The stage was not yet set either for large private investment in manufacturing enterprises or for the operation of large industries by private Turks on a competitive basis. Neither the capital resources nor the necessary initiative had yet appeared.

One immediate result of the first Five-Year Plan was that, from 1937 to the beginning of World War II, there was a spate of "year plans" along this line and that. These were, however, produced with more enthusiasm than discretion. Also many of the projects tended to lapse during the war, and never thereafter to reshape themselves in their original form. Only one of them merits special comment. That is the Four-Year Agricultural Plan, produced and instituted in 1937.

FOUR-YEAR AGRICULTURAL PLAN

The importance of this plan is mainly due to the fact that it constituted the first strong effort of the Turkish Government to give agriculture and agriculturists (who constitute over three-quarters of the entire population) their due share of official attention. The plan was to involve an expenditure of T.L. 100,000,000. A variety of projects were roughly outlined.

In spite of the outbreak of the war, which balked a good part of the scheme, there were some consequential specific achievements. For example, two irrigation projects have been completed or substantially advanced. Also, during the war, the government took over a 750,000-acre tract of uncultivated land, part of which has been converted into efficiently operated state farms. These extended over at least 40,000 acres in February, 1949, and probably now cover a much larger area.

But even these accomplishments have been valuable not so much because of their own intrinsic merits as because of the direction in which they have led or are leading. Most important, the agricultural needs of the country are now being recognized as of immediate importance.[13] A good example of the indirect results is the fact that, owing to well-substantiated foreign criticisms of the manner in which the irrigation schemes were planned and executed, the government has now put into actual practice a policy of integrated planning for entire river systems. Advice can apparently produce much better effect when it is based upon actual trial and error.

THE FIVE-YEAR INVESTMENT PLAN

During World War II, Turkish developmental activity was considerably handicapped both by the difficulties encountered in obtaining essential supplies from abroad and by the greatly increased needs of the army for man power. Nevertheless, by virtue of Turkey's alliance with Great Britain, and of a Lend-Lease agreement with the United States, the government was enabled to continue with certain forms of development.[14] Although the financial and technical aid which Britain and America furnished was primarily for military purposes, it also had the results of (1) reducing the burden of military expenditures from the ordinary budget and (2) facilitating an efficient performance of some work, notably road and port construction, which was useful for both military and civilian objectives. While the general pace of advancement was slowed down considerably during those years, at least part of the accomplishment was of an important character. Turkey's roads and ports, and to a lesser extent her railways, were wholly inadequate in 1939 for the stage of development which had been reached; and plans for improving that situation had

[13] An important source of detailed information in regard to present-day situations in certain rural areas in Turkey has been the Institute of Current World Affairs, 522 Fifth Ave., New York City. A representative of the institute, Mr. Richard D. Robinson, conducted exhaustive firsthand studies of social and economic conditions in selected villages.

[14] British financial assistance to Turkey from 1939 to 1947 amounted to £90,-500,000. American wartime Lend-Lease aid amounted to $34,800,000. Cf. Lingeman, op. cit., p. 10; Economic Cooperation Administration, op. cit., Table XII-1.

lagged well behind the industrial phases of modernization. The war, with its closure of all ports other than Iskenderun and Mersin to Allied shipping, served to emphasize, both at the time and thereafter, the urgency of more and better communications and transport facilities. An additional result was that, by the end of the war, the government had become fully conscious of all major aspects of the general developmental problem.

A further important consequence of the wartime arrangements was the alteration which they wrought in Turkey's policy with regard to borrowing abroad. The close economic relations with Great Britain and America had not proved at all detrimental to Turkey's independence; and in 1945 and 1946 there seemed to be little fear of any adverse effects of future loans, no matter how large, issuing from those nations. A large loan was, moreover, urgently needed at that time, since Turkey's dollar-exchange resources were far from sufficient to enable her to go ahead with development at the rapid pace which was desired.

NEW FIVE-YEAR PROGRAM INITIATED IN 1946

In 1946 the Turkish Government prepared a general five-year plan involving all fields of economic endeavor, as well as public health measures. This plan was apparently designed to supersede all previously announced year plans still uncompleted. The main declared purpose was the raising of living standards. The development of agriculture was to have accounted for about $32,000,000 of the total foreign-exchange expenditure of $500,000,000 under the scheme.

An attempt was then made to obtain a loan of $500,000,000 from the Export-Import Bank for the necessary dollar-exchange expenditures under this plan. However, an examination of the Turkish economy which was being conducted at the time by the Twentieth Century Fund (an American private organization) gave indication that the projects in question were poorly coordinated with Turkey's needs and that it would be desirable to review the whole question of Turkish development before concluding any definite loan agreement. The Export-Import Bank granted a loan of $25,000,000 in 1946 to cover Turkey's most immediate dollar-exchange needs, but the question of the general developmental loan was apparently deferred pending the results of further inquiry and an effort by the Turkish Government to revise its planning along lines of better integration. The next major developments as to comprehensive planning took place in 1948, after an integrated plan of a more restricted character had already been put into effect, following the Truman declaration of March, 1947.[15]

INVESTMENT PROGRAM REVISED UNDER MARSHALL PLAN

In April, 1948, the four-year European Recovery Plan was enacted by the United States Congress and made applicable to Turkey. The Economic Cooperation Administration, the administrative organ for this plan, proceeded to conduct its own inquiry into all aspects of the Turkish economy. During the course of this investigation the Turkish Government presented a revised proposal for a large-scale five-year developmental program. It involved an investment of $730,-000,000 in capital equipment and public works over a period of five years, 1948-53.

The Economic Cooperation Administration, after a tentative examination of this investment program in the light of its findings in regard to the Turkish economy, referred the matter to the International Bank for Reconstruction and Development for its consideration. The bank, in order to form an estimate of the merits of the scheme, conducted a preliminary inquiry of its own in Turkey in 1949. Apparently this study satisfied the bank officials that the Turkish proposals offered a suitable tentative basis for loan negotiations. Accordingly, the bank instituted in 1950 a much more thorough survey of social and economic conditions in Turkey, and it was generally understood that the Turkish Government would give favorable consideration to a revision of its program along the lines which the bank would propose after completion of the survey. The bank itself would presumably then furnish a part of the finances

[15] See later discussion of the Turkish Roads Program. The Truman Doctrine aid also facilitated some port construction activities which had value other than military.

needed and also provide helpful suggestions (possibly in cooperation with E.C.A. and the Export-Import Bank) as to sources of additional funds.

TURKISH INDUSTRIAL BANK ORGANIZED

Closely related to the preparations for a five-year plan of general development was the establishment in April, 1950, of the Turkish Industrial Development Bank. This bank, the founding of which was sponsored by the International Bank, is a device designed to help wean Turkey away from statism in industry by offering more attractive facilities than had ever previously been made available to private investors. Privately owned and operated, the bank has backing and guarantees from the government. Also it has a $9,000,000 dollar-exchange credit, extended in October, 1950, by the International Bank on a loan basis. The services will be in the nature of financial facilities and managerial assistance to private entrepreneurs. According to present prospects, the latter form of assistance will probably be the more important, as the bank's lending capacity will not exceed $18,000,000 at the uppermost—at least for the present. An American, Mr. Norman M. Tucker, was appointed general manager of the bank; and there is to be a staff of foreign technical and managerial experts. The bank has authority, in exceptional cases, to establish and operate enterprises of its own.

INTERNATIONAL BANK PROGRAM FOR TURKEY

The report of the International Bank survey, made in the summer of 1950 by the Barker Mission, was still being awaited at the end of that year. Meanwhile, since there were certain projects which it was felt should not be delayed pending decision on the general investment program, the International Bank had, on July 7, 1950, extended two loans to Turkey. One, in the amount of $12,500,000, was for port development and construction. The other, amounting to $3,900,-000, was for construction of grain storage facilities in many parts of the country. These loans cover only foreign currency costs. The total estimated expenditures for the projects are $38,600,000 and $10,-000,000 respectively.

The Five-Year Investment Program, as it will stand until the Barker Report is issued and acted upon, provides for the following expenditures:[16]

Agriculture	$100,600,000
Mining	105,870,000
Transportation	416,030,000
Power production	41,910,000
Industry	60,640,000
Studies and control	4,850,000
TOTAL	$729,900,000

Of this total amount of $730,000,000, it was proposed that $363,000,000 should be defrayed by internal financing, with the remainder, i.e., $367,000,000, financed by foreign loans or grants. It is noteworthy that, although the total amount estimated for foreign-exchange costs was considerably lower than in the 1946 draft, the estimate for agricultural requirements on that account has been more than doubled.

Public health projects are apparently no longer included in the comprehensive planning for general development. Such projects, which are of great importance, will presumably be conducted separately.

THE ROADS PROGRAM

Perhaps the most crucial of Turkey's current plans is the Roads Program, which was put into effect in 1948. This project has been financed partly by American military aid, partly by E.C.A., and partly by the Turkish Government. It calls for the construction of 14,300 miles of all-weather arterial highways over a period of nine years. The annual foreign-exchange expenditure is about $7,500,000.

One of the immediate objectives of this plan, as it is being carried out, is to produce a large nuclear skilled labor force, highly trained both as to techniques and as to attitudes and capable of passing these along to others. Another is to insure that, as soon as possible, the Turkish highway administration will constitute, in its executive aspects, a model of departmental efficiency. As far as the American

[16] E.C.A., *Turkey: Country Study* (Washington, 1949), p. 37.

advisers are concerned, these objects are being accorded priority over the matter of mileage constructed.

Commenting on the problems which have been encountered in connection with the project, Mr. Kerwin writes:

Individuals are often lost because of insufficient pay scales over which the Roads Department has no control. All salaries of government employees are set by a civil service law, now unrealistic in the face of rising costs of living. In addition, taxes absorb about one-third of the gross salary of a government functionary. This insufficiency of pay opens the door to graft and bribery.

A Turkish project engineer . . . generally has little chance to acquire practical experience. He is strictly an executive by virtue of his education, one who dictates work to be carried out by others. It is not an exaggeration to say that an engineer or surveyor seldom even drives a stake for himself. . . .

A serious deficiency in the economic development of Turkey has been the almost complete absence of cost accounting or of what may be termed "cost consciousness." . . .

Despite expressed intentions to do so, Turkey may not be able to carry on alone when the aid runs out, presumably in 1952, because the program may be far from completion by that time and may still be too costly for the Turks to finance by themselves. The roads program is greatly different from the short-term aid projects being financed by ECA. . . .

The road program, like many other aspects of American aid to Turkey, indicates that technological aid to under-developed countries involves careful and patient work over a long period of time.[17]

Still another problem has been that of developing new attitudes on the part of workers unaccustomed to the tempo and processes of modern mechanical efficiency. This problem is being met in some measure by the establishment of training centers at suitably scattered points throughout the country. It is questionable, however, that the psychological obstacles will be completely overcome in short order. It is the exceptional foreign technician who is qualified to handle problems of that nature expertly.

Nevertheless, in their determined pursuance of the fundamental objectives previously stated, the American advisers have at all times

[17] Robert W. Kerwin, "The Turkish Roads Program," *Middle East Journal*, April, 1950, pp. 201-208.

had the full backing and confidence of the Turkish Government at its highest level, and to a large extent even at lower official levels. Also, apparently the road developments are being welcomed more and more enthusiastically by the rural villagers whose lives are to be affected thereby. According to a recent newspaper report, on several occasions mayors have petitioned the national authorities to route highways through their respective villages.[18]

From the viewpoint of preparing the way for large-scale elevation of Turkish living standards on an enduring basis, the Roads Program probably exceeds even the Five-Year Investment Plan in potential importance.

ADDITIONAL OBSERVATIONS

THE ROLE OF E.C.A.

Unquestionably the Economic Cooperation Administration has made a substantial contribution, both financial and advisory, to the campaign for higher living standards in Turkey. The integration of its activities with those of the other lending and advisory bodies (American Military Aid Administration, Export-Import Bank, and International Bank) on the whole has been effectively handled. E.C.A. has, in fact, since April, 1948, been the *de facto* central coordinating body for outside aid extended to Turkey. In this role it has probably also been instrumental in paving the way to closer integration on the Turkish side. In January, 1949, a Minister of State was appointed to coordinate the handling of matters pertaining to foreign and international aid. In the following month, an Inter-Ministerial Committee was established to coordinate all economic planning.

E.C.A. has participated in, or helped in the formulation of, both of the current major plans for raising living standards. Also it has implemented its own smaller-scale projects, some of which might otherwise have had to await the final decision on the Five-Year

[18] Farnsworth Fowle, "New Turkish Road Points Up U.S. Aid," *New York Times*, May 7, 1950; also "Turkey Improves Ancient Highways," *New York Times*, April 30, 1950.

Investment Plan.[19] Between April 1, 1948, and September 30, 1950, E.C.A.'s total authorizations amounted to $103,100,000.

Planning with respect to living standards, however, has not been E.C.A.'s main function—which was to promote Turkish exports of essential commodities in short supply in western Europe. Further, E.C.A.'s role is a temporary and short-lived one.[20]

CULTIVATED AND CULTIVABLE AREAS; IRRIGATION; POPULATION

The cultivated acreage in Turkey was estimated at 31,440,000, as of February, 1949. From the viewpoint of farm size, this was divided as follows:[21]

	Number of Farms	Acreage	Percentage of Total Acreage
Over 1,200 acres	418	1,530,000	5
240 to 1,200	5,764	4,140,000	13
Less than 240	2,000,000	25,770,000	82
TOTALS	2,006,182	31,440,000	100

There is also a large amount of unused cultivable land, much of which would not require irrigation. While the precise quantity in the latter category has not been accurately determined, the following statement in E.C.A.'s *Turkey: Country Study*, prepared in February, 1949, provides partial (and probably conservative) information in regard to the subject:

"According to the Turkish Government there is presently about 10,400,000 acres of land that is described as 'not cultivated but easily tillable by means of proper machinery.' Some of this is land not farmed in the usual sense. Other is land privately owned but

[19] One policy of E.C.A.'s which does not appear to have been examined adequately by unbiased experts, as to its efficacy for raising living standards, is the campaign to mechanize Turkish agriculture. During the first twenty-one months of the four-year Marshall Plan, tractors accounted for more than one-third of the total authorizations for Turkish purchases from all countries under the E.C.A. program. Cf. Economic Cooperation Administration, *op. cit.*, Table XIV-1.

[20] The status of this matter, as of November 1, 1951, was that E.C.A.'s successor, the Mutual Security Agency, would be conducting a program in Turkey until June 30, 1954.

[21] E.C.A., *op. cit.*, p. 32.

which is not cultivated for crop-growing purposes at all because of the lack of equipment, or which is only intermittently cultivated, that is, every second or third year."[22]

Certainly, between February, 1949, and the end of 1950 some of the land in this category has been brought under cultivation. A fulfillment of Turkish intentions expressed in 1948 would mean that about 3,000,000 acres had been added to the dry cultivated area. It is, however, doubtful that the increase has even closely approached that figure.

There is believed to be great scope for the introduction of additional irrigation facilities. Irrigation is, in fact, in its infancy in Turkey. Although the available statistical data on this subject are somewhat confused, it is clear that, at the beginning of 1949, the total area irrigated under all schemes, both large and small, did not exceed 900,000 acres out of a total irrigable area estimated at 6,750,000 acres. It is equally plain that the projects subsequently completed, or now under way or under serious contemplation for the near future (as reckoned from the end of 1950), would not increase the 1949 figure by more than 700,000 acres at the utmost.

Turkey's population in 1940 was 17,821,000. By 1949 it had grown to 19,623,000.[23] The results of the 1950 census have not yet been published.

PER CAPITA INCOME

According to estimates published in December, 1950, by the Statistical Office of the United Nations for all countries of the world, Turkey's per capita income is $125, which is the same as Lebanon's but higher than that of any other Middle Eastern country, Israel excepted. It is only slightly lower than Greece's per capita income ($128), and considerably higher than Japan's ($100). Apart from Israel and Lebanon, no other Asiatic country had a higher or equal per capita income.[24]

According to calculations made by the Economic Cooperation Ad-

[22] Ibid.

[23] Statistical Office of the United Nations, Monthly Bulletin of Statistics, December, 1950.

[24] "Income per Person in Soviet Held $308," New York Times, December 4, 1950.

ministration, the gross national product, based on the 1936 value of the Turkish lira, rose from T.L. 1,295,000 in 1936 to T.L. 2,915,000 in 1947, then dropped to T.L. 2,294,000 in 1948. The 1936-48 differential thus amounted to 77 per cent, while the rise in population in those years amounted to only 18 per cent.[25]

These data provide evidence that Turkey's high rank among Asiatic countries is at least partially attributable to relatively rapid developmental progress in pursuance of official planning, with general living standards an item of important consideration.

The Turkish Bureaucracy[26]

In the days of the Ottoman Empire, appointments to civil governmental positions were regarded as the exclusive prerogative of families of the then ruling classes, that is, army officers, religious leaders, and great landowners. These positions were generally thought of by the holders as conferring rights rather than imposing duties. The three classes, to a considerable extent, overlapped one another.

However, after the republic had been instituted and Mustafa Kemal's (Ataturk's) People's party had assumed power on a single-party basis, the main general criterion of eligibility for appointive positions was altered. Loyalty to the party was now what mattered, not the economic, social, or professional class to which one belonged. This change was made completely effective by Ataturk's successful struggle against the religious leaders, which had also the result of reducing the importance of the great landowner class.

The change has not yet produced any complete revision of the general underlying concept regarding the nature and purposes of government positions, largely because, in the early days of the republic, the positions were still monopolized by persons of aristocratic background, who constituted the only sizable educated group in the country and who were incapable of discarding all their customary assumptions to meet the need of the reform program. Although the

[25] Economic Cooperation Administration, *op. cit.*, Table III-2a.
[26] This discussion is based in considerable measure upon a reading of the following passage and article, which provide criteria for evaluating bureaucracies: Max Weber, *The Theory of Social and Economic Organization* (Oxford, 1947), pp. 331-340; Richard Bendix, "Bureaucracy: The Problem and Its Study," *American Sociological Review*, October, 1947, *passim*.

base of the bureaucracy has subsequently been broadened, the result of that development has apparently been in large measure an adaptation of newcomers to somewhat remodeled old traditions, not an elimination of the traditions. In short, while the precise basis for determining a person's fitness for a certain position has been altered, there is often, even now, a wide gap between (1) the factors which decide eligibility, on the one hand, and (2) the formally prescribed functions of the office, on the other. The former are still mainly political.

As a result, most Turkish officeholders are still, at least to some extent, beneficiaries of patronage rather than technically competent professionals—who, moreover, regard the positions they hold not as a public trust but as a personal right. Also the general public, taken as a whole, does not appear to have reached the point of expecting any different situation in this respect. It is, in fact, even doubtful that the public expects the bureaucracy to be free from all-pervading corruption.

In short, the Turkish bureaucracy still does not operate entirely along lines which Max Weber would regard as "rational," that is, based on ability and readiness to render substantial service along specialized lines.[27] But, although there is still not enough competence and not enough sense of responsibility on the part of officials, it is equally true that there is no longer any marked prejudice in favor of any special interests, other than their own individual interests in such matters as prestige, power, pay, and so forth. These are probably favorable indications for the future of planning, since—assuming a favorable political climate—once a greater degree of technical competence is acquired by the bureaucracy, there is every likelihood that it will be exercised on an impartial and impersonal basis.

CONCLUSIONS

Perhaps the most difficult problem of all in connection with Western attempts to assist Middle Eastern countries has been the existence in those countries of a fanatical, hypersensitive, and suspicious nationalism in all sections of the population above the peasantry. The inevitable result of nationalism of that nature has been the

[27] Weber, *op. cit.*, p. 332.

constant recurrence of a vicious circle which has nearly always proved impossible to break. No less in Turkey than in most of the other Middle Eastern countries was this a fact of the highest importance during the between-wars era.

The vicious circle in question has consisted of the following circumstances and conditions:

1. The many poor are exploited by the wealthy few, who control the government.

2. The gradual worsening of this situation increases the menace of revolution by violence.

3. Ordinarily it has proved that the situation can be remedied only by foreign intervention.

4. But foreign intervention is resented even more by the poor than by the rich.

5. Hence, unless it is carried out in the interests of the rich, it causes deterioration rather than improvement of internal conditions.

6. But, if it is carried out in the interests of the rich, the exploitation of the poor becomes identified with the foreign intervention. The ruling group assists in this process.

7. Thus, no matter what policy is adopted by foreign powers, the revolutionary trend is favored.

8. The growth of such a trend favors the interests of foreign powers which are interested in utilizing revolutionary situations to the advantage of their own particular ideologies.

9. Activities of this sort, by altering the world balance of power as between opposed ideologies, tend to promote total war.

10. Up to the time of actual crisis, the political life of the country is pervaded throughout by fears and frustrations, which serve as effective bars to economic progress.

Probably most worthy of note in the present Turkish situation is the strong evidence that this circle has at last been broken in one Middle Eastern country. This fact is apparent from the cordial support which has been extended by the government to the American advisers.[28]

[28] This is fully reflected in the articles printed in 1950 in the Turkish Government's weekly information bulletin, *News from Turkey*, published by the Turkish Information Office at New York.

This attitude is certainly due in large measure to political considerations—the realization that Turkey's successful defense against the U.S.S.R. will probably be largely dependent upon the closeness of Turkish-Western ties. However, such intellectual realizations do not necessarily alter established emotional patterns. Hence it is particularly noteworthy that nearly four years of experience with American aid, in the forms and manner in which such aid is now extended, seem from all available evidence to have lessened Turkish apprehensions rather than increased them.

While due credit must go to the American advisers, there has also undoubtedly been an autonomous change within Turkey itself. The Turkish Government is showing itself less and less inclined to resent criticism directed against itself, its subordinate officials, or Turks in general and to be tolerant of the human shortcomings which are usually found among groups of persons rendering technical and specialized assistance in countries different from their own. In short, gains of the utmost importance have been made. What has caused them?

One part of the answer seems to be that, even in the darkest and most degenerate days, the Turkish people were never entirely lacking in spiritual strength of a sort which has not been at all discernible in most other Middle Eastern countries. The Turkish performance in World War I was at times magnificent, as particularly manifested in the defense of Gallipoli. The conduct of the later War of Liberation was even more creditable.

However, in 1923, and for some time thereafter, these symptoms of inner strength seemed far more than counterbalanced by the forces which were moving Turkey in the directions of bankruptcy, inertia, and despair. In general, the conditions most easily discernible were substantially the same as those preponderantly unhealthful ones prevailing in the rest of the Middle East.

What, then, has been mainly responsible for the recent change?

The answer seems to lie largely in the unusual career of Kemal Ataturk, as ruler of Turkey for over fifteen years. After taking all possible steps, first to gather exclusive power firmly into his own hands and those of his most loyal associates and thereafter to maintain that power on the same exclusive basis, Ataturk utilized the power to an extraordinary extent for the public good rather than for his own interests. In this he was, of course, greatly aided by the chaotic situation which prevailed when he first assumed control—a situation in which it was relatively easy to put an end to old precedents. Thereafter he dealt drastically, and at times ruthlessly, with all forces which threatened to reestablish the influence of landed wealth, the Moslem church, foreign nations, racial minorities, or even poorer groups in matters of government. There remained only the classless bureaucracy, discussed in the preceding section.[29] To the extent that it understood his ideas, this bureaucracy was completely loyal to Ataturk, whose popularity was thoroughly genuine. By the time of his death, a definite pattern had been established.

Since Ataturk's death, this pattern has been continued and, according to all indications, there have been no external groups with sufficient potential influence to entertain serious hopes of challenging the structure thus established.

This policy, made possible by Ataturk's attractive personality, his disinterestedness, his strength of character, and his competence, has made for political stability and a government which has little or nothing to gain by confusing issues, misleading the poorer classes, or rejecting foreign assistance proffered in good faith without ulterior motives.

The question which remains is whether this happy result is attributable mainly to Ataturk's special genius, or whether the way has been partially indicated toward a solution of general applicability.

[29] Mr. Thornburg is inclined to question the "classlessness" of the Turkish bureaucracy. His ideas, which are at variance with those of practically all other authorities on Turkey, seem to be based on the fact that a large percentage of the higher officials are, even now, of families which belonged to the old Ottoman ruling classes. Even Mr. Thornburg, however, never suggests that the present-day "ruling class" is an exclusive body, closed to persons of different family backgrounds or dedicated to the obstruction of such persons' economic interests. Cf. Thornburg, Spry, and Soule, op. cit., passim.

CHAPTER XI

❖

Regional Planning

Regionalized planning for the Middle East has been the subject of many strong pleas by Westerners interested in, or concerned with, the future well-being of the region.[1] The outlook, however, is somewhat nebulous.

THE OUTLOOK AT THE END OF WORLD WAR II

In 1945 the prospects for improved living standards resulting from major regional undertakings seemed highly favorable. During the war, both the Middle East Supply Centre and the Allied military authorities had achieved distinctly gratifying results through integrated treatment of the Middle East as a whole, mainly for the purposes of (1) supplying the Allied armies in the region, (2) conserving shipping space, (3) preventing famine among the inhabitants of Middle Eastern countries, and (4) protecting the health of the Allied armed forces.[2]

[1] Among those who have recently expressed themselves strongly in favor of Middle Eastern regional planning is Trygve Lie, Secretary-General of the United Nations. Cf. Introduction to his *Annual Report on the Work of the Organization*, July 7, 1949, quoted in *International Organization*, November, 1949. Also cf. footnote 8.

[2] E. B. Worthington, *Middle East Science* (London, 1945), pp. 7, 148; "Review of the Work of the Middle East Supply Centre," *Department of State Bulletin*, September 30, 1945.

In these endeavors the Allied authorities had enlisted the cooperation of the national governments and had apparently created among
officials a strong impression favorable to regional planning as a
general principle for future application.[3] Anticipating a marked postwar development in that sense, the M.E.S.C. had appointed in
1943 a Scientific Advisory Mission to conduct a preliminary survey
for the guidance of Middle Eastern governments in their future
decisions on desirable cooperative activities. The Mission was
specifically instructed to examine (1) the principal scientific problems
within the Middle East, irrespective of political boundaries, (2) the
principal scientific and technical resources available within the area,
and (3) the available organization for supplying scientific and technical information and advice from all sources.[4]

The survey was not completed until the war was nearly over. It
was at that time decided to release the Mission's reports to the
general public in the form of books by individual members of the
Mission. The main ones were *Middle East Science* by E. B. Worthington and *The Agricultural Development of the Middle East* by
B. A. Keen. A comprehensive postwar book along parallel lines, also
based on work done for the M.E.S.C. during the war period, is *Land
and Poverty in the Middle East* by Miss Doreen Warriner. In all
three works the desirability of regional cooperation along economic
and social lines is strongly stressed.[5]

Meanwhile there had been important local developments. In
1943 the M.E.S.C. had sponsored a conference of Middle Eastern
nations to consider the matter of improving the statistical data for
the region. This led to the appointment of a standing committee
to advise the governments in regard to statistical methods.[6] In the
following year, a regional Conference on Middle East Agricultural

[3] Harold Beeley, "The Middle East in 1939 and in 1944," *Journal of the Royal
Central Asian Society*, 1945, Part I, pp. 12, 15; Keith A. H. Murray, "Feeding
the Middle East in War-Time," *Journal of the Royal Central Asian Society*, 1945,
Part III-IV, p. 246; B. A. Keen, *The Agricultural Development of the Middle
East* (London, 1946), p. 103.

[4] Worthington, *op. cit.*, p. xi.

[5] *Ibid.*, p. v; Keen, *op. cit.*, p. vii; Doreen Warriner, *Land and Poverty in the
Middle East* (London, 1948), p. 132.

[6] Worthington, *op. cit.*, p. 195.

Development was held at Cairo. Finally, in March, 1945, when the Arab League was established, the seven Arab nations of the Middle East agreed that the League should be a vehicle for extensive regional cooperation in economic and developmental matters. Organs were established for the detailed planning and execution of such cooperation.[7]

THE POSTWAR DETERIORATION

Subsequent developments, however, have not been at all in harmony with the 1945 appearances. Generally speaking, such active regional cooperation as has come into being has been promoted not by the Arab League or by any other purely regional body but by the United Nations and its specialized agencies. The activity, moreover, has been on a small scale, and, except in the matter of conferences, institutes, and seminars, there has been an increasing tendency for these international bodies to focus their attention upon individual Middle Eastern nations rather than upon regional groupings.[8] Two specialized agencies, namely FAO and WHO, have established Middle Eastern regional offices, but they have been handicapped by the limited funds at their disposal.[9]

A controlling reason for this change in orientation has been the continuously strained relations between the seven Arab states and the Jewish community of Palestine (later the state of Israel). With Israel occupying a key position from the standpoint of any rational communications network for the Middle Eastern region, most forms of major pan-regional planning would be somewhat futile without that nation's participation and subsequent cooperation.

[7] Arab Office, *The League of Arab States* (pamphlet) (Washington, 1946).

[8] The United Nations Economic Survey Mission for the Middle East, 1949, was instructed "to make recommendations for an integrated programme . . . to promote economic conditions conducive to the maintenance of peace and stability in the area." After close inquiry into local conditions, the Mission recommended that all developmental projects should be conducted on national bases, with coordination confined to regionally integrated recommendations by external authorities to the individual nations. Cf. United Nations, *Final Report of the United Nations Economic Survey Mission for the Middle East*, 1949, Part I, pp. 1, 3.

[9] *International Organization*, August, 1949, p. 546.

However, as matters stand at present, the Arab governments do not—at least officially—even envisage a permanent existence for the state of Israel.

Under the circumstances, it is hardly worth while to discuss any possibilities for greatly expanded intra-regional cooperation before relations between Israel and the Arab League states have improved materially. But whether that event will prove to be a decisive factor is also a matter of considerable doubt. This statement is made in the light of the entire history of regional cooperation in the Middle East after the end of World War I.

THE BETWEEN-WARS PERIOD

During the period between the two world wars an outstanding feature of the relations among the Middle Eastern nations was the almost complete absence of multilateral regional pacts or arrangements in regard to economic and social matters. Apart from broadly international conventions, usually operative on a more or less world-wide basis, the only agreements of such a nature were the 1929 Beirut accord for the sanitary regulation of pilgrimages to Mecca, concluded by the three mandated countries (Iraq, Syria, and Transjordan) through which pilgrims pass in transit, and the 1926 pact which established the *Bureau International de Reseignements sur les Sauterelles*, with headquarters at Damascus. The latter agreement was only short-lived, despite the importance of the activities for which it provided.[10] Apart from the locust-control office there were no regional bodies of an official nature, and no regional conferences were held for consideration of economic and social (other than religious) problems.[11] Perhaps the most pointed illustration of the absence of regionalism in action and sentiment during the between-wars period is the fact that not a single book was published on

[10] Ministère des Affaires Etrangères, *Rapports sur la Situation de la Syrie et du Liban, 1921-1938* (Paris, 1923-1939), 1927, p. 94; 1932, p. 20.

[11] During the early part of the period the existence of two great religious problems, namely, the succession to the caliphate and the protection of pilgrimages to Mecca after Ibn Saud's capture of that city, served to promote regionalism in the Moslem religious sphere. However, after 1926 those problems rapidly declined in importance.

economic and social conditions in the Middle East as a whole, or in any group of Middle Eastern countries.[12]

Since it has often been stated that at least the northern and central parts of the Ottoman Empire formed a natural economic unity,[13] the extreme disunity among the "balkanized" fragments of that empire requires some explanation. For one thing, of course, this "balkanization," as arranged between Britain and France, had in part been designed to produce precisely such a result, particularly insofar as relations between Turkey and her southern neighbors were concerned. Equally important was the fact that Turkey and Iran, desirous as they were of achieving speedy results in Westernization, were disinclined to associate themselves with the more conservative developmental policies of the states under League of Nations mandates. A probable third factor was the absence of great faith on the part of the Middle Eastern peoples in the future political stability of the Middle Eastern nations. It may be added that, during most of the between-wars period, the Western world was not setting a particularly good example in the matter of international cooperation. There was, to be sure, an abundance of inconspicuous cooperation among Western nations; but this was overshadowed by the conflicts which developed in the political and economic spheres. As far as the Middle Eastern region was concerned, Britain and France conspicuously failed to implement a formal agreement made by them in December, 1920, to appoint a joint commission to consider the equitable distribution of water supplies in the areas under mandate. Furthermore, with the growth of the Jewish National Home in Palestine, fears developed among the Middle East Arabs that regionalization—especially in economic matters—would be tantamount to conferring complete domination of the region upon the Palestinian Jews, or possibly upon world Jewry as a whole.[14]

A possible alternative would have been a partial regional integra-

[12] The pioneer work along such lines was *The Economic Development of the Middle East* by Alfred Bonné (London, 1945).

[13] Said B. Himadeh, *Economic Organization of Syria* (Beirut, 1946), pp. 177, 199, 200; United Nations, *op. cit.*, Part I, p. 1.

[14] James B. Hays, *T.V.A. on the Jordan* (Washington, 1948), p. 20; Arnold J. Toynbee, *The Islamic World Since the Peace Settlement* (London, 1927), p. 466.

tion with both Turkey and Palestine excluded. Such a prospect, however, was not of a nature to arouse really strong interest. The remaining seven countries now had substantially similar economies —predominantly agricultural and with more or less the same types of crop. Moreover, their problems as to health, education, and general development were—or at least appeared on the surface to be—also substantially similar. Only Saudi Arabia and Yemen, more backward than their neighbors, found value in assistance from other Middle Eastern countries along those lines.[15] This could be handled through simple bilateral arrangements—as could nearly all the other obvious national needs in which action beyond the national frontier was an element. As for the many forms of regional cooperation which are valuable though lacking in spectacular qualities, there was no state of readiness for them. What was needed first, but not forthcoming, was striking demonstration of the great value of regional cooperation in general.

In the result, autarchic policies were adopted, which had the effect of strengthening the centrifugal tendencies already at work. Public attention, in economic and social matters, became focused upon the problems of the national unit, not those of the region or of a large part thereof.[16]

Present Tendencies and the Underlying Factors

Although the developments of the Second World War aroused considerable interest in the possibilities of regional cooperation, one highly important aspect was generally overlooked at the time. This was that the Allied authorities during the war were particularly favorably situated, in that they possessed a high degree of power, and in some cases actual control, over the national governments of the region.[17] When seven or eight independent nations, all unaccustomed to voluntary cooperation, attempt to duplicate such a

[15] *Oriente Moderno*, May, 1936, p. 295; K. S. Twitchell, *Saudi Arabia* (Princeton, 1947), pp. 108, 171.

[16] Himadeh, *op. cit.*, pp. 252-258.

[17] The British mandate for Palestine and Transjordan had not yet been terminated. Also, owing to war developments, Britain had acquired preponderant control in Egypt, Syria, Lebanon, Iraq, and part of Iran. In all of those countries she had large armed forces. The Allied governments controlled most of the major transportation facilities.

performance under different conditions and with different objectives, the result is bound to be somewhat less satisfactory,[18] and would have been so even if relations between the Arab states and the Jews of Palestine had been much better than they actually were. As it is, the complete failure of the much-publicized attempts by the Arab League to institute an effective regionalization has unquestionably destroyed much of the faith generated during the war period.[19]

An additional element in the situation is the fact that, as far as the most conspicuously profitable forms of cooperation are concerned, the main benefits pertain to a hypothetical future state of affairs which may never materialize. If Lebanon develops its hydroelectric power; if the oil resources of the region come under the control of *stable and efficient* Middle Eastern governments; and *if* Iraq and Syria develop their wastelands *for the benefit of the cultivators*, there would doubtless be many possibilities for profitable cooperation—in the form, for example, of a customs union between Syria, Lebanon, and Iraq. Under these conditions additional desirable forms of cooperation would become sufficiently obvious. Lebanese might appreciate the need of assisting in measures to eliminate insect pests in Syria. Syrians might feel concerned over an assured supply of Iraqi oil for power needs in Lebanon which could not be met from its own supplies of hydroelectric power. But, desirable as it may be to begin now to pave the way for these eventualities, it is difficult to arouse true enthusiasm over such nebulous prospects. Meanwhile, as far as the *foreseeable* future is concerned, there is even expert dissent as to the desirability of a mere Syro-Lebanese customs union.[20]

[18] An additional factor has been the demonstrated inability of the Arab leaders and their followers to establish any balance between political strategy and economic development which was not heavily weighted against the latter. This is largely ascribable to historical background conditions which have been discussed in other chapters. Cf. Warriner, *op. cit.*, p. 2.

[19] Paul Seabury, "The League of Arab States: Debacle of a Regional Arrangement," *International Organization*, August, 1949, p. 633 *et seq.*; Albion Ross, "Jordan Ban Held Blow to Arab Pact," New York *Times*, May 17, 1950.

[20] Cf. Charles Issawi's book review of Menassa's *Plan de Réconstruction de l'Economie Libanaise et de Réforme de l'Etat* in the *Middle East Journal*, January, 1949, p. 95.

It now seems probable that formal regionalization, as manifested by the many new regional organs and the numerous regional conferences which have been held since the end of the war, is being kept alive mainly by considerations of national prestige.[21] One important indication that this is the case is the marked paucity of published statements in the Arab countries or Iran to the effect that regional peace would be desirable for economic reasons. Also there seems to be no widespread disposition among Arabs or Iranians to deplore the fact that, as a result of Turkey's inclusion in the Marshall Plan, her economy is now being closely coordinated with western Europe's on what appears to be a permanent basis. It is significant, too, that the proposal to establish an Economic Commission for the Middle East, under the Economic and Social Council of the United Nations, has now been virtually dormant for over two years.[22] The tangible accomplishments along regional lines seem to have been mainly in the start provided toward assembly of essential regional data. In this general connection the following paragraphs, quoted from an article in the August, 1949, issue of *International Organization*, are of interest:

Economic, cultural and social projects undertaken by the League of Arab States have been numerous and ambitious. . . . Economic, Transportation and Communications, and Finance Committees of the League have drafted far-reaching plans for the closer integration of the Arab economies. . . . In 1948, a proposed investigation of the feasibility of currency unification was approved by the League Council. Accordingly, Paul van Zeeland, former Premier of Belgium, was directed to study the question. M. van Zeeland's report, made public in November 1948, provides valuable comment upon the marked disparity between the declarations and fulfilment of League undertakings. While emphasizing the difficulties of such a plan, the report concludes that a monetary union could be realized "if the Arab States are disposed to adopt the principles which they extol."

It is not known what success has been obtained in securing member

[21] Examples of the types of conferences are: an FAO regional conference in 1948; an ILO regional conference in 1947; conference of an Expert Committee on Pilgrimages in 1947; conference on the Moroccan locust in 1949; U.N. social welfare seminars in 1949 and 1950 for the Arab states; Annual Conferences of Arab Engineers.

[22] *International Organization*, May, 1949, p. 311.

294 CHALLENGE AND RESPONSE IN THE MIDDLE EAST

governments' ratification of the above schemes, but it is apparent that most of the League's economic and social activities have either been abandoned or pigeonholed due to the pressures of the Palestine venture. While this is probably the case, it is also evident that too many Arab leaders today, nurtured in a climate of agitation and conspiracy, have found collaboration on the hum-drum practical tasks somewhat un-palatable.[23]

In April of the current year the following report appeared in the *Middle East Journal:*

There was little evidence in 1949 of contributions by the Arab League to the cause of economic integration. However, the Islamic Economic Conference sponsored by the Government of Pakistan in the fall brought together official and business representatives from Pakistan, Iran, Afghanistan, Turkey, and the Arab countries, and observers. . . . It worked out various plans of economic cooperation and set up a permanent International Islamic Federation of Chambers of Commerce and Industry. . . .

A bulletin of the Conference's secretariat issued on December 2 stated: "The first need is to raise the standard of life by the best technical means known to the western world, but the remedy must be applied to Muslim conditions by Muslim agencies pursuing the principles of Islam.[24]

There are at present no indications as to the progress being made by the new organization just mentioned. Probably it has not embarked upon any major undertakings.[25] As for regionalism in the realm of private enterprise, there is no evidence that this has made any marked progress.

ISRAEL'S INTEREST IN THE REGIONAL APPROACH

The only Middle Eastern nation which appears to be genuinely interested in regional integration is Israel.[26] However, even if peace should be restored in the near future, there would remain the fears that such integration would be solely for Israel's benefit and to the detriment of the rest of the Middle East. Unfortunately, some of the

[23] Seabury, *op. cit.,* p. 639.
[24] Dorothea Seelye Franck and Peter G. Franck, "The Middle East Economy in 1949," *Middle East Journal,* April, 1950, p. 243.
[25] If it has, the fact has certainly not been given much publicity.
[26] "Morgenthau Asks East Pact," New York *Times,* January 22, 1950.

pronouncements by Palestine Jews and by persons working in their behalf have conveyed an impression of that very nature, even to some neutral observers. The report of the Clapp Mission, for example, contains the following statement: "An engineering plan has yet to be devised for the Jordan and its tributaries which treats the system as a whole without prejudging specific political interests. Until that is done the countries concerned will not be aware of the possible alternative costs, losses or benefits any particular scheme for development might involve."[27]

Miss Warriner makes even more pointed comment:

The idea of "absorptive capacity," which influences so much of the discussion of Middle East prospects, tends to ignore the . . . low standard of the existing population and the existing social institutions. It is greatly to the credit of the economists of the Jewish Agency, in particular to Dr. Bonné, that they have assembled the economic data of the Middle East countries and analyzed them from the standpoint of what additional population could be supported. . . . But by making their starting point the need for living space for immigrants they have ignored these important limiting factors.[28]

It is further to be noted that even the idea of integrated treatment of the Tigris-Euphrates-Karun river system is to some extent regarded by Arabs as a Jewish idea advanced for exclusively Jewish reasons. This notion arose partly because the popularization of "TVA's for the Middle East" began with the Jewish-sponsored proposal for a "Jordan Valley Authority." It is also partly due to the fact that specific suggestions have been made, notably by former President Hoover, for development of the international Tigris-Euphrates-Karun basin for the purpose of solving the Palestine problem in a manner satisfactory to Jews.[29] These factors may constitute a partial reason why regional cooperation in matters involving that river basin has been so little advanced up to the time of writing.[30]

[27] United Nations, op. cit., Part I, p. 4.
[28] Warriner, op. cit., pp. 3-4.
[29] Arab Office, "Mr. Hoover's Plan," Arab News Bulletin (Washington, January 1, 1946).
[30] Feliks Bochenski and William Diamond, "TVA's in the Middle East," Middle East Journal, January, 1950, pp. 78-79; United Nations, op. cit., Part I, pp. 71-72, 89-92.

IMMEDIATE PROSPECTS OF REGIONALIZATION

In summary, the prospects for extensive regional cooperation of a voluntary nature seem rather dim at present. Moreover, a great part of the value of such cooperation would necessarily be lost if both Israel and Turkey, the nations most advanced in industrialization and general modernization, were, as appears likely, to remain outside of the main attempts at regional integration. Possibly, of course, the very fact of greatly increased contacts in conferences and study groups will in time promote a general insistence upon more thoroughgoing cooperation. It is difficult, however, to see how this pressure can be brought into being unless new and spectacular illustrations of the importance of greater regionalization are forthcoming. This importance is probably already realized by many specialists in the region, each as to his own field. But such realization is unlikely to produce major results until the specialists can gain the support of the top-level politicians and of the politically conscious public in general, which may not be until drastic political changes have taken place in the region.[31]

Finally, in the case of Egypt, there would appear to be some doubt as to whether her proper orientation, from the viewpoint of regional integration, is with the other Middle Eastern states or with the African countries to the south, particularly the Sudan and Ethiopia.[32]

THE ROLE OF MIDDLE EASTERN OIL

As to the possible future role of oil in the elevation of Middle Eastern living standards through regional planning, the following statement by Miss Warriner, in *Land and Poverty in the Middle East*, published in 1948 by the Royal Institute of International Affairs (London and New York), still holds substantially true:

[31] It is possible, for example, that a political union among several of the Arab states would weaken the present unbalance as between political strategy *directed against* Israel and the Western powers and statesmanship *directed toward* development in the social and economic spheres. With such a union, Arabs might lose some of their present feeling of insecurity.

[32] See the chapter on Egypt.

The other big factor which is likely to change the economic outlook in the Middle East is the forthcoming great expansion of oil production. . . . In the eight years 1938–46 the oil output from the Middle East territories doubled, from 16 million tons to 32 million tons. By 1951 it is anticipated that the total output of oil will reach 77 million tons, much of the increase coming from Saudi Arabia and Kuwait.[33] . . .

The rights of exploitation of these supplies are held by a few foreign companies, some of which are new in this area. Most of the increase will come from new oil fields which have hitherto been unexploited. The most important of these are in Bahrein[34] and Saudi Arabia where exclusive rights are owned by . . . American companies. . . .

Under present conditions, it seems unlikely that this new investment will be related to the general economic development of the Middle East area, for two reasons. One is that most of the new money which investment brings in the form of royalties will go into countries which have almost no other resources, the sparsely populated desert kingdom of Saudi Arabia, and the tiny area of Kuwait, virtually without agriculture or industry. Much of it will doubtless be spent on direct personal consumption, and it is unlikely to find its way into long-term investment in the neighboring countries with large populations and possibilities of agricultural development. The political divisions between territories of the Middle East thus stand in the way of long-term development; if they were economically and politically more unified, the benefits accruing to the rulers of Saudi Arabia and the sheikhdoms might be spread more evenly, and lead to a long-term rise in living standards. This presupposes, however, a progressive policy on the part of the Governments concerned.

Another reason why the expansion of oil production is not likely to stimulate general development is that since the companies are foreign all their profits will presumably be invested outside the Middle East territories. The danger is that the main mineral resource of the territories will be drained away, without contributing towards an increase in the supply of capital and the long-term investment needed to provide for a general rise in the standard of living. It is estimated that the oil reserves may be exhausted in the course of two generations; by that time local populations, more than double their present size, will have sunk into irremediable poverty unless agriculture has been more productive, and other branches of industry have been built up. If the expansion of oil production is to promote a balanced development and relieve the general shortage of capital, it is necessary that a part of the profits from

[33] Kuwait is a small, semi-independent Arab shaikhdom under British protection, lying between Iraq and Saudi Arabia.

[34] Bahrein Island is a British protectorate in the Persian Gulf. British possession of it is disputed by Iran.

oil as well as part of the royalties accruing to the local Governments should be reinvested in the development of agriculture, where the return is necessarily low and long-term, and in consumption goods industries, which could expand if the general standard of living were rising. To secure such a general expansion, as part of the terms of a governmental agreement covering the relations of the oil companies with each other and with the Middle East Governments, was the object of a proposal made by the British Government in 1945; this recommended the setting up of a bank for general economic development, covering all the territories concerned, in which the companies would have assigned a proportion of their profits, for investment in long-term development projects. A scheme of this kind would be the only way of securing that the development of the chief resource of the territories would directly promote a general rise in the standard of living. Unfortunately this proposal was not carried out because the general Anglo-American oil agreement, of which it was a part, was not ratified.[35]

A resumption of the negotiations for an acceptable Anglo-American oil agreement is apparently not contemplated at the time of writing.[36]

The Potential Roles of Israel and Turkey

With regard to the role which the Jews of Palestine might play in the development of the Middle East, T. E. Lawrence made the following statement in 1920:

They hope to adjust their mode of life to the climate of Palestine, and by the exercise of their skill and capital to make it as highly organized as a European state. The success of their scheme will involve inevitably the raising of the present Arab population to their own material level, only a little after themselves in point of time, and the consequences might be of the highest importance for the future of the Arab world. It might well prove a source of technical supply rendering them independent of industrial Europe, and in that case the new confederation might become a formidable element of world power. However, such

[35] Warriner, op. cit., pp. 137-139.
[36] The attempts to produce an agreement which would give substantial satisfaction to all parties immediately involved proved virtually hopeless. Cf. Raymond F. Mikesell and Hollis B. Chenery, Arabian Oil: America's Stake in the Middle East (Chapel Hill, 1949), passim; Herbert Feis, Petroleum and American Foreign Policy (Stanford University, March, 1944), passim.

a contingency will not be for the first or even for the second generation, but it must be borne in mind in any laying out of foundations of empire in Western Asia. These to a very large extent must stand or fall by the course of the Zionist effort.[37]

This statement seems, even today, to represent a fair appraisal. A problem for Israel will be how to make adequate use of the great amount of technically skilled man power which she will be capable of producing, in view of the paucity of natural resources within her own boundaries. The Arab states' greatest need along developmental lines, on the other hand, will be those very skills which Israel has much better prospects of acquiring in relatively short order. The skills would, moreover, be in the hands of persons having a strong interest in promoting the maximum development of the Middle Eastern region.

Thus, because of the proximity of Israel, the Arab states (and probably Iran as well) have an opportunity of a sort which has been denied to most of the world's underdeveloped countries. The scope of this opportunity could, moreover, be enhanced as Turkish development advanced and Turkey graduated to the status of a semi-developed country.[38] In relation to this point, there is well-grounded authority for the view that the best assistance to underdeveloped countries can often be rendered by nationals of newly developed or semideveloped ones—in other words, by those who have only recently succeeded in coping with analogous problems. The strength of this argument is increased if the countries of the latter type are of the same geographical and cultural region. Aside from the technical advantages, there is the advantage of greater direct apprehension

[37] Quoted by Alfred Bonné in "Some Aspects of the Recent Socio-Economic Changes in the Middle East," *Journal of the Royal Central Asian Society*, 1940, Part III, p. 299.

[38] With the marked advances made in 1951 toward the establishment of a military command for the region (i.e., The Middle East Command) linked to the North Atlantic Treaty Organization, there is, as of December 1, 1951, a growing possibility that Turkey's interest in Middle East regional affairs will increase greatly during the coming years. In fact, some manifestations of increased interest have already become evident. Turkey's role might even, conceivably, become one of leadership in the region.

of the human problems involved. The Arabs of Israel could, no doubt, be helpful in this respect.[39]

This whole argument, however, is at present purely theoretical, since few Arabs are favorably inclined toward development of the region on such a basis. The greatest need is for *objective* analyses of the Arab fears in this matter, together with assessments as to the validity of the various factors entering into those fears. The difficulty is that, in view of the multiplicity of elements in this situation, immense versatility, both as to scholarship and as to familiarity with the peoples concerned, would be an essential ingredient of any such study. Under the present conditions of virtually complete nonintercourse between Israelis and subjects of the Arab states, it would be practically impossible for any third party to keep in intimate touch at all times with the subtler aspects of the thought currents circulating in each camp.

The Role of International Law

In view of the unfavorable prospects for any thoroughgoing voluntary regional cooperation in the Middle East in social and economic matters, it is pertinent to consider whether there are any principles of international law which might be invoked to facilitate regional development on a more cooperative basis. If noneconomic factors are disregarded, it may be assumed that, with the possible exceptions of Turkey and Egypt, the countries of the Middle East would all be greatly benefited by closer coordination based upon the region—or at least a substantial portion thereof, which would in any case include Israel—as the economic unit.

This question has three important aspects: (1) the right of an individual Middle Eastern state to the cooperation of its neighbors in matters particularly vital to the state's development; (2) the right of states outside the region, or of the United Nations, to take steps to promote cooperative attitudes, either in the particular interests of

---

[39] The Near East Foundation, in its village development schemes, has operated on the principle that the instruction of the masses is often best accomplished by those who have just completed the learning process themselves. In such cases the psychological obstacles are fewer. Cf. also William L. Lawrence, "Scientists Warned on Point Four Plan," New York *Times*, December 27, 1950.

individual states or in the interests of the general world welfare (any such steps would probably involve coercive measures); (3) the duty of states outside the region to manage their economic interests therein in such a manner as to benefit the inhabitants of the region and to promote harmony among the governments.[40]

Rights and duties of this nature would have the purpose of providing maximal satisfaction of the needs and wishes of all interested states with regard to such matters as: utilization of water resources; location of ports and access thereto; routing of railroads and highways; exploitation of mineral resources; preventive measures against communicable diseases; educational standards; reasonable stability of national laws and national policies with respect to social and economic matters of international concern; free access of persons to all parts of the region for benevolent or innocent purposes.

Probably the best example of the importance and complexity of these questions is afforded by the present large-scale exploitation of oil resources in Iran, Iraq, and Saudi Arabia by American and European firms on a concession basis. Because of the need for pipe lines to the sea, and because of local requirements of power for industrial, agricultural, and domestic purposes, practically all of the other Middle Eastern nations would also have to be regarded as parties at interest in any revised oil arrangements which might be made, if the present ones prove too unsatisfactory.[41] In the formulation of such arrangements, broad questions would arise as to the relative priorities to be accorded to: (1) the geographical sovereignty of the government in whose territory the petroleum fields are located, (2) the rights of the general populace of that territory to benefit from the oil revenues, (3) these same matters with respect to the territories crossed by pipe lines, (4) the rights of other near-by governments and populaces, (5) the rights of the persons or groups through whose

[40] The foreign oil companies operating in the Middle East have tended to support the political policies of whatever governments happened to be in power in the respective concession areas. Cf. Mikesell and Chenery, op. cit., p. 40.

[41] There have never been any integrated national or international policies with respect to the many problems associated with the extraction of Middle Eastern oil. For a detailed discussion of this question cf. Mikesell and Chenery, op. cit., passim.

initiative the crude petroleum is converted into usable forms, (6) the rights of industrial consumers of petroleum products in all parts of the world, (7) the rights of ordinary consumers in all parts of the world, and (8) the proper methods of enforcing these rights, once they are determined.

Similar questions arise in connection with water resources. To cite a single example, Israel may require, for maximal development of her industries and agriculture, hydroelectric power based upon the Litani River, of which the entire flow is in Lebanon. It is, moreover, possible that Lebanon would have nothing to gain, from the purely economic viewpoint, by withholding the necessary facilities from Israel.[42] Under the circumstances, would Lebanon, as geographical sovereign, have the right to deny these facilities to Israel, without even being required to state her reasons for so doing?

The answer is that, in customary international law, every sovereign state has the right to exercise virtually unfettered jurisdiction in such matters within the confines of its own territory, as well as to uphold its "vital interests" therein. These, moreover, are often defined according to generous legal principles not related, either in origin or in logic, to the prevailing situations.

The only pertinent duties of states are those of (1) abiding by the terms of international treaties, so long as the conditions upon which a given pact was based have not altered to the state's substantial detriment; (2) refraining from arbitrary or discriminatory treatment of foreign nationals and firms in the state's territory; (3) preventing the commission in the state's territory of certain limited categories of action inimical to other states' interests, as, for example, counterfeiting of foreign currencies or the formation of private armed bands for unlawful expeditions across the territorial state's frontiers. Generally speaking, there is no obligation upon states under customary international law to be constructive in their attitudes vis-à-vis social and economic questions of mutual concern to themselves and other states.[43] Also, as far as the Middle East is concerned, there are

[42] See chapter on Lebanon.

[43] The preamble of the United Nations Charter seems to contain an implied pledge of constructive attitudes. The body of the Charter, however, has little to offer as to the manner of implementation of the pledge. Cf. also Charles G. Fenwick, *International Law* (New York, 1948), p. 493.

no international conventions which have supplemented the customary law in an important manner.

Clearly the net result of this situation is that, in a region such as the Middle East which contains many small independent states, social and economic development may be greatly hampered by the "veto power" now conferred by international law upon each of them.

There seems to be a nascent tendency on the part of general international law to move in the opposite direction. Up to the present, however, such a trend is discernible in only one sphere of economic activity, namely, the utilization of water resources derived from international rivers. Even in this case, apart from the navigational aspects which are of relatively little importance in the Middle East,[44] there has been a striking paucity of authoritative commentary. The most recent major work on the subject, which may indeed be the only comprehensive authoritative treatment of the topic, is Mr. H. A. Smith's *The Economic Uses of International Rivers.*[45] Of outstanding interest is this author's opinion as to the most probable principles of a future international law governing the utilization of such rivers.[46] Those predicted principles, together with the general philosophy underlying them, might also provide some guidance in the regulation of other major economic matters of regional concern, as, for example, the equitable distribution and utilization of oil revenues.

The code which would finally result from such a trend would conform substantially with Mr. J. L. Brierly's ideas, expressed in 1945, as to the general character which the international law of the future must assume if it is to serve a truly worth-while purpose. His central theme was that the "vital interests" of states in the social and eco-

[44] Under long-established customary international law, a state may not divert the waters of a boundary river in such a manner as to reduce the navigability by nationals of the coriparian state. Also every state is required by customary international law to permit navigational use of its portion of a boundary river by nationals of the coriparian state. These principles would almost certainly take precedence over any new rules which might be adopted according equality in general as between navigational and other economic uses. However, as far as the Middle East is concerned, these limitations would probably never be serious ones in practice.

[45] London, 1931, pp. 150-152.

[46] The same general principles, appropriately modified, might be equally well applied to rivers which are not, strictly speaking, international, but which, like the Litani, are capable of serving the interests of two or more states.

nomic spheres should be assessed largely on their individual merits, rather than on the basis of rules of law designed to cover every case arising within a certain broad category, and taking no account of the special conditions which invariably obtain.[47]

THE IMMEDIATE NEEDS

The most immediate present needs along the lines of regionalization in the Middle East are probably the following: (1) coordination of internal transport; (2) agreements in regard to the siting of new ports for the benefit of the region as a whole; (3) arrangements for labor migration from overcrowded areas to areas where labor is needed for development; (4) preliminary arrangements for an equitable allocation of the region's water resources; (5) arrangements to insure adequate and cheap fuel supplies for the entire region from local sources; (6) preliminary arrangements for an equitable sharing of the mineral resources, as they are developed; (7) procedures for eradicating diseases on a pan-regional basis; (8) coordinated arrangements for promotion of tourism throughout the Middle Eastern region.

If the will, the faith, and the experience existed, considerable progress could probably be made within a relatively short time through cooperative endeavor in all of the spheres above mentioned. In some other cases, however, the achievement of a high degree of regionalization would take much longer because of "the mass of information on social structure, custom, legal systems, land tenure, and the like which is required as a basis for planning economic and social developments."[48]

[47] J. L. Brierly, *The Outlook for International Law* (Oxford, 1945), p. 43 *et passim*.
A broadly international convention which tended in this direction was the Geneva Convention of December 9, 1923, on hydraulic power. Cf. *League of Nations Treaty Series*, XXXIX (1925), 76 *et seq*.
[48] Worthington, *op. cit.*, p. 195.

CHAPTER XII

❖

The Future[1]

THE POINT FOUR CONCEPT

In his inaugural address of January, 1949, President Truman proclaimed the now famous "Point Four" policy, to the effect that the United States must, as a highly important matter of self-interest, render substantial assistance to underdeveloped countries in their efforts to develop themselves, and in particular to raise living standards. Later in the same year, by a unanimous vote of the General Assembly, this policy received United Nations endorsement as a relationship to be established between all the developed nations of the world, on the one hand, and all the underdeveloped ones, on the other. Generally speaking, major activities along Point Four lines had not been commenced at the time of writing (December 1, 1951) but were about to begin in the near future.

"Developed" and "Underdeveloped" Countries

The concept of "development" here applied relates basically to social and economic criteria, and more specifically to the per capita

[1] This chapter takes into consideration occurrences in the Middle East up to December 1, 1951. The rest of the book, except for a few explanatory footnotes, deals with the situation as of December 31, 1950.

real purchasing power of the national community. The term "social" applies to matters classifiable under the heads of health, security, morals, and social justice, all of which are considered to have an intimate bearing upon general economic progress.[2] Economic and social situations are determined not only by the richness or poverty of the natural resources exploitable but also to a considerable extent by the prevailing mental attitudes of the people concerned. The latter may be derived from such varied sources as religion, climate, language, occupational mores, and so forth.

As for the precise line of demarcation between the "developed" and the "underdeveloped" nations, the accepted practice has been to place the United States, Canada, Australia, New Zealand, and most of western Europe in the former category and the rest of the world in the latter. In terms of per capita income, a developed country is one in which the average annual income is $400 or higher.[3] In such terms, all of the Middle Eastern countries must be regarded as underdeveloped. In the 1949 compilations of the United Nations,[4] Israel's per capita income, which was by far the highest for the Middle East, was reckoned at $389. The other countries range downward from Turkey and Lebanon with $125 each to Saudi Arabia and Yemen with $40 each. In the same year the per capita income in the United States was $1453, and in Canada $870.

THE SCOPE OF ECONOMIC AID PROGRAMS

It was contemplated that the assistance rendered to underdeveloped countries should be both technical and financial, with the relative proportions of these types of aid to be determined on the merits of the individual situations dealt with. The term "technical" was to be construed in its broadest sense, with an inclusion of assistance in the removal of basic traditional, psychological, and institutional obstacles

[2] This definition of "social" matters is taken from International Law, by Charles G. Fenwick (New York, 1948), p. 488.

[3] Comparisons of the computed per capita incomes in the different countries afford, it is true, only a rough test of the relative degrees of advancement. However, where the computed differences are considerable, these figures are probably more satisfactory measures than any of the other available criteria.

[4] Will Lissner, "Income per Person in Soviet Held $308," New York Times, December 4, 1950, p. 1.

to progress, no matter what forms such impediments might assume.[5]

There was also the clear intention that all action taken under aid programs should contribute toward a goal of ultimate self-sufficiency, both financial and technical, for the governments and peoples assisted. For example, a certain underdeveloped country may actually possess capital resources which, in theory, would be ample for a complete working out of all stages of fundamental economic development in the foreseeable future. But the resources may be in such forms, e.g., private treasure hoards, unrecorded investments in foreign securities, or unrecorded income applied largely to unproductive uses, as to be in fact unavailable for the needs of the people as a whole. One of the functions of a well-considered aid program would be to assist the government to devise ways and means of uncovering such resources, both present and potential, and putting them to useful service.

By contrast, one of the other underdeveloped countries may have within easy reach the technical wherewithal but may be unable to utilize it effectively because of an absolute shortage of capital. In some of these cases additional funds may be needed for avoidance of imminent economic collapse. In most of them, integrated and rounded developmental programs could eventually provide the means of adequate capital accumulation for the essential purposes. Here the role of the assisting bodies would be either to interest foreign commercial firms in the possibilities of profitable investment in the country concerned or, if that proved impossible because of the low rate of return, to supply the funds needed in the form of grants or of long-term, low-interest loans, with provisions for relief or moratoria in the event of the recipient's inability to make the debt and interest payments.

As a third example, it may be that the deeply rooted customs of a certain underdeveloped country are of such a nature as to make it virtually impossible to establish the types of institution needed for economic progress. This problem is particularly acute where, as in

[5] The main official publications on this matter are: U.S. Dept. of State, *Point Four—Cooperative Program for Aid in the Development of Economically Underdeveloped Areas* (Washington, 1950); United Nations, *Technical Assistance for Economic Development* (Lake Success, N.Y., 1949).

some parts of the Middle East, the forces of resistance are to a large
extent centered in the government itself. Where that situation prevails, it becomes difficult at times to distinguish between the planners
and the human obstacles to the success of plans. Generally speaking,
the only permissible function of the aiding bodies would be to extend
all possible help and encouragement to those exceptional government officials who have workable ideas, linked to the necessary degree
of authority, for overcoming major resistances by legal and legitimate
methods.

THE DETERIORATION OF MIDDLE EASTERN LIVING STANDARDS

According to all surface appearances, there is now a strong and
mutual[6] desire for the inauguration or continuance[7] of cooperative
programs between the West and the Middle East along Point Four
lines. Still more important, however, is the compelling evidence of
urgent need for such programs.

The shockingly low living standards which prevailed in the Ottoman and Persian empires in 1918 were the product of centuries of
decadence and neglect of the common people's needs both by the
governmental authorities and by the upper classes in general. Yet it is
now abundantly clear, from the analyses just completed, that in five
of the ten countries considered (Egypt, Iraq, Syria, Lebanon, and
Iran) the standard of life has undergone a further marked decline
during the period 1919-50! This deterioration has occurred in spite
of the remarkable expansion of modern technology and of communications facilitating greatly increased general knowledge of conditions in all parts of the world. Nor have the spectacular oil developments in two of the countries mentioned had any observable effect
upon the prevailing trend.

[6] "Mutual" refers not only to governmental attitudes but also to popular ones
among the educated classes.
[7] The announcement of "Point Four" did not signalize the commencement of
a completely new activity. Already a considerable amount of scattered work along
Point Four lines had been undertaken, both governmentally and by private
organizations. The International Bank for Reconstruction and Development, the
Export-Import Bank of Washington, the Rockefeller Foundation, and the Near
East Foundation, for example, had rendered assistance to underdeveloped countries.

These are facts fraught with great danger for the developed nations. For, although the main blame is possibly attributable to the governing classes of the countries in question, the far more glaring statistical fact is that the income differential between the average American and the typical Middle Easterner has been increasing rapidly and sharply by virtue of marked centrifugal tendencies at both ends of the scale. The only possible conclusion, therefore, is that there is now a situation which, in these days of heightened consciousness of social inequalities, would hardly be tolerated for long within the domestic sphere of one of the advanced nations. It may be added that, during the period 1939 to 1950, there has apparently been a decline in per capita living standards in two additional Middle Eastern countries, namely, Israel and Jordan. The facts about Yemen are not clear. Only in Turkey and Saudi Arabia does the prevalent tendency from 1919 through 1950 appear to have been upward.

THE APPLICATION OF ECONOMIC AID TO THE MIDDLE EAST

THE CONSERVATIVE VIEWPOINT VS. IMPATIENCE FOR RESULTS

It is now relevant to consider in what manner an integrated regional program might be conducted for achievement of the best possible results.[8] It is all very well to say, as is not infrequently said by Western economists, engineers, and scientists, that all growth in the countries must in any case be from small beginnings and gradual.[9] Although the statement is partially correct, it hardly expresses a practical viewpoint for present-day planning, in view of the great and obvious psychological forces of these times. The successes of Soviet communism in underdeveloped countries, notably China, have been due in large measure to its promise of speedy and spectacular changes. Further, the popularity of "year plans" in Middle Eastern countries

[8] The word "integrated," as here used, does not imply treatment of the whole area as a single unit without regard to political boundaries, but refers rather to an appropriate distribution of funds, personnel, and projects among the countries to be aided.

[9] E. B. Worthington, *Middle East Science* (London, 1945), p. 6; United Nations, *Final Report of the United Nations Economic Survey Mission for the Middle East* (Lake Success, N.Y., 1949), Part I, p. viii.

provides testimony of a yearning for visible, tangible, and important results during a time period sufficiently brief and definite for retention of both patience and enthusiasm. Hence it is unlikely that large economic aid programs[10] would be accorded the necessary degree of sustained support unless at least a few of the achievements were of a highly convincing nature on a short-range—say, three to five years—basis. Here, too, the question of public opinion in the developed countries must be considered. If there is only a world-wide showing of painfully slow progress, along with the inevitable failures here and there, surely the whole Point Four concept will be greatly weakened as far as popular appeal anywhere is concerned.

Except where political considerations dictate otherwise, it would seem to be simple prudence to steer clear of grandiose and unattainable objectives in countries where, because of factors ascertainable in advance, they would probably not be realized. But it would be equally wise to plan somewhat ambitiously for countries where, because of specially propitious conditions and attitudes, the opportunities for achievement are greatly in excess of superficial indications. If this analysis of major planning from 1919 through 1950 for the elevation of Middle Eastern living standards can produce any clues as to the precise applicability of these criteria, the labor of unearthing the data and coordinating them will have been justified.

Local Sources of Finance

Probably the question of foremost immediate importance, in connection with the economic aid programs for the Middle East, is the matter of effective financing.

Manifestly much of the external financing of Middle Eastern programs, at least for the present and near future, would have to be provided either by the United States Government or by international

---

[10] There have been no official indications as to the magnitude which such programs might ultimately assume. It was reported in September, 1950, that the State Department was studying a proposed aid program which would provide $250,000,-000 to $300,000,0000 a year for four or five years to Asiatic countries alone. Cf. Stringfellow Barr, *Let's Join the Human Race* (Chicago, 1950); Walter H. Waggoner, "Aid to South Asia and Mid-East Seen," New York *Times*, September 15, 1950; Benjamin A. Javits, *Peace by Investment* (New York, 1950).

agencies with important American participation. But it is quite clear that assistance in this form would not of itself solve many of the really basic problems. Whereas for some Middle Eastern countries (e.g., Iraq and Saudi Arabia) the main near-future needs will be other than monetary, others (e.g., Jordan and Israel) may for some time to come require outside help on a scale larger than that generally regarded as forthcoming from sources now open (including United States aid). It must, therefore, be considered whether there is any additional source which might be tapped in order to establish a proper balance.[11] Particularly desirable would be an economic development agency *within the region,* having an assurance of the resources, both financial and technical, needed to inaugurate and carry out a substantial program for the entire area on a nondiscriminatory basis.

The most obvious possibility for additional development capital is still the one suggested by the large oil revenues in prospect for the rulers of three small British protectorates, namely, Kuwait, Bahrein, and Qatar.

The importance of this question has been greatly increased during 1951 by the recent nationalization of oil in Iran and by the precedent now being rapidly established that any country from which petroleum is extracted is entitled to at least a 50 per cent share in the profits from oil exported by foreign concessionaires. As a result of these developments, which have both increased the world demand for non-Iranian oil and greatly improved the financial terms to which governments or rulers of producing countries may hopefully aspire, there is now a distinct possibility that the Shaikh of Kuwait will soon be receiving *an average daily payment* well in excess of half a million

[11] United States economic aid to the Middle East (including Turkey) will amount to about $230,000,000 in the fiscal year 1951-52. It is improbable, however, that the allocations from this sum will be suitably proportioned to the various countries' relative need for financing. Short-range political considerations, both domestic and international, will necessarily play an important role in this question. As for large-scale aid from the United Nations, other than for special temporary purposes, that is apparently not likely to be forthcoming within the foreseeable future.

At the time of writing, the American aid programs for 1951-52 had hardly begun. As far as could be determined, the plans as to types of activity were still incomplete.

dollars! Corresponding improvements, though at lower levels and possibly not so soon, may be looked for in the financial positions of the shaikhs of Bahrein and Qatar respectively.[12]

The shaikhdom of Kuwait has an estimated population of 170,000; Bahrein has 110,000 inhabitants, Qatar only 20,000. Bahrein is an important center of the declining natural pearl industry; Kuwait has a fine harbor which, under suitable political conditions, might serve Iraq's needs to some extent. Otherwise the three shaikhdoms have no consequential resources, apart from oil, which could be developed. In all three cases, the elevation of purely local living standards to a fairly high point should be a relatively simple and inexpensive process, unless there is extreme negligence or inefficiency. But, once certain maximum levels had been achieved, it would not be desirable to attempt any further elevation of those standards on the basis of subsidy or expenditure for unproductive services, which might be the only conceivable means. Nor is it likely that such an attempt would be made.

Thus, even after all practicable expenditures had been made for the local welfare, and even after heavy outflow for the benefit of relatives and retainers, there should still be large annual sums—in Kuwait's case, probably $150,000,000 or more—uncommitted for local production and consumption needs, real or fancied.[13]

Clearly the disposition of these large annual surpluses will depend upon the shaikhs' assessment of their international political positions. If they fail entirely to appreciate the political implications of their

[12] Average daily output of crude petroleum, in thousands of barrels, in the three shaikhdoms during 1950 was: Kuwait—350.3; Qatar—33.1; Bahrein—30.7. It is now anticipated that Kuwait production, which was not commenced until 1946, will have risen to 1,000,000 barrels a day before the end of 1955. The present royalty to the Shaikh of Kuwait is only nine cents a barrel, but an even division of profits would give him at least fifty cents a barrel and possibly much more.

The oil company operating in Kuwait is 50 per cent British, 50 per cent American. A British company has the Qatar concession, while an American one operates in Bahrein.

[13] The annual amount theoretically available from this source for general Middle East development would be at least equal to the $160,000,000 economic aid to be furnished by the United States to the Middle East, excluding Turkey, during fiscal 1951-52.

new wealth, they will almost unquestionably suffer fates similar to those of the Indian native princes who paid no heed to external forces. If, however, they make an earnest attempt to conduct their affairs prudently, they can hardly escape the following observations:

1. In view of the small populations and exposed positions of their countries, the shaikhs, in order to maintain their autonomous status, must conduct themselves in a manner which will be deemed satisfactory by: (a) the governments and people of the neighboring states, (b) the shaikhs' Western protectors, and (c) the foreign oil concessionaires.

2. The main interest of the neighboring Middle Eastern states is that the shaikhs' great wealth should not be applied wholly to wasteful local purposes while the financial needs of the Middle East as a whole remain so acute. Pressures arising from this interest may be either governmental or popular. If they are of the latter type, they will surely receive governmental support.

3. The interests of the United States, Great Britain, and the other Western powers, and those of the foreign oil concessionaires, have many elements in common. All desire a maintenance of peaceful conditions within the territories of the shaikhdoms and an absence of external pressures threatening to alter the existing political status of those areas.

4. The necessity of satisfying all of these interests will force upon the shaikhs the following alternatives: paying out a large proportion of their income for straight protection purposes; participating actively and extensively (through investments, contributions, and counsel) in the affairs of the entire region; or losing their autonomous status.

5. If the autonomous status is lost, it is unlikely that oil revenues will still be paid to the shaikhs.

The ideal solution, of course, would be the establishment of an effective Middle East Development Board, financed to a large extent by grants made from the shaikhs' resources, supplemented by those of the oil companies and of international organizations. A parallel institution might be a development bank, possibly having close ties with the International Bank for Reconstruction and Development. This would have the function of making loans for meritorious projects of a self-liquidating character. The controlling board might be comprised of representatives of the three shaikhs, of each independent Middle Eastern country, and of interested international organizations, and a number of neutral experts.

But, while these facts are fully appreciated by nearly everyone concerned with the development of the Middle East, the writer knows of no workable proposal that has been advanced thus far for realizing such an outcome. The most difficult obstacle is to be found in the geographical positions of the three shaikhdoms. The only close neighbors of Kuwait and Qatar are Iraq and Saudi Arabia. Those are the Middle Eastern states in which financial needs are least, and which would probably not be greatly benefited by additional sources of income of the unearned sort. Bahrein's close neighbors are Saudi Arabia and Iran, the latter having a long-standing claim to Bahrein as her own territory.

Even if this particular obstacle could be overcome, there would still remain others of a consequential nature, as, for example, the role of Israel in any far-reaching scheme for development of the Middle East.

Any satisfactory solution to these difficult problems would certainly require the extreme in ingenuity. However, in view of the magnitude of the stakes, the total problem should be regarded as a challenge to be squarely faced by persons having knowledge of the region and a desire to render benefit to it.[14]

The Obstacles to Economic Aid

For the present, in view of the prevailing situation, economic aid programs for the Middle East must be largely on a country-by-country basis. Only as conditions within the individual countries improve will it become feasible to make plans involving close regional integration without too much regard for national frontiers.

Even as regards the prospects for country programs there are some distinctly unfavorable indications. Clearly the record of major planning in the Middle East during the period reviewed in this study is

[14] In particular, the problem should be regarded as a challenge to American and British policy makers.

not, in all its aspects, one which augurs well for the future, particularly with respect to Egypt, Syria, Lebanon, Iraq, Iran and Yemen.

Yemen is in a somewhat different category from the rest. As for the first five, the history of planning is in close conformity with a frequent expert observation in regard to the Middle East. It has often been pointed out that social and economic progress meets with the greatest obstacles where (1) the prevalence of large landed estates is coupled with landlord domination of the government and (2) morbidly xenophobic attitudes prevail. The usual simultaneous presence of these two phenomena is by no means purely coincidental.

It is unfortunate, too, that the 1950 and 1951 records give little indication of any improvement in underlying conditions in those five countries since the end of World War II. The most significant recent test cases (which will be discussed in the paragraphs on individual countries) have involved Iran, Syria, and Lebanon. But there is no reason to believe that the results of similar tests would be any better in Egypt or Iraq. In all of the countries, the overt eagerness for development has increased;[15] but there is apparently little change in the matter of willingness and ability to establish the necessary conditions for development.

It is therefore not easily predictable that more favorable climates for planning will soon appear, unless there are definite revolutions of long duration.[16] It is unlikely, moreover, that the Western powers could either foster such revolutions or steer them in the direction of their desires, once they had broken out. The identification of the revolutionary leaders with Western support would in all probability be more harmful than helpful to them. A Communist revolution, on the other hand, would doubtless profit from the xenophobia of

---

[15] Even this trend may have passed its peak in at least one of the countries. In Egypt there are some distinct indications that the Moslem Brotherhood and similar organizations are gaining in public favor, on a basis of thoroughgoing opposition to all phases of Westernism.

[16] The government now in power in Iran, i.e., Mosadeq's, is not, in general, representative of landlords' interests. Nevertheless it would be premature to regard Iran as a country which has ceased to be landlord-dominated. Not only is Mosadeq himself a great estate owner, with a poor record in the matter of reforms on his own lands; also the majority of Majlis members are concerned mainly with the narrow interests of landlords.

the urban groups, since this is mainly a sentiment of distrust of the Western powers which have exercised governmental control or had large commercial interests in the Middle East.

OTHER ASPECTS; THE INDIRECT APPROACH

There are, however, three somewhat happier aspects of this general question. The first is the fact that, in a few of the countries, the prospects are considerably more favorable. The second is the possibility of utilizing technical and financial assistance for important secondary or subsidiary purposes, even in cases in which the main problems are for the moment insoluble. The third is the possibility of undermining obstructive vested interests, as well as obstructive mental attitudes, through the use of indirect approaches.

The occasional efficacy of indirect methods is well illustrated in the country chapters of this study. In Saudi Arabia, for example, where the powerful vested interests were nomadism and tribalism, these forces of conservatism were greatly weakened by linking an appeal to religious sentiments with assurances that basic interests (as opposed to institutional interests) would be fully preserved. The basic interests were religion, the spirit of brotherhood, and the love of warfare. But, as Ibn Saud had predicted, even these values began to change, once the alteration of institutions had taken place. There are similar examples of effective indirect approaches in the chapters on Egypt, Jordan, and Turkey.

COUNTRY PROGRAMS

It is now in order to reexamine, in the light of the Point Four concept and of forthcoming economic aid programs, the present status of each country as regards prospects, both theoretical and realistic, for improved standards of life.

EGYPT

Egypt's future development will apparently depend in the main upon how much progress can be made in the alteration of land tenure. A partition of the large estates into viable small holdings would, according to all indications, lead to improved agricultural production, higher per capita income from agriculture, substantial and rational industrial development, and far greater general interest in education and health conditions.

However, the political conditions which have thus far prevailed in Egypt are unsuitable for attempts at land reform of the more meaningful sort. Thus, until this situation is altered in marked degree, economic aid programs must be largely along lines of secondary importance. The current planning and projects described in the chapter on Egypt offer some clues as to forms of useful assistance which might be provided. Of particular interest, as an example, is Dr. Ahmed Hussein's Village Improvement Scheme. The important achievement of this undertaking was the reduction of educated city dwellers' unwillingness to render necessary help in the improvement of the rural areas.[17]

Although this scheme has apparently failed of its main ends, and although other schemes with similar purposes may also fail, the encouragement of such projects would nevertheless serve the double purpose of keeping the door open for future major aid programs and promoting some of the conditions precedent to an ultimate attack upon the main bulwarks of resistance.

SAUDI ARABIA

Ibn Saud has shown great interest in the modernization of his country's agriculture, the quest by scientific methods for additional supplies of water, and the development of modern communications. While the possibilities of the country are still not well known, there are clearly opportunities for valuable technical assistance in these spheres. Certain cautions are, however, in order.

In the first place, it would be most unfortunate if economic aid should become a medium for the promotion of "landlordism" in Saudi Arabia. This event could easily happen, since already quite a number of Saudi Arabians are ready and eager to divert the programs into such channels. For avoidance of this result, perhaps the best

[17] This was accomplished by removing two of the deficiencies of rural life, as viewed by city dwellers, namely, (1) the nature of the dwelling-places available; (2) the lack of companionship with persons of urban background.

procedure would be to review carefully the history of the growth of landlord dominance in some of the other Arab countries, and then to make sure that no encouragement, direct or indirect, is given to the inauguration of similar historical processes in this less advanced area.

Additionally, Saudi Arabia differs from the other Middle Eastern countries (except Yemen) in that most of the people have not yet experienced the effects of Western penetration, at least in the more drastic forms. The xenophobia which inevitably results from initial Western impact under such circumstances does not usually make for a highly suitable climate wherein to attempt to elevate living standards by processes of wide scope. It is, moreover, improper to assume that actual imperialism is the only root-cause of xenophobia; it can probably be produced just as easily by the mere flagrant and wholesale disregard by Westerners of local sensibilities[18] which are too little understood.

Although a program of economic aid for Saudi Arabia is certainly desirable, it would apparently be unduly hazardous to start out with objectives of a lofty nature, the attainment of which might be overshadowed by untoward by-product results. Finally, the aid program should be accompanied by the continuous accumulation of a much greater fund of knowledge about the country and its people—particularly in regard to the prevalent attitudes and trends, and the background factors underlying them.

YEMEN

In view of the well-established isolationist policies of the successive governments, there is no likelihood of sizable economic aid programs in Yemen for some time to come.

[18] Sir Ramaswami Mudaliar describes the result as follows: "There are worse things than cannibalism; when the soul of man is destroyed, his identity gone away, an inferiority complex established in him and he is made to feel, dinned into his ears by various methods, that he can never aspire to the position enjoyed by those who rule over him—that is the destruction of the human soul; that is the greatest disaster to any of those who have been bondaged in the most favorable of circumstances by the most benign of authority." (Mid-Century: The Social Implications of Scientific Progress, edited by John Ely Burchard [Cambridge, 1950], p. 161.)

LEBANON

Because of the enormous potential supply of hydroelectric power, the geographical position of the country, and the presence of suitable raw materials, Lebanon's outlook for industrial development would be excellent if there were only a greater general determination to realize the potentialities, as a matter of putting first things first.

It must be recalled in this connection that, by assuming antagonistic and unconstructive positions vis-à-vis the much-publicized Clapp proposals, Lebanon greatly lessened the possibility that funds would be forthcoming from the United Nations in 1951 for the highly important Litani River development. This was a particularly disappointing showing for a country where Westernization had had such an early start, dating back to the nineteenth century. Indeed, to the average observer, Lebanon's continued record of failure in economic planning must be quite astonishing, in view of all the superficially favorable factors in her case. What this record certainly demonstrates is the ability of the controlling landed interests to hold their own, and to enlist extreme nationalism in their service, even in a country where a large part of the populace is fairly well educated.

Nevertheless, from the standpoint of economic aid, it is still an important and relevant fact that appreciable numbers of Lebanese have philosophical values similar to Western ones. Because of this fact, there should be even better possibilities here than in Egypt for effective cooperation between assistance bodies and high-level officials involving the solution of secondary problems, partial progress in the rational development of water resources, and an eventual clearance of the political atmosphere.

At the same time, however, it should be borne in mind always that no *major* achievements are to be expected from economic aid extended to Lebanon under existing conditions.

SYRIA

What has been said about Lebanon's industrial possibilities applies with even greater force to Syria's agricultural potentialities. Moreover, if the two developments were to take place contemporaneously, the two countries' economies would complement each other admirably. It is true that Syria's theoretical prospects are not as brilliant as Iraq's. On the other hand, the Syrian development would require much simpler technical processes and could be achieved in a much shorter time—mainly because Syrian agriculture is not dependent, to nearly so great an extent, on irrigation.

A corollary fact is that, because of this theoretical possibility of rapid agricultural development, Syria could play an important role in the permanent settlement of Arab refugees from Israel.

Once more, however, it is clear that the continued strength of both landlord domination and fanatical nationalism prevents these possibilities from being realized. Syria, like Lebanon, was unconstructive in her attitudes toward the United Nations-sponsored Clapp plans.

Under the circumstances, it would seem inadvisable to base many hopes upon the economic aid program for Syria.

IRAQ

As has already been stated, Iraq seems to be the only country in the Middle East where Western-style living standards would be even theoretically possible in the foreseeable future. The Iraqi Government, moreover, unlike the other landlord-dominated governments of the region, has a project (the National Development Plan) which may assume a form conducive to the elevation of general standards of living. This would be the case if the scheme should lead to irrigation development and land reclamation on a grand scale, without any commensurate increase in population. Since the likelihood of such an outcome is considerable, foreign technical assistance to Iraq in connection with the working out of this plan might yield rich rewards. This possibility is particularly attractive because there would be little need in Iraq's case for financing through grants. Occasional loans might be advanced on the security of the large future oil revenues.

There is, of course, no certainty that the present developmental plans will advance in a desirable direction. One distinct danger, for example, is that, while both landlords and peasants may stand to gain, their gain might not be at all shared by the majority of the educated middle classes. Landlords would probably experience rising labor costs before realizing any increased profits, and the result might be an effort to transfer this additional expense to the middle class in the shape of increased income tax in the lower income brackets, lower real wages of minor government employees, and similar measures affecting mainly "white-collar" workers and professional people. Any such measures might well produce a powerful political opposition based on policies antagonistic to any form of success for the main projects. Xenophobia might enter strongly into the question, since it would almost certainly be remembered that the assignment of places to Westerners on Iraq's National Development Board was intimately connected with International Bank pressures. As far as the sources of aid and advice are concerned, most Middle Eastern peoples make little distinction between the West on the one hand and the United Nations and its specialized agencies on the other.

But, in spite of such adverse possibilities, a cordial and thorough-going support of Iraq's plans through extensive technical assistance would seem to be a calculated risk well worth taking. If success is achieved, the resultant example of a country's transformation should be remarkable. If, on the other hand, the plans should fail, valuable material would have been acquired for analysis of situations which might militate against the success of major planning in some other countries of the world.

IRAN

Iran's theoretical economic possibilities are in the same general category as Iraq's and Syria's. But the over-all importance in Iran's case may be even greater, since it is a considerably larger and more populous country than either of the others. Also its geographical position, with a long common frontier with Russia, gives Iran a special significance.

An even more important aspect of the matter is that major foreign assistance, in the spirit of the Point Four concept, has already been supplied to Iran. Thus the prestige of that concept is at stake in Iran, as it is not to nearly the same extent anywhere else in the Middle East. Particularly is this the case since the grandiose Seven-Year Plan, which involved intimate collaboration between the Iranian Government and a group of American engineering firms, is now seriously threatened with failure. A final collapse would also constitute a major blow to the prestige of the United States and of the West in general in Iran. This outcome, moreover, would surely have serious repercussions in the rest of the Middle East.

Because of these circumstances, a departure from the usual criteria of aidworthiness would seem to be in order, as far as Iran is concerned. Otherwise all economic aid programs for Middle Eastern countries may be placed in jeopardy.

It is true that the political atmosphere, particularly following the main 1951 occurrences, could hardly be less auspicious. After having taken up with enthusiasm the pioneer Seven-Year Plan for reconstruction and rehabilitation of the country, Iran, by expelling the Anglo-Iranian Oil Company, has proceeded to destroy the very foundations upon which the project was to have been built, namely, the revenues from petroleum. Moreover, because of the extreme nationalism which has even been on the increase since the country chapter was written, there is at the moment no clear-cut method available for a full-scale reinstatement of the plan in its original form.

The only obvious course which suggests itself at this time is to take full advantage of the success of the Near East Foundation's Village Betterment Scheme, and to apply technical assistance to expanded projects of that nature, to the limit that the Iranian Government will approve. This procedure, as a matter of fact, is already in contemplation by the United States Department of State.[19] It is not certain, however, that Iranian governments would approve such schemes beyond the point where, because of the slight impact on the economy as a whole, they would have little effect on the general question of rural population relationships and absentee profits from agriculture.

One other point, however, should be noted. In the summer of 1950 an excellent opportunity was apparently missed, not only for keeping the Seven-Year Plan alive and vigorous, but also for instilling much-needed confidence into the Iranian advocates of genuine reform

[19] As of December 1, 1951, it seemed probable that Iran would receive $23,000,-000 in United States grant aid for utilization before July 1, 1952. It also seemed likely that at least an equal amount would be forthcoming during the American fiscal year 1952-53.

and development. Had a large-scale loan or grant (which President Truman had, at least by implication, promised) been made to Iran in July or August, 1950, the whole psychological atmosphere might have been improved considerably. The powerful landlord group, for achievement of ends which seemed unattainable in the absence of large foreign aid, had, in order to attract such aid to the country, just consented to the appointment of a reform cabinet with potential armed support. The landlords were, no doubt, gambling against the possibility that that government would be able to dominate the scene completely.

Although not predictable at present, it is certainly possible, in view of Iran's increasing economic difficulties, that similar opportunities may again be offered. In such an event, it would seem to be a legitimate function of the assisting bodies to supply immediate financial aid in the amount needed to sustain an improved political climate and thereby facilitate a resumption of Seven-Year Plan activities on a large scale, with wide scope, and along suitable lines. Since the amount of money required for effective application might be large (perhaps $100,000,000), and since there would be no assurance that the moneys granted would thereafter be wisely expended, this sort of policy is not to be recommended except for countries where, as in Iran's case, the stakes are particularly great.

The fact must, of course, be recognized that the original end objectives of the Seven-Year Plan may be impossible of attainment in even twice or three times seven years, in view of the many obstacles which would have to be overcome. But in that event the prestige of the Point Four concept would still be preserved if, by virtue of competent technical assistance, Iranians could be brought to recognize the facts and to alter the bases of their development projects so as to make them conform with realities. What is mainly important is that the Seven-Year Plan should not be permitted to collapse while there is nothing at hand to take its place in a fitting manner.

ISRAEL

Seen from the long view, Israel's prospects of successful development, on an economic basis somewhat similar to Switzerland's, seem quite favorable. Nor is there any doubt that foreign assistance—technical as well as financial—could help materially toward the attainment of such an objective.

Good cooperation on the part of the Israeli populace could be expected because, despite the eastern European rather than Western origin of the majority of the population, there is a close approach to Westernism in the prevailing social and economic outlook. This results partly from the cosmopolitan nature of Judaism and Zionism and partly from the presence of sizable Western elements in the populace.

Because of this favorable basic situation, it would be highly desirable to regard the economic aid program for Israel as one to be emphasized above most others for the Middle East. However, two important points must be noted in this general connection. One is that, for the next few years, Israel's need for foreign technicians will be negligible as compared with her need for foreign capital in large amounts. Hence the only really vital function of any near-future aid program would be the supply of investment funds in the form of loans or grants. The other point is that a successful economic aid program for Israel would not offer as fair a test of the validity of the Point Four concept as would a successful program in almost any other Middle Eastern country.

Because of these two factors, Israel does not appear to be the Middle Eastern country most suitable for demonstration purposes. In the first place, any "model program" should, if at all possible, be based on patterns comprising more or less typical proportions of the different kinds of economic aid. In the second place, what really needs to be demonstrated is that the West can offer substantial and effective help in countries *where customs, culture, and traditions are greatly dissimilar to Western ones.*

Turkey

Of all the Middle Eastern countries, Turkey offers the strongest possibilities, from the viewpoint of direct and general usefulness, for a successful economic aid program conducted on a grand scale. The agricultural, mineral, and industrial potentialities are present, and the human factors are favorable.

These are fortunate circumstances, because Turkey's strategic position is such as to offer the greatest dangers to the rest of the world, were the country to constitute a political vacuum. The same has been true practically throughout historic times. A strong, self-reliant, and unified Turkey is a virtual necessity from the standpoint of world peace.

An additional factor in this question is the great desirability of gradually transferring Middle East technical assistance programs from the broadly international basis to a predominantly regional basis. Under such an arrangement, the Middle Eastern countries which became "developed" earliest would then proceed to assist in bringing the others up to their own levels of development. The matter could thus be handled more efficiently, since the advanced countries of the region would have much more direct interest in the question than outsiders could ever conceivably have. As has already been pointed out, Turkey's consciousness of the Middle East as a region has increased considerably during 1951. Until recently there had been a protracted period of conspicuously limited relations with the Middle Eastern neighbors.

Turkey is, moreover, the only Middle Eastern country which, as matters now stand, seems at all eligible for the role of leadership. Israel was once deemed suitable, but it is now difficult to believe that the Arab states would provide the necessary reciprocity at any near-future time. True, Turkey's relations with Iran and some of the Arab countries are not wholly cordial at the time of writing, but on the other hand there is no indication of any serious breach in the making. In the matter of keeping on fairly good terms with both Israel and the Arab countries, Turkey's performance has been somewhat remarkable. The fact that Turkey is nominally a Moslem country is particularly significant.

As for the more immediate prognosis, Turkey's economic planning record has shown a consistent improvement; and per capita income in Turkey has been rising more or less steadily since the inauguration of the republic in 1923. There is direct evidence, too, that the basic attitudes now prevailing in Turkey with regard to cooperation for raising living standards are mature ones. Finally, the country has a democratic form of government which appears to be genuine in most respects. Apparently all that Turkey now requires for full development is guidance, financial assistance, and time.

It is strongly to be recommended, therefore, that a comprehensive economic aid program be conducted in Turkey on the largest scale practicable, and that it be continued in effect until its purposes have been served. Two slight qualifications are, nevertheless, in order.

Satisfactory as the results of an aid program for Turkey would be, if efficiently conducted under present conditions, it is probable that more *conspicuous* effects could be achieved in a smaller and less advanced country, given equally favorable basic factors.

The second reservation is that, if aid to Turkey were allowed to overshadow all other aid programs for the Middle East, the impression might well be conveyed that major aid was being largely confined to nations which advocate Westernism in all its aspects, including the cultural, philosophical, and even sartorial and culinary. The dangers of any such implication are obvious.[20]

JORDAN

Jordan appears to be a suitable country for a model program along Point Four lines, as long as the favorable conditions of December 1, 1951, remain substantially unchanged.[21] The following are the principal reasons for such a conclusion:

[20] What is too often overlooked is that mental and spiritual health, no less than physical health, is an important condition precedent to balanced progress along social and economic lines. Nor can it be assumed that, because some of the most obvious aspects of Orientalism constitute obstacles to progress, the decreed abolition of all Orientalism would necessarily produce a more favorable situation. This matter has not yet been sufficiently analyzed. From the philosophical viewpoint, Professor Northrop argues in favor of a synthesis between the scientific rationalism of the West and the emotional estheticism of the East. Mr. Gibb holds that the argument advanced is, as a whole, valid for the Moslem countries of the Middle East. Cf. F. S. C. Northrop, *The Meeting of East and West* (New York, 1946), *passim*; also book review by H. A. R. Gibb, *Middle East Journal*, July, 1947, pp. 336-337.
[21] The writer originally reached this conclusion as of December 31, 1950, when an important element in the situation was the leadership of King Abdullah. Although Abdullah was assassinated in July, 1951, the basically favorable conditions are apparently little altered.

1. Jordan's record as to plans has been good.

2. The xenophobia which usually results from Western impact upon an Oriental country has been much less marked in Jordan than elsewhere. This situation does not seem to have been decisively changed by the annexation of Arab Palestine. The Palestine Arabs have apparently been influenced favorably by Jordan's calmer atmosphere.[22]

3. Land tenure in Jordan is now well established on a basis of small individual holdings. The great landlords are not a major problem.

4. There are no such extremely delicate problems as those which would have to be faced in Saudi Arabia or Yemen. The religious attitudes are not as fanatical as in Saudi Arabia; and Western ways are not the complete novelty that they would be in Yemen.

5. The country has a relatively homogeneous populace.

6. Jordan, according to direct evidence, is the Arab country least disinclined to come to terms with Israel.[23]

7. Since Jordan, next to Yemen and Saudi Arabia, is now the least developed of all Middle Eastern countries, any marked improvement in that status might well serve as a spur to her Arab neighbors to elevate their own living standards.

8. Jordan has particularly acute economic problems at present. While facing the prospect of bankruptcy, she must continue in her efforts to absorb the 325,000 Arab refugees from Israel now destitute in her territory. She must also attack the many problems connected with the integration of Arab Palestine with Transjordan. This is a particularly difficult matter because the Arab Palestine population is more numerous than the Transjordanian.[24] Finally, her normal channels of trade have been severely disrupted by the termination of the Palestine mandate and thereby of Jordan's close economic rela-

[22] The leadership is also a factor. The rival Husseini and Nashashibi factions were the controlling powers in Arab politics in pre-Israel Palestine. The nationalism of the Nashashibis was always much more moderate than that of the Husseinis. The former have now accepted absorption into Jordan; but the Husseinis' main leader, Haj Amin el-Husseini (the ex-Mufti of Jerusalem), now lives in Egypt.

[23] Albion Ross, "Jordan Seen Ready for Israel Accord," New York Times, March 4, 1950.

[24] Royal Institute of International Affairs, The Middle East: A Political and Economic Survey (London, 1950), p. 419; United Nations, op. cit., Part I, p. 18.

tionship to the whole Palestine area. An economic aid program which would succeed in spite of all these problems would surely contribute greatly to the prestige of the Point Four idea.

9. In all Middle Eastern countries except Israel and Turkey the outcome of technical assistance programs would apparently depend in some measure upon the employment of Western personnel well versed in the matter of dealing tactfully and efficiently with local sensibilities and local limitations as to capacity. But the combination of such competence with specialized technical ability will probably be, for some time to come, a relatively rare one. Under the circumstances, it would be desirable at the outset, if at all feasible, to concentrate men of this type mainly in small countries where the total amount of work to be done would not impose an excessive strain on the available stocks of that sort of man power. Jordan, as it happens, is, next to Lebanon, the least populous of all the independent Middle Eastern countries.

FINAL SUMMARY

Stated in the briefest possible form, the main conclusions of this study are as follows:

1. Low as living standards in the Middle East were in 1919, in at least five of the ten countries they have undergone a marked further decline since that year. In at least two additional countries the standard of life in 1950 was below the 1939 level.

2. Under present conditions, economic aid programs for Egypt, Lebanon, Syria, Saudi Arabia, and Yemen should be of somewhat limited scope. In the first three countries the political climate is not suitable for cooperative attempts to reduce the main resistances by direct methods. In the last two there is danger that progress in any particular aspect of development would be outweighed by harmful by-product results of projects undertaken.

3. In Iran, although political conditions are even less propitious than in Egypt, Lebanon, and Syria, a different and more positive type of approach to economic aid is in order because the prestige of the Point Four concept is at stake in Iran to a much greater extent than in any other Middle Eastern country.

4. Because of the enormous absolute magnitude of Iraq's future economic possibilities, large-scale technical aid extended by America and western Europe vis-à-vis National Development Plan undertakings would, at the least, facilitate the conduct of an experiment of outstanding significance.

5. Israel is well qualified for a large program of economic aid. Her case is, however, an atypical one, because the need for technical assistance is negligible as compared with the need for investment funds.

6. Turkey is the Middle Eastern country in which the most directly important results could be achieved from a large-scale program of economic aid. It is, however, not the most suitable country for demonstration purposes.

7. The Hashemite state of Jordan is a suitable locale for a model program along Point Four lines. This should be conducted on an adequate scale to produce readily visible improvement in the general living standards of the country. An important requirement of such a program would be the recruitment of personnel qualified not only as to technical skills but also as to capacity for sympathetic understanding of the Jordanian people, their aspirations, and their human problems.

8. The outlook for Middle Eastern living standards could be considerably improved if the prospective resources of the shaikhs of Kuwait, Qatar, and Bahrein were to be applied to development of the region. Ways and means should be explored of formulating a suitable draft program which might prove attractive to those three rulers on a basis of enlightened self-interest.

Appendix

THE MIDDLE EAST STATISTICAL DATA

	Egypt	Iran	Iraq	Israel	Jordan
Pop. 1950 (in millions)	20.4	ca. 18.5	5.1	1.5**	1.3
Area—sq. mi. (in thousands)	360.0	586.8	156.6	7.6	37.5
Cultivable land (in mil. acres)	7.3	123.5	30.0	1.0-1.5	2.4
Cultivated area (in mil. acres)	6.0	41.0	10.0	.6	1.3
Irrigated area (in mil. acres)	6.0	5.4	4.3	.075-.1	ca. .07
Exchange rate, 1951	£E=$2.87	US. $1=Rial 57.50*	Dinar=$2.80	I.£=$2.80	Dinar=$2.80
Foreign receipts, 1950 (in mil. $)	ca. 650.0	ca. 310.0†	ca. 110.0	ca. 120.0	ca. 15.0
Foreign payments, 1950 (in mil. $)	ca. 720.0	ca. 330.0†	ca. 100.0	ca. 320.0	ca. 40.0
Principal exports	(cotton, rice)	(oil, carpets)	(oil, barley)	(citrus fruits, diamonds)	(wheat, olive oil)
Prod. of electricity (in mil. kwh)***	642.0	200.0	69.0	329.0	30.0

	Lebanon	Saudi Arabia	Syria	Turkey	Yemen
Pop. 1950 (in millions)	ca. 1.3	ca. 6.0	3.2	20.9	ca. 4.5
Area—sq. mi. (in thousands)	3.6	556.6	67.3	296.5	70.2
Cultivable land (in mil. acres)	.8	n.a.	12.0	33.0	n.a.
Cultivated area (in mil. acres)	.6	n.a.	6.2	60.0	n.a.
Irrigated area (in mil. acres)	.1	n.a.	.8	.75-1.0	n.a.
Exchange rate, 1951	US. $1=£L3.60*	Riyal=$ .27	US. $1=£S3.60*	Lira=US. $ .357	n.a.
Foreign receipts, 1950 (in mil. $)	ca. 70.0	ca. 125.0	ca. 90.0	ca. 305.0	n.a.
Foreign payments, 1950 (in mil. $)	ca. 95.0	ca. 100.0	ca. 95.0	ca. 345.0	n.a.
Principal exports	(invisibles, fruits)	(oil, dates)	(cotton, wheat)	(tobacco, wheat)	(hides, coffee)
Prod. of electricity (in mil. kwh)***	86.0	n.a.	79.9	676.0	neg.

* Free rate
** Israel population is as of September 30, 1951
*** Annual-most recent figures available

† For fiscal year ended March, 1950
n.a. = not available

Map of Egypt and of the Nile River system from Lake Victoria to the Mediterranean Sea.

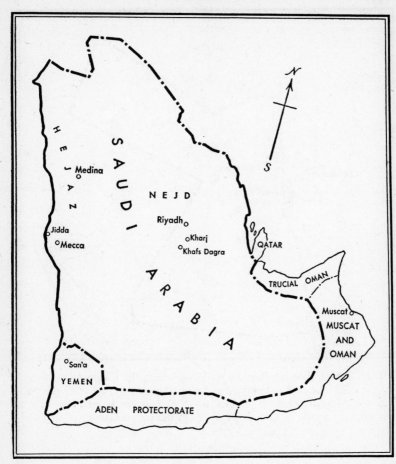

Map of Arabia. The political boundaries are only approximate. Most of them have never been officially delimited.

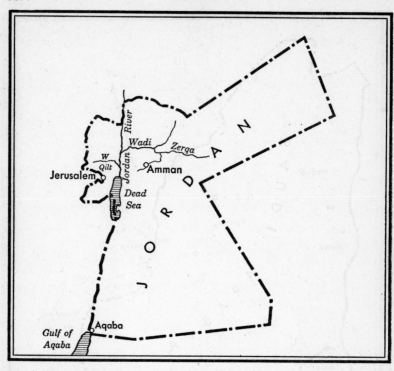

Map of Jordan showing the two wadis on which the Clapp plans of 1949 were based. The rest of the Jordan River system, together with the political frontiers involved, is shown on the map of Israel. The city of Jerusalem is partly in Israeli, partly in Jordanian, territory.

Map of Lebanon. The Hasbani River is part of the Jordan River system. All the main features of that system are shown on the map of Israel.

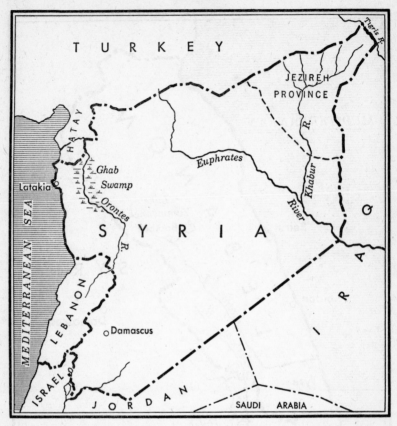

Map of Syria showing the locales of the Ghab Valley and Jezireh schemes.

Map of Iraq showing the projected canal (A) which will divert water
from the Tigris River into Wadi Tharthar Depression (B).

Map of Israel and the Jordan River system. The old frontier between Palestine and Transjordan followed the center of the Jordan River from Tel-Or to the Dead Sea, then passed through the center of the Dead Sea. The Hasbani River, which has its source in Lebanon, runs parallel and close to the Litani River until the latter turns westward to the sea. Southward of the Hasbani-Banyas confluence, the combined stream is called the Jordan River. (See map of Lebanon.)

Map of Iran showing the respective locales of the Khuzistan Scheme and the Near East Foundation Village Betterment Scheme.

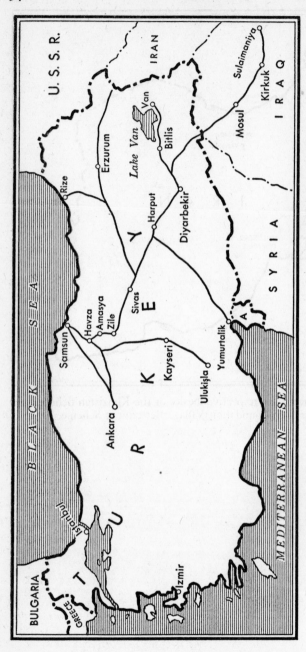

Map of Turkey showing approximate routes of the proposed railway lines involved in the Chester Concession of 1923. The proposed branch to Mosul and Kirkuk was to have terminated at Sulaimaniya, Iraq, almost due east of Kirkuk, near the Iranian frontier. The area designated A is the Vilayet of Hatay, formerly the Sanjaq of Alexandretta, which was transferred from Syria to Turkey in 1939.

BIBLIOGRAPHY

Public Documents

EGYPT, GOVERNMENT OF. *Population Census of Egypt, 1937.* Cairo, 1942.

GREAT BRITAIN, FOREIGN OFFICE. *Despatch from the Earl of Cromer Respecting the Water Supply of Egypt.* Cd. 3397. The Earl of Cromer to Sir Edward Grey, March 15, 1907. London, 1907.

GREAT BRITAIN, FOREIGN OFFICE. *Exchange of Notes Between His Majesty's Government in the United Kingdom and the Egyptian Government in Regard to the Use of the Waters of the River Nile for Irrigation Purposes.* Cmd. 3348. *Treaty Series,* No. 17 (1929). London, 1929.

INTERNATIONAL BANK FOR RECONSTRUCTION AND DEVELOPMENT. *WB— Loan Number 26 IRQ (Wadi Tharthar Flood Control Project)—Loan Agreement—June 15, 1950.* Washington, 1950.

INTERNATIONAL BANK FOR RECONSTRUCTION AND DEVELOPMENT. *WB— Loan No. 27 TU—Grain Storage Project—Loan Agreement—July 7, 1950.* Washington, 1950.

INTERNATIONAL BANK FOR RECONSTRUCTION AND DEVELOPMENT. *WB— Loan No. 28 TU—Port Development and Construction Projects— Loan Agreement—July 7, 1950.* Washington, 1950.

IRAQ, MINISTRY OF ECONOMICS. *Statistical Abstract—1946.* Baghdad, 1948.

ISRAEL, GOVERNMENT OF. *Statistical Bulletin of Israel, January to July, 1950.* Tel Aviv, 1950.

LEAGUE OF NATIONS. *League of Nations Assembly Records, 1920–1938.* 20 vols. Geneva, 1921–39.

LEAGUE OF NATIONS. *League of Nations Monthly Summary, 1928–1939.* 12 vols. Geneva, 1928–39.

LEAGUE OF NATIONS. *League of Nations Official Journal, 1920–1938.* 19 vols. Geneva, 1920–39.

343

TURKEY, OFFICE OF STATISTICS. *Istatistik Yilligi—1948 (Annuaire Statistique—1948)*. Ankara, 1949.

UNITED NATIONS, STATISTICAL OFFICE. *Monthly Bulletin of Statistics, December, 1950*. Lake Success, N.Y., 1950.

UNITED STATES CONGRESS. *Hearings on Foreign Aid Appropriations for 1951*. Washington, 1950.

UNITED STATES DEPARTMENT OF STATE. *Foreign Relations of the United States, 1922–24*. 3 vols. Washington, 1938–39.

Reports

FRANCE, Ministère des Affaires Etrangères. *Rapports sur la Situation de la Syrie et du Liban, 1921–1938*. 18 vols. Paris, 1923–39.

GREAT BRITAIN, COLONIAL OFFICE. *Reports by His Britannic Majesty's Government to the Council of the League of Nations on the Administration under Mandate of Palestine and Transjordan, 1924–38*. 15 vols. London, 1925–39.

GREAT BRITAIN, COLONIAL OFFICE. *Special Report by His Majesty's Government in the United Kingdom of Great Britain and Northern Ireland on the Progress of Iraq During the Period 1920–1931*. London, 1931.

GREAT BRITAIN, FOREIGN OFFICE. *Reports by His Majesty's Agent and Consul-General on the Finances, Administration, and Condition of Egypt and the Soudan in 1906*. Cd. 3394. London, 1907.

GREAT BRITAIN, PALESTINE ROYAL COMMISSION. *Palestine Royal Commission Report, July, 1937*. London, 1937.

HAYS, JAMES B. *T.V.A. on the Jordan*. Proposals for Irrigation and Hydroelectric Development in Palestine. A Report Prepared Under the Auspices of the Commission on Palestine Surveys. Washington, 1948.

INTERNATIONAL BANK FOR RECONSTRUCTION AND DEVELOPMENT. *Fifth Annual Report, 1949–50*. Washington, 1950.

INTERNATIONAL BANK FOR RECONSTRUCTION AND DEVELOPMENT. *Fourth Annual Report, 1948–49*. Washington, 1949.

INTERNATIONAL BANK FOR RECONSTRUCTION AND DEVELOPMENT. *Report of Third Annual Meeting of Board of Governors*. Washington, 1948.

IONIDES, M. G. *Report on the Water Resources of Transjordan and Their Development*. London, 1940.

MACDONALD, SIR MURDOCH. *Nile Control*. A Report by the Adviser, Egyptian Ministry of Public Works, to the Minister of Public Works. Cairo, 1920.

NEAR EAST FOUNDATION. *Annual Report of Educational Director*. New York, October, 1950.

NEAR EAST FOUNDATION. *Foreign Director's Annual Report, 1949–1950*. New York, 1950.

NILE PROJECTS COMMISSION. *Report of the Nile Projects Commission.* London, 1920.

OVERSEAS CONSULTANTS, INC. *Report on Seven Year Development Plan for the Plan Organization of the Imperial Government of Iran.* 5 vols. New York, 1949.

ROYAL INSTITUTE OF INTERNATIONAL AFFAIRS. *Nationalism.* A Report by a Study Group of Members of the Royal Institute of International Affairs. London, 1939.

UNITED NATIONS, SECRETARIAT. *Economic Development in Selected Countries.* Lake Success, N.Y., 1947.

UNITED NATIONS, SECRETARIAT. *Technical Assistance for Economic Development.* Lake Success, N.Y., 1949.

UNITED NATIONS, STATISTICAL OFFICE. *Population and Vital Statistics Reports.* Lake Success, N.Y., December 1, 1949.

UNITED NATIONS CONCILIATION COMMISSION FOR PALESTINE. *Final Report of the United Nations Economic Survey Mission for the Middle East.* 2 vols. Lake Success, N.Y., December 28, 1949.

UNITED STATES, ECONOMIC COOPERATION ADMINISTRATION. *Turkey— Country Data Book.* Washington, March, 1950.

UNITED STATES, ECONOMIC COOPERATION ADMINISTRATION. *Turkey: Country Study.* Washington, February, 1949.

UNITED STATES, EXPORT-IMPORT BANK OF WASHINGTON. *Semi-Annual Reports, July, 1945, to December, 1950.* 11 vols. Washington, 1945–51.

UNITED STATES, LEND-LEASE ADMINISTRATION. *Reports to Congress on Lend-Lease Operations, 1941–45.* 20 vols. Washington, 1941–45.

UNITED STATES DEPARTMENT OF STATE. *Point Four-Cooperative Program for Aid in the Development of Economically Underdeveloped Areas.* Washington, December, 1949.

VOGT, JOSEPHINE. *A Study of Home and Family Life in Rural Iran.* A Report by the Supervisor of Home Making for the Near East Foundation. New York, 1950.

Books

ABBOTT, NABIA. *Aisha, the Beloved of Mohammed.* Chicago, 1942.

ABOUCHDID, EUGENIE ELIE. *Thirty Years of Lebanon and Syria (1917– 1947).* Beirut, 1948.

ALLEN, H. B. *Rural Education and Welfare in the Middle East.* London, 1946.

Americans and the Middle East: Partners in the Next Decade. A series of addresses and panel discussions on cultural and technical cooperation presented at the Fourth Annual Conference on Middle East Affairs, sponsored by the Middle East Institute. Washington, 1950.

ANDRAE, TOR. *Mohammed, the Man and His Faith.* Translated by Theophil Menzel. New York, 1936.

ANTONIUS, GEORGE. *The Arab Awakening.* London, 1938.

ARNOLD, T. W. *The Preaching of Islam.* New York, 1913.

BELDING, DAVID L. *Textbook of Clinical Parasitology.* New York, 1942.

BEN HORIN, ELIAHU. *The Middle East.* New York, 1943.

BONNÉ, ALFRED. *The Economic Development of the Middle East.* London, 1945.

BONNÉ, ALFRED. *State and Economics in the Middle East.* London, 1948.

BOVERI, MARGRET. *Minaret and Pipe Line.* London, 1939.

BOYD, MARK F. *Malariology.* Philadelphia, 1949.

BOYKO, E., AND MAYER, E. J. *The Negev: Facts, Hopes and Plans.* Tel Aviv, 1950.

BREASTED, JAMES H. *The Conquest of Civilization.* New York, 1938.

BREASTED, JAMES H. *A History of the Ancient Egyptians.* New York, 1908.

BRIERLY, J. L. *The Law of Nations.* Oxford, 1949.

BRIERLY, J. L. *The Outlook for International Law.* Oxford, 1945.

BURCHARD, JOHN ELY (ED.). *Mid-Century: The Social Implications of Scientific Progress.* Cambridge, Mass., 1950.

CHANG, PEI-KANG, *Agriculture and Industrialization.* Cambridge, Mass., 1949.

CHILDE, V. GORDON. *What Happened in History.* London, 1942.

CLARK, COLIN. *The Conditions of Economic Progress.* London, 1940.

CLARK, COLIN. *The Economics of 1960.* London, 1944.

CLELAND, W. W. *The Population Problem in Egypt.* Lancaster, Pa., 1936.

CROMER, EARL OF. *Modern Egypt.* Vol. II. New York, 1908.

DAVIS, HELEN MILLER. *Constitutions, Electoral Laws, Treaties of States in the Near and Middle East.* Durham, N.C., 1947.

DAVIS, W. S. *A Short History of the Near East.* New York, 1923.

EAGLETON, CLYDE. *International Government.* New York, 1948.

ELWELL-SUTTON, L. P. *Modern Iran.* London, 1941.

ESSAD-BEY, MOHAMMED. *Rezah Shah.* London, 1938.

ESSALEH, SALAH. *L'Etat Actuel de l'Economie Syrienne.* Paris, 1942.

FEIS, HERBERT. *Petroleum and American Foreign Policy.* Stanford University, Calif., 1944.

FEIS, HERBERT. *Seen from E. A.* New York, 1947.

FENWICK, CARLES G. *International Law.* New York, 1948.

FERENCZI, IMRE. *The Synthetic Optimum of Population.* Paris, 1938.

GIBB, H. A. R. *Modern Trends in Islam.* Chicago, 1947.

GIBB, H. A. R. *Mohammedanism, An Historical Survey.* London, 1949.

GLUBB, JOHN BAGOTT. *The Story of the Arab Legion.* London, 1948.

GRANT, ELIHU. *The Orient in Bible Times.* Philadelphia, 1920.

GROBBA, FRITZ. *Irak.* Berlin, 1941.

GRUENBAUM, LUDWIG. *Outlines of a Development Plan for Jewish Palestine.* Jerusalem, 1946.

GUPTA, RAJ NARAIN. *Iran, An Economic Study.* Allahabad, 1947.

HAAS, WILLIAM S. *Iran.* New York, 1946.

HANSEN, ALVIN H. *America's Role in the World Economy.* New York, 1946.

HELL, JOSEPH. *The Arab Civilization.* Cambridge, Mass., August, 1926.

HICKMAN, CHARLES ADDISON. *World Economic Problems.* New York, 1947.

HIMADEH, SAID B. (ED.). *The Economic Organization of Palestine.* Beirut, 1938.

HIMADEH, SAID B. (ED.). *The Economic Organization of Syria.* Beirut, 1936.

HOURANI, A. H. *Minorities in the Arab World.* London, 1947.

HOURANI, A. H. *Syria and Lebanon, A Political Essay.* London, 1946.

HUXLEY, JULIAN. *TVA Adventure in Planning.* London, 1945.

IBN MUNQIDH, USAMAH. *An Arab-Syrian Gentleman and Warrior in the Period of the Crusades.* Translated by P. K. Hitti. New York, 1929.

IKBAL ALI SHAH, SIRDAR. *Fuad: King of Egypt.* London, 1936.

IONIDES, M. G. *The Regime of the Rivers Tigris and Euphrates.* London, 1937.

ISSAWI, CHARLES. *Egypt, An Economic and Social Analysis.* London, 1947.

JAVITS, BENJAMIN A. *Peace by Investment.* New York, 1950.

KEEN, B. A. *The Agricultural Development of the Middle East.* London, 1946.

KIRK, G. E. *A Short History of the Middle East.* London, 1948.

KOHN, HANS. *Nationalism and Imperialism in the Hither East.* London, 1932.

KOHN, HANS. *Orient and Occident.* New York, 1934.

KONIKOFF, A. *Trans-Jordan, An Economic Survey.* Jerusalem, 1943.

LEVY, R. *The Sociology of Islam.* London, 1931.

LINGEMAN, E. R. *Turkey: Economic and Social Conditions in Turkey.* London, 1948.

LUKE, HARRY CHARLES, AND KEITH-ROACH, EDWARD (EDS.). *The Handbook of Palestine and Trans-Jordan.* London, 1930.

MACDONALD, DUNCAN B. *Muslim Theology.* New York, 1903.

MAIN, ERNEST. *Iraq: From Mandate to Independence.* London, 1935.

MATTHEWS, RODERIC D., AND AKRAWI, MATTA. *Education in Arab Countries of the Near East.* Washington, 1949.

MENASSA, GABRIEL. *Plan de Réconstruction de l'Economie Libanaise et de Réforme de l'Etat.* Beirut, 1948.

348 BIBLIOGRAPHY

MIKESELL, RAYMOND F., AND CHENERY, HOLLIS B. *Arabian Oil: America's Stake in the Middle East*. Chapel Hill, N.C., 1949.
MIKUSCH, DAGOBERT VON. *Ibn Saud*. Leipzig, 1942.
MILLSPAUGH, A. C. *Americans in Persia*. Washington, 1946.
MUENZER, GERHARD. *Labor Enterprise in Palestine*. New York, 1947.
NATHAN, ROBERT R., GASS, OSCAR, AND CREAMER, DANIEL. *Palestine, Problem and Promise*. Washington, 1946.
NEWHOUSE, F. *The Training of the Upper Nile*. London, 1939.
NORTHROP, F. S. C. *The Meeting of East and West*. New York, 1946.
OGBURN, W. F. (ED.). *Technology and International Relations*. Chicago, 1949.
PIRNIA, H. *A Short Survey of the Economic Condition of Iran*. Teheran, 1945.
RONDOT, PIERRE. *Les Institutions Politiques du Liban*. Paris, 1947.
ROYAL INSTITUTE OF INTERNATIONAL AFFAIRS. *The Middle East: A Political and Economic Survey*. London, 1950.
SAMPTER, JESSIE (ED.). *Modern Palestine: A Symposium*. New York, 1933.
SCHMIDT, NATHANIEL. *Ibn Khaldun*. New York, 1930.
SERTOLI SALIS, RENZO. *Italia, Europa, Arabia*. Milan, 1940.
SHARP, WALTER R., AND KIRK, GRAYSON. *Contemporary International Politics*. New York, 1940.
SMITH, HERBERT ARTHUR. *The Economic Uses of International Rivers*. London, 1931.
SOUSA, AHMED. *Irrigation in Iraq, Its History and Development*. Baghdad, 1945.
THORNBURG, MAX WESTON, SPRY, GRAHAM, AND SOULE, GEORGE. *Turkey, An Economic Appraisal*. New York, 1949.
TOUKAN, B. A. *A Short History of Trans-Jordan*. London, 1945.
TOYNBEE, ARNOLD J. *The Islamic World Since the Peace Settlement*. London, 1927.
TOYNBEE, ARNOLD J. *The Western Question in Greece and Turkey: A Study in the Contact of Civilizations*. London, 1923.
TWITCHELL, K. S. *Saudi Arabia*. Princeton, 1947.
WARBURG, JAMES PAUL. *"Point Four"; Our Chance to Achieve Freedom from Fear and What You Can Do About It*. New York, 1949.
WARRINER, DOREEN. *Land and Poverty in the Middle East*. London and New York, 1948.
WEBER, MAX. *The Theory of Social and Economic Organization*. Oxford, 1947.
WILBER, DONALD N. *Iran, Past and Present*. Princeton, 1948.
WORTHINGTON, E. B. *Middle East Science*. London, 1945.

Newspapers and Periodicals

American Economic Review.
American Journal of International Law.
Arab News Bulletin. Washington: Arab Office.
Chicago Daily Sun-Times.
Department of State Bulletin.
Economic Journal.
The Economist.
Egypt News Bulletin.
L'Egypte Contemporaine. Cairo.
Great Britain and the East.
Hadassah Newsletter. New York: Hadassah Women's Organization of
America.
Harvard Business Review.
International Organization.
Journal of Political Economy.
Journal of the Royal Central Asian Society.
Middle East Journal.
Middle Eastern Affairs.
Modern Egypt News Bulletin.
National Bank of Egypt Economic Bulletin.
New York Times.
News from Turkey. New York: Turkish Information Office.
Oriente Moderno.
Quarterly Journal of Economics.
Turkey To-day. New York: Turkish Information Office.

Articles in Other Publications

"Agricultural and Industrial Activity and Manpower in Iran," International Labor Review, May, 1949.
"Another 'Emek' in the Making," Life in Israel, Tel Aviv, December, 1950.
BASCH, ANTONIN. "International Bank for Reconstruction and Development," International Conciliation, No. 455, November, 1949.
BENDIX, RICHARD. "Bureaucracy: The Problem and Its Setting," American Sociological Review, October, 1947.
BERENSTEIN, M. "The Levant States Under French Mandate and Problems of Emigration and Immigration," International Labor Review, May, 1936.
CLARK, BLAKE. "Lyle Hayden, Shirt-Sleeve Ambassador," Reader's Digest, December, 1949.

DANINOS, A. "L'Utilisation Intégrale des Eaux du Bassin du Nil," *Bulletin de l'Institut d'Egypte*, Vol. XXX, Cairo, 1949.

FAY, SIDNEY B. "Egypt and the Arab League," *Current History*, August, 1947.

HOSKINS, HALFORD L. "Point Four with Reference to the Middle East," *Annals of the American Academy of Political and Social Science*, March, 1950.

IVES, RONALD L. "The Palestinian Environment," *American Scientist*, January, 1950.

KUZNETS, SIMON. "Measurement of Economic Growth," *Journal of Economic History*, Supplement to Vol. VII, 1948.

PIQUET, HOWARD S. "Point Four and World Production," *Annals of the American Academy of Political and Social Science*, March, 1950.

REUTHER, VICTOR G. "The World's Most Successful Trade Union," *United Nations World*, September, 1950.

VUCINICH, WAYNE S. "Turkey 1948," *Current History*, January, 1949.

Encyclopedias and Year Books

Encyclopaedia Britannica. 1946 ed.

Encyclopaedia Britannica Book of the Year. 7 vols. 1944–50.

The New International Year Book. New York.

Unpublished Material

EDIDIN, THEODORE. "The Greater Syria Scheme." Unpublished Master's thesis, Committee on International Relations, University of Chicago, 1949.

GRUNEBAUM, GUSTAVE E. VON. "Attempts at Self-Interpretation in Contemporary Islam." A study in two sections, the first of which was published as chap. 67 of *Approaches to Group Understanding*, edited by Lyman Bryson, Louis Finkelstein, and R. M. MacIver, New York, 1947. Section II has not been published.

MADINA, MAAN ZILFO. "A TVA in Syria." Unpublished Master's thesis, Committee on International Relations, University of Chicago, 1949.

Index

Abdullah, King, 14, 25, 122 (n. 44), 147 (n. 4), 326 (n. 21)
Acreage, cultivable, 50, 56 (n. 5), 66, 80, 92, 109 (n. 17), 133, 146, 164, 168, 179, 181, 193, 198, 224, 225, 234, 279, 280, 333
Afghanistan, 16, 294
Africa, 296
Agricultural banks, see Banks, agricultural
Agricultural Workers Association (Palestine), 210
Agriculture, Middle Eastern (see also individual countries):
  inadequacy of communications, 48
  problems of, general, 36-45
  production, uniformity of, 291
Agudas Israel, 210 (n. 17)
Ahmed, Imam, 100, 101 (n. 26)
Aid, financial (see also Point Four):
  American, successful aplication of, 284
  contributions from abroad, 208, 209, 215, 227, 228, 232
  E. C. A., 265 (n. 7), 276, 279
  foreign, rejection of, 157, 237, 238, 268
  foreign loans, 55, 227, 228, 232, 248, 250, 252, 253, 263, 269, 273
  grant aid, foreign, 253, 255
  International Bank, 275
  Lend-Lease, 272
  needed for development, 121, 231

Aid, financial—Continued
  Point Four program, prospects for success of, 305-329
  Truman Doctrine, 259 (n. 1)
Aid, military, 259 (n. 1), 260, 272, 276, 278
Al-Azhar University, 25, 73
Al-Mamun, 29
Alawi state, 6, 147 (n. 3), 149
Alawis, 11 (n. 6), 148
Aleppo, 151, 169
Alexandretta, Sanjaq of, 4, 147
Algeria, 229 (n. 75)
Allen, Dr. Harold B., 77, 78, 255
Amasya, 268
American Advisory Commission (Iran), 235
American economic mission (Iran), 250, 251
Americans, 198 (n. 67)
Amman, 107, 114
Anatolia, 4, 160, 234, 265
Ancylostoma, 68, 70
Anglo-Iranian Oil Co., 49 (n. 72), 238, 249, 253, 322
Animals, farm, 42
Ankara, 268
Anthropologists, 1, 2
Anti-Corruption Board (Iran), 248, 251, 252
Anti-Westernism, 13, 59, 61, 62, 98, 99, 118, 143, 147, 150, 156, 157, 174, 175, 251-254, 260, 284, 296, 315, 316, 318, 321, 327
Anti-Zionism, 13, 157

"Developed" nations, 306, 325
Development agency, 311, 313
Development boards, 107, 194-196, 244, 270, 321
Dictatorship, 23, 155 (n. 23), 235, 239, 250, 262, 264 (n. 6), 284, 285
Diplomacy, Turkish, 260 (n. 2)
Diyala, 188
Diyala River, 191
Diyarbekir, 268
Dowson, Sir Ernest, 107
Drainage, 186, 188, 190-191, 199
Druze, Jebel, 6, 147, 148
Druzes, 11 (n. 6)
Dujayla Plan (Iraq), 186-189, 200

Economic Commission for the Middle East, 293
Economic Cooperation Administration (E.C.A.), 265 (n. 7), 274-276, 278-280
Economic development, Middle Eastern (see also Landlords, Peasants, Planning):
before 1919, 9, 10, 27-29
impact of West, 31-33
obstacles to regional approach, 291, 292 (n. 18)
prospects for future, 36
role of international organizations, 314
role of oil, 297, 298, 311, 314
underdevelopment of countries, 306
unique position of Iraq, 320
Economists, 142, 269
Education, 29, 32, 38-40, 69, 72, 73, 77, 78, 92, 95, 115, 124, 128, 145, 166, 173, 176-178, 209, 239, 245, 255, 256, 291, 319
Education, Universal Free, Scheme (Egypt), 77, 78
"Effendi" class, 173, 174, 184
Eggs, 36
Egypt, 7, 8, 10, 11, 14, 18, 20-24, 28, 33, 34, 36, 38-40, 44, 45, 47, 50, 51, 53-84, 99, 119 (n. 37), 127, 296, 300, 308, 315, 316, 319, 327 (n. 22)

Elections, 127
Electricity, production of, Middle Eastern countries, 333
Emigration, 30, 61, 83, 84, 124, 129, 130, 304
Engineers, 142, 173, 194, 236, 242-244, 269, 277, 293 (n. 21)
Erivan, 159
Erosion, 45
Erzurum, 268
Estheticism, emotional, 326 (n. 20)
Ethiopia, 60, 296
Euphrates River, 17, 28, 134, 151, 184, 185, 188, 191, 192, 197, 295
European Recovery Plan (E.R.P.), 274, 279, 293
Exchange controls, 125, 152, 227
Exchange rates, 333
Expansionism, 198 (n. 67), 259
Experimental station, 162
Export-Import Bank, 275, 278, 308, (n. 7)
Exports from Middle Eastern countries, 333

Famine, 113
Farms, size of, 50
Farms, state, 271
Farouk, King, 14, 62, 63 (n. 26), 65, 73, 77
Fatalism, 30, 39
Feisal I, King, 147
Feisal II, King, 14 (n. 11)
Fellahin, see Peasants
Fertile Crescent Scheme, 14
Finance, governmental, 52-53, 57, 72, 78, 88, 95-97, 105, 106, 128, 145, 152, 183, 184, 195, 206, 235, 237, 240, 244, 245, 249, 253, 254, 269, 272, 311, 314, 320, 324
Finances, local, Middle East, 310-316
Five-Year Investment Plan (Turkey), 272
Five-Year Plan (Egypt), 72, 73
Five-Year Plan, First (Turkey), 268-271
Flood control, 136, 137, 139, 189, 190, 192